PROFESSIONAL PRACTICE IN FACILITY PROGRAMMING

PROFESSIONAL PRACTICE IN FACILITY PROGRAMMING

Edited by
Wolfgang F. E. Preiser
University of Cincinnati

VNR VAN NOSTRAND REINHOLD
New York

Library of Congress Catalog Card Number 92-16174
ISBN 0-442-00936-4

Printed in the United States of America.

Van Nostrand Reinhold
115 Fifth Avenue
New York, New York 10003

Chapman and Hall
2-6 Boundary Row
London, SE1 8HN, England

Thomas Nelson Australia
102 Dodds Street
South Melbourne 3205
Victoria, Australia

Nelson Canada
120 Birchmount Road
Scarborough, Ontario MIK 5G4, Canada

16 15 14 13 12 11 10 9 8 7 6 5 4 3 2

Library of Congress Cataloging-in-Publication Data

Professional practice in facility programming / [edited] by Wolfgang
    Preiser.
        p.   cm.
    Includes indexes.
    ISBN 0-442-00936-4
    1. Architectural design—Research.   2. Architectural design—Data
processing.   I. Preiser, Wolfgang F. E.
NA2750.P75   1992
    720—dc20   92-16174
                                                            CIP

CONTENTS

Preface   ix

Contributors   xi

Introduction   1

Wolfgang F. E. Preiser, Johanna W. Looye, and David G. Saile,
Center for the Study of the Practice of Architecture,
University of Cincinnati, Ohio

PART I: NEW DEVELOPMENTS IN FACILITY PROGRAMMING   21

Chapter 1   23
   Strategic Asset Management: An Expanded Role for Facility Programmers,
   John P. Petronis, Architectural Research Consultants, Albuquerque,
   New Mexico

Chapter 2   47
   Applying the Problem-Seeking Approach to Engineering Programming,
   Conny R. Brown and Timothy K. Scarbrough, CRSS Architects, Inc.,
   Greenville, South Carolina

Chapter 3   65
   NCR Corporation Worldwide Facilities Design Guidelines,
   Janet Mackey Brown, CUH2A, Inc., Princeton, New Jersey

Chapter 4   85
   Facilities Managers and New Developments: The Experience of
   Broadgate and Stockley Park
   Francis Duffy, DEGW, Ltd., London, England

Chapter 5   103
   Computer Usage in Facility Programming,
   Ched Reeder, Los Angeles, California

Chapter 6   131
Participatory Programming of Campus Child-Care Facilities,
Henry Sanoff, North Carolina State University, Raleigh, North Carolina

Chapter 7   153
Programming Office Space: Adaptive Re-Use of the H-E-B Arsenal
Headquarters
John Zeisel and Marc A. Maxwell, Boston, Massachusetts

PART II: PROGRAMMING CASE STUDIES   185

Chapter 8   187
Interior Programming, Stacking, and Blocking for Society National Bank,
Richard C. Maxwell and David J. Wyckoff, Gensler Associates, Houston,
Texas

Chapter 9   227
Programming: The Third Dimension
Wilbur H. Tusler, SMP, San Francisco, California, with Frank Zilm,
James T. Hannon, and Mary Ann Newman

Chapter 10   249
Programming Processes for Military Health Care Facilities,
Clarence E. Maxwell and Dale R. Brown, United States Army,
Washington, D.C.

Chapter 11   279
The Fit-Up for the World Headquarters of British Petroleum Company plc
Gary A. Miciunas, Hellmuth, Obata, & Kassabaum, St. Louis, Missouri

Chapter 12   303
Facility Master Plan for Mattel Toys Worldwide Headquarters,
William T. Coleman and Branka V. Olson, Sindik Olson Associates,
Santa Monica, California

Chapter 13   337
A Facility Planning Framework for Programming the Office Environment,
Peter McLennan, DEGW, Ltd., London, England

Chapter 14   357
Planning for a Captive Audience: Approaches and Problems in
Programming Correctional Facilities,
Mark Goldman, Rosser Fabrap/Justice Systems, Atlanta, Georgia
Frieda D. Peatross, University of Florida, Gainesville, Florida

PART III: ISSUES IN FACILITY PROGRAMMING   381

Chapter 15   383
The Impact of the Client Organization on the Programming Process,
Jay Farbstein, Jay Farbstein & Associates, San Luis Obispo, California

Chapter 16   405
The Role of the Programmer as Interpreter and Translator,
Raymond Bertrand, CGO D'Organisations, Inc., Montreal, Canada

Chapter 17   427
Creating Decision-Support Systems,
James Paterson Murray, University of Reading, England
Roderick M. Gameson, University of Manchester, England
John Hudson, Lancashire Polytechnic, England

Chapter 18   453
Research-Based Programming and Design,
Uriel Cohen, University of Wisconsin-Milwaukee

Chapter 19   471
Programming for Safety,
Roger L. Brauer, Board of Certified Safety Professionals, Savoy, Illinois

Chapter 20   491
Programming Architectural Security in Facilities,
Randall Atlas, Atlas Safety & Security Design, Inc., Miami, Florida

Chapter 21   511
Programming Considerations for Energy Conservation,
Fuller Moore, Miami University, Oxford, Ohio

Epilogue   525

Robert G. Hershberger, University of Arizona, Tucson, Arizona

Index   533

Preface

The idea for this book originated from the simple fact that the previous two volumes on facility programming published by this editor in 1978 and 1985 are out of print and thus no longer available.

Some significant developments have taken place during the past seven years that warrant a new collection of case studies in facility programming for use by professionals. Also, a number of schools of architecture and planning in North America have started to offer facility programming through technical "how-to" courses for undergraduate students. A few master's level programs in the country have been created, such as that at Florida A&M University, which reflects an increasing appeal and need for instruction in facility programming. After publication of this book, it is expected that the textbook by Robert Hershberger entitled *Programming for Architecture* will follow in due time, constituting a companion volume to this one.

Two groups of readers appear to like programming books that use the case study format:

1. Professionals who are looking for information on precedents of particular building types.
2. College students in need of a textbook that presents a variety of programming approaches and situations, rather than books on more idiosyncratic programming approaches that were published by Sanoff and Pena in the 1970s, but which have seen no significant updating since.

A great number of colleagues have assisted with this book—not just those who contributed chapters, but also members of the facility programming community around this country and in the United Kingdom. This includes members of the American Institute of Architects and the Environmental Design Association, as well as others who are too numerous to be mentioned individually. Credit is given to many of these people in the acknowledgment sections of the respective chapters.

I wish to thank the School of Architecture and Interior Design and the Center for the Study of the Practice of Architecture at the University of Cincinnati for their support of this publishing effort, especially the secretarial support staff, including Fabian and Celeste. Credit is given to Eric Muschler for statistical work on the survey reported in the introductory chapter.

Thanks are also owed to my fax machine, without which instant communication with my colleagues would not have been possible, thus facilitating adherence to a rather tight publication schedule.

Lastly, I wish to thank my wife, Cecilia, for her encouragement and assistance during demanding times and for making possible the successful conclusion of this book project.

Cincinnati, Ohio

Contributors

Randall Atlas, Ph.D., AIA, CPP, is a registered architect in Florida and Vice President of Atlas Safety & Security Design, Inc., in Miami, Florida. He is a Certified Protection Professional (CPP) with the American Society of Industrial Security and an appointed member of its Architect/Engineer Committee. Atlas is also an appointed member of the American Institute of Architects' Architecture for Justice Committee. He earned his doctorate in criminology from Florida State University after obtaining his master's in architecture from the University of Illinois. He currently serves as Adjunct Professor of Criminal Justice at both the University of Miami and Florida International University. Atlas is a nationally recognized trainer and consultant in crime prevention through environmental design, environmental security, and premises liability.

Raymond Bertrand is a Conseiller of CGO D'Organisations, Inc., in Montreal, Canada. He obtained his master's degree in architecture at McGill University and a bachelor's degree in environmental design at University of Quebec at Montreal, where he also teaches. His present research interests include values and organizational culture in the office setting and evaluative research.

Roger L. Brauer is the Technical Director for the Board of Certified Safety Professionals, Savoy, Illinois, and an Adjunct Professor teaching safety engineering in the Department of Mechanical and Industrial Engineering at the University of Illinois at Urbana-Champaign. He was involved in facility planning and management research for nineteen years at the U.S. Army Construction Engineering Research Laboratory. He is the author of *Safety and Health for Engineers* and *Facilities Planning—User Requirements Method*.

Mr. Roger Brauer received his Ph.D. in Mechanical & Industrial Engineering from the University of Illinois at Urbana-Champaign, his M.S. in Mechanical & Industrial Engineering also from Illinois, his B.A. in Psychology from Valparaiso University. Also from this university he received his BSME in Mechanical Engineering.

Conny R. Brown, PE, is Vice President and Director of Engineering Programming with CRSS Architects, Inc., in Greenville, South Carolina. He has over twenty-one years of experience and is responsible for client requirement analysis and ultimate program development. He has brought his expertise in engineering and programming to major projects for clients such as IBM, Chrysler, Motorola, Cummins Engine, 3M, NASA, and the U.S. Department of Energy.

Brown is a Fellow of the American Society of Heating, Refrigerating, and Air-Conditioning Engineers and has received that organization's Distinguished Service Award. He earned his bachelor of science degree in mechanical engineering at Texas A&M University and is a registered professional engineer (mechanical) in four states.

Dale R. Brown currently teaches health facility planning at the U.S. Army Medical Department's Academy of Health Sciences in Washington, D.C. He has a Ph.D. in architecture as well as a master's in health care administration, and an extensive professional background in hospital operations, and health facility design and construction.

Major Dale Brown received his Ph.D. in Architecture from the University of California, Berkeley, his M.S. in Business Administration from the University of Northern Colorado, and his B.A. degree in Experimental Psychology from the University of California at Santa Barbara.

Janet Mackey Brown is the Director of Facility Planning at CUH2A in Princeton, New Jersey. She applies her training in environmental psychology and organizational analysis to help her corporate and institutional clients make well-informed, appropriate facility decisions. She has also taught architectural programming and problem-solving courses at the Pennsylvania State University and the Washington University School of Architecture in St. Louis.

Dr. Brown received her Ph.D. in Man-Environment Relations from Pennsylvania State University, her M.S. in Housing & Interior Design from University of Kentucky, and her B.S. degree from the University of Missouri.

Uriel Cohen is a Professor of Architecture and Director of the Center for Architecture and Urban Planning Research at the University of Wisconsin-Milwaukee. He is the author and co-author of six books as well as numerous monographs, chapters, and articles, and is the co-recipient of four *Progressive Architecture* awards for applied research.

Dr. Uriel Cohen received his Doctorate in Architecture from the University of Michigan, Ann Arbor, his M.Arch in Architecture from the same university, and his B.Arch in Architecture from the University of Illinois, Chicago.

William T. Coleman, AIA, is a Principal of Sindik Olson Associates, a facility programming and planning consulting firm based in Santa Monica, California. He is a licensed architect with a specialty in pre-design services. He is currently Chairman of the National AIA Practice sub-committee on programming.

Mr. William Coleman received his Masters in Architecture from Harvard University, and his A.B. in Independent Concentration: Architectural History, Theory & Criticism from Brown University.

Francis Duffy is the founder and Chairman of DEGW Architects, Ltd., in London, England. He is known internationally for architectural research—ORBIT studies and the Responsible Workplace—and facility management. He is founding editor of *Facilities,* and has authored numerous publications on commercial architecture, including *The Changing City* and *The Changing Workplace.*

Dr. Duffy received his Ph.D. in Architecture from Princeton University, his M.A. in Architecture from University of California-Berkeley, and his AA Dipl (Hons) in Architecture from the Architectural Association in London.

Jay Farbstein, Ph.D., AIA, is President of Jay Farbstein & Associates, a San Luis Obispo, California, firm specializing in facility programming and post-occupancy evaluation. He is the author of *Correctional Facility Planning and Design* (1986) and *People in Places* (1978).

Mr. Farbstein received his Ph.D. in Environmental Studies from the University of London, his M.A. in Architecture from Harvard University, and his B.A. degree in Fine Arts from the University of California at Los Angeles.

Roderick M. Gameson is Lecturer in the Department of Building Engineering at the University of Manchester Institute of Science & Technology in England. Before joining the University of Manchester, he worked for eight years for a contractor in site management on building and civil engineering projects. He lectures to undergraduate and post-graduate students on construction engineering and construction management-related subjects. Research activities include interaction between potential building clients and construction professionals (Ph.D. research). He is also involved in the use of expert systems to improve communication between clients and construction professionals during the architectural programming process.

Mr. R. M. Gameson received his BSc in Building Construction & Management from Reading University.

Mark Goldman, Director of Planning and Programming for Rosser Fabrap/Justice Systems in Atlanta, Georgia, develops master plans, needs assessments, operational and architectural programs, and evaluations for jails, prisons, and juvenile detention facilities. To date, he has contributed to over $3 billion worth of correctional facilities. Between studying sociology and architecture, he worked with juvenile delinquents and adult inmates.

Mr. Mark Goldman received his M.Arch in Architecture from Georgia Institute of Technology, his M.S. in Urban Life from Georgia State University, his B.A. in Sociology from Clemson University, and his B.S. in Architecture also from Georgia Institute of Technology.

James T. Hannon, APA, is a Vice President of Stone Marraccini Patterson, Architects, in San Francisco, California. He currently directs SMP's planning and programming studio. He completed undergraduate work at the University of California at Berkeley, and obtained a master's in urban and regional planning from the University of Wisconsin at Madison.

Robert G. Hershberger is Professor and Dean of the College of Architecture at the University of Arizona in Tucson, Arizona. In addition to a career in teaching, he has done research in the area of meaning and architecture, and has maintained a practice in which programming has been offered as an essential service. He is recipient of a number of AIA design awards, which he credits to his value-based programming approach.

Mr. Robert Hershberger received his Ph.D. and M.Arch in Architecture from the University of Pennsylvania, his B. Arch in Architecture from the University of Utah, and his A.B. in Architecture from Stanford University.

John Hudson is Senior Lecturer in the Department of the Built Environment at Lancashire Polytechnic in England. He gained a First degree in undergraduate architectural planning, building, and environmental studies and a master's degree in advanced architectural studies at University College London. He later gained a master's degree in computing science at the University of Newcastle-upon-Tyne. His career has encompassed research into several aspects of the built environment and work for a local authority planning department.

Mr. J. Hudson received his MSc in Computing Science from the University of Newcastle-upon-Tyne, his MSc in Advanced Architectural Studies from the University College of London, and his BSc in Architecture/Planning Building & Environmental Studies also from the University College of London.

Johanna W. Looye is Assistant Professor in the School of Planning at the University of Cincinnati, where she teaches graduate-level quantitative methods and international development planning. Her interests center on urbanization and small-scale business development in Third World countries, especially Brazil.

Dr. Looye received her Ph.D. in City and Regional Planning from Cornell University, her Master of Regional Planning (MRP) from the same university and her B.A. in Spanish and Latin American Studies from Grinnel College.

Clarence E. Maxwell is the Commander, U.S. Army Health Facility Planning Agency, Office of the Surgeon General in Washington, D.C. He also serves as the health facility planning consultant to the Surgeon General. An architect with a Ph.D. from Texas A&M University, he has over twenty years' experience in health planning, health care facility design, and construction management — both as an architect-planner and as hospital CEO.

Colonel Cem Maxwell received his Ph.D. in Architecture from the Texas A&M University, his MHA in Health Care Administration from Baylor University, and his B.Arch degree in Architecture also from Texas A&M University.

Marc A. Maxwell, AIA, is both an architect and a planner, holding an undergraduate degree in urban planning from the University of Cincinnati and a master's in architecture from the Massachusetts Institute of Technology. As Vice President/Design at Building Diagnostics, Inc., he managed the delivery of master planning, facility programming, design, and project review for office buildings and senior citizen housing. Prior to this position, Maxwell had served as Director of Construction and Design for USA Cinemas and as senior space planner/designer for The Boston Company, a large financial investment company with a comprehensive in-house facilities management and design department. He is a frequent lecturer on the sick building syndrome and the team approach to design. Since 1990, Maxwell has headed his own consulting firm in Somerville, Massachusetts, providing project planning and management, facility programming, and architectural design services to a wide range of public and private clients.

Richard C. Maxwell is a Vice President and Partner with Gensler and Associates/Architects in Houston, Texas. A member of the American Institute of Architects and the American Planning Association, he is primarily involved in facility programming and building design consultation.

Mr. Richard Maxwell received his M.Arch in Urban Design from Washington University, and his B.Arch in Architecture from Tulane University.

Peter McLennan is a Senior Facility Planning Consultant for DEGW, Ltd., in London, England. He is interested in developing models to help optimize facility planning decisions by studying how organizations use space over time. He is a member of the Association of Facility Management in the United Kingdom and serves on the Education, Training, and Research Committee.

Mr. Peter McLennan received his M.S. in Facility Planning from Cornell University, and his B.A. in Art History from the University of Connecticut, and his B.S. in Interior Design from the same university.

Gary A. Miciunas is currently a Senior Associate with Hellmuth, Obata & Kassabaum, Incorporated, a multidisciplinary planning, design, and engineering firm headquartered in St. Louis, Missouri. His experience centers on corporate projects, including strategic planning and pre-design programming assignments in America, Great Britain, and Japan.

Mr. Gary Miciunas received his M.S. in Environment Design from Southern Illinois University, and his B.S. in Urban Studies from the University of Wisconsin.

Fuller Moore is Professor of Architecture at Miami University in Oxford, Ohio, and is the founding Director of the Center for Building Science Research there. A registered architect, he specializes in the design of energy-efficient buildings, several of which have received national design awards. He is the author of several books on the subject, including *Concepts and Practice of Architectural Daylighting* and *The Responsive Envelope.*

Mr. Fuller Moore received his M.Arch and B.Arch in Architecture from Virginia Polytechnic Institute.

James Paterson Murray is Lecturer and Course Director (Master of Science) in MSc Construction Management in the Department of Construction Management and Engineering at the University of Reading in England. Initially qualified as a quantity surveyor with a background in construction economics, he worked in private practice before taking an honors degree in architecture. He has had many years of experience as a project architect, in both local authority and private practice. Joining the University of Reading as a research fellow, he is now a lecturer in construction management and construction technology with a special interest in the early stages of project development and the architectural programming process.

Mr. Jim Murray received his B.Arch in Architecture from Heriot-Watt University.

Mary Ann Newman, RN, BS, MPH, is currently Assistant Vice President for Planning and Institutional Studies at the University of Texas/M.D. Anderson Cancer Center. Previous positions include Administrative Analyst/Planner, the University of Texas Medical School-Houston (1982-1987); ten years' nursing experience, including two years in Navy Nurse Corps; and three years as a research nurse at M.D. Anderson. A diploma nursing graduate, she received a bachelor's in health services administration from the University of Houston and a master's in public health from the University of Texas School of Public Health.

Branka V. Olson, AIA, is President of Sindik Olson Associates in Santa Monica, California. She is a licensed architect with a specialty in pre-design Services. In addition to working with Mattel Toys, she has recently developed needs assessment programs for millions of square feet of public- and private-sector space for organizations including CCH Computax, American Honda Motor Company, and the State Bar Association of California.

Ms. Branka Olson received her Master degree in Architecture from the University of Michigan, Ann Arbor, and her B.A. in Interior Design from the University of Illinois, Champaign-Urbana, and her B.S. in Architecture from the same university.

Frieda D. Peatross, Assistant Professor in the Department of Interior Design at the University of Florida and a planner with Rosser Fabrap/Justice Systems in Atlanta, Georgia, works on operational and architectural programs and evaluations for jails, prisons, and juvenile detention facilities. A Ph.D. candidate in architecture at the Georgia Institute of Technology, her research interests focus on the morphology of buildings and their social logic.

Ms. Dita Peatross received her Ph.D. in Architecture from the Georgia Institute of Technology except for dissertation, her M.A. in Art Education &

Design from Florida State University, her M.S. in Interior Design from Indiana University, and her B.A. in Art History & Fine Arts from University of North Carolina.

John P. Petronis is President of Architectural Research Consultants, Inc., based in Albuquerque, New Mexico. He is an architect and certified planner who has directed many large-scale strategic asset planning projects, primarily for public-sector clients.

Mr. Petronis received his M.Arch in Architecture from the University of New Mexico, his M.B.A. in Management from the same university, and his B.A. in Philosophy from Gettysburg College.

Wolfgang F. E. Preiser is Professor of Architecture at the University of Cincinnati. He is co-founder and Director of Research with Architectural Research Consultants, Inc., in Albuquerque, New Mexico. Mr. Preiser holds a Ph.D. in Man-Environment Relations from the Pennsylvania State University, as well as master's degrees in architecture from Virginia Polytechnic Institute and the University of Karlsruhe in Germany. His bachelor's degree in architecture is from the Technical University in Vienna, Austria.

Preiser has extensive experience related to the fields of design research, post-occupancy evaluation, and facility programming, both in academia and in private practice. He co-authored the book *Post-Occupancy Evaluation* (1988) and edited both *Facility Programming* (1982) and *Programming the Built Environment* (1985), as well as *Building Evaluation* (1989), *Pueblo Style and Regional Architecture* (1989), and *Design Intervention: Toward a More Humane Architecture* (1991).

Ched Reeder currently heads the Reeder Consulting Group, based in Los Angeles, California. Trained as an architect, he has over twenty years of experience in using computers to aid in the design and construction process. As a founder of Mitchell, Reeder, Hamer, The Computer-Aided Design Group (CADG), he has consulted in computer usage to many design firms and corporations. He also teaches courses at the Southern California Institute of Architecture. He has one of the best 3D collections going.

Mr. Reeder received his M.Arch in Architecture from the University of California at Los Angeles, and his B.Arch in Architecture from University of Kentucky.

David G. Saile is Associate Professor in the School of Architecture and Interior Design at the University of Cincinnati. He is Executive Director of the Center for the Study of the Practice of Architecture (CSPA) and is currently a member of the Board of Directors of the Environmental Design Research Association (EDRA) and of the Built Form and Culture Research Conference Steering Committee.

Dr. Saile received his Ph.D. in Architecture from the University of Newcastle-upon-Tyne, in England, and his M. Arch degree in Architecture from the University of Illinois at Champaign-Urbana.

Henry Sanoff is Professor of Architecture at North Carolina State University and Director of the architecture graduate program. He is a recent recipient of a Distinguished Fulbright Award to Korea. His most recent publications include *Visual Research Methods in Design, Participatory Design: Theory and Techniques,* and *Learning Environments for Children.*

Professor Sanoff received his M.Arch in Architecture from Pratt Institute, and his B.Arch in Architecture from the same Institute.

Timothy K. Scarbrough, AIA, is an Associate and Senior Analyst with CRSS Architects, Inc., in Greenville, South Carolina. He has over ten years of architectural experience, including long-term strategic analysis, architectural and interior programming, and numerous special studies. He has worked on office buildings, manufacturing facilities, research and development facilities, military installations, hotels, and schools for clients such as Bell Northern Research, Chrysler, IBM, Baylor College of Medicine, Arizona State University, and Dade County (Florida) Public Schools. He leads a programming group that is applying the problem-seeking process to industrial engineering projects.

Scarbrough received his bachelor of science and master of architecture degrees from Florida A&M University.

Wilbur H. Tusler, FAIA, is a Senior Vice President of Stone Marraccini Patterson, Architects, in San Francisco, California. He served as the firm's President from 1981 to 1991. Prior to that period, he led SMP's programming activities for many years. He holds bachelor's and master's degrees from Virginia Polytechnic Institute and a master's of architecture degree from the Massachusetts Institute of Technology.

David J. Wyckoff is a Senior Associate and space programming specialist with Gensler and Associates/Architects in Houston, Texas. Having programmed over 12 million square feet of office space, he is primarily involved in facility programming, space planning, and building design consultation.

Mr. David Wyckoff received his Masters in Interior Architecture from Texas A&M University, he also received from the same university his Bachelors in Environmental Design.

John Zeisel received his Ph.D. in sociology from Columbia University and a post-doctoral Loeb Fellowship from Harvard University's Graduate School of Design. He has been on the faculty at McGill University in Montreal, at Yale, and at Harvard in the Department of Architecture. Based in Boston, Massachusetts, he is the author of *Inquiry by Design: Tools for Environment-Behavior Research.* He has won several *Progressive Architecture* awards for his research efforts.

Frank Zilm, AIA, received his bachelor's of architecture from the University of Kansas and his doctorate in architecture from the University of Michigan. He is currently President of Frank Zilm & Associates, Inc., specializing in the planning of health care and educational facilities. Zilm also serves as an adjunct faculty member in the school of architecture and urban design at the University of Kansas.

INTRODUCTION

Recent Developments in Facility Programming

Wolfgang F. E. Preiser
Johanna W. Looye
David G. Saile

SYNOPSIS

The intent of this book is to create a dialogue between practitioners, educators, and clients, in the quest to improve the building delivery process and, ultimately, the quality of buildings themselves. The chapters included here—written by a mix of practitioners, programming specialists, and educators—reflect the values, approaches, and experiences of each group, and they provide useful insights for the reader. This introductory chapter addresses three topics regarding professional practice in facility programming.

First, recent and new developments and emerging trends in the industry are highlighted, as exemplified by chapters in Part I of this book. This section is followed by a short discussion placing facility programming into the larger professional context of education and training for architectural practice. It raises questions about who should do facility programming: Should it be an in-house specialist or a hired consultant? How should programming best be practiced—as a dynamic activity that is integrated and that evolves with design, or strictly as a pre-design activity? How should students be educated in schools of architecture with the technical skills and know-how that permit them to apply facility programming methods in professional life? Where and when in the curriculum should this area of specialization be introduced, and how can it be integrated with the design studio and other course work in architectural education? We hope that these and other questions will be

1

answered through the collective efforts of the authors who have contributed to this book. The third part of this introductory chapter is a presentation of the results of a survey on facility programming that was conducted by the American Institute of Architects (AIA) through the *AIA Memo*, a newsletter that reaches the organization's approximately 53,000 members. This survey attempted to identify issues surrounding programming practice. Questions included, for example, the following: Who does facility programming? What is the training of these programmers? How much time and money is devoted to programming in a typical project? What is the nature of projects and clients who benefit the most from facility programming?

FACILITY PROGRAMMING:
A CHANGING AND MATURING FIELD

This is the third in a series of volumes on facility programming published over the past fourteen years by Van Nostrand Reinhold, Publishers. The first volume was entitled *Facility Programming,* and was originally published in 1978 by Dowden, Hutchinson & Ross, Publishers, who were later acquired by Van Nostrand Reinhold. *Programming the Built Environment* was published in 1985, and it also followed the case study format. Now, several years later, we endeavor to update the reader on new developments in the field of facility programming and to present a new set of case studies, especially from the corporate sector. Finally, we wish to raise questions surrounding facility programming and its application to highly specialized fields such as security and safety in buildings.

Considering the relatively short history of the field of facility programming—dating back to approximately the mid-1960s—it is useful for the reader to revisit the introductions of the previously published volumes to become familiar with the main points, which will not be repeated here:

- The evolution of the field of facility programming
- A generic process description of programming
- An introduction of the major actors in programming
- The principal beneficiaries of programming
- A discussion of who pays for facility programming

Of particular interest may be the observations made by John Eberhard in the final chapter of the 1978 book entitled *Prospects for the Field of Facility Programming.* Perhaps the most important of his prognoses was the potential for computerized database development as the brains for decision support systems that would link facility programming, design, and post-occupancy evaluation into a coherent, comprehensive system. This system was to allow the designer to apply the lessons learned from the successes and failures in building performance in the past to the design of future buildings, as well as the remodeling of existing ones.

Integrated databases of this nature are indeed becoming a reality now with the arrival of sophisticated, high-speed work stations that permit networking and the merging of graphic and text data, including moving images at a high rate of speed. Such database development projects are underway at several universities, including California Polytechnic State University (San Luis Obispo), Carnegie Mellon University, and the University of Cincinnati, to name just a few. For instance, the post-occupancy evaluation database project at the University of Cincinnati (Preiser and Krishnan, 1992) involves the development of an expert system to interface with CAD and POE knowledge-base systems. The system can be used by designers and planners to accomplish better designs by learning from past experiences as well as from comprehensive design information made available during the design process. The project is made up of two phases—the development of an expert system to use design knowledge-bases, and the development of the knowledge-bases themselves. Development of the knowledge-bases is a process of collecting information from various sources, such as design analysis and user responses, and collating them to be of effective use in the design process. The knowledge-bases would consist of information categorized under various design aspects as well as levels of expertise. The evaluation system would consist of rule sets formed out of these knowledge-bases.

The evaluation system envisioned consists of an expert systems shell interfacing with CAD-database systems. The expert system would essentially evaluate designs against the above rule sets, suggest alternatives, and provide access to design-related information. An important aspect of the system would be the introduction of object-oriented design. This concept would allow designs to be viewed from the perspective of what they represent—entities, relationships, and attributes—rather than being viewed as what they are—lines and surfaces—and hence be valuable information sources.

In the future, such computer systems are expected to play a key role in facilities management—in planning, design, and maintenance processes. Such systems could be of great impact, not only in terms of impressive benefits in planning and operation, but also in terms of long-term cost savings.

Furthermore, recent developments bring facilities management into the picture to the point where in the foreseeable future it may dominate the creation of appropriate software systems and modules. The reason for this is quite simple. It is the facilities managers who have to live with planning, programming, and design decisions throughout the useful life of a building, decisions that affect operations and maintenance in a significant way. Thus, it can be expected that in the future facilities management software systems will add modules for facility programming and post-occupancy evaluation to those already in existence, as exemplified by the Accugraph MountainTop software.

Once the base building plan has been developed, the software supports the following applications:

Facility development plan
Five-year plan
Architecture and engineering
Human resource management
Interior planning   } Integrated with base building plan
Interior installation
Maintenance and operations
Hazardous materials management
Fire and safety
Activation

In the mid-1980s the Building Research Board at the National Academy of Sciences, under the directorship of John Eberhard, undertook several investigations into "opportunities for improvement" in programming and post-occupancy evaluation processes, linked to database development. The results of these committee deliberations, with input from both private and public sectors, were published in reports that contained a number of important policy implications, some of which are contained in Table 1 on page 5.

In recent years there have been major requests for proposals such as the National Museum of the American Indian, a Smithsonian-sponsored building that will be placed in a prominent spot on the Mall in Washington, D.C. The first and critical step was a competition for conducting a rather extensive programming effort to clarify client objectives, to inventory the artifacts to be housed, and to specify the expected building performance prior to initiation of architect selection and design. Furthermore, most states now require that extensive programming efforts be undertaken before architect selection can take place for public building commissions. Today, large firms avail themselves of facility programming, either as an in-house function or in collaboration with highly specialized facility programmers. This is particularly true for such sectors as health facilities and laboratory design.

One of the authors was an invited observer during sessions of the "Design Excellence in the Architecture of Interiors" roundtable organized by the American Institute of Architects in October 1990 at Georgetown University. There was a distinct impression that the interior design firms that were represented at the roundtable were much more concerned with programming than were many more specifically architectural firms. Pre-design, "front-end" client communication was consistently stressed as a factor in influencing design quality. It was also observed that during periods of economic depression, new building slows down, but renovated facilities, or buildings "repositioned in the market," tend to increase the work of interior designers. Much of the work that these firms receive is from repeat clients. This means that client

TABLE 1   Recent Developments in Facility Programming

Strategic asset and management tool: The role of the facility planner/programmer is increasingly important in strategic planning for corporate and institutional clients. Thus, the process of post-occupancy evaluation (POE) as a complement to facility programming represents a new diagnostic tool in strategic asset management.

Programming in engineering: An innovative application in the field of engineering of an established programming approach called "problem seeking" is exemplified by the high-purity-water building case study (Chapter 2).

Design guidance: Design guidelines in the public and corporate sectors are gaining increasing acceptance and use. In-house design guides are available, with which contracting architects are required to comply in order to create systemwide identity of image and compatibility of design concepts. This is particularly true for organizations with recurring building programs. Again, post-occupancy evaluation is used to test and fine-tune prototype buildings, programs, and databases, which represent the cumulative experience of the organization with a given building type.

Computer usage: Computer usage in facility programming is driven by extending the use of computers in facility management. Comprehensive software systems available now cover strategic planning functions, programming, design, occupancy, and operation and maintenance, as well as the post-occupancy evaluation phases of the building delivery cycle.

Participatory programming: In the corporate sector, especially with health care providers, one can detect certain signs of a renewed emphasis on user input and participation in the planning, programming, and design process in the quest for "getting it right" the first time. The reasons for this participation are fierce competition for the health care dollar, as well as the patients' satisfaction and the organization's implied concern for the quality of care received.

Adaptive re-use: In addition to new construction, an important part of building activity is the adaptive re-use of existing building stock, where the application of programming techniques is equally beneficial.

Special programming applications: Some highly specialized applications can be observed that use facility programming techniques in making sure that safety, security, or other critical concerns—such as energy conservation—are being met in building design and operation.

---

relations, post-occupancy evaluation, and programming services may be especially important for the survival of interior design firms.

We can conclude that facility programming, as has been stated in many places, fills an ever more important need by establishing effective communication among all the players involved in the building delivery process, including clients, funding groups, designers, builders, facilities managers, and—last but not least—the actual occupants of buildings. New and recent developments in facility programming are summarized in Table 1.

PROGRAMMING IN THE ARCHITECTURAL CURRICULUM

Having briefly addressed new developments in the field of facility programming, we now turn to the implications for architectural education. What, if anything, are we doing to better equip future professionals with skills and knowledge about programming methods and applications?

Without a deeper and more comparative study of programming as an area within architectural education, it is difficult to ascertain what emphasis is placed upon the subject matter and how it is integrated with other areas of the curriculum in any comprehensive manner. From our experience in various schools of architecture, however, we know that there are at least three major ways in which programming becomes part of architectural education programs (each with a range of variations).

What is taught under the heading of "programming" and what is related to the topic, but taught in other course areas, such as "design," "theory," and "professional practice," also raises some crucial pedagogical *and* architectural questions. We cannot address them in any detail here, but some of the doubts and questions are summarized following the three strands of programming in educational curricula outlined next.

Programming: As Part of a Final Design Project

Final design projects, culminating in the last or penultimate quarter or semester of educational programs, require substantial preparation regardless of particular architectural and pedagogical philosophies. In most B.Arch. and M.Arch. professional degree programs incorporating a final project, a specific preparatory exercise is undertaken for academic credit. Sometimes this is a linked but separate course taken prior to the studio course. In other cases this is credit given for submission of a program document undertaken with a tutor or committee under the heading of "independent study." In some cases, submission of a final design program is a prerequisite for entry into the final design studio.

The preparation varies, but often has the following stated goals:

- Immersion of the student in the human, technical, and environmental aspects of the design situation (and encouragement of an ability to question different design approaches)
- Clarification of the different participants and perspectives related to the project, especially the sponsor, user, builder, and designer, as well as broader social groups
- Development of criteria for performance of the design in terms of these values, participants, and contexts

The more or less elaborated program document that results usually contains behavioral information and summarizes technical, climatic, and physical contexts. From our experience, the document is as likely to be a justification for a particular approach to the project as it is to be a reasoned and well-justified exploration of the design situation and the goals of the major actors.

In any case, the document is not frequently referred to during final reviews of the project, although it may have served as a reference and discussion document earlier. Critics and reviewers often behave as if the qualities, values, and contexts of the design project are self-evident in the drawings, simulations, or models. Visiting reviewers are often not given copies of the program in advance, nor do they have the time to digest the contents (Anthony, 1987).

Courses in Programming: Introduction to a Field

In addition to final project programming, and independent of it, many schools have a course running parallel to the middle design studios that is an introduction to the field called programming. Through readings, exercises, and field study, such courses look at examples of programming activity in the practice of architecture, at the techniques and approaches of programming specialists, and at programming as a specialized professional field itself.

Generally these courses are about programming *as it is*. The implications of technical and information-handling advances are usually mentioned, but conceptual reappraisals of design approaches and "programming" are left for other course areas to tackle. Course work in these introductions is not coherently or consistently linked with design studio (except occasionally with final design projects) nor with either theoretical work or the study of history. It is more consistently linked with courses in human, social, and behavioral factors in design.

Courses in Programming: As a Specialization

In a handful of architecture programs, programming is offered as an emphasis and as a possible area for graduate study (for example, Florida A&M University, University of Wisconsin-Milwaukee). In these programs the subject is treated not only as preparation for normal architectural design activity but also as a possible career path. The programs deal with systematizing the wealth of information that can be gathered about the performance of buildings in use, or in relation to special user groups, for the purpose of developing guidelines or databases for future development or design activity. Such an educational focus can also be found in a few large professional firms (for example, CRSS).

The academic programs lead their students toward careers in facilities management, project management, building diagnostics, post-occupancy evaluation, and professional facility programming, or as a building type specialist.

Educational Questions

Programming is not as fully integrated as it might be with architectural curricula because of the fluid nature of questions raised in architectural education. Questions currently surround a large philosophical shift. On the one hand, the field of programming grew from an era that focused on systematic design methods, increasing computer applications, and overlap of design with psychological and social issues. It assumes a scientifically knowable world and it suggests that better ways of handling large numbers of data will help building design become more responsible (to users, to environmental change, and to complex social and technical processes).

On the other hand, educators and professionals with broad humanistic and scholarly backgrounds consider that deeper understanding of the human, social, and cultural roles of architecture is what matters most. For them, enlightened discourse and richer theory is more valuable than more data and more applicability in an established design process.

Programming in schools sits nervously neither inside nor outside this debate. Certainly there is a need for philosophical and political rethinking in architecture, and there is an equal need for inclusion and discussion of a wider and more complex body of evidence. In the meantime there is an almost inevitable increasing specialization in all professions. Our survey respondents consist of firms that are at the larger end of the size spectrum and that have multiple departments and services. It is also likely that programmers' education will continue to be interdisciplinary: Evidence from our pilot survey shows a quarter of respondents having non-architecture degrees.

Those schools that emphasize programming, and its links with post-occupancy evaluation, facility performance databases, and building-diagnostic processes, are likely to find their graduates most welcomed by firms with large and continuing clients in the institutional and corporate worlds. Such schools are few in number, and at the moment it appears that many students pursue their programming interests (beyond an initial introduction) in elective courses and degree programs in other departments.

CURRENT TRENDS IN FACILITY PROGRAMMING: A PILOT SURVEY

Who Responded to the Survey?

In an attempt to identify issues surrounding programming practices, this pilot survey was intended "to identify current trends in facility programming methods, personnel, costs, and benefits." It was published in the July 1991 issue of the *AIA Memo* (see the appendix for the actual survey form). Of the 53,000 members (firms and individuals) of the American Institute of Architects who receive the *AIA Memo*, eighty-three responded to the survey. Because respondents were self-selected, it is probably safe to suppose that they are people or firms that either do programming or have some particular interest in it. The principal findings of the survey are as follows:

- Firms that responded to the survey are not representative of architecture firms in general. Respondents were more likely to be in firms with multiple services like architecture/interior design and less likely to be solely architecture firms. Responding firms are also larger than the average architectural firm.

- Most firms have no programmer. Of those that do, firms with two to nineteen employees have one or two programmers, while firms with twenty employees or more have six or seven programmers.
- Programming clients are predominantly institutions and corporations.
- Most of the respondents do not bill programming as a separate design service.
- Few firms offer programming as a consulting service separate from design.
- Nearly half of respondents estimate that between 2 and 5 percent of billable time is devoted to programming.
- Nearly 60 percent of the firms estimated the overall cost of programming to be over 2 percent of total project costs.
- Most programmers have first professional degrees—B. Arch. or M. Arch. —in architecture, but one-fourth of programmers have non-architecture degrees.

These results are examined in greater detail below.

Type of Firms

Because the self-selected respondents in this survey do not represent a random sample of architectural firms, it is useful to compare their characteristics to those of architectural firms in general, as reported by the *Architecture Factbook* (American Institute of Architects, 1990). Figure 1 shows that the firms that answered are not representative of the profession as a whole. Firms that responded to the survey are more diverse than those in the *Factbook,* and consist of a lower proportion of solely architecture firms and a higher proportion of architecture/interior design firms. This suggests that interior design firms are more inclined to do programming than are other types of architectural firms. It is interesting to note that the third most frequent response was "other." This category included firms that simply combined two or three of the mentioned categories. Just under half of the firms in the "other" category included either architecture or architecture/interior design within their combination.[1]

Firm Size

In terms of the number of employees, the eighty-two firms that reported this information range in size up to 11,000 employees, with an average of 213. If the firms with over 250 employees are eliminated, the average—now thirty-three employees—is still quite high, considering that over one-third of all architectural firms employ two to four people (see Figure 2).[2]

---

[1]Planning was deleted as a category since 0 percent of respondents identified themselves as strictly planning and the *Factbook* does not use the category in its analysis.

[2]The zero employees category arises from the fact that it is not clear if the proprietor is included in the number of employees. Some firms included the proprietor as an employee, while others clearly did not.

TABLE 2   Number of Programmers by Firm Size

No. of Programmers*	Firm Size (No. of Employees)						Total
	0	1	2-4	5-9	10-19	> 20	
0	2.5	1.2	7.4	13.6	4.9	7.4	37.0
1	0	2.5	6.2	2.5	1.2	0.0	12.3
2	0	0	2.5	3.7	6.2	3.7	16.0
3-5	0	0	0	4.9	2.5	13.6	21.0
6-10	0	0	0	0	1.2	6.2	7.4
11-15	0	0	0	0	0	2.5	2.5
16-20	0	0	0	0	0	0	0.0
21-24	0	0	0	0	0	0	0.0
25-30	0	0	0	0	0	3.7	3.7
Total	2.5%	3.7%	16.0%	24.7%	16.0%	37.0%	100.0%

Facility Programming

Programming Specialists

In addition to reporting the total number of employees, firms reported the number of programming specialists. They are shown in Table 2, using the same size categories as Figure 2.[3] The table indicates the number of programmers in each firm size category for the eighty-one firms that reported this information. The stair-step downward illustrates how the number of programmers increases along with the firm size.

The table shows that over one-third of the firms have no programmer. In addition, results show that most small firms (two to nineteen employees) have one or two programmers, while most firms with over twenty employees have six or seven programmers. The average for all firms is three or four programming specialists.

Programming Clients[4]

Figure 3 shows that, of a total of 82 responses, institutional and corporate clients predominate, representing nearly two-thirds of the responses. The

---

[3]The survey provided no definition for this job category, so people are classified according to the criteria of the respondents, who may have identified as a programmer only someone with that job title, at one extreme, or someone who carried out (some unspecified amount of) programming activities, at the other extreme. It is worth noting that the *Factbook* does not list programmer as a separate position title (see pp. 33-35). The average for the forty-six firms with between two and nineteen employees was 1.3 programmers; for the thirty firms with over twenty employees, 6.7 programmers; and for all firms, 3.2 programmers.

[4]The categories used in the *Factbook* were assigned to the survey categories as follows: Institutional (Public Institutions); Corporate (Developers, Private Institutions); Government (Federal, State, and Local Government); Industrial (Business, Industrial); and Other (Engineers, Other Architects, Construction Companies, Private Individuals).

"other" category includes health care, religious, or some combination of the given choices (such as commercial/industrial), which probably reflects the need for elaborate programming in highly specialized fields with particular space requirements. Compared with the profession as a whole, the survey respondents are much more likely to have institutional clients and much less likely to have industrial clients. The data appear to indicate that there is a need for programmers in institutions where lines of communication are complex and networking is prevalent. Design for factories seems to be treated as puzzle-solving, while design for institutions is people-focused because of the methods of communication and diffused patterns of decision making.

Methods of Data Gathering

Firms were asked to rank their most prevalent methods for data gathering. Figure 4 shows that, of a total seventy-four responses, the first-place ranking was given, in order, to:

interviews,
surveys,
document analysis,
behavioral observation,
visiting a similar state-of-the-art project, and
literature search.

One-quarter of the responses fell in the "other" data-gathering category, in which interactive techniques were more frequently mentioned than other techniques. Group interactive techniques mentioned include work sessions, user design forums, charettes, interactive discussions, workshops, and consensus building. Interestingly, four respondents indicated that they were developing in-house database systems.

Formats for Communicating
Programming Information

Figure 5 shows that, of seventy-four firms reporting, the first-place ranking of formats for communicating programming information were as follows:

text,
planning information,
sketches,
photography,
bar graphs, pie charts, etc., and
video.

Video appears to be used only in educational institutions. The in-house data collection mentioned above gives rise in this question to different ways of communicating computer spreadsheets and databases. It is worth noting that although verbal presentation was not listed explicitly on the questionnaire, it is an important tool in communication of information. Eight respondents listed it explicitly in the "other" category.

Billing for Programming

When asked about how their programming is billed, the respondents exhibited a tendency not to bill for programming separately. About one-quarter of the firms responded that over 90 percent of their programming is *not* billed separately, while 45 percent of the firms stated that only between 0 and 10 percent is billed separately (that is, they *do not* generally bill it as a separate service). Only 11 percent of the firms bill over half of their programming as a separate service.

Few firms offer programming as a consulting service separate from design. Over 80 percent of the firms report doing so in less than 30 percent of their business. In fact, only 8 percent of the firms report offering programming as a consulting service over half of the time.

Programming-Intensive Projects

When asked to rank the types of projects that require the most in programming services, eighty firms responded. As Figure 6 shows, the programming-intensive project types are, in rank order:

institutional,
commercial,
residential,
industrial, and
other.

"Other" responses here included government, health care, corporate, and religious projects. Government and health care go along with the notion of institutional projects being the most programming-intensive. The complications of institutional networks demand programming work.

Time and Cost

Asked to estimate how much time is devoted to programming as a percentage of total billable time for an average project, nearly half of the respondents estimate that between 2 and 5 percent of billable time is devoted to programming (see Figure 7).[5]

Firms were also asked to report the estimated overall cost percentage of programming as part of total project cost. Nearly 60 percent of the respondents estimated overall cost of programming to be more than 2 percent of total project costs (see Figure 8).[6]

---

[5]The way in which these two questions were phrased leaves us with no category for 3 percent or 4 percent, and with 5-plus to 100 percent as one single category.

[6]See footnote 5.

Educational Level of Programmers

Table 3 shows the number of programmers with a certain level of training and the number of firms with at least one person holding the indicated degree.

Other survey data show that the majority of the firms that responded had one or two programmers with B. Arch. degrees. Nearly 40 percent had one person with a B. Arch., although over one fourth had none. One firm reported having twelve programmers with B. Arch. degrees.

Nearly half of the firms responding had no programmers with an M. Arch. degree. Twenty percent of the firms reporting had one programmer with an M. Arch. degree; over 30 percent had one or two such individuals. One firm reported eleven programmers with M. Arch. degrees.

The vast majority of firms (86 percent) had no programmers with a Ph.D. Ten percent of the firms reporting had one programmer with a Ph.D. One firm reported having six programmers with doctorates.

Most significant in the education of programmers is the diversity of background. Over one-quarter of programmers had degrees such as a B.A. or B.S. in design-oriented fields, an M.B.A., or degrees in health care-related fields, facility management or public administration, engineering, and planning. One programmer even had a background in cultural anthropology. The diversity in the background of programmers seems to reflect the programmer's role in facilitating communication across areas of specialization.

Future Research

While the survey answered many questions about facility programming, it gave rise to many more. In future research, it would be useful to further investigate the following:

• It appears that programming is gradually becoming part of standard architectural practice. However, as programming becomes increasingly complex, its inclusion as an un-itemized activity comes into question, especially as governments and institutions require programming before

TABLE 3   Number and Percentage of Programmers by Degree and Firms by Type of Degree

Degree	B.Arch.	M.Arch.	Ph.D.	Other	Total
No. of Degree Holders	112	97	17	77	303
Percentage of Total Degree Holders	37%	32%	6%	25%	100%
No. of Firms	71	37	10	29	83 *
Percentage of Firms	86%	45%	12%	35%	NA

* This total represents the number of firms responding, not the sum of the firms in each category. For example, a firm may have two programmers, one with a B.Arch. and one with a M.Arch.

releasing funding. This raises the question of whether the real costs of programming, especially in terms of time expended, are reflected in client fees. Research is needed to investigate the relationship between cost, fees charged, and time spent on programming.

- There is a need to know the extent to which programming is becoming a recognized field in the architectural profession. Future research should compare the use of the job title with the number of people actually doing programming.
- We do not know whether it is likely that young firms, which may be smaller and consider themselves as "cutting-edge," do less programming, while older firms, often operated as business enterprises, are likely to carry out more programming. Research is needed to investigate the relationship between the orientation, size, and age of a firm and its use of programming.
- Further research is required to determine whether specialized firms (such as those that specialize in hospital design) have a greater number (or a higher percentage) of programmers than do general architecture firms.
- Many argue that a conflict of interest arises when a firm that does the programming also carries out the design and construction documentation. There is a need to investigate whether firms that do programming follow the projects through other phases or work only at their initiation.
- Architecture schools need to examine whether architecture curricula should change to reflect increased use of programming or whether the profession should rely upon on-the-job training. This calls for a survey of programmers about their education.

References

American Institute of Architects, Office of Research & Planning. 1990. *Architecture factbook: Industry statistics, 1990 edition.* Washington, D.C.: The American Institute of Architects.

Anthony, K.H. 1987. Private reactions to public criticism. *Journal of Architectural Education,* 40:3, pp. 2-11.

Atienza, T.S. 1990. Computer-aided facility management in a hospital environment. Miami, Fla.: VA Medical Center.

Eberhard, J.P. 1978. Prospects for the field of facility programming. In *Facility programming,* edited by W.F.E. Preiser. Stroudsburg, Pa.: Dowden, Hutchinson & Ross, Inc.

Preiser, W.F.E., and R.G. Krishnan. 1992. Post-occupancy evaluation database development project. Cincinnati, Ohio: University of Cincinnati (in preparation).

APPENDIX

The Survey Questionnaire

WHAT DO YOU THINK?

In an effort to identify current trends in facility programming methods, personnel, costs, and benefits, The Center for the Study of the Practice of Architecture at the University of Cincinnati would appreciate your help. Please take a few moments to complete this questionnaire. A summary of the results, in addition to appearing in a future issue of MEMO, will be published in Wolfgang F.E. Preiser's forthcoming book, *Professional Practice in Facility Programming* (Van Nostrand Reinhold, 1993). Please return your completed form—by Sept. 1, 1991—to Douglas Gordon, at the AIA, 1735 New York Ave., NW, Washington, DC 20006, fax: (202) 626-7421.

1. Name, address, phone and fax numbers of your firm (optional)

   _____

   _____

2. Please check the designation that best describes your firm.
   - ☐ Architecture
   - ☐ Architecture/Interior Design
   - ☐ Interior Design/Space Planning
   - ☐ Other _____
   - ☐ A/E
   - ☐ E/A
   - ☐ Planning

3. Approximately what percentage of the programming you do is:

   Offered as a design service, not billed separately   _____

   Offered as a design service, billed separately   _____

   Offered as a consulting service separate from design   _____

4. How many employees does your firm have?   _____

5. How many programming specialists do you employ?   _____

6. What is the training of your programmers? (Please provide numbers in the appropriate category.)
   - ☐ BArch   ☐ MArch   ☐ PhD
   - ☐ Other _____

7. Please estimate how much *time* you devote to programming as a percentage of total billable time for an average project.
   - ☐ ½%   ☐ 1%   ☐ 2%   ☐ 5%   ☐ Over 5%

8. What is the estimated overall *cost* percentage of programming as part of total project cost?
   - ☐ ½%   ☐ 1%   ☐ 2%   ☐ 5%   ☐ Over 5%

9. What are your most used or prevalent methods for data gathering? Please rank the applicable items 1 to 7.
   - ☐ Document analysis
   - ☐ Behavioral observation
   - ☐ Visiting similar, state-of-the-art projects
   - ☐ Surveys
   - ☐ Literature search
   - ☐ Interviews
   - ☐ Other _____

10. Which are your most used or prevalent formats for communicating programming information? Please rank the applicable items 1 to 7.
    - ☐ Text
    - ☐ Photography
    - ☐ Video
    - ☐ Plan information
    - ☐ Sketches
    - ☐ Bar-graphs, pie charts
    - Other _____

11. What types of clients do you provide most programming services for? Please rank 1 to 5.
    - ☐ Government   ☐ Corporate   ☐ Institutional   ☐ Individual
    - Other _____

12. Which types of projects require the most in programming services? Please rank 1 to 5.
    - ☐ Commercial   ☐ Residential   ☐ Institutional   ☐ Industrial
    - Other _____

13. Has your firm developed innovative approaches in facility programming? If so, please describe:

    _____

    _____

    _____

    _____

Should you wish to submit an example of what you consider to be your best and most innovative programming effort for possible inclusion as a case study in Dr. Preiser's upcoming book, you may contact him at CSPA, The University of Cincinnati, Cincinnati, OH 45221-0016, (513) 556-6426, fax (513) 556-3288.

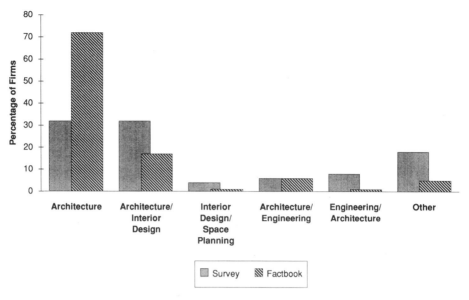

FIGURE 1.   Distribution of Firms by Type

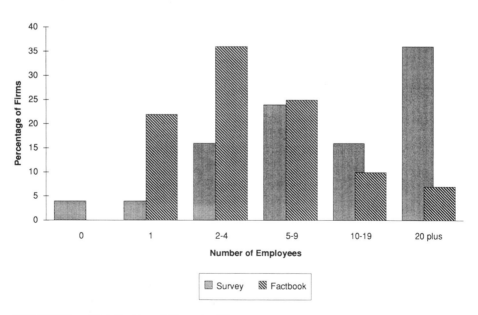

FIGURE 2.   Distribution of Firms by Size

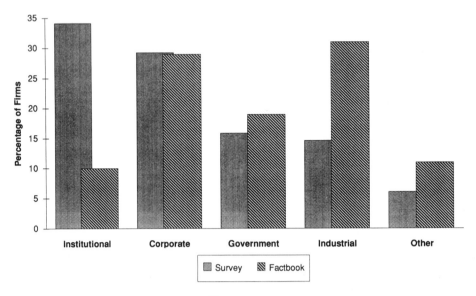

FIGURE 3.   Types of Programming Clients

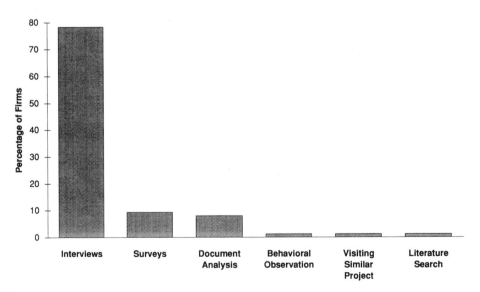

FIGURE 4.   Methods of Data Gathering

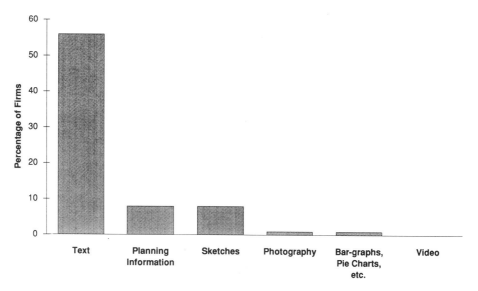

FIGURE 5.   Formats for Communicating Programming Information

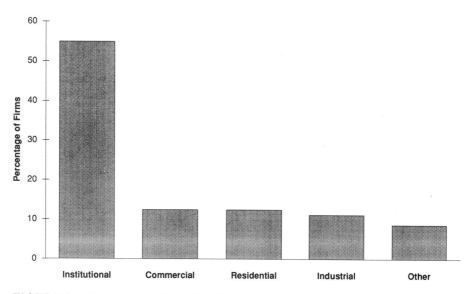

FIGURE 6.   Programming Intensive Projects

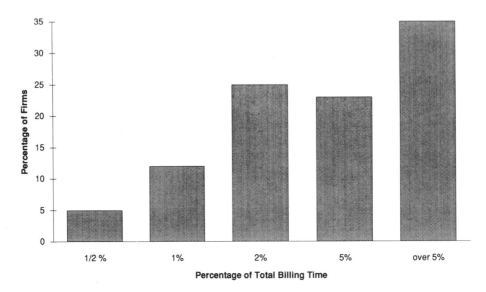

FIGURE 7.   Programming Time as a Percentage of Total Billing Time

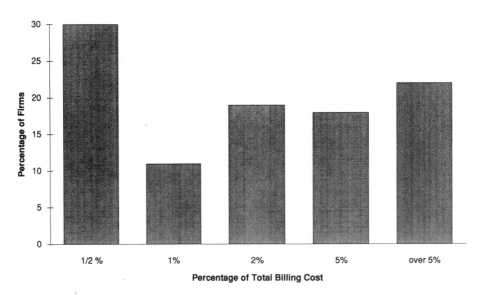

FIGURE 8.   Programming Costs as a Percentage of Total Billing Cost

PART I

New Developments in Facility Programming

CHAPTER 1

Strategic Asset Management: An Expanded Role for Facility Programmers

John P. Petronis

INTRODUCTION

A facility program makes explicit the goals, facts, concepts, and facility needs of a building in a way useful for making design decisions. It is an important and increasingly accepted step in the facility delivery process. While we acknowledge that facility programming itself is an important activity, it is also important to recognize that programming exists within a larger planning perspective. The purpose of this chapter is to define and describe the process of *strategic asset management* within an institutional framework, its relationship to facility programming, and the planner's role within this process.

Background

Facility programming is an important step in the facility delivery process. Facility programming provides essential information to the client and designer about the building requirements necessary to support required functions. As such, it is an important step in the facility delivery cycle. This cycle incorporates all the activities of bringing a facility from conception to occupancy and the evaluation of this effort to feed-forward to the next project (Figure 1-1).

The focus of facility programming has been most often directed toward defining the *design* requirements for specific facility projects. Trained primarily as architects or in the environmental sciences, facility programmers may tend to view their tasks as an effort to identify and support the functional and environmental requirements of the existing and projected functions rather than in the broader context of the building's entire life cycle. While programmers are cognizant of the economic consequences of their recommendations, the focus of their efforts is generally at the single building complex scale. While this perspective is proper and necessary for the programming effort, it is also important to recognize the larger institutional decision-making framework.

The facility delivery cycle is part of a larger institutional strategic asset management process. From an institutional and business standpoint, buildings are assets that support the mission and programs of the institution. *Assets* are defined as economic resources that have the potential of providing future services or benefits. An accountant would classify a building as a noncurrent asset, or something that is held for a number of years. This is contrasted to a current asset, which is cash or something that can readily be turned into cash.

As part of an overall strategic plan, an institution may use current assets (cash) to create or maintain noncurrent assets (infrastructure, buildings, land, major equipment). An institution must manage its assets to maintain their value and their usefulness to the institution. From this perspective, facilities have both functional and economic importance. In a sense, when institutions build a new facility or renovate an existing one, they are *investing* in the future. They are translating a short-term asset into long-term value.

Buildings require periodic investment to maintain their value and usefulness to the institution. Since buildings are physical entities, they tend to wear out over time. Buildings need to be maintained and renewed. The ongoing operating investment in a facility (such as repainting, roofing, etc.) is called *maintenance.* Periodically, a greater level of investment is required to replace major building system(s), adapt to new codes or level of performance, or to adjust to new functional requirements. The ongoing planned process of capital investment that ensures that facilities will function at levels commensurate with the priorities and mission of an institution is called *capital renewal.* Continual investment of operating and capital resources is required in this management process. These funds generally come from a separate capital budget that is allocated for improvements of a nonmaintenance nature.

If regular maintenance or portions of regular maintenance are deferred, eventually the accumulated effects of time and neglect can lead to faster-than-normal deterioration of the building, resulting in greater capital needs. If maintenance and/or regular reinvestment is deferred long enough, then the cost of returning the asset to useful life may exceed the asset's value. In this case, it may be more economical for the institution to build a new structure than to reinvest in the old one. (Figure 1-2).

There are many competing uses for an institution's resources. Many facility maintenance and capital needs may be deferred in the budgeting process. Economic forces place capital and operating budgeting constraints on many institutions, particularly those in the public sector. Numerous studies have documented that a capital investment "crisis" exists in higher education, with a $60 billion backlog of maintenance and repair required. In 1988, a typical university campus deferred $4 of needed maintenance for every $1 spent. In other words, a typical campus requires reinvestment of up to 25 percent of its replacement value (Rush, 1988).

While no definitive studies exist, it is clear that many public institutions (higher education, primary and secondary education, municipal, or state) are deferring necessary maintenance and capital investment because of competing demands for their limited resources. When compounded over time, this deferred maintenance and capital investment may become critical, adversely affecting health, safety, or the ability of a facility to support its mission.

There is a growing need to understand the overall institutional need for maintenance and capital investment and to determine strategies of how to fulfill needs. This process, called strategic asset management, will be described in the following section.

STRATEGIC ASSET MANAGEMENT

Strategic asset management is a process for making timely decisions about institutional assets to meet institutional needs. The strategic asset management process identifies how the physical assets of an institution can be developed, maintained, and enhanced to meet institutional goals.

The focus of strategic asset management is broader than facility programming. It begins earlier, at the time when initial needs are identified, and extends through the life of the facility. Whereas facility programming tends to focus on facility-specific requirements, strategic asset management seeks to understand the current and long-range needs of the institution and to secure suitable resources to maintain and augment its assets to support the institutional mission (Figure 1-3). Strategic asset management addresses the following questions:

- What is the asset base?
- What are the physical conditions of the facilities?
- Are land/facilities adequate for existing and projected functions?
- What capital improvements are required to meet needs?
- Should land be purchased/sold to meet institutional needs?
- What needs are most important?
- Where are funds coming from?
- How should needs be communicated in a manner useful for securing funds?

The steps of this process are shown in Figure 1-4 and are described as follows.

Prepare an Institutional Audit

Facilities exist to support the mission of the institution. This step documents the mission and internal and external forces that may affect the need for facilities. In an academic context, external forces include long-range trends affecting programs; competitive factors affecting the provision of services; or national, state, or local political impacts. Internal forces include existing institutional strategic plans, academic plans, or desires of key institutional bodies or individuals. For example, the trend for continuing development of new learning technologies (computer, video, voice communications) is an important external force that has tremendous current and future impact on how educational institutions teach and consequently on the facilities that need to support changing programs.

Prepare an Asset Audit

This step inventories and assesses the condition of the institutional assets and their capacity to meet the existing and projected functional needs. A number of facility audit procedures exist for higher and lower educational systems; if appropriate, a customized system can be developed. Generally, this assessment is conducted by trained teams that visit every facility and "grade" the facility with respect to pre-defined physical and functional criteria. The need for specific projects and their associated costs is systematically documented.

Assess Growth and Change

This step seeks to identify parameters of future change, such as enrollment, staffing projections, or legislative or market impacts that may affect the demand for the institution's services and, therefore, its facilities.

Determine Needs

Based on the analysis of the previous steps, specific maintenance and capital needs can be identified, including the following:

- facility renewal (deferred maintenance, or other projects having to do with the facility "wearing out")
- health/safety issues
- growth/change (new or expanded facilities to meet new functions), and
- facility adaptation (projects related to adjusting to new code or functional requirements)

Formulate Plan

During this step priorities are determined, funding strategies agreed upon, and the needs are documented and communicated for implementation.

Implement the Plan

Now the plan is acted upon. Necessary resources are secured and individual projects are implemented over a determined schedule.

The formula for a successful strategic asset management process stresses bringing the right people together with the right information at the right time to make the right decisions (Figure 1-5).

Participation of the "Right People"

Top-level management support is required, as is a clear understanding of what the decision-making sequence will be. Participation of key members of the administration, physical plant, planning staff, and appropriate consultants should be carefully considered and thoughtfully managed.

Collection of the "Right Information"

The "right information" is whatever is required to assist final decision making. Major elements of the information required are collected in steps 1, 2, and 3 of the process. Planners are fortunate that the tools available to assist in the planning process have proliferated, and include a variety of computerized database systems to aid in tracking and sorting of needs, geographic information systems and facilities management programs that tie databases to maps and floor plans, and programs to communicate requirements.

Managing the Process

The bringing together of all the elements at the proper time is an important management consideration. The entire process should be pre-planned and all the elements should be carefully managed. An overview of a typical work plan is shown in Figure 1-6. The timing of initial planning activities may vary substantially, depending upon the magnitude of an institution's assets, and range from a minimum of six months to more than a year. However, it is important to recognize that planning never really stops, and continued institutional commitment is required to keep information current and relevant. Computerized databases require updating and maintenance as individual projects are implemented and as needs are refined over time. The benefit of this investment is information that can be used for ongoing facilities management purposes.

The strategic asset management approach provides an institution with a comprehensive picture of the condition of its assets as well as a specific list of prioritized actions, costs, and timing to maintain the assets' value. Armed with this information, the institution will be able to communicate these needs in a manner appropriate for securing required funding and, once funds are acquired, allocating them in a rational and equitable manner. The databases that are established have continuing usefulness for facilities management purposes. With an institutional strategic asset plan in place, a facility programmer can work within a framework that clarifies overall institutional needs and puts individual projects within a larger context.

CASE STUDY

Purpose

This case study will describe the strategic asset management process for a large (90,000 student) public school system.

Context

This large, growing, public school system in the southwestern United States has more than 90,000 students and 125 schools totalling over 9 million square feet. After the defeat of a local mill levy election to fund new schools and renovation of existing structures, the district recognized that it required a better understanding of its capital needs so that it could effectively communicate these needs to the community. The district initiated a facilities master plan process that was based on strategic asset management concepts.

Highlights of the Planning Process

The overall planning process is shown in Figure 1-7; highlights follow.

Conduct an Institutional Audit
Existing information on the curriculum requirements was determined by studying existing documents and meeting with representatives of each curriculum area. Working papers were prepared that discussed potential facility impacts of educational trends, capital financing alternatives, and growth and change.

Conduct an Asset Audit
Information regarding existing facilities was compiled and placed on computerized spreadsheets and databases. Based on assessments of national standards, existing practices, and meetings with school-based committees, facility guidelines were established that described prototypical elementary, middle, and high schools. These guidelines were policy-based and provided a means to compare all the schools to a common standard (Figure 1-8).

Evaluation forms based on the standards were prepared and evaluators were trained so that consistent results would be achieved. All schools were then evaluated with respect to the guidelines and "graded" for their compliance. Results were placed on a computerized database (Figure 1-9).

Assess Growth and Change
This step included conducting enrollment projections and utilization analysis.

ENROLLMENT PROJECTIONS
Concurrent with the facility evaluation, long-range enrollment projections were prepared. While five-year enrollment projections already existed, long-range projections (fifteen years) were prepared for each high school, middle school, and elementary school by middle school feeder area. These projections provided a long-range perspective with which to make facility planning decisions, as well as providing some basis for planning for special education needs, which were not addressed in the five-year projection (Figure 1-10).

UTILIZATION ANALYSIS
For facility planning purposes, enrollment numbers and projections are only part of the picture. Since each facility has a certain potential capacity to accept students that depends on the nature and number of classrooms, utilization analysis is necessary. This process entailed developing spreadsheets that included the number of existing classrooms at each facility and the capacity of each facility to accept students based on formulas regarding acceptable pupil-teacher ratios. Projected enrollment numbers were then used to determine the number of classrooms that would be needed at each school to accommodate anticipated enrollment (Figure 1-11).

Determine Needs
Based on specific school-by-school analysis, itemized capital requirements were determined to meet existing and projected needs totalling more than $280 million. Capital projects were categorized and placed in a computerized database to assess relative measures of priority (Figure 1-12). Major categories of projects included the following:

- growth (projects required to accommodate an expanding student population)
- educational/programmatic (projects required to meet essential elements of the educational program)
- health/safety (projects addressing specific health/safety requirements),
- facility renewal (deferred maintenance, or other projects having to do with the facility "wearing out")
- educational/support (projects supporting primary educational requirements)

Formulate Plan
Based on conservative revenue estimates, it was determined that the district could expect $125 million of revenue in the next five years without raising taxes. The challenge of this step was to agree upon which projects could be

implemented during the coming five-year implementation cycle, given this revenue constraint.

Using the codes established during the previous steps, a strategy was agreed upon that funded (Figure 1-13):

all health/safety projects,
anticipated growth needs,
facility renewal projects to the extent possible, starting with the schools in
   the poorest condition (those schools with the lowest evaluation scores), and
a special allocation to each school to be used at its discretion.

The facility master plan was endorsed by the school administration and adopted by the Board of Education.

Implement

Implementation of any plan depends on resources and institutional support. A key implementation element was to organize to ensure a successful passage of the mill levy to fund the plan. Using the facilities master plan as a basis, a year-long (and ultimately successful—4 to 1 in favor) voter campaign was waged. It contained the following elements:

- The election effort began early.
- A committee of community volunteers was created to raise money and get out the vote via using phone banks to call registered voters.
- A variety of informational materials were prepared for community distribution, including leaflets, signs, and bumper stickers.
- Administrators visited schools to meet with parents, presenting the mill levy package and answering questions and concerns.
- Administrators made successful passage of the mill levy a priority for school principals. The principal's efforts for the mill levy election (for instance, disseminating information, encouraging parents and teachers to vote) were included in each principal's performance evaluation.

After having funded the program, the school district continues to support the implementation of the plan. It has established a facilities master planning office responsible for monitoring the plan and implementing a process to keep the plan current and to suggest modifications as required.

CONCLUSIONS

Strategic asset management provides a structured process for identifying operational and capital requirements to support institutional goals. An institution benefits from strategic asset management because it provides a detailed, comprehensive picture of the institution's assets as well as a plan for maintaining their value. The plan is vital both for securing funds and for allocating and managing resources that are obtained in an equitable manner. Databases developed in the process have immediate usefulness for ongoing real property and facilities management.

The strategic asset management process benefits the facility programmer by establishing the larger context within which an individual project resides. With an understanding of the big picture, a programmer can identify and accommodate interrelationships that may previously have been obscure. From a service standpoint, strategic asset management is fertile ground for an expanded role for facility programmers. Strategic asset management applies the same rigor in analysis that is required in facility programming, but it is broader in nature. A facility programmer is well equipped from training and experience to step into an asset management role that expands responsibilities from an individual project to the needs of an institution.

References

Architectural Research Consultants, Inc. 1989. *Albuquerque public schools facilities master plan*, Albuquerque, New Mexico.

Burgdorf, Kenneth, et al. 1990. *Scientific and engineering research facilities at universities and colleges*. Washington, D.C.: National Science Foundation.

Callnan, Michael T., and J. Stephen Collins. 1986. A clear challenge for the future: Capital asset management and planning at colleges and universities. *Planning for Higher Education* 14:3, pp. 30-38.

Dunn, John A. 1989. *Financial planning guidelines for facility renewal and adaptation*. Ann Arbor, Mich.: The Society for College and University Planning.

Hyatt, James. 1988-89. Financing facilities renewal and replacement. *Planning for higher education* 17:3, pp. 33-42.

Kaiser, Harvey H. January 1982. Funding of facility repairs and renovation. *Business officer*, pp. 22-24.

Kaiser, Harvey H. 1984. *Crumbling academe: Solving the capital renewal and replacement dilemma*. Washington, D.C.: Association of Governing Boards of Universities and Colleges.

Kaiser, Harvey H. 1987. *Facility audit manual: A self-evaluation process for higher education*. Alexandria, Va.: Association of Physical Plant Administrators of Universities and Colleges.

Meyerson, Joel, and Peter M. Mitchell. 1990. *Financing capital maintenance*. Washington, D.C.: National Association of College and University Business Officers.

Petronis, John P. 1985. Facility planning on a large scale: New Mexico facilities master plan. In *Programming the built environment*, ed. Wolfgang F.E. Preiser, 82-106. New York: Van Nostrand Reinhold.

Rush, Sean. 1988. *The decaying American campus: A ticking time bomb*. Alexandria, Va.: A joint report of the Association of Physical Plant Administrators of Universities and Colleges (APPA) and the National Association of College and University Business Officers (NACUBO), with the assistance of Coopers and Lybrand.

Rush, Sean, and Sandra Johnson. 1989-90. Campus facilities: A diminishing endowment. *Planning for higher education* 18:1, pp. 35-49.

Sherman, Douglas R., and William A. Dergis. 1981. A funding model for building renewal. *Planning for Higher Education* 9:3, pp. 21-25.

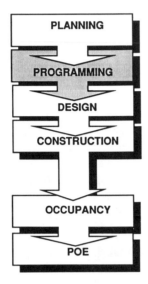

FIGURE 1-1.   Facility Programming Is an Important Step in the Facility Delivery Cycle

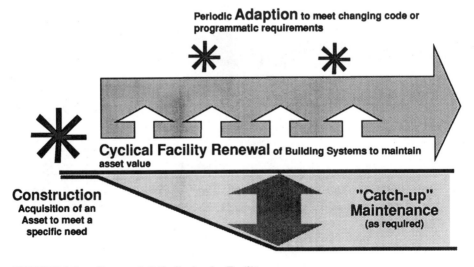

FIGURE 1-2.   Economic Life Cycle of a Facility

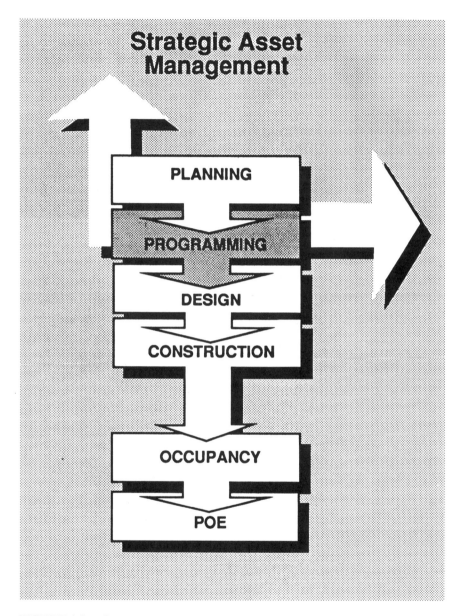

FIGURE 1-3.   Strategic Asset Management

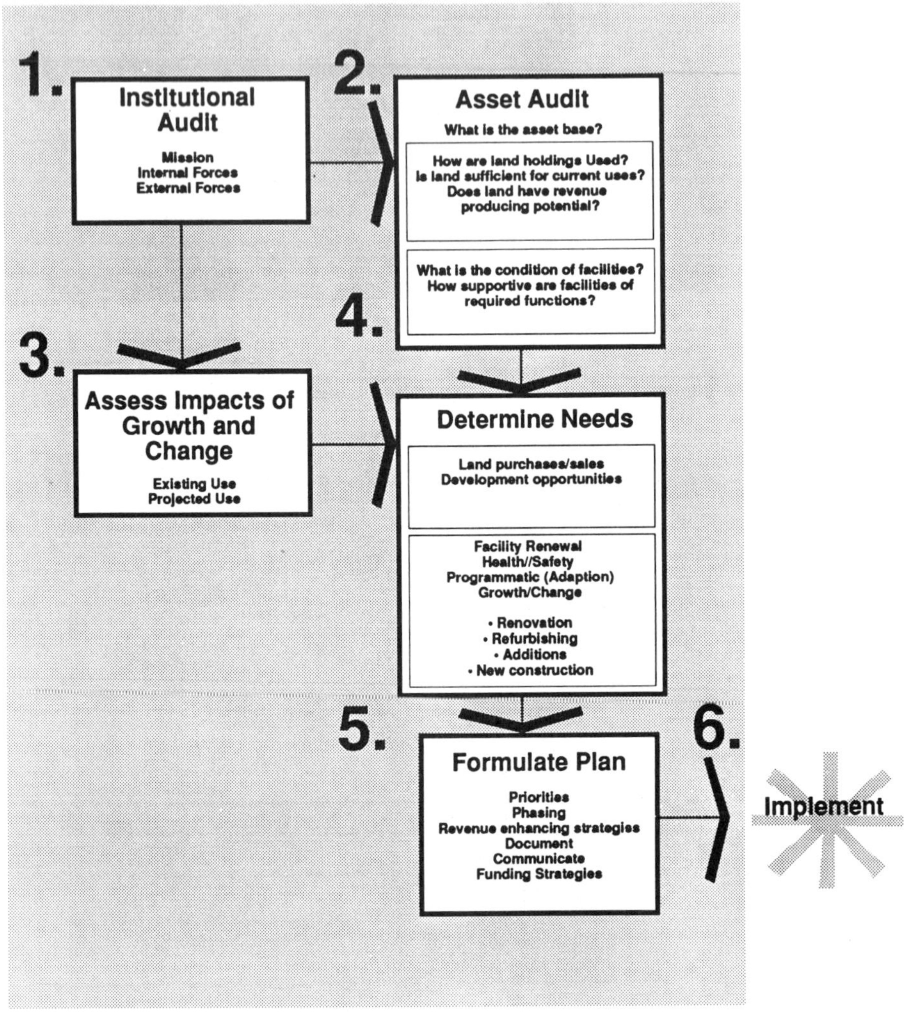

1. Institutional
Audit

Mission
Internal Forces
External Forces

2. Asset Audit

What is the asset base?

How are land holdings Used?
Is land sufficient for current uses?
Does land have revenue
producing potential?

What is the condition of facilities?
How supportive are facilities of
required functions?

3. Assess Impacts of
Growth and
Change

Existing Use
Projected Use

4. Determine Needs

Land purchases/sales
Development opportunities

Facility Renewal
Health//Safety
Programmatic (Adaption)
Growth/Change

• Renovation
• Refurbishing
• Additions
• New construction

5. Formulate Plan

Priorities
Phasing
Revenue enhancing strategies
Document
Communicate
Funding Strategies

6. Implement

FIGURE 1-4.   Strategic Asset Management Considerations

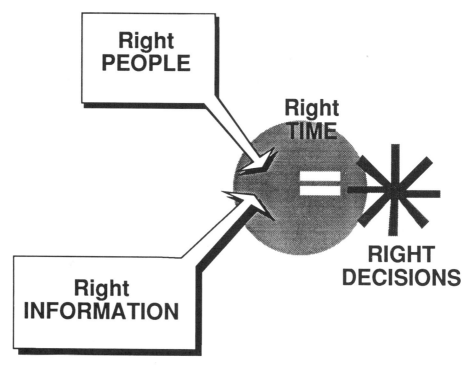

FIGURE 1-5.   Formula for Successful Planning

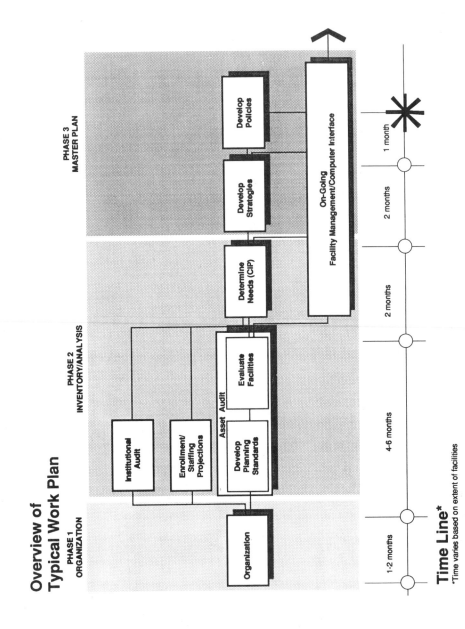

FIGURE 1-6.   Typical Management Plan

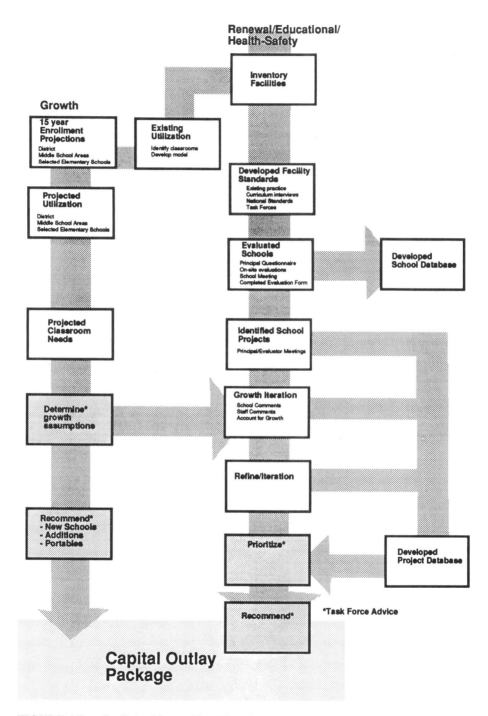

FIGURE 1-7.   Facilities Master Plan Flow Chart

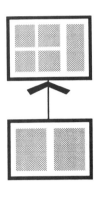

Provide Flexibility To Meet
New Circumstances

Policy 3.1   Plan for Flexibility
School facilities should provide ability to adjust to programmatic (instructional and community) and technological change.

School facilities must provide a learning environment supportive of the District's educational programs and curricula. While it may be impossible to predict with certainty the types of programs and technological changes that may occur in the future, it is a realistic goal to build into our facilities opportunity to adjust to many demands including:

-    Internal flexibility
-    Ability to expand and contract
-    Ability to accommodate future technology.

Guideline 3.1.1   Flexibility of Classrooms
Educational areas should allow internal flexibility for program adaptations: Factors to consider include:

-    *Classrooms are sized to allow a variety of grade levels.*
-    *Classrooms and support areas are designed to allow different programs to occur.*
-    *Classrooms can be varied in size through use of demountable partitions.*
  - *1/2 size classrooms that can be made into full classrooms;*
  - *Full classrooms that can be made into double size (for team teaching)*
  - *Appropriate plumbing stub-outs*
-    *Classrooms that allow the positive use of walls and ceilings*
-    *Flexibility in furniture arrangement.*

Note:
In recent APS schools there are classrooms with demountable partitions in each "wing" of the school to allow some classrooms to expand to meet new purposes.

38

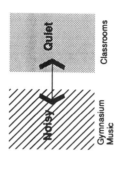

Centralize key support activities

Classrooms — Quiet

Gymnasium Music — Noisy

Separate Noisy Activities from Quiet Activities

Policy 3.2 **Site/Facility Organization**

School sites and facilities should be organized in a clear and consistent manner that is conducive to learning and allows proper supervision (see exhibits on following pages).

Guideline 3.2.1 **Centralization of Common Use Facilities**

Common use facilities should be centralized to population served:

- Media Center
- Work Room
- Cafeteria
- Student Rest Rooms
- Staff Rest Rooms

Guideline 3.2.2 **Noisy-Quiet Separation**

"Noisy" activities (gymnasium, music, assembly areas) are separated from learning areas.

Guideline 3.2.3 **Kindergarten Pick-up/Drop-Off**

Kindergarten classrooms should be close to parent pick-up/drop-off areas.

Guideline 3.2.4 **Covered Circulation**

Covered circulation with hard surfaced sidewalks should connect all school activity areas.

FIGURE 1-8.   Example of Facility Standards

39

APS Elementary School Evaluation Form

School Name

Location Number   **Area/Cluster**

Telephone Number

Address

Evaluator Names

Team Leader   Member

Evaluation Date

Appraisal Summary
Excellent = 100 - 90%   Poor = 30 - 49%
Satisfactory = 89 - 70%   Very Inadequate = <29%
Borderline = 50 - 69%

	Possible Points	Total Earned	%	Rating Category
The School Site	271			
School Plant Assessment	354			
The Adequacy and Environment for Education	375			
Total	**1000**			

School Data

Site Acreage

Building Area (SF)

1988-89-40 Day Enrollment | Permanent | Port. | Total |

Dates of Construction | Kinder. | Reg. | C&D |

Number of Classrooms | Regular | 1/2 |

No. of Portables | Double | Singles | Toilets |

Energy Sources   Gas   Electricity   Oil

Air Conditioning   Central   Window Units   Central

Heating   Roof   Roof   Individual

Construction
Steel Frame
Concrete Frame
Masonry
Other
Exterior Surfacing
Floor Slab on Grade
Floor Structural Slab
Floor Steel Joists
Floor Wood Joists

A   B   C

Notes and Comments

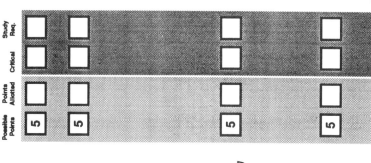

Possible Points	Points Allotted	Critical	Study Req.
5			
5			
5			
5			

Standard 1.7.3 Kindergarten Playground
There should be a fenced kindergarten area with appropriate equipment.

Standard 1.7.4 Playground Safety
The playground equipment should be located and designed to minimize hazards.

Factors to consider include:

- *Proper spacing between equipment*
- *Cushioned 'soft' ground surfaces beneath the equipment*
- *Metal rather than wood play structures to minimize hazards of splinters and minimize maintenance*
- *Designs that are free of obstacles.*

Standard 1.7.5 Hard Surfaced Play Areas
There should be hard surfaced play areas located near the building with southern sun exposure. Areas should include:

- *1 concrete pad (60' x 80') or 2 pads (each 40' x 60') with 12 basketball goals (6 around each pad)*
- *Asphalt play area (25,000 sf, or about 160' x 160') with painted game lines.*

Standard 1.7.6 Grass Playing Field
There should be one grassed game field not to exceed 180' x 320' with a 8'-10' running track around the perimeter.

FIGURE 1-9.   Example of Asset Audit Evaluation Form

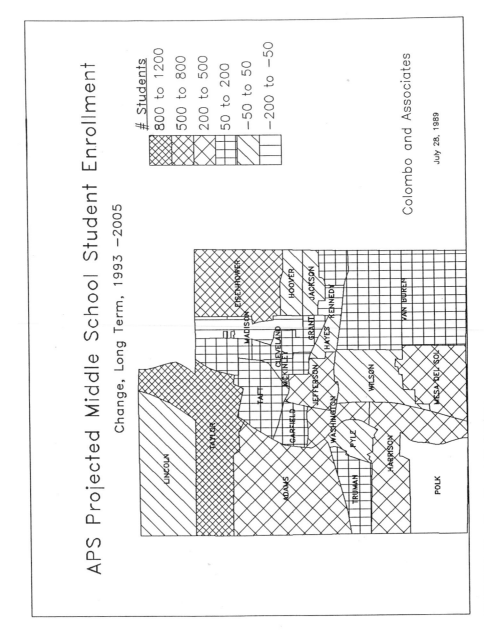

FIGURE 1-10. Enrollment Projections

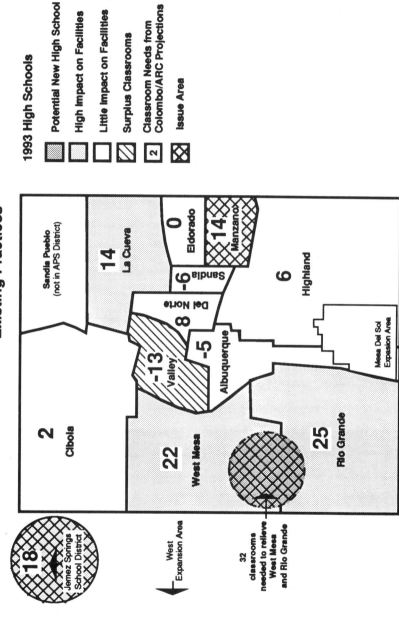

FIGURE 1-11. Classroom Need Projections

43

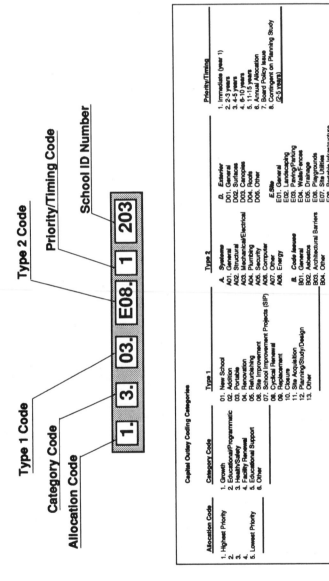

FIGURE 1-12. Example of Capital Project Coding Scheme

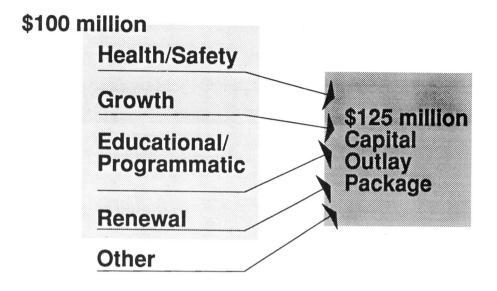

$100 million

- Health/Safety
- Growth
- Educational/ Programmatic
- Renewal
- Other

$125 million Capital Outlay Package

$25 million

Contingency ($5 million)
Equipment
Support Facilities
Special Requests

FIGURE 1-13.   Capital Outlay Plan Overview

CHAPTER 2

Applying the Problem-Seeking Approach to Engineering Programming

Conny R. Brown and Timothy K. Scarbrough

INTRODUCTION

When William Peña wrote the first edition of *Problem Seeking* in 1969, he intended it as an architectural programming primer for clients. Now in its third edition (1987), the work has become a standard text on architectual programming in colleges and universities nationwide.

The simplicity of the problem-seeking process has demonstrated itself over the years in architecture and in many other venues as well; for instance, its use in engineering has proven very successful. This chapter provides an example of how the problem-seeking method was used to do the following:

- establish the real requirements for a high-quality water system,
- develop the equipment and flow requirements for the system,
- determine the area requirements of a building to house the system,
- choose the best site location for the building, and
- select an operating and maintenance strategy for the system.

PROBLEM SEEKING: THE BASIS OF PROGRAMMING

Design is a problem-solving process. In order to have a successful design, it is necessary to have a clear definition of the problem to be solved, whether it is engineering, architectural, or operational in nature. Programming is a means of seeking to define the problem, an organized method of uncovering and stating a project's requirements. It is a process to seek out and define design criteria. The goals of programming are to:

- collect all pertinent information available from all sources
- identify good ideas to be considered
- obtain consensus among all parties involved
- develop the big picture without getting bogged down in details
- establish quality level expectations with the client
- identify issues and assign them to someone for timely resolution

Experience has shown that problem seeking is best approached as a specialty — one performed by programmers, not involving the designers who will do the problem *solving*. This approach prevents a distorted or inaccurate solution from arising out of a possible preconception of the problem to be solved. It also keeps the designer from developing misconceptions based on incomplete information. The program is a key element in the overall system of planning, which builds on previous decisions in a true "building-block" fashion.

While each situation and individual project has its own unique factors and influences, the programmer's approach to problem definition is consistent. Problem seeking employs a systematic, five-step process.

Step 1: Establish Goals

The establishment of clear goals for a project is of utmost importance, for the goals constitute the light by which all subsequent developments will be guided. One might see such goals as the project's desired destination, and they will strongly influence the selection of the means to reach that end.

Step 2: Collect, Organize, and Analyze Facts

Relevant facts are dates, parameters, and assumptions that influence the design of a project. The information derived from this step is primarily quantitative; it describes existing conditions and standards that must be met. The goals established in step 1 are valuable aids in determining what types of facts to collect.

Most members of the programming team collect and assemble information; however, the programming specialist has the greatest responsibility for data analysis and documentation. The programmer must sift out irrelevant material and hold details in abeyance until more comprehensive input is clearly required by the designer.

Factual data encompass specific project requirements, such as existing conditions, manpower, space needs, budget, and operations and maintenance strategies. They also involve knowledge of utility service, redundancy requirements, site considerations, and the existing codes and standards that must be met. To address all the factors that may influence the design of a process, product, or facility, the programming team must gather a great deal of information.

Step 3: Uncover and Test Concepts

Concepts are qualitative ideas for achieving goals. The creative opportunities for the client or user reach their high point during this phase of programming. Inspiration can come from any and all team members to produce a variety of alternatives.

Often a developing concept may point to the need for collecting certain related facts. A see-saw process must take place, for collection of facts and development of concepts cannot be completed in isolation.

Once the concepts are enumerated, the team must test them, analyzing them in terms of which can best satisfy the stated goals. A "recycling process"—reviewing goals in terms of concepts—also helps uncover invalid goals and suggests concept revisions.

The development and documentation of the concepts is one of the most crucial segments of the program. The designer's efforts will be based on these concepts, and subsequent reviews of his or her submittal will be made relative to them. The development of programmatic concepts expressing material flow, functional relationships, flexibility, material handling, centralized or decentralized operations, environmental controls, and levels of safety or security should constitute the conceptual segment of the program. The programming team must be alert to avoid providing the designer with physical solutions as input.

Step 4: Determine Needs

The purpose of step 4 is to differentiate what is truly necessary from what is merely desirable. The team defines needs in quantifiable terms, such as building area, quality of construction, list of equipment components, equipment and construction cost, and time. To do so, team members must prioritize goals and set a preliminary budget.

During the activities of the first three steps, it is probably best not to impose constraints on input from the various members of the programming team. Potential users should be free to express their desires related to the scope of the project, even when the emerging requirements may result in an ambitious program of far greater scope than that which can be supported financially. This is not an unusual occurrence, but it is imperative that the final program, as provided to the designer, be balanced within the budget.

Step 5: State the Problem

The problem statement provides a summary of the unique and essential criteria for design. It is developed jointly by the programming team and the design team at the project handoff. These statements serve as the premise for design and can be used later as design criteria to evaluate the design solution.

While the requirements should be stated and clearly analyzed by the programming team, considerations leading to the design should be presented in a factual manner, which requires the designer to analyze them also. This activity provides a valuable interface between problem definition (programming) and problem solution (design), and ensures that the design team clearly understands the program.

THE PROBLEM-SEEKING APPROACH

The problem-seeking process uses a variety of proven communication techniques that allow for easy presentation and scrutiny of material. One of the most valuable benefits of programming is the promotion of consensus building. The communication techniques foster participation within large project groups by providing ways to collect input, analyze and illustrate options for decision making, and inform those involved of the results of their efforts. Operational groups frequently do not see facilities requirements the same way management or facilities personnel do. Programming creates understanding between the two groups, leading to project buy-in on all levels.

Goal Setting and Decision Making by Management

It is crucial for management to buy into the project. Without this acceptance, chances for project approval and funding are very slim. One way to get management involvement and buy-in is to have them establish the goals that the project is to accomplish. By providing an early establishment of these goals, programming defines the direction for the project team. When these goals are incorporated into the design of the project, there is a better chance for management approval of ultimate project development.

The other main role for management during programming is in decision making and issue resolution. As items that need resolution before the completion of the program come up, they are collected and tracked as *issues*. A "feasibility test" meeting is scheduled as part of the interactive work sessions. At this time, these issues are either resolved or assigned to a particular individual or committee with a scheduled resolution date.

The key to management involvement is to make the best use of their time and only involve them at the appropriate times during the programming phase of the project.

Interactive Work Sessions

Interactive work sessions, sometimes called "squatters," bring together all pertinent groups in an organized manner. These work sessions help identify each group's perspective on the project and encourage input from both users and workers. The sessions keep information in front of the "public" and stimulate ongoing examination of issues. The process includes graphic analysis, documentation, and presentation during "on-the-spot" sessions. This approach allows the most accurate feedback and maximizes user involvement over a relatively short period of time. It also enables the project team to come to terms with any problems confronting the project, and provides the client or user with all the relevant data needed for timely, informed decision making.

Wall Displays of Analysis Cards

The analysis cards technique is a method of graphically recording and presenting information. A wall display of cards allows for easy presentation and scrutiny of project information at any time during the progress of a project. This information is intended to be discussed, decided upon, and sometimes discarded during interviews and work sessions. The cards contain abstract diagrams and symbols along with written comments.

Why Use a Specialist?

Although the techniques mentioned sound relatively simple, it is generally advantageous to hire a specialist to implement them. Consultants offer unbiased analysis. They have no positions to defend, no hidden objectives to prove. Moreover, they manage the process in an organized fashion. Users are more willing to adjust their schedules to come to meetings with specialists, since they perceive the "outsiders" to offer benefits.

In summary, the problem-seeking method of programming is an organized method of analysis that defines the problem to be solved by the design team. It has five basic steps that apply to architecture, engineering, or any other type of project. By using this method, you are sure of dealing with the whole problem and eliminating false starts.

ENGINEERING PROGRAMMING: A CASE STUDY OF A HIGH-QUALITY WATER SYSTEM PROJECT

Engineering programming is the use of problem-seeking methods and techniques for systems, manufacturing processes, or other nonfacility engineering studies. It is led by engineers who are familiar with engineering terminology, design criteria needed to do engineering design, and engineering design costs. Specialists from CRSS Architects, Inc., working with engineers from its sister company, CRS Sirrine Engineers, Inc., have successfully applied problem seeking to engineering issues many times. The following case study of a high-quality water system demonstrates the process well.

Project Summary

A client asked CRSS to meet with its user and utility groups to determine outstanding issues that needed to be resolved to define the requirements for the high-quality water system. By using the problem-seeking programming process, the diverse client groups reached a consensus on the requirements for the system. CRSS used its "squatters" technique of continuous, intense work sessions to collect and analyze data rapidly, organizing information according to its standard programming format (see the Engineering Information Index, Figure 2-1). Key schedule milestones revealed an immediate need for the development of system components and a preliminary layout to establish the size of the building shell. The well-organized and proven programming methodology was instrumental in completing the project within stringent time limits.

Problem Seeking in Action

The planned completion of a new building (Building C) with major high-quality (HQ) water demands triggered the need for the client to analyze its HQ water availability on the client's site and propose a new facility to augment supply. Frequent changes in the HQ water project, however, concerned all groups involved. Because CRSS previously had completed several effective programming studies for this client, management awarded the firm a contract, with the following missions:

- set goals for the project
- identify the concerns of each group involved
- identify key project issues
- identify critical decisions, who should make them, and when
- establish performance requirements for the HQ water system
- identify and confirm key schedule milestones
- collect and organize information available on the project

At an executive briefing and kickoff meeting held to initiate the study, all parties involved reviewed the project mission and scheduled individual work sessions for the week (Figure 2-2). Meeting attendees included representatives from Building C users, utilities, architectural and engineering services, project management, property development, industrial safety, and maintenance engineering. This group set the following preliminary goals for the project:

- to provide an HQ water system for line-of-business requirements through 1995
- to locate the HQ water system in the right location
- to provide the water required by Building C to start process commissioning in October 1989
- to provide the water required by Building C to start product accreditation in April 1990 (Figure 2-3)

The programming team conducted nine intensive work sessions in one week to deal with the various issues confronting the project (Figure 2-4). The subject of the first squatters was the location of the HQ water system. The client had chosen a preliminary site, but there were some problems with it: One issue discussed during the first work session was solvent and chemical unloading and storage in the vicinity.

The next work session concerned water requirements for all the buildings that required HQ water: buildings A, B, and C. The team deliberated the specification for the water required by these facilities, as well as the need for process/product quality control to show that water meets the specification. Team members determined that three types of water were required—filtered, softened, and high-quality. They also established water demand.

The Building B requirements were the topic of another meeting. Since the proposed water facility site was adjacent to Building B, it was necessary to make sure that the HQ water building would not block future expansion plans the client had for Building B.

A fourth work session was held to discuss the utility services that would be required at the new HQ water building. On the agenda as well were material handling and dock requirements, the number of personnel required to operate the facility, what temperatures should be maintained in the facility, and what chemicals would be used there.

At the following session, construction and project management representatives studied what impact the addition of a new building would have on construction of Building C and other planned projects in the area. Owing to the mature nature of the site, there are few locations for laydown areas for construction projects, and rerouting of vehicular and pedestrian traffic must be closely coordinated over the entire area.

Trucking and traffic—specifically the effect of construction of a new HQ water building on trailer deliveries and routing to existing docks—was the subject of a sixth meeting. Attendees determined proper clearances and needed turning areas for the sizes of trucks and trailers used.

As the amount of time required to select a site, design and construct the building, and receive, install, and debug the HQ water system became evident, the client realized just how stringent the time limits of this project would be. Hence the purpose of another session was to establish the schedule required to construct a new HQ water building. Long lead items were enumerated at this meeting.

The engineering team for the HQ water project also conducted a squatters. They developed a list of questions that needed to be answered before designing the facility.

At the final work session, the participants discussed the location for the facility. They defined twelve potential sites and analyzed the strengths and weaknesses of each. The evaluation criteria established by the team included two "musts" and eleven "wants" (Figure 2-5). The "musts" were that contiguous area had to be currently available owing to the schedule (there was no time to relocate existing operations) and that the schedule must be able to be met (there was no time for additional permitting or impacting the Building C construction project). Those criteria eliminated all but three sites. The eleven "wants" were given a value between 1 and 10. After each site was rated on how well it met these criteria, it became clear which of the three sites was best suited for the project. However, the team pointed out that a detailed evaluation of every potential site must be conducted to confirm preliminary ideas about each.

The week ended with an in-process review of the preliminary findings by all participants. At this meeting, the project goals, the key decisions required, the outstanding issues, and the information needed to design the building were presented. The summary recommendations were as follows:

- Obtain all *key decisions* by the dates shown on the schedule.
- Perform *site analysis* of the most likely sites immediately, select a site, and obtain approval of the site committee.
- Develop the *cost differences* between the various own versus lease options.
- Provide worst-case scenario *building design criteria* to the building design team if multiple vendors bid on the system.
- Develop a *critical path* of decisions and design requirements for the softened water system to meet October 1989 schedule requirements.
- Coordinate *construction activities* through the appropriate construction manager.

System Definition

One week after the review meeting, the client asked CRSS to come back and use its problem-seeking programming process to define the HQ water system according to the following mission statement:

- to meet the *management philosophy* on redundancy and reliability
- to satisfy the *quality and cost needs of the users*, especially on the Building C project
- to have the HQ water system *installed according to the schedule* set by the Building C project
- to *answer questions* presented by the building/facility portion of the design team by November 1, 1991
- to allow *bid packages* to be written upon completion of the team's work
- to allow management to make a *decision on the operation and maintenance strategy* for the HQ water process

Key additions to the project team were made to accomplish this mission. A CRSS process engineer who specialized in HQ water systems, as well as engineers from a firm that specializes in the design of HQ water systems, joined the team. The client's process engineers, utilities managers, and existing HQ water system operators joined these specialists for four intense days of meetings.

Following the standard five-step process, the team first reviewed and agreed upon goals for the project. The goals from the previous study were still appropriate, but one goal was added: to have an HQ water system that will meet the *capacity requirements* and will also meet new *quality requirements*.

Factual data were then collected to provide a basis for the design. Assumptions for the project included operational dates for the system. Team members concurred that a redundancy philosophy of "$N + 1$" should apply to all major components. Documented problems arising from putting storage tanks outside the building led to a decision to locate all storage tanks on the interior. Water requirements for buildings A, B, and C established quality and quantity requirements, for both the October 1989 and April 1990 dates. Then the team analyzed the raw water supplied to the system. Compilation of detailed specifications for the filtered water, softened water, and HQ water followed. After studying flow demands on a minute-by-minute basis over a typical eight-hour shift, team members determined peak and overall usage. They also established HQ makeup requirements; evaluated three different primary deionized water systems; investigated the advantages and disadvantages of three reverse osmosis systems; and developed process utility requirements for steam, condensate, electric power, and wastewater.

This all led to the development of the actual water system. Three options for softened water, including a temporary system, were developed. The recommendation was to *not* supply softened water from the new HQ water building, because a new system could not be operational in the required time frame. Instead, the programmers recommended a closed loop system in Building C with makeup water from the demineralized water system.

Development of the equipment definition for the system occupied the majority of the four-day session. A very preliminary flow diagram provided a starting point (Figure 2-6). Then the team went through the system on a component-by-component basis. As participants defined additional bleed or supplemental system requirements, they reworked the sizing of the upstream components to provide the total system flow required. Isometric sketches gave floor plate and height requirements for the flow at each step.

The overall system consisted of the following components (Figure 2-7):

water supply	degassifier
chlorine	regeneration equipment
coagulant (lime softening was rejected)	submicron filters
multimedia filters	ultraviolet
filtered water tank	HQ storage tanks
heat exchanger	booster pumps
pre-treatment skid	polish system
reverse osmosis	micron filters
chemical cleaning	ultrafiltration
reverse osmosis water storage	recovery unit
chlorine scavenger	chemical cleaning
primary deionized water	recirculation pumps
neutralization tank	sterilization unit
mixed beds	sterilization area
mixed-bed regeneration	support spaces

Following the development of the equipment definition, the team studied where to divide the HQ water system if it would not all fit into one building. They determined that there were two potential division points that could lead up to three locations for the system. In addition, they enumerated the disadvantages of dividing the system.

System location was addressed again. Although they identified sixteen additional potential sites, the team still felt that the one recommended in the first study was the most suitable.

Although many HQ building issues were resolved during the work sessions, some were not—despite days of discussion. The team assigned these problems to the proper groups or individuals for solution by a set deadline.

After the four days of process definition, the process engineers went back to their respective offices for three days to verify the sizing of equipment. The team then returned to the client's offices for two more days to develop block layouts for the facility. Using the footprints developed during the equipment sizing exercise, they generated several possible layouts. The recommended facility shape was triangular in nature and two stories high. However, this footprint eliminated the minimum number of executive parking spaces in the existing parking lot proposed as the site.

The following week, CRSS presented the results of the study to the client's site and manufacturing management. During this executive review, management gave one last consideration to locating the system inside Building C.

Ultimately, the facility was designed in the recommended footprint and located on the suggested site. It met all of the goals for the project, including providing HQ water in the quality and quantity needed for the users at the client's site.

System Operation and Maintenance

Two months after the completion of this programming project, the client again called on CRSS to use its problem-seeking techniques. This time the object was to determine the operating and maintenance strategy for the HQ water system.

In brief, the operating and maintenance programming sessions established that HQ water is a critical component to the manufacturing operations at the client's site. The quality of HQ water is a consideration that should not be published to outside sources. There is added value to having the client operate and maintain the HQ water system.

SUMMARY

The problem-seeking method of programming works very well for the analysis of engineering problems. It is an organized method of uncovering and defining a client's project requirements. An engineering programmer who is familiar with the process being defined should lead the sessions; otherwise, the team might not recognize what is a "big idea" or concept that should be documented and what is a detail that is not important to the development of the system or process.

For CRSS' client, the interactive work sessions brought together all pertinent groups involved in the project so that they could hear each other's ideas and concerns firsthand. The analysis card technique of public display of information kept each group's ideas out in front of all involved for discussion and scrutiny. All groups were able to develop a better understanding of the total project and agree on what the "real" requirements for the project were.

CRSS and the client team considered six operating and maintenance strategies:

- vendor-owned, -operated, and -maintained
- vendor-owned technology and process strategy operated and maintained by the client
- third-party lease operated and maintained by the client
- vendor-owned, client-operated, and vendor-maintained
- vendor-owned, joint vendor-client operation and maintenance
- client-owned, -operated and -maintained

Parties involved rejected the last three strategies after the initial consideration and the first after more investigation; however, they did not feel that they could make a final recommendation without more information on the initial and operating costs of the two remaining options.

Additionally, team members developed concepts concerning the following:

- various contract options
- an organization chart
- staffing requirements
- responsibilities for the various staff positions
- specifications for the operating and maintenance contract

	Goals	Facts	Concepts	Needs	Problem

Function
People
 	
Process
 	
Systems
	Mission
	Maximum number
	Individual identity
	Interaction/privacy
	Hierarchy of values
	Operations
	Efficiency
	Security
	Continued service
	Reduced downtime
	Reliability
	Compatibility
		Statistical data
		Area parameters
		Manpower/workloads
		User characteristics
		Process analysis
		Time-motion study
		Impact of loss
		Equipment support
		  requirements
		Consumer service
		  requirements
		Equipment maintenance
		  requirements
		Equipment lists
			Maintenance grouping
			Operation grouping
			Separated flow
			Sequential flow
			Mixed flow
			Security controls
			Degree of reliability
			Maintain/availability
			Relation of systems
				Space requirements
				Parking requirements
				Engineering system
				  capacity
				Security system capacity
					Unique and important performance requirements which will shape design solution.

Form
Facility
 	
Site
 	
Quality
	Facility elements (source,
	  supply points, other
	  systems)
	Efficient space use
	Site elements (trees, water,
	  open space, existing
	  facilities, utilities)
	Neighbors
	Projected image
	Level of quality
		Facility analysis
		Climate analysis
		Code survey
		F.a.r. and g.a.c.
		Site analysis
		Utility availability
		Soil analysis
		Cost/system
		Facility efficiency
		Functional support
			Climate control
			Safety
			Density
			Accessibility
			Interdependence
			Special techniques
			Character
			Quality control
				Facility and site influences
				  on cost
				Quality (system security)
				Quality (system efficiency)
				Quality (system cost)
					Major form considerations which will affect building design.

Economy *Initial budget* *Operating Costs* *Life Cycle Costs*	Extent of funds Cost effectiveness Maximum return Return on investment Minimize operating costs Maintenance and operating costs Reduce life cycle costs	Cost parameters Maximum budget Time-use factors Market analysis Energy source-costs Process and climate factors Economic data	Cost control Efficient allocation Multi-function Cogeneration Energy conservation Merchandising	Cost estimate analysis Energy estimate analysis Entry budget Operation costs Life cycle costs	Attitude toward the initial and life cycle costs and their influence on the fabric and geometry of the facility.
Time *Past* *Present* *Future*	System reuse Static/dynamic Change Growth Occupancy date	Maintenance schedule Replacement schedule Operation schedule projections	Adaptability Tailored/loose fit Convertibility Expansibility Linear/concurrent scheduling	Spare capacity Phasing Escalation System life expectancy Expansion capacity	Implications of change/growth on long-range performance.

FIGURE 2-1. Engineering Information Index

Week	Monday	Tuesday	Wednesday	Thursday	Friday
1	3 October	4	5	6	7
	← Project Issue Management Worksessions →				
2	10	11	12	13	14
	← Prepare Issue Document →			Review Meeting	
3	17		Develop Process Definition, Flow Diagram & Information to Size Building		
4	24	25	26	Develop Block Layouts & Select Site	
	← Equipment Sizing Verification →				
5	31	1 November	2	Executive Review	Refine System Equipment
	Refine Block Layouts	Select / Hire A/E			
6	7	8	9	10	11
	← Refine Block Layouts, Determine Building Shell & Develop Request For Bid for HP Water System →				
	← Prepare Process Definition Program Document →				Publish Program
7	14	15	16	17	18
	← Finalize Building Shell →				
		Request Bid	← Conceptual Building Design →		
8	21	22	23	24	25
	← Conceptual Building Design →			Holiday	Holiday
9	28	29	30	1 December	2
	← Conceptual Building Design →			A/E Fast Track Design	
10	5	6	7	8	9
	← A/E Fast Track Building Design →				
11	12	13	14	15	16
	← A/E Fast Track Building Design →				
12	19	20	21	22	23
		Operating and Maintenance Strategy Analysis			

FIGURE 2-2.   Programming Schedule

59

Task	Year / Month	1988 O N D	1989 J F M A M J J A S O N D	1989 J F M A
Bldg. C				
Debug & Start-Up			*	
Process Accreditation			▬▬▬▬▬▬▬	
Start Product Accreditation				*
Softened Water System				
Order Equipment		*		
Water Available for Bldg. C			*	
HP Water System				
Request for Bids		*		
Award Bid			*	
Receive Vendor Drawings			*	
Sign Contract			*	
Order Equipment			*	
Receive Equipment				*
HP Water System Building				
Site Selection		*		
A/E Proposal		*		
A/E Selection / Hire		*		
Block Layouts		■		
Conceptual Engineering Design		■		
A/E Design (Fast Track)			▬▬▬	
Order Steel			*	
Order Load Center			*	
Excavation Approval			*	
Site Preparation			*	
Start Foundations			*	
Steel Delivery			*	
Steel Installed			*	
Floor Slabs			*	
Shell Completion			*	
Receive / Install Load Center			*	
Load Center Complete			*	
Receive HP System Equipment				*
Equipment Installed				*
Provide HP Water to Bldg. C				*

60

FIGURE 2-3. Project Schedule

Phase I Worksessions

#1   Solvent & Chemical Unloading & Storage
#2   Water Requirements
#3   Bldg. C Building Requirements
#4   Utilities
#5   Construction Impacts
#6   Trucking/Traffic
#7   Schedule
#8   Engineering Team Meeting
#9   System Location (Site)

FIGURE 2-4.   Phase I Work Sessions

Criteria	Must	Want	Value	Site 1	2	3	4	5	6	1	2	3	6
1. Area Available	X			Y	Y	Y	Y	N	Y				
2. Can Meet Project Schedule	X			Y	Y	Y	N	Y	Y				
3. Permitting		X	10	3	10	9			5	30	100	90	50
4. Potential Process Impediments		X	9	3	9	9			10	27	81	81	90
5. Length of Pipe Run		X	7	10	6	1			5	70	42	7	35
6. Traffic Impact		X	9	3	3	9			5	27	27	81	45
7. Material Handling		X	7	3	2	9			4	21	14	63	28
8. Water Availability		X	5	6	6	9			7	30	30	45	35
9. Safety		X	4	1	9	8			6	4	36	32	24
10. Operating Cost		X	8	7	7	6			6	56	56	48	48
11. Construction Cost		X	6	2	5	10			4	12	30	60	24
12. Other Utility Availability		X	3	6	6	4			7	18	18	12	21
13. Expansion Capability		X	6	2	5	9			1	12	30	54	6

Total: 307   464   573   406

FIGURE 2-5.   Site Selection Criteria

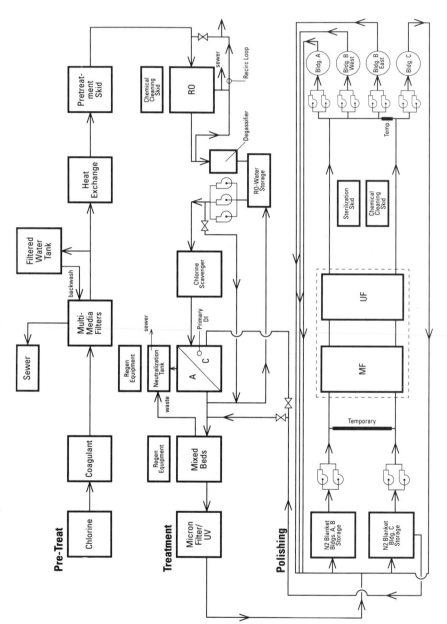

FIGURE 2-6. Process Flow Diagram

RO WATER STORAGE

- PUMP SUCTION FOR PRIMARY DI
- 5 MINUTES AT PEAK FLOW
- N_2 BLANKET NOT REQUIRED
- PROVIDE AIR FILTER
- 4,000 GAL. FOR MAX RECIRCULATION
- 1150 GAL × 5 MINUTES = 6,000 GAL.
- SIZE FOR 6,000 GALLONS

- 8 FT. ϕ × 17 FT (H) - 1990
- 304 STAINLESS STEEL
- 51,000 # TOTAL
- 1,000 # / SQ. FT.
- PUMPING STATION
  - 3 CENTRIFUGAL PUMPS @ 50%
- FOOT PRINT :
  8 FT × 12 FT × 17 FT (H) · (1990)
  W/ 3 FT OVERHEAD CLEARANCE

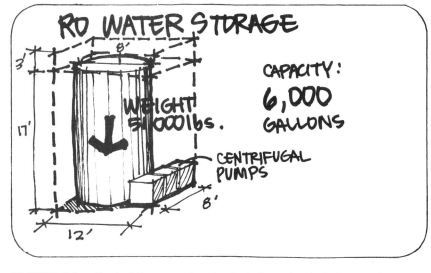

RO WATER STORAGE

CAPACITY: 6,000 GALLONS

WEIGHT 51,000 lbs.

CENTRIFUGAL PUMPS

63

FIGURE 2-7.   Typical Programming Analysis Done for Each Process Step

CHAPTER 3

NCR Corporation Worldwide Facilities Design Guidelines

Janet Mackey Brown

INTRODUCTION

"A great style must first of all be clear. It must be appropriate." — Aristotle

NCR Corporation, a Fortune 100 computer company with yearly sales of more than $6 billion, retained Hellmuth, Obata & Kassabaum (HOK) to develop corporate image and design guidelines for its 1,200 worldwide facilities. NCR was acquired by AT&T as a wholly owned subsidiary in 1991.

NCR's management philosophy is to direct, teach, and support decision makers throughout the organization rather than to issue rules and regulations. HOK's design guidelines reinforce this philosophy by presenting a strong, clearly articulated design philosophy that allows a wide range of design solutions, thought, and creativity.

In response to NCR's goals, HOK programmers, site designers, architects, and interior and graphic designers worked as a team, developing a comprehensive corporate facilities program that enables NCR to present one common corporate image. The design guidelines program creates an image for all of NCR's facilities that is compatible with the company's corporate values and traditions. At the same time, the guidelines help corporate managers and design consultants improve facilities, making them more supportive work environments for NCR employees. The program may be applied to any of NCR's facilities, from their Dayton, Ohio, headquarters to a sales office in New Guinea to a manufacturing plant in Scotland.

The actual programming or problem-definition phase was an important part of this design effort, since a thorough understanding of NCR's mission, culture, values, and operations was critical in developing the design. The impact of the programming effort was reinforced throughout the project, since the lead programmer was also the project director. Indeed, the complete guidelines package is really a program or pre-design tool that is used by designers all over the world. The following sections describe the purpose of the program, the methods used in developing the guidelines, and a report of the results to date.

CONTEXT

"By projecting the same quality image in our products, our facilities, and our communications, we create value and contribute to the continuing success and growth of NCR."—Charles E. Exley, NCR Chairman and C.E.O.

In the mid-1980s, NCR was just coming out of a period of austerity. Severe financial hardship accompanied the transition of changing from a mechanical products company (producing cash registers) to a computer company. NCR's facilities staff responded to this financial crunch by bringing facilities on-line at the lowest possible cost—with image, design quality, and employee satisfaction having relatively low priority.

Once the company had turned around financially, NCR wanted to upgrade their facilities. The real estate staff began as—individual, decentralized groups—to improve the quality of their new projects. It soon became clear, however, that while each individual project was making a good attempt at upgrading, a lack of consistency and quality control kept these projects from being a set or family of buildings with a focused message.

The need to improve design quality in facilities followed closely and was substantially influenced by another important NCR design improvement project: their product design guidelines. Until the early 1980s, NCR had not focused on product design quality. A major turnaround began with the redesign of their entire line of products and the development of guidelines for a decentralized industrial design staff so that they could individually design products that belong visually to the set or family of NCR products.

This product design program was so successful that NCR was hailed by the *Wall Street Journal* and others for their design leadership and, according to Chuck Exley, NCR's former C.E.O., went from having among the worst-looking products in the industry to having the best. According to Exley, "If you look at the appearance of NCR products today, I think you would agree that we deserve the recognition we have received as a leader in industrial design."

Exley recognized the potential of facilities to make the same quality statements about the company that NCR achieved with their product and graphic design programs. Two enthusiastic designers in the Corporate Real Estate Group, Kevin Barker and Dan Accrocco, AIA, took up the challenge, leading the development and implementation effort for NCR.

One of NCR's dilemmas regarding issuing design guidelines was that it seemed somewhat contradictory to their intention of decentralizing and push-ing decision making as low as possible in the organization. Historically, NCR has been a somewhat paternalistic and hierarchical corporation—fitting, perhaps, for an old, Midwestern corporation with a history of leaders with long tenures. While the current leadership continues to take pride in the company's conser-vative, "Midwestern" values, they are convinced that the people who are closest to a problem can best solve that problem. As Exley put it, "I believe that everybody functions better if you explain to them what their job is all about and how it fits into the picture."

The guidelines are intended to tell users what is important to the company and what is to be achieved by NCR facilities. Autonomy is given to the project teams in how to accomplish the task. Exley's introductory letter at the front of the guidelines emphasizes this point:

> Our facilities must be a confirmation to the people of NCR and to our customers of our respect for the individual, and that we seek to attain the highest standards of quality in everything we do. This guideline describes the ideas and the look that can help us meet these goals in our facilities. It has enough "rules" to assure some consistency and recognizability, and many suggestions, recommendations, and ideas. We are depending on you, as a manager or design professional, to apply these guidelines with creativity, intelligence, and thoughtfulness.

Scope of the Guidelines

NCR has approximately 1,200 facilities worldwide; one can hardly find a country so remote that NCR is not there. The majority of their facilities are sales offices, but they also have the following:

- headquarters facilities
- development and production facilities
- data centers (both in-house data centers and service bureaus)
- training facilities (for both technical and management training)
- distribution centers
- customer service centers (for repair and maintenance)

The guidelines focus on the sales office but are applicable to all NCR buildings. The "Guidelines Structure," illustrated in the guidelines manual, shows the scope of the topics covered, from site entry design to computer room interior design (Figure 3-1).

Guidelines Users

A wide variety of people use the guidelines manual to understand what is acceptable for an NCR facility and how to create one. The guidelines are directed to the following people:

- Executives and other managers, who need to understand the philosophy and goals of the program and the criteria on which they should evaluate plans and facilities. These people are experts on NCR but are rarely design professionals.

- Facility managers, who play a major role in maintaining the quality and consistency of the design and therefore should be familiar with the philosophy and goals as well as the design specifics. These people tend to have administrative or financial rather than design backgrounds.
- Project managers, who are pivotal in the implementation of the guidelines and need to know it all. These are the people who know a lot about both NCR and facility design.
- Designers, both in-house and outside consultants, who need to be familiar with the overall image goal and the details of how to achieve that image. These people are knowledgeable about design, but may or may not be very familiar with NCR—its image, goals, culture, functions, etc.

One of the challenges in planning and writing the manual is to communicate clearly to all users, regardless of their level of design expertise or NCR sophistication, without seeming to condescend. The audience can range from a sales office manager in some remote country, working with a local designer and limited to local products, to a very sophisticated design firm in a cosmopolitan city with a complete range of international products at their disposal.

The structure of the manual is designed so that people can selectively read only those portions relating to their particular mission. The writing style attempts to be simple, and we ask for indulgence when we tell the reader things he or she may already know.

Application of the Guidelines

NCR does not intend to replace or renovate all 1,200 of its facilities at once. The intention of the guidelines program is for the guidelines to be used whenever facilities are replaced or renovated for business reasons.

The applicability of the guidelines varies by situation. In some cases, NCR may develop a site, construct a building, and furnish it for their own use. In this case, every element in the environment can follow the guidelines. In another case, an NCR facility may be a suite of leased rooms inside someone else's building. Here the application of the guidelines may be limited to interior design. In each case, whenever NCR needs a new or renovated facility, they should follow the guidelines in any area over which they have control.

APPROACH AND METHODOLOGY

"It is always safe to assume, not that the old way is wrong, but that there may be a better way."—Henry F. Harrower

The purpose of the programming phase was to familiarize the HOK team with NCR: its history, its mission, its goals, its values, and its operations. Another important part of the programming phase was to work with NCR executives and real estate staff to determine the proper focus, priorities, and range of application of the guidelines. Figure 3-2 illustrates the process from Phase 1: "Visual Concept Development," which includes the programming and design concept phases, to the "Implementation" phase.

Information Gathering

In order to establish an appropriate "visual image concept," we learned about NCR by using a variety of programming methods.

We began the data-gathering effort by doing a literature search. Most of the articles published about NCR were in the business press—useful for information on recent events but limited in giving an overview or history. Coincidentally, NCR had just published a set of books for their hundredth anniversary, and they provided a good introduction to the company's history and products.

NCR, like other corporations, was able to supply us with a wealth of published material, mostly marketing-oriented. We read employee newsletters, annual reports, product brochures, human resources recruiting packages, etc. Readily available materials are very useful in the early stages of a project to familiarize the team with the company before conducting interviews and work sessions. Reviewing these materials builds credibility and self-confidence, demonstrating that the team members are generally informed about the company.

We encountered one of the more entertaining forms of data gathering the day we spent going through NCR's photographic archives. Since the company has a long and colorful history, as well as a strong and well-established corporate culture, it was useful for us to learn as much as possible about its past. The nineteenth-century photo of an elephant swimming across a river in India with a brass cash register strapped to its back was amusing, but it also made us keenly aware that NCR has been distributing American technology to the rest of the world for a very long time. It also suggests that while we may create a new image for their facilities, the image must be faithful to the long and consistent character that NCR has developed over the course of a century if it is to be credible.

Another very helpful way to gather data was to tour NCR facilities. We saw several facilities in Dayton: a manufacturing facility, training center, service bureau, sales office, and then, of course, their world headquarters. We also saw facilities in Canada and across America, from Orlando to Seattle. In addition, we reviewed hundreds of photos of NCR's facilities in other countries. The facility tours and photo reviews were useful in establishing our frame of reference, making us aware that the guidelines need to be more than just a superficial image program: They need to be functionally based as well. We saw problems such as employee parking that was unnecessarily distanced from the employee entrance, without any protection from the weather; site and building entries that did not make clear how to get into the building; receptionists' desks that seemed to be hidden from view; lunch rooms that doubled as storage rooms, etc. We felt that these signs of design insensitivity and lack of focus on user needs made more of a statement about the company than superficial "decorating" items would.

To help us as we developed the design, we talked informally with many of the people who were in charge of operating and maintaining facilities. To determine the priorities, focus, common elements, etc., we worked with the real estate staff.

Perhaps our most important form of data gathering was our executive interviews. We talked with forty senior managers, who represented every branch of the organization, in individual, one-hour, structured interviews. We discussed what they thought about NCR, their goals, their forecasts, their reputation, etc.—and *not* directly about what they thought NCR facilities should look like. The topics we discussed and some of the questions we asked were the following:

- Goals and objectives: What are you hoping NCR can achieve in the next five years? Ten years? What are NCR's strengths? Weaknesses?
- Drivers of growth and change: What kind of growth patterns do you expect in the next ten years in terms of number of employees and level of employees? In terms of geographical region?
- Stakeholders in the NCR look: What groups have a stake in NCR's future?
- Image: Do customers think of NCR as you would like them to? Do employees think of NCR as you would like them to? What is the most important thing to change about NCR's image? What is the most important thing to preserve about its image?
- Competitors: Who are your competitors? In what way is it important to you that NCR compares favorably to competitors? How do NCR facilities compare, in general, to those of your competitors?
- Facilities: How might NCR facilities enhance and support your business goals? Your desired image?

Through our asking these managers about what they know best—NCR— they freely discussed what NCR is already doing right and what things they were hoping to change.

Data Analysis

The content of these executive interviews was analyzed, and composite statements were produced for each of the items. These composites were presented to the executive committee for review and approval. This was an important part of the process, since it confirmed that we had gotten a clear picture of what NCR is and what it wishes to be, and it established the team's credibility with NCR's executives, demonstrating our understanding of their company before we even began to consider design elements.

On a more informal basis, we understood NCR facilities by the end of the data-gathering phase. We knew where their priorities were, the general cost level they found acceptable, and the elements that were found most commonly in NCR facilities of different types.

The Design Process

Converting this organizational understanding into generic design solutions proved to be the most difficult part of the process. The effort began by holding a design charrette where the core team was joined by a collection of senior HOK designers and specialists for an intense work session to quickly generate design ideas. The team built on those ideas in subsequent weeks.

The team, which was composed of a programmer/project director, a site planner, an architect, an interior designer, and a graphic designer, established a team studio space where we could work side by side, sharing our efforts. It was exemplary of the best in multidisciplinary efforts where we all worked on each part of the problem, each feeling "ownership" of the whole design solution. It was also exemplary of the best of client relationships, with the NCR project manager spending many hours actually working with the team. By the time the team presented design ideas to management, he felt ownership as well.

One tactic that was effective in making the design effort more "real" and less abstract was to use existing facilities as test cases. We used plans and photographs of several existing NCR facilities to illustrate how they might have been designed if our design team had been doing it. We worked iteratively between designing specific things and stepping back to formulate general principles that were then applied to "project" specifics.

We made numerous design presentations to the executive committee, refining and developing the concepts with their guidance. For example, when we first presented the idea of red front doors, one executive wisely questioned if red doors or even the use of red on building exteriors might have negative connotations in some cultures. We knew that in China and other Asian countries red doors are a symbol of welcome, which was quite appropriate, but we were not sure if some countries might have "red" taboos. As a result, we did an exhaustive literature search on the multicultural symbolism of red. This included looking at the literature on the psychology of color and confirming visually that, at least in major regions of the world, one can find pictures showing red being used on the exterior of buildings. We found that while red symbolizes everything from love to hate, it is not a mistake to use red on the exterior of buildings anywhere in the world.

Documenting the Guidelines

After the design concept was completed and approved, the arduous task of writing and illustrating the manual began. We confirmed the obvious: Knowing how to design and knowing how to write about how to design are very different things, requiring substantially different talents.

Designing the structure of the manual was difficult. Should we, for example, discuss floor coverings as a topic, describing the kind of floor covering to use in every type of NCR space—or should we discuss a room type, such as a training room, and cover type of flooring, along with wall treatment, lighting, furnishings, etc.? If we discussed floor covering for every room type, the reader who is designing many different rooms becomes fatigued by the redundancy. On the other hand, for a reader who is only designing one type of space, it is ideal to find everything about that space type in one place. To resolve this problem, we present "default" guidelines near the beginning of each chapter, which establish the norms, and then focus on those elements that are exceptional when discussing each room type.

We also found that architectural drawings, a communications mainstay for designers, are not very effective when reduced in size to fit an 8½'' by 11'' format. We also wanted to achieve graphic consistency, which the drawings, created over the course of the project, lacked. In addition, we wanted the illustrations to carry a great deal of weight in communicating the essence of the program—allowing the reader who was browsing through the manual, looking only at the illustrations, to understand most of the point without reading the narrative.

Late in the process, when the draft was nearly complete, the team had a work session to consider the two or three most critical points in each section. We then designed illustrations and captions to clearly make those points. Finally, the drawings were executed by a single artist, using one style.

The completed manuals were distributed within NCR, and their project managers began the implementation process. In many cases, NCR retains outside design consultants to do their design work; but often, particularly in sales office interiors projects, design is performed by the NCR staff.

ELEMENTS AND OUTCOMES

"Always design a thing by considering it in its larger context—a chair in a room, a room in a house, a house in an environment, an environment in a city plan."—Eliel Saarinen

In the transition phase from programming to design, the team developed a set of descriptors—words we think describe NCR at its best (Figure 3-3). If one were to visit an NCR facility and get the impression that these words describe the *company* perfectly, then the building design would be ideal. These words then, served as criteria as we were developing the design guidelines.

The question was this: What physical environmental qualities bring these words to mind? The products of the design effort are documented in the guidelines manual, discussed previously. The manual is a self-contained package that covers the gamut from philosophical to pragmatic (Figure 3-4).

Figures 3-5 through 3-6 are from the manual and exemplify the guidelines' focus on accommodating user needs.

The guidelines manual is a handsome document that has been well received. The real product of the program is, of course, the resulting facilities.

The Facilities

Many facilities have now been designed through the use of the guidelines, and both the NCR Real Estate people and we at HOK think that the buildings have achieved an acceptable level of consistency, with marked individual differences. We also believe that the overall design quality is much improved from their former level. The composite photographs in Figures 3-7 through 3-10 are taken from projects throughout the country.

As these photos show, a marked degree of visual or aesthetic consistency is apparent. The program has enjoyed a great deal of support and has had few detractors within NCR. Most NCR people seem to accept completely the purpose and philosophy of the guidelines; however, some occasionally dislike particular design elements (such as having white as the primary exterior building color). In one case, a senior regional manager, who prided himself on his design sophistication, directed his design consultant to disregard the guidelines—much to the chagrin of the NCR Real Estate people. Ultimately a compromise was achieved, and given the latitude allowed in the guidelines, the revised project does fit into the program—more or less.

Naturally, the program has a long way to go and will evolve and become more refined over time. If facilities are replaced or renovated at the rate of one a week, it will take over twenty-five years to bring all 1,200 into the program, so the final chapter has clearly not yet been written.

SUMMARY AND CONCLUSIONS

"A company that is proud of itself and its culture will reflect that pride through its environment."—Terrence E. Deal and Allan A. Kennedy

NCR is a leader in recognizing the value of design. In a videotaped interview, James O'Toole, author of *Vanguard Management*, compliments Chairman Exley for being the only American C.E.O. he has ever heard say that design is an important business tool. How will AT&T's recent acquisition of NCR affect NCR's programs to create and control its image through consistent design? Only time will tell.

It is difficult (and undesirable) in a project such as this one to separate programming from design. The whole project is really a program that will be used to guide designers as they plan NCR facilities in years to come. The facility aesthetic we created for NCR clearly has to fit the essential qualities of the organization. The truth is that NCR is conservative and frugal, and their facility image reflects that. They are also quality-oriented, innovative, thoughtful, and international, and their facilities need to reflect that as well.

Only by thoroughly understanding the company's past, present, and hopes for the future could we create a design aesthetic and plan a program that is custom-fit to NCR and is likely to remain a part of their strong culture.

APPENDIX

NCR LOOK AGENDA FOR VALUES & MISSIONS INTERVIEWS

July 1986

The purpose of the meeting is to discuss your values and goals for NCR in preparation to our developing an "NCR Look."

Discussion will focus on the following topics:

1. **Goals and Objectives**
   - What are you hoping NCR can achieve in the next five years? Ten years?
   - How are you planning to reach these goals?
   - What are NCR's strengths? Weaknesses?
2. **Drivers of Growth and Change**
   - What kind of growth patterns do you expect in the next ten years in terms of number of employees and level of employees? In terms of geographical region?
3. **Stakeholders in the NCR Look**
   - What groups have a stake in NCR's future?
   - It is our understanding that customers and employees are the two primary target groups for this project. Which other group(s) would you like to target for the "NCR Look?"
4. **Image**
   - Do customers think of NCR as you would like them to?
   - Do employees think of NCR as you would like them to?
   - What is the most important thing to change about NCR's image?
   - What is the most important thing to preserve about the image?
5. **Competitors**
   - Who are your competitors?
   - In what way is it important to you that NCR compares favorably to competitors?
   - How do NCR facilities compare, in general, to those of your competitors?
6. **Facilities**
   - How might NCR facilities enhance and support your business goals? Your desired image?

NCR Facility Design Guidelines
Draft Evaluation

	YES	NO
Can you easily find specific topics in the guidelines?	X	☐
Is the text clear and straightforward?	X	☐
Are the illustrations clear and useful?	X	☐
Do the guidelines give you sufficient latitude so that you could produce a good project?	X	☐
Do you believe these guidelines would be useful to you if you were doing a facility project?	X	☐
Are the guidelines too restrictive?	☐	X
Would you recommend covering some topics in more depth?	X	☐

Which subjects?

It would be very helpful to have drawings, schemes, and illustrations in color. This would ensure better interpretation to non-professional people.

Are there additional topics that should be covered?   no

What would be the most useful part of the guidelines to you?   All parts of the guidelines are very useful to show the NCR philosophy of facility design—especially for the involved people, such as local management, architects, consultants, etc.

Are the guidelines technically correct?

yes

Do you have additional comments?

These new guidelines are exactly what we were waiting for!

PLEASE GIVE US INFORMATION ABOUT YOU

Name ___Bill Werther___

Title ___Manager, Real Estate—Germany___

Years with NCR? ___30___

Recap your previous experience with NCR facilities.
As far as the facilities of NCR-Germany are concerned, we tried hard to

bring the corporate identity from the "cash register"—standard to

today's advanced "computer-company"—standard.

New projects and refurbishments in recent years brought us to very

improved accommodations.

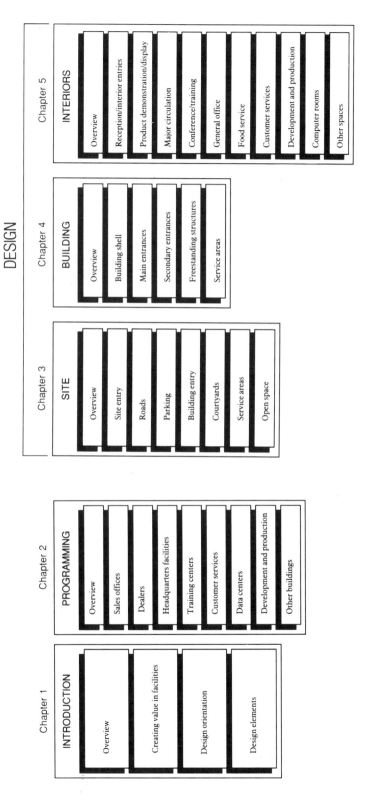

FIGURE 3-1. The Structure Shows the Broad Range of Topics and Space Types Addressed by the Guidelines

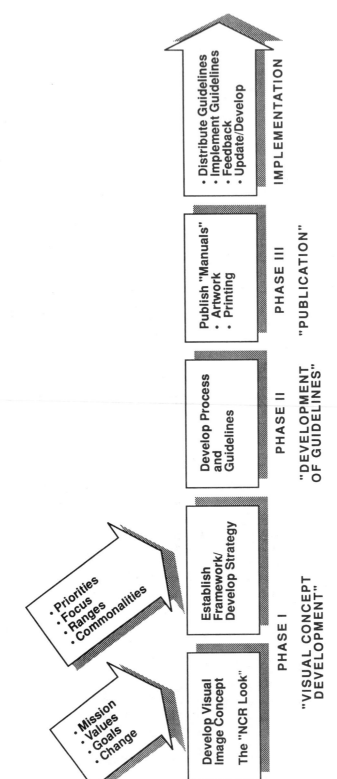

FIGURE 3-2. Process Diagram

HUMAN
- People Oriented
  - Friendly • Humane • Inviting
  - Inviting • Individual Freedom
- User Friendly
  - Error Forgiving
  - Accommodates Ad Hoc Nature
- Appropriate
  - Culture • Region • Function

NCR

TECHNICAL
- Organized
  - Systematic
  - Engineered
  - Precise
  - Attention to Detail
- Intelligent
- Informative
- Geometric

QUALITY
- Successful
- Innovative
  - "State of the Art" • Vital
  - Progressive • Flexible
- Professional
- Conservative
  - Traditional • Durable
  - Consistent • Frugal

FIGURE 3-3.   These Words Would Describe the Ideal NCR Facility

FIGURE 3-4.   Documenting the Guidelines Was as Much of a Challenge as Developing the Design

FIGURE 3-5.   The Site Entry Should be Evident to Approaching Visitors

FIGURE 3-6.   Reception Areas Should Welcome, Accommodate, and Impress Visitors

FIGURE 3-7.   Typical Building Exteriors Following the Guidelines

FIGURE 3-8.   Examples of Lobbies and Major Circulation

FIGURE 3-9.   Meeting Areas Applying the Guidelines

FIGURE 3-10. Food Service Areas That Follow the Guidelines

CHAPTER 4

Facilities Managers and New Developments: the Experience of Broadgate and Stockley Park

Francis Duffy

INTRODUCTION

The role of facilities management in the development process has been relatively little explored, perhaps because of the widening gap between what most developers strive for (exchange value) and the day-to-day purposes (use value) for which office buildings are constructed.

Two exceptions to this general rule have occurred recently in the rather particular circumstances of the United Kingdom property industry: Broadgate, a 4 million square feet development in the City of London, and Stockley Park, a 1.5 million square feet business park near London's Heathrow Airport. What both projects have in common—apart from their very considerable commercial success, excellent architecture, and the same developer (Stuart Lipton)—is a very solid basis of user research. The conduct of this research coincided with and was made possible by the emergence in the United Kingdom of the articulate new profession of facilities management.

Focus group discussions were used in both projects to elicit priorities from respondents—drawn in the case of Broadgate from the financial services sector, and in that of Stockley from the new knowledge-based industries attracted to that site by excellent national and international communications. It was clear from these priorities that existing models of City office buildings and of the "industrial estate" were considered by the facilities managers and other senior managers interviewed to be totally inadequate in plan form, section, level of servicing, amenities and imagery. User dissatisfaction and user aspirations were the basis for the briefs for the new buildings eventually erected on both sites. They were also the justification for what have turned out to be two entirely new classes of office buildings. The crystallization of these new office models represents a major step in the modernization, and indeed globalization, of the European property market. In the case of Stockley Park, user input had a significant input on British planning controls because the need for new locations and new types of buildings for high-tech firms was conclusively demonstrated.

This chapter describes the conditions under which these major changes were carried out, how user input and particularly the priorities of facilities managers were solicited and analyzed, and how the briefing process for the new types of buildings was conducted. The results in terms of the science of workplace design are particularly satisfactory: Not only are Broadgate and Stockley Park models of their kind, but their excellence can be said to be derived directly from user research and facilities feedback.

GIVING DEVELOPERS A BAD NAME

Facilities managers don't usually have many good words to say for developers. This is hardly surprising, given first the inevitable loyalty of all developers to the iron logic of building supply and second, and in the United Kingdom more importantly, their enslavement by the dictates of the investment institutions. Conventional developers maximize the exchange value of buildings—constructed at the least cost in the quickest time—rather than their long-term utility. Facilities managers view the same transactions from a very different perspective—that of the user.

That some of the most rapid advances in the measurement of building use, building capacity, and building performance should have been initiated and supported by developers is, therefore, very surprising. Nevertheless, this is exactly what happened between 1985 and 1990 at Stockley Park and Broadgate—two of the largest and most important office developments in the United Kingdom.

This chapter sketches the intellectual as well as the commercial background to these two highly successful British projects. It explains the importance of facilities managers in their conception and shaping, and also why the user-based methodologies on which they are founded will be of continuing significance to both owners and users of buildings everywhere.

THE CONTEXT

On the surface Broadgate and Stockley Park are locationally and physically very different. The first is a centrally located, City of London office development for the financial and professional services industry; the second, a business park at the junction of two vitally important motorways, very near London's Heathrow Airport. In their formation, however, both projects have much in common.

Both projects are the product of one man: the developer, Stuart Lipton (whose partner on Broadgate was the no less famous—in British real estate circles at least—Godfrey Bradman). Lipton is the developer who will be remembered for rediscovering the user.

The context at the time that both projects were conceived was one of extraordinary change. British real estate practice since the second World War had been shaped, protected, and smothered by a coincidence of interests between a powerful planning system and some very unusual allies. The planners were biased for political reasons against white-collar employment and granted with reluctance planning permission for new office buildings. Their surprising allies were the temperamentally risk-averse developers who enjoyed the certainty of leasing whatever office space they could persuade the planners to accept. This cozy and regressive alliance of socialism and capitalism resulted in one of the worst assortments of office space in the world. In the City of London, Britain's (and indeed Europe's) most important office center, the office buildings that resulted from this alliance tended to be small, fragmented, underserviced, and value-engineered in totally the wrong way—their configuration generally more influenced by external site planning consideration rather than by utility. Faced with such indifference to the user, City tenants would take anything they could get. For similar reasons, outside central London, business park buildings designed for rapidly growing, high-tech enterprises hardly existed. A planning land-use category—the industrial estate, designated in the 1940s by planners and perpetuated by reactionary developers— meant little more than basic sheds laid out without style, imagination, or landscaping on barren concrete roads. Use values were nowhere to be seen.

FACTORS FOR CHANGE

What happened? Broadgate and Stockley Park are large-scale evidence of the changes that took place in the United Kingdom in the 1980s: partly as a result of Thatcherism, partly because of international influences, and very much to do with the extremely rapid diffusion of information technology (IT). The epoch-making 1981 decision by IBM to market the personal computer and local area networks made IT the catalyst of change. Rapid change was most evident in the quickly expanding and globalizing financial services industry (for which Broadgate was designed) and the highly value-adding and vigorous sectors of electronics, pharmaceuticals, and other knowledge-based industries (at which Stockley Park was directed).

Broadgate and Stockley Park may be regarded as symbols and indicators of the extent of the changes that transformed all developed economies, and not least that of the United Kingdom, in the last decade. Of much more interest to the international building community is that these two developments were designed, internally and externally, in direct collaboration with facilities managers. As a result, both projects are extraordinary, not just in their architectural quality—great in both cases as this certainly is—but because they break, for the user, for facilities management, and for market reasons, most real estate conventions. Behind these breaches of rules lies innovative architectural programming, based on user research. This research, much of it conducted by the firm DEGW, could not have been conducted without the help of the growing facilities management profession. Facilities management hardly existed in the United Kingdom as a serious vocation in the early 1980s. By the end of that decade, the profession was well established, and facilities managers had demonstrated their ability to influence the quality and shape of buildings.

INTELLECTUAL PRECEDENTS

The programming of Broadgate and Stockley Park was based on a long, hard-won, and very self-conscious methodology of user studies of the design of the workplace. The six chief characteristics of these methods, developed by DEGW, are the following:

- a strong emphasis on time as a critical aspect of design: Buildings are regarded not so much as totally integrated and timeless entities but rather as being capable of being analyzed and broken down into several independent layers of longevity
- an equally strong evenhandedness in balancing on the one hand data that have to deal with people and, on the other, the variables that constitute design: Design decisions are only relevant when directly related to user choice
- a reliance on typologies—typologies to describe the forms of organization as well as to characterize building forms. Generalizations about the relation of user to design variables depend upon typological analysis
- an insistence on empirical data: Fieldwork, interviews, observations, and measurements are highly valued and much used, with equal weight given to both social and design indices and, above all, to linking the two
- a dependence on a model of supply and demand in which the design activities of architects are seen to straddle the gap between changing user expectations, individual as well as collective, and the resources of the construction industry
- a deliberate orientation of user research to design in action, to ensuring that executive decisions about the procurement and use of design resources are directed to achieve organizational purposes

Practically all of DEGW's programming and "user-based, design-oriented" research have been related to the place of work. The greater proportion of this work has been carried out for large, corporate space users.

Some critically important user-based design studies, which were the foundation of the Broadgate and Stockley Park breakthrough in involving facilities managers in the development process, were the following:

- ORBIT 1[1] (1983-84), a study of the impact of information technology on office design, carried out with much fieldwork, but contributing most significantly a first crude approach to the measurement of the capacity of office buildings to accommodate information technology
- ORBIT 2[2] (1985), a North American version of ORBIT 1 that carried the measurement of building performance to a more sophisticated level, allowing user priorities to be determined and thus avoiding the implicit assumption that there exists a perfect building or facilities management procedure that suits all requirements equally well
- investigations[3] (carried out in the late 1970s for various British industrial development agencies) of the emerging needs of the newer sort of business enterprise and of how these complex and mixed needs could best be accommodated in simple, long-term buildings with various options for fit-out
- studies,[4] done in the late 1970s, of the capacity of older buildings for "adaptive reuse." This work involved understanding patterns of entrepreneurial activity and then estimating the capacity of different sorts of existing buildings to accommodate emerging enterprises

All four of these precedents were characterized intellectually and methodologically by the six features of user research noted previously.

THE BROADGATE EXPERIENCE

The beginning of Stuart Lipton and Godfrey Bradman's work at Broadgate coincided with the publication in early 1984 of the findings of ORBIT 1. These two important developers had realized the importance of the ORBIT findings

---

[1]ORBIT 1 was a multiclient study carried out in 1983-84 by DEGW, Building Use Studies, and EOSYS. The topic was the impact of information technology on the design of office buildings. A summary report was published privately in 1984 by DEGW and EOSYS.

[2]ORBIT 2 followed in the tradition of ORBIT 1 but was conducted by DEGW, Harbinger, and FRA in the context of North America. A summary report by Franklin Becker, Gerald Davis, Francis Duffy, and William Sims was published by Harbinger (a subsidiary of the Xerox Corporation) in 1985. The ORBIT 2 method of matching building capacity to user priorities has undergone several stages of development since 1985.

[3]Particularly those carried out by DEGW between 1975 and 1980 for the Welsh Development Agency (WSA), Warrington Development Corporation, and the Scottish Development Agency (SDA).

[4]From DEGW's point of view, much of this work was summed up in Eley, P., and J. Worthington. 1984. *Industrial rehabilitation.* London: Architectural Press. The best of this work was carried out in collaboration with Nicholas Falk and URBED, the innovative consultancy he founded to achieve inner-city regeneration through liberating underused resources of unemployed people and underused buildings.

for their project at Broadgate—which was to grow continually in scope over the next five years—because this important development in the City of London coincided with the globalization of financial services, the opening up of the London market to international securities trading, and the intensive and unprecedented diffusion of IT through all City organizations and institutions.

The most important single methodology in the programming of Broadgate was the use of small *focus group* discussions to examine the emerging needs and priorities of the kinds of firms that seemed likely to be attracted to the development.[5] Sixty-seven financial and professional firms were interviewed. The objective of these user discussions was threefold: to ascertain user priorities so that the design specification could be improved; to inform architects, leasing agents, and other skeptical vendors of the need to listen to the demands of users; and above all to change the climate of opinion within which potential tenants made their property acquisition decisions. It seemed better to base these decisions on systematically organized, user-derived knowledge than on the folklore of tenant requirements that had previously satisfied the London real estate market.

The focus group technique, well known in other branches of user and market research, was a novelty in 1985 in the London real estate market. Facilities managers and other senior managers and directors from many of the leading financial services organizations were invited to a series of lunches held in the prestigious surroundings of the City of London Club. A typical meeting involved about ten such managers. A brief presentation was made by the author about trends in office design, particularly in relation to information technology. This talk was designed to stimulate a wide-ranging discussion among the facilities managers about their problems in finding and planning suitable office accommodation to satisfy their firms' changing requirements. After about an hour of general (and invariably lively) discussion, which was recorded on flip chart sheets hung up as they were completed until the room was lined with a record of the discussion, the presenter got each participant to list in order of importance the three most vital priorities for his or her organization for improving the effectiveness and quality of the office environment.

Priorities frequently listed included large, simple floor plates; better and more controllable levels of servicing to accommodate information technology; deep, but not too deep, floor space; staff amenities; and capacity to accommodate changing needs. All priorities were assessed and related to the requirements of different subsectors of the financial services industry.

The consequences of these focus group discussions were profound. The fragmented, small-floored, underserviced office buildings that had been the staple of the United Kingdom property market were found to be disliked by the

---

[5]Focus groups as a methodology for studying the use of buildings were much used in the late 1970s and early 1980s by Peter Ellis and his colleagues at Building Use Studies (a company founded in 1982 by two architectural practices, DEGW and ABK) to assist architectural design through the systematic study of building use.

managers interviewed. The focus groups were designed to elicit user priorities. The collective priorities of the users interviewed related directly to operational matters—that is, to *demand*, rather than to the discredited assumptions of a *supply*-dominated real estate industry.

This information validated Stuart Lipton's and Godfrey Bradman's sense that a new quality of office space was necessary to meet emerging demand, helped the architects (initially Arup Associates and later SOM) to refine their designs to better meet user requirements, and encouraged an ongoing dialogue between developer and users (most of whom, incidentally, were professionalizing themselves as procurers of office space, either through acquiring project management skills or through membership in the newly formed Association of Facilities Managers).

Important as the focus groups were to the development of Broadgate, several other major methodological innovations were spun off from this large and extremely fruitful project:

- sectoral studies—partly funded by the developers and partly by DEGW's own initiatives, a number of innovative user studies of sectors of the financial services industry in the City of London. Examples include the *Professional Offices Study* (1987),[6] which examined the needs of lawyers and accountants, as well as two major studies of the requirements of trading floor design. One of these studies[7] involved visiting four leading American, four British, and four Japanese trading houses in New York, London, and Tokyo to make a twelve-way comparison of practice in the design of trading floors.
- comparative building appraisal—equally powerful was the invention of comparisons of building capacity to accommodate user needs. This appraisal was done initially, using the datum of the requirements of financial services, for eleven of the first London buildings to be designed specifically for the post-Big Bank City of London. The results were published by Lipton and Bradman's joint company, Rosehaugh Stanhope Developments, as *Eleven Contemporary Office Buildings*.[8] This study was prepared in parallel to ORBIT 2, and shares with that study the distinction of being an early use of avowedly consumerist techniques—for instance, by using graphics imitating the way in which factual comparative information about refrigerators and cars is habitually presented in consumer magazines—in the assessment of architecture. Building appraisal as a service to

---

[6]This is a typical example of the kind of sectoral user studies being carried out by DEGW in relation to Broadgate in the mid-1980s. The findings were based on interviews and surveys in the largest and most important firms of accountants and lawyers in the City of London.

[7]This was *Trading in Three Cities*, a study carried out by DEGW in 1987 for Rosehaugh Stanhope Developments as part of the background briefing for Broadgate.

[8]This was perhaps the most significant and influential—and certainly the best produced—of all the early DEGW building appraisal documents. It was published privately in 1986 by Rosehaugh Stanhope Developments (RSD).

developers as well as tenants has been taken much further by DEGW since.[9]

- post-occupancy evaluation—of two kinds: The first was rather less successful, perhaps because of the complexity of the constituencies of interests involved (developers, tenants, members of the design team), which depends on the evaluation of the performance of the Broadgate buildings in use. The second sort of evaluation has been more successful because it is simpler and involves the observation, measurement, and comparison of different patterns of use on typical floors by typical tenants. The precedent has been established at Broadgate of routine post-occupancy studies—a practice now becoming less rare in the United Kingdom.

All these methodologies are of direct interest and relevance to facilities managers.

A considerable literature has been built up on the user studies that are the real foundation of Broadgate. Of this perhaps the most ambitious so far is the book, *The Changing City*,[10] which not only describes the space requirements of seven sectors of the economy of the City of London but establishes a typology of office building forms that meet these requirements.

Broadgate is now substantially complete—over 4 million square feet—and 90 percent leased. The project is well known for urbanistic reasons (introducing three major squares inserted into the dense fabric of the City of London); for architectural quality (winning many design awards); and for constructional innovation (Broadgate is renowned worldwide for the successful application of fast-track techniques of building). However, from a facilities management perspective, it is the influence of articulate user pressure on design and the persistence of the developer in closing the feedback loop between those who suffer and those who provide the working environment that makes Broadgate a world leader among office developments.

THE STOCKLEY PARK EXPERIENCE

Stockley Park is part of the Green Belt surrounding London. It was in 1985 also literally a garbage dump: a gravel pit near Heathrow Airport that had been used for depositing household waste—up to thirty feet of active fill. An able developer, Peter Jones, who had spotted the potential of the site as early as 1980, enlisted the support of the local authority by responding to their desire to repair a ravaged site and provide recreational amenities for the community. He ran a successful architectural competition (won by DEGW) and won the backing of the local authority. Eventually, in a complicated series of moves, Peter Jones was superseded as developer by Stuart Lipton. By that time

---

[9]Building appraisal is now the major function of one of the most important units of DEGW London. Well over 200 significant office buildings have been appraised in the last five years.

[10]Duffy, F., and A. Henney. 1989. *The changing city*. London: Bulstrode Press.

DEGW's particular contribution to the project was no longer as architects but as interpreters of the complex emerging space needs of the high-value-adding international firms likely to be attracted by a site as well located as Stockley Park.

The function performed by DEGW at Stockley Park was exactly the same as at Broadgate: to translate underarticulated, and sometimes incoherent, facilities needs into terms to which the developer and his or her architect could respond, while at the same time using data about user needs to challenge artificial planning constraints based on planners' outdated assumptions about the needs of industry.

There is an exact correspondence between Stockley Park and Broadgate in methodology:

- focus group sessions with facilities managers from potential tenants in various sectors held to measure their satisfaction and dissatisfaction with their existing accommodation and to establish their priorities for change. Information produced in these sessions not only greatly influenced building design and specification but was also critical in negotiations with the planners, who were moving toward a new definition of business use (B1) that acknowledged the reality of what had previously been considered an unacceptably high office component in buildings for knowledge-based industries.
- comparative building appraisal (that is, applying what had been learned from the sectoral studies of knowledge-based users to the design of particular buildings at Stockley Park). A very similar exercise to *Eleven Buildings*[11] was prepared; it evaluated the Stockley Park buildings systematically on user criteria against what might be considered by potential tenants as competing projects. The advantage of the Stockley Park analysis compared with the Broadgate work is that it emphasized both first and occupancy costs from the point of view of users and facilities managers.
- post-occupancy evaluation—particular care was taken at Stockley Park to investigate and report back to the developer about patterns of space use that had actually emerged at Stockley Park: density, cellularization, proportion of support and specially serviced or accessed areas, etc.

Stockley Park, at 1.5 million square feet, is by no means complete. Although smaller than Broadgate, it has more individual buildings, many of which have been applauded internationally. Architectural glory, however, from the point of view of facilities managers, is less important than the evolution of new building types and the provision of a supportive urban environment. Tenants see both developments as considerably enhancing their chances of organizational success in a highly competitive international business environment.

---

[11]DEGW. 1986. *Business buildings compared: A review of nine developments for high technology firms.* London: DEGW.

LESSONS LEARNED

The United Kingdom has a long tradition of innovative programming, more often than not initiated by architects for the benefit of their clients. Numerous design bulletins[12] and guidelines in education, housing, and health are evidence of the excellence of this work, as is the technical information published for decades by the excellent weekly, the *Architects Journal.* The development work upon which Broadgate and Stockley Park are built continues this tradition. However, in the market-oriented economy of the 1980s and 1990s, the best new user studies are being carried out in the private sector rather than in the public domain of schools, hospitals, universities, and housing.

Today's problems in building up a body of architectural knowledge that is also accessible to facilities managers are practical, ethical, and epistemological:

- practical: demonstrating to clients, even to those who employ enlightened facilities managers, the continuing economic benefit of understanding user needs, of scanning the horizon for change, and of establishing feedback from the existing building stock into new projects
- ethical: such information, once gained, has an immediate financial and commercial value for both architects and facilities managers, which could be an impediment to free communication and exchange
- epistemological: consequently, peer review, validity testing, generalizing from particular cases, and theory building are likely to be delayed, hampered, and potentially distorted

Broadgate and Stockley Park demonstrate that while these problems exist, they can be overcome, even in an intensely competitive real estate environment. In fact, the enthusiasm with which hundreds of facilities managers contributed to the projects is evidence of a huge and still largely untapped source of data about building use and building design.

The proprietary problems faced at Broadgate and Stockley Park are no greater than those in the computer and pharmaceutical industries—and could be solved for the same reason. It is in everyone's ultimate interests, in order to build better working environments, that user data should be shared, promulgated, and built upon.[13]

In the cases of Broadgate and Stockley Park, an enlightened and unusually active developer was the agent by which access to user-based, design-oriented knowledge was achieved. The results have been spectacular—new building types, a new quality of urban environment, and major steps forward in the professionalization of facilities management. Success breeds success. Let us

---

[12]The best account of British architectural ideals in this period is Saint, Andrew. 1987. *Towards a social architecture.* New Haven and London: Yale University Press.

[13]This argument is developed in: RIBA. 1991. *Policy for architectural research,* which was approved in 1991 and is available from John Veal, Royal Institute of British Architects, 66 Portland Place, London W1.

hope that the examples of Broadgate and Stockley Park will stimulate facilities managers as well as developers and architects everywhere to forget their old habits and prejudices and learn to love and value knowledge about buildings and their use.

Nothing could be more practical.

References
DEGW, Building Use Studies, and EOSYS. 1984. *ORBIT 1.* London: DEGW.

DEGW. 1987. *Trading in three cities.* London: DEGW.

DEGW. 1986. *Business buildings compared: A review of nine developments for high technology firms.* London: DEGW.

Duffy, F. 1992. *The changing workplace.* London: Phaidon.

Duffy, F., and A. Henney. 1989. *The changing city.* London: Bulstrode Press.

Duffy, F., F. Becker, G. Davis, and W. Sims. 1985. *ORBIT 2.* Norwalk, Conn.: Harbinger Group, Inc.

Eley, P., and J. Worthington. 1984. Industrial rehabilitation. London: Architectural Press.

RIBA. 1991. *Policy for architectural research.* London: RIBA.

Saint, A. 1987. *Towards a social architecture.* New Haven and London: Yale University Press.

FIGURE 4-1. Broadgate

(photograph by Peter Hall, Stonegate Properties, PLC.)

1. 1985 **Accommodating the Changing City**, DEGW

    the first report on the results of the focus groups together with a study of locational

    trends in the City of London, sector by sector.

2. 1986 **Eleven Contemporary Office Buildings**, DEGW

    a comparative, consumerist analysis of the first generation of post Big Bank offices

    based on criteria from larger organisations in the financial services sector.

3. 1986 **Services on the City Fringe**, DEGW

    a survey of the space needs or network of smaller service organisations which support

    the major space occupiers in the City.

4. 1986 **Trading in Two Cities**, DEGW

    an analysis of trading floor requirements of financial services firms in London and New

    York.

5. 1987 **Professional Offices Study** DEGW

    report on a survey of the space requirements and priorities of accountants and lawyers.

6. 1988 **Trading in Three Cities** DEGW

    an expansion of (4) to take into account Tokyo. Four British, four US, and four Japanese

    financial houses were visited, studies and compared in London, New York and Tokyo.

7. 1988 **Post Occupancy Evaluation** DEGW

    a report on POEs of Broadgate and five other buildings in the City from the point of view

    of Facilities Managers, Services Engineers, Space Planners etc.

8. 1988 **Managing Urban Change** DEGW

    studies of the process by which interest groups and constituencies in the changing city

    can achieve their objectives.

9   1989 **The Changing City** Bulstrode Press

    the most complete account of the requirements of seven sectors of the City economy -

    leading to recommendations on building types and a review of the planning process.

FIGURE 4-2.   Key Broadgate User Research Documents

STEMMING FROM BROADGATE USER RESEARCH

These vary from sector to sector : the purpose of this selection is to illustrate the order of change in office specification from before the Broadgate to afterwards.

1.   **Size of Floor Plate** : from 700 - 1000 sq m to 2500 - 4000 sq m.

2.   **Depth of Space** - from 13.5 m perimeter to perimeter to 18 m perimeter to perimeter and 12 m from perimeter to core.

3.   **Configuration of Floor Plate** - from fragmented - designed outside in - to continuous simplicity - designed inside out.

4.   **Floor to Floor Height** - from 3.5 m to 4.1 m.

5.   **Environmental Servicing** - greatly increased cooling loads to accommodate IT, much finer zoning of HVAC controls.

6.   **IT Servicing** - from 3 compartment trunking at 2 m intervals to full access floors provision 150 mm clear.

7.   **Subletting** - enhances ducts etc designed to facilitate sub letting to accommodate growth and change.

8.   **Access and Security** : enhances ducts etc designed to Facilitate sub letting to accommodate growth and change.

9.   **Access and Security** much greater emphasis on goods handling (goods lifts, loading bays) and on security systems (BMS).

10. **Image** - clear identity for tenants.

11. **Amenities** - office buildings no longer isolated entities but designed as part of a place with shared amenities.

FIGURE 4-3.   Typical City Office Design Recommendations

FIGURE 4-4.   Stockley Park

1. 1983 **Accommodation Requirements of Modern Industry** JLW Research

summary of intensive interviews with ISS top UK individual corporations operating in high technology and related growth sectors.

2. 1984 **Understanding Tenant Needs** DEGW

an in depth review of space usage and premises requirements of 26 firms in electronics, pharmaceuticals, controls and instrumentation, research and development, computer hardware and software - chiefly in the early stages of such firms' development.

3. 1984 **Stockley Park and the future of the London Economy** URBED

detailed exploration of the impact of a major business industrial centre at Stockley Park.

4. 1984 **Profile of Potential Occupancy** DEGW, JLW Research & Arup Economic Cons.

summarises extensive research on high tech industries and other growth sectors. Investigates the size and character of demand.

5. 1985 **Meeting the Needs of Modern Industry** DEGW

a full summary of user research and design recommendations.

6. 1987 **Business Building Compared** DEGW

7. 1987 **A Working Guide to Stockley Park** DEGW

a summary for potential tenants of design and locational recommendations devised from the Stockley Research.

FIGURE 4-5.   Key Stockley Park User Research Documents

STEMMING FROM STOCKLEY USER RESEARCH

1. **Adequate Car Parking** - 1 space per 315 sq ft GFA.

2. **Room for Expansion** - scope for expansion by subleasing as well as longer term options for expansion eg leaving alternative plots vacant.

3. **Individual Identity** - using architecture to establish identity; attraction for customers and staff.

4. **Building Configuration** - large (1500 sq m to 2000 sq m) uninterrupted spaces; medium depth floors ie 15 to 18 m; two to three storey buildings; not hard boundaries between support and production; ease of sub division; flexible floor to ceiling heights within generous floor to floor heights (4m to 4.6m);

5. **Servicing** - finely zoned air handling; capacity to accommodate additional plan; space for cabling horizontally and vertically; provision for kitchen; easy access for goods and equipment; external service areas.

6. **Occupancy Arrangements** - flexible lease arrangements, ease of fitting out; shared services.

FIGURE 4-6.   Typical Business Park Design Recommendations

CHAPTER 5

Computer Usage in Facility Programming

Ched Reeder

INTRODUCTION

Computer tools have been used in facility programming for a long time. I headed a team that wrote a computer program for an architecture firm in 1972 to record and project future space needs for a major oil company. Since those days of batch Fortran files, computers and facility programming applications have come a long way. Database management systems and spreadsheets are now in common use. But much progress still lies ahead. Computer programs, used properly, provide the user with ability to deal with more data and to explore more alternatives. This ability can provide facility programmers with the power to greatly improve the quality of the service they deliver to the customer organization.

Facility programs vary in the amount and type of detail required, and computers can support and integrate this variety. The ongoing use of the data in the day-to-day facility operations is a powerful concept, greatly increasing the value of expensively collected information. Integration with other facility management functions is a key to success. There are many benefits to such application, but they must be contrasted to the costs. Off-the-shelf versus homegrown software is one consideration. Most off-the-shelf programs share a set of common features; most users share a set of problems when they try to use such computer tools. As facility programming opportunities are realized, we will move forward with ever increasing software and hardware capabilities.

TYPES OF PROGRAMMING TECHNIQUES AND AMOUNT OF DETAIL

The application of any facility programming technique at any level of detail can be accomplished without a computer, if one has enough time and resources. With limited time and resources, more can be done with a computer. In the next section, we will discuss the many benefits to using the computer. However, two of the main benefits that show up in all computer applications are the ability to deal with more data and the ability to explore more alternatives. These general benefits have influenced the facility programming process by allowing for a wider breadth of techniques to be applied in greater detail in a limited time frame. Quantitative information is emphasized by the addition of the computer to the process. I see this effect as neither bad or good, as long as the user appreciates the fact of the situation. Of the various types of programming techniques—surveys, interviews and focus groups, simulation, archival record analysis, and structured observation—some are aided more by the computer than others. These areas are discussed in the next section in order of most common usage.

Besides the different programming techniques, there are also different levels of detail in the programming information required for the various design and planning functions within facility management (FM). Three distinct functions in FM use this programmatic information: master planning, architecture (building shell) planning, and interior/space planning.

Shortly, we will discuss the characteristics of these planning functions and their relationship to programming.

Surveys

A survey, employing the standard questionnaire or form, is the technique most frequently used by facility programming groups. Most often a selected representative from the user organization acts as the contact point for gathering the survey data. These contacts often have limited training in design and planning, but their knowledge of the group they represent is usually quite good.

The information gathered is mostly quantitative. Usually this information consists of head count or area required by function. For specialized areas, equipment or auxiliary spaces may be listed.

Sometimes a general section that discusses more qualitative information is included. This section may cover general growth variables, communication, privacy, and other location selection issues. A frequent problem is that these issues are seldom expressed purely in requirement terms; often, suggested design solutions accompany the programmatic data. Since the contacts have limited design experience, and since they are unaware of many larger organizational issues, these suggested design solutions are often of little value. Separating these proposed solutions from programmatic statements is a key to good interview technique.

General surveys are usually scheduled on a calendar basis, once or twice a year, and are usually done at a fairly high level in the organization. More detailed surveys are done on a project basis. Figure 5-1 shows a page from a typical survey form.

Interviews and Focus Groups

Interviews are usually used to clarify survey data. More detailed quantitative and more qualitative data are usually gathered in the interview process. Interviews are often used to enrich the survey data for space planning purposes. However, for most in-house FM organizations, this is still an unstandardized, designer-by-designer process, where little of the information is available in a form for general, multiple use. Interview and survey data are often stored on computer disc or tape.

Focus groups are not often used by FM groups. When they are used, it is to help solve expensive or personnel-sensitive issues. From a programming standpoint, focus groups sometimes come into play with the selection of new furniture systems, office standards, or common usage spaces (cafeteria, break room, fitness facilities, etc.), and they most often meet when a new major building is being programmed. The information that results from a focus group can be very valuable to the design process. However, the data are not massive and contain a large amount of qualitative results. Therefore, the data seldom find their way into a computer, other than being word-processed or desktop-published.

Simulation

Because we can only try to predict the future, there is much use for simulation in FM programming. These simulations can range from simple extrapolation of existing conditions based on various growth rates (Figure 5-2) to component flow analysis of complex manufacturing or information processes (Figure 5-3). This area of computer application often blurs the programming/planning boundary. Feedback from the simulation can affect the program. In other cases, schematic design solutions are the product of the simulation process.

Simulation requires an understanding of the component parts of a process and the interaction of these parts. This understanding has only recently been developed within the field of facility management. This appears to be an area with a very large potential growth in application.

Archival Record Analysis

For organizations with a relatively stable function, historical data can be a good predictor of the future (Figure 5-4). However, most FM groups using computers work for organizations marked by rapid functional evolution and consequential high churn rates. These groups may use archival records, but as only one small input to the analysis process. As better facility inventory data are captured, more useful statistical analysis of historical data can be

done. This analysis can look at the growth and movement of groups, maintenance history and usage of equipment and furnishing, rate and type of work
requests, etc.

Structured Observation

Structured observation is used in FM mainly for work station redesign and
circulation flow analysis. While a useful technique, it is representative of a
number of techniques seldom used by FM groups. Structured observation
provides a valuable input to broad studies such as the Steelcase (1978-1981)
and Bosti (1985) studies. The results of this general work can find specific
application for facility managers. The rest of this chapter will deal with the
information that results from the four other processes mentioned previously.

THREE LEVELS OF SPACE NEED PROGRAM FOR FACILITY MANAGEMENT

FM groups should deal with three programmatic levels of detail. On the
highest level—master planning or long-range facility planning—FM today is
generally doing a poor job. In the case of all three types of programs, information often is lost and must be collected again, the collection process often is not
systematic, and there are many opportunities for improvement.

The most exciting opportunity is the potential of better integration of the
data from all three levels of programs through the use of the computer.

Master Planning Program

The master plan or long-range facility plan supports the long-range strategy of
the organization. This plan is based on current conditions and anticipated
future needs. It should provide strategic direction as to the moves, construction,
and real estate activities of the organization. Unfortunately, this plan is very
often "after the fact" of other business planning. Many times, shockingly, it is
not done in a formal way at all. Often, when done, the plan is provided by an
outside firm. This process requires the least detail and specificity of all the
programs. The formal planning cycle for facilities almost always coincides with
the fiscal year, corresponding to the business plan.

The value of a facility program that goes into the "distant" future of two to
five years is not in its accuracy; it is the ability to quickly model alternative
futures that is of value. With alternative future views we can question the
critical points at which alternative solutions must be found. For example, "If
we grow faster than we expect in the next two years, how will we handle the
overflow?" or "Is it better to retain some [how much?] expansion space after a
consolidation, or shrinkwrap the facility to the downsized organization?"
These "What difference makes a difference?" questions are the kind that
alternative modeling can help answer.

The master plan program usually consists of some head count or other productivity measure and an area requirement by group or organizational unit (Figure 5-5).

Architectural Program

When a new building or major renovation is undertaken, an architectural program is the one required. This program is often provided by an outside architecture firm. There is no regular planning cycle involved, because this programming is done only when a new or extensively remodeled building is being considered. An *architectural program* is a mix of detailed and general data as needed to support architectural building shell design (Figure 5-6).

More *detailed data* about areas with special requirements are captured in an architectural program than a master planning program. Areas such as cafeterias, computer rooms, and vaults would be covered because of their special requirements. Areas with impact on building subsystems (HVAC, plumbing, structure, etc.) must be covered in more detail so that the building can accommodate them. Only *general data* are collected about the standard areas of the building (offices, conference rooms, storage areas). These are programmed for sizing, only with much less detail. For example, a 400-square-foot library area with heavy floor loading and special fire prevention requirements may be programmed so that a detailed structural analysis can be performed. However, the 4,000-square-foot standard office space to be located next to the library may be but a single-line entry in the same architectural program. Since these large architectural projects occur infrequently for most organizations, it does not make sense to maintain an up-to-date program of all space at this level of detail.

Interior/Space Planning Program

The interior/space planning program has the greatest level of detail of the three forms. Reports at this level of detail are used by facility designers and move coordinators on a day-to-day basis. For office space this program will typically list all existing employees and other on-site workers, along with their standard and special space requirements. Future hires (or reductions) are listed by type. Individual adjacency data would be captured at this level. This program will also list existing equipment, with power and other building subsystem requirements enumerated. Future equipment is listed generically or specifically, depending on where the equipment is in the procurement process. Auxiliary or support spaces are also itemized. Future requirements are usually added to the base of current inventory information after interviews with group managers (Figure 5-7). This program may be used for a small or large interior space planning project. For manufacturing space, equipment, rather than employees, is the main element driving need. For hospitals, a mix of equipment and special spaces is in the forefront of the facility program. Thus, the exact emphasis of the data of a facility program seems to vary with facility type.

The interior/space planning program supports detailed layout (move and expansion) projects. There is no standard planning cycle to this program type; it is done when required. Because of the massive amounts of information involved in a large interior/space planning program, this was the type of facility program that was first augmented by computer processing.

Cost of Data Gathering and Processing

Data gathering is usually the most expensive part of the facility programming process. Because of this cost, there is a strong desire to use the data in many ways for as long as possible. We found in the early days of using computers to process detailed programmatic data that we could reduce the initial data-gathering and processing costs from $0.25 per square foot to $0.10 per square foot. This savings resulted from an overall system design that smoothed the flow of data by using a structured interview process, a flexible questionnaire, an open data structure, and a speedy update process. While reducing the gathering and processing costs, we were assembling better and more detailed quantitative *and* qualitative information than we had been able to do manually.

One extremely exciting idea from a computer usage viewpoint is this: Ongoing facility management can make much more efficient use of data than a project-oriented approach. The next year, the entire database could be updated for less than $0.03 per square foot. Information was then readily available for the day-to-day layout and move projects. This approach provided a significant data collection savings over a project-oriented method. It also had the effect of standardizing the form and content of the programming reports. Group managers improved their forecasting abilities with a standard set of procedures. However, twenty years later, many organizations are still not taking advantage of this improved approach to facility programming.

Typical Aging of Information

If a typical organization (with a 30 percent churn rate and a 5 percent growth rate) used all the techniques mentioned previously to maintain ongoing programmatic data, it would possess a database of programmatic information that was aging as shown in Table 1.

TABLE 1   Aging of Information

Type of Program	Amount of Organization	Average Age
Master planning	100%	6 months
Architecture planning	20%	2½ years
Interior/space planning	30%	6 months
	20%*	1½ years
	10%*	2½ years
	etc.*	

*The rate of this decline depends on distribution of churn rate and growth rate within organization.

BENEFITS OF COMPUTER USAGE

The general benefits of computer usage in design have been thoroughly discussed, but they boil down to the ability to work with *more data* in *less time*. All facility programming benefits derive from these two large benefit areas. Certainly, having more data is good when it comes to making an accurate program for a facility; questions of accuracy and relevancy of the "more" data are not a computer issue. Some of the saved time can be used to explore more alternatives, and the ability to explore alternatives is of unquestioned value. To forecast the future facility needs of an organization requires looking at alternatives as well as the implied downside risk of being wrong in one's forecast.

There are other, secondary benefits. The computer often allows (some say, forces) a common format to the information and a clearer methodology to the data collection methods. It imposes an understanding of the data to be collected *before* it is collected. It also provides for a centralized data source, better than scattered project files and margin notes on as-built drawings. This centralized data source, out of the hands of individual project managers and designers and available for the collective use of the organization, creates many ongoing savings for that organization. These secondary benefits can be obtained without a computer, but in practice they seldom are. It seems that the computer is the catalyst for many procedural improvements.

All the benefits in facility management can be classified in three areas: labor savings, implementation savings, and operational savings. Labor savings from the application of computer processing in the facility programming area are fairly well known—the time involved can be cut roughly in half over a purely manual method. We were able to show this magnitude of savings in the early 1970s at Morganelli-Heumann and Associates on projects for such customers as ARCO and Owens-Illinois. Since that time, refinements in computer software have improved the quality and scope of work, rather than just reducing its cost further. But what do we do with this savings? Do you do the same work for much less or do better work for somewhat less? Most designers would pick the latter option. By taking some of the time saved, we can explore a few more options in more detail. By making some better decisions based on this exploration, we can save much more in the implementation and ongoing operational costs.

Facility implementation covers the move, remodel, refurbishing, and construction portion of supporting an organization's evolving functions. The cost of one unnecessary medium-sized move can overshadow the cost of a complete facility program. But can a better program help avoid that unneeded move? Here is where we get into difficult cause and effect. However, my experience with many facility managers has been that their response is an unqualified "Yes!" Every facility manager can tell stories of the unneeded double move or construction project that could have been avoided with an improved up-front programming study. The programmatic information to stop the unnecessary action was available within the organization, but it was not uncovered using the existing programming process.

Finally, the largest potential area of savings (and most difficult in which to prove cause and effect) is in the facility operations area. This area contains huge potential savings in such aspects as real estate costs, employee productivity, and maintenance costs. A tiny percentage decrease in any of these costs will dwarf entire facility management budgets. Can a better program contribute to this reduction? A closer fit between the environment and the functional needs of the occupants should yield more productivity in the minimum space, and a better programmatic statement will contribute. Most managers should agree with this reasoning, but the argument has still not been put before many of them.

COSTS OF COMPUTER USAGE

Labor Costs

Costs for compiling the data for different facility programs vary with the current status of information within the organization. One organization may have interview procedures and data-processing procedures in place and may already be producing standard manual reports; another organization may have none of that work done. Obviously, the cost for the two organizations would be significantly different. There are two costs involved: the initial data collection and processing cost and the ongoing data maintenance cost.

Initial cost for compiling, analyzing, and reporting an *interior/space planning facility program* (as mentioned earlier, the most detailed and data-intensive program) ranges from $0.05 to $0.25 per square foot. The range in cost is related to the type and function of space, the amount of qualitative data required, and the form of the "final" report. A major part of this cost is the time spent in the interview process. In general, the data-gathering costs are the biggest item in the programming project budget. They typically account for one-third to one-half of the costs. Ongoing maintenance of the space planning data should range from $0.01 to $0.05 per square foot per year, depending on the churn rates and the informational goals of the organization. However, these maintenance costs can almost all be covered in move and remodel project charges, which can be "billed" back to the space user.

An *architectural program* costs between $0.01 and $0.10 per square foot for initial processing. If the organization is mostly made up of a few standard space types, the costs would be toward the lower end of that range. As the amount of custom space or building subsystem-dependent space rises, so does the cost. Other studies are often involved in the early stages of an architectural project. These services are often bid together with architectural programming as a schematic design or feasibility study.

The cost of a *master plan program* (just the facility programming piece, not the complete plan) is in the $0.01 to $0.05 per square foot range. As mentioned earlier, the generation of alternative future scenarios, not overly accurate data, is the thrust of master plan programming. Maintenance costs for both of these program types are very low. In fact, data updating is done only on the planning cycle for master plan programs and as needed for architectural programs.

Tool Costs

There is a range of computer tools available for facility programming applications. Off-the-shelf tools vary in sophistication and ease of use. Some programs are one module in a suite of programs focused on FM and Computer Aided Design and Drafting (CADD). As is the case with the use of most computer programs, the procedures are a key part of a successful implementation. The procedures help fit the application to the specific use of the organization, and not all vendors supply them. However, consultants are available to help with this crucial step of correct application. The cost of an off-the-shelf package ranges from $1,500 to $25,000. The off-the-shelf program sometimes makes the user wish for something more perfectly fitted to their needs.

To customize a package, some users build in-house tools from more general computer programs. Database management systems (DBMS) and spreadsheets are at the heart of many of these efforts. Although its initial cost is lower, in-house custom coding quite often brings along high hidden costs. Maintenance and enhancements to these in-house developed tools are very expensive to carry out and consequently are often not done.

Documentation and training materials for in-house systems are usually poor or nonexistent. These items usually end up costing the user of the in-house code much more over time than would an off-the-shelf package.

GENERAL CHARACTERISTICS
OF PROGRAMS

Most of the computer programs available have features in common. The base data (or objects) that make up the forecast are some mix of data consisting of people, equipment, and functional spaces. One of these three elements is usually the focus of the facility program. The focus varies by type of space: For office space, the concentration is on people; for manufacturing and laboratories, the focus is on equipment; for hotels, schools, and prisons, the emphasis is on functional spaces. Do not be confused—all programs contain all elements, but one of the elements simply becomes more dominant as the "core" of the program.

The programs use a variety of formulas for projecting growth and space required. Capacities and unit areas are used to project net space. Circulation factors and other markups are used to compute usable and gross areas required.

Information about adjacency requirements (and desires) also finds a home in most of these programs (Figure 5-8).

There are usually areas for unrestrained text comments so that qualitative information can be recorded. The amount of structure applied to qualitative data varies with each facility program and programming team.

Some programs can use functional drivers to derive needed capacities over time. For example, medical functional drivers are the demographics of the community. By looking at characteristics of the potential population being served, the amount and types of equipment, space, and staff can be determined. For example, from the local demographics, the annual number of heart attack patients coming into the facility can be projected. Facility requirements to service one heart attack patient are derived from earlier usage statistics. By combining these data, the number of beds, surgical suites, etc., that will be needed over time can be predicted. In this case, changing demographics equals a new and changing building program. The functional drivers for community service facilities are also demographics.

For businesses with an office or manufacturing orientation, the drivers are more complex, and are usually tied to confidential marketing forecasts. This area remains a custom application at this point, and several consulting/computer firms offer the service. More often, the organization's managers are left to interpret the general business plans into people, equipment, and space needs. Going to the individual manager for such interpretation does open the process to more confusion and conflict, but it also opens up organizational communication in very constructive ways.

The computer programs that support facility programming are usually based on database or spreadsheet tools. Programs built on database tools tend to have better reporting and data-integrity features. Programs built on spreadsheet tools tend to have better modeling (what if) features. A third set of programs is just appearing. It makes use of both databases and spreadsheets as underlying tools. Data links directly into CADD systems are now also reasonably accomplished. This multitool approach holds much promise as the next generation of programs provides the advantages of all the underlying tools.

Perhaps the software and data model integration that has been discussed in computer use for architecture over the last twenty years is finally appearing.

EVOLUTION OF COMPUTER USAGE

Files (1970-1980)

The earliest programs for facility programming were Fortran- and Cobol-based batch file processes (Figure 5-9). These early programs exhibited similar reporting functionality to today's versions. The programs automated much of what was being done in the late 1960s with manual forms and calculators. The ease of use, procedural standards, and data integrity were all very underdeveloped. Specialists with computer training were required as key programming team members in order to use such programs.

Database (1978-)

As DBMS tools became available, many vendors migrated their products to those platforms. The early versions of databases required significant computing resources, but they did make reporting and generating graphics much better and easier. The user interface and data integrity also made advances. The user interface was usually handled by screen forms. Data checking, user security, backup, and journaling functions reduced (but didn't eliminate) the need for computer specialists.

Spreadsheet (1982-)

Soon after the introduction of databases, early spreadsheets were being applied to the programming effort. They allowed for much more straightforward modeling of alternatives. Early spreadsheets were inadequate, both in capacity and throughput, for most serious facility programming applications. The early spreadsheets were overloaded by a typical facility program at the interior design/space planning level of detail. Because of the lack of controls at the product level, these applications were restricted to custom consulting contexts, and some were a bit idiosyncratic.

Current spreadsheets, such as Excel, Improv, Lotus for Windows, and Wingz, are extremely powerful tools. These programs have many useful features such as macro languages, which allow for building custom applications, excellent built-in business graphics, simple database capabilities, and data linking within spreadsheets as well as to external applications (such as database and CADD programs). These features have allowed some smaller firms using such tools to build excellent facility programming capabilities (Figure 5-10).

OVERVIEW OF SOME EXISTING PROGRAMS

Although this chapter is not meant to be a product survey, a brief discussion of some currently available computer programs seems appropriate. Most of the companies mentioned here offer other FM computer programs to support other areas of facility management and environmental design. Discussion is limited here to the facility programming area. This is not intended as an exhaustive survey, and I apologize for any omissions. New releases of programs and capabilities are being introduced every year.

Accugraph distributes Mountain Top CAD Information Management, which provides tools for FM in the UNIX environment including Hewlett-Packard and IBM hardware. It provides for reporting in response to queries using Lotus spreadsheets and graphics. The company brings over twenty years of experience to the problem.

FM:Systems offers FM:Space-Management for the PC environment. Reporting is flexible and links are provided to AutoCAD and other CAD systems. Many years of architectural and facility management experience are reflected in the software.

As of this writing, *Intergraph* provides a range of work station solutions and is ready to release a new set of modules. The STPL module is a mainstay of the programming arena. It supports a range of hardware options, including the UNIX and VAX operating systems as well as the PC, both IBM and Macintosh. Reporting is flexible and links are provided to planning and CAD modules. Intergraph is one of the pioneers in computer applications to design.

Thirteen-year-old *Ospro/CADG* distributes CADG+FM for facility applications. Various modules run in the IBM and Digital hardware environments, including work stations and PCs. The Facility Requirements Programmer provides facility programming capabilities. Links are provided to other CADG+FM modules and to many CADD systems. Output includes reports and business graphics.

Prime distributes Prime FM +, a series of FM tools. Perhaps needless to say, the software runs on Prime computers. It is based on software licensed from MicroVector, one of the pioneers of FM software.

Sigma Design provides the ARRIS F/X package, a UNIX-based CADD and FM system made up of many modules. It will exchange data with other CADD packages. The forecasting module provides growth projections based on growth increments and standards.

Whidden•Silver provides a series of modules and consulting services for facility programming. Based on Excel, the programs run in both the Mac and IBM PC hardware environments. In fact, many design firms (such as *CRSS, Gensler, HOK,* and *SOM*) have services and computer software available. The professionals in these firms have deep and diverse experience, which is vital to a successful facility programming project. Computer software is worth nothing without knowledge of the appropriate procedures and trained staff to apply it to the problem.

INTEGRATION WITH OTHER FACILITY MANAGEMENT AREAS

Facility programming has a data and process relationship with many other functions in facility management. It is important to support these links in a computer context so that data does not have to be redundantly entered. The key relationships for facility programming data are to the inventory and to early planning functions, such as master planning, layout (schematic design), and space planning (Figure 5-11).

Inventory

An important application area in FM is the tracking of current inventory data. This reflection of current status of the facility is certainly a key starting point for a facility program. (You can't know where you are going, if you don't know where you are!) These data, sometimes in a summary form, should be easily accessible to the facility programming computer program. Information about space and equipment standards, including capacities, is often contained in the facility inventory database and can be of use to facility programming. The savings in not having to reenter the data are significant: Transfer of data from the inventory can reduce the cost of developing a facility requirements program by 5 to 30 percent.

Master Planning, Layout, and Space Planning

Master Planning
Facility programming uses the facility inventory as one of its inputs, but it is itself an input to several other processes. High-level (less detailed) programs

form one of the key inputs to a facility master plan. The facility program forms the basis for the entire master planning process, along with inputs from the inventory and direction from upper management of the organization as to trends, goals, and strategies.

Layout (Schematic Design)

More detailed programmatic data on the sizing of the elements to be placed as well as adjacency preferences are an important input to the schematic design or layout process. The only additional key inputs are budgetary constraints and any other fixed physical elements.

Space Planning

A detailed interior program is the main problem-specific input to the space planning process. It should be the primary source of information about the needs of the group(s) for the space planner. Additional programmatic information that may be uncovered in the space planning process should be placed back in the facility program. If this project-specific input is recorded as it is used, the cost of maintaining up-to-date information is greatly reduced.

CURRENT PROBLEMS WITH COMPUTER APPLICATIONS IN FACILITY PROGRAMMING

Problems are opportunities for improvement and positive change. There are many such opportunities in the current state of facility programming and computer usage. Problems fall into three categories, by users of the information: general management, facility management group, and end user.

General Management Problems

The biggest opportunity in most organizations is the current lack of integration of facility programming and planning into the business planning process. In many organizations, facility programming and planning is seen mainly as an effect or result of business planning output. Thus, it is seen as supportive or secondary in nature. The whole of facility management (of which facility programming is a part) is looked upon as a fixed cost that is minimized only by doing less.

Once the true cost of facility-related decisions is understood, and its causal properties recognized, better integration into early business planning decisions will be desired. Today, however, this is not the case in most corporations and other organizations.

There is a tendency still to be reactionary rather than proactive in FM processes. Since programming is only of much use in a proactive or planning mode, a reactive attitude severely limits the value, and hence the potential positive impact, of any computer tools.

To compound the problem, electronic and communication technology has an ever accelerating impact on work function. Most upper management is only vaguely aware of the facility implications of this impact. Facility programming provides the best structure for relating technological impact to the organization in concrete terms.

Facility Management Group Problems

Current practices in the facility programming area provide many opportunities for improvement. Space planners and "facility coordinators" in many organizations act alone to solve their customers' "space problems." This leads to isolation of programmatic information in many small pools. Sometimes the only repository of the programming information is in the head of the person who collected it. With the data scattered and disorganized in this way, information is less likely to be reused or looked at in a broad or summary context. Since the programming data are costly to gather and valuable for multiple purposes, there is much waste and missed opportunities in this state of affairs. Even when stored on personal computers, this information can exist in isolated pockets.

Another problem that exists within facility management groups is poor general training on spreadsheets and databases. People waste time using tools improperly or not at all. The examples I have seen in my personal consulting experience at some organizations are frightening.

Facility groups balk at the workload of building a detailed programmatic database. They don't realize that most of the cost is already hidden in their existing, inefficient methodologies. Of course, there are many organizations that have already realized these opportunities within their work, but there are golden opportunities awaiting many more firms.

End User Problems

End users have many opportunities for better facility programming. In general, they lack training and understanding of the total process in which the information is used. Armed with this understanding, they would probably be less protective of information about their group's future plans. I have found that when proper procedures are in place for the updating of this information, the managers providing the input improve in their efficiency and accuracy over the first few years of operation. Finally, like the facility management group, the end users could also have better training on the tools.

THE FUTURE OF FM PROGRAMMING AND COMPUTER USAGE

Talking about the future of computer usage in any area focuses on a near horizon. Change is taking place so quickly that imagining five or ten years in the future conjures up science fiction images for most people. The area of FM programming is no different. On the near horizon, here are a few things I see.

Distributed and centralized implementations will provide a combination of tools for facility programming. Large organizations will be decentralizing control and function, but they will still want to oversee operational data. To paraphrase a well known slogan for the 1990s, facility programming will be done locally, but monitored globally. Because of this monitoring function, some data and tools will reside on a central accessible machine; but because of the local application, some data and tools will reside in individual work stations. For example, the facility program for a Lexington, Massachusetts, subsidiary facility may be kept locally. Summaries of that data are linked to the New York headquarters location. Each group can use the same data for different study purposes. This type of implementation will involve new underlying tools.

Spreadsheet/database hybrids: The database portion will be implemented in a client/server architecture. The spreadsheet portion will be a customized, three-dimensional, macro-driven modeling program. The underlying tools to support the development of these programs are just becoming available.

Finally, the end users of the facility or their representative will have direct input to the updating of programmatic data (and feedback on their input), using the same tools that the facility managers use.

In general, the field of FM will show much process improvement, and new powerful tools to support the process changes will be there to help speed that improvement. The use of these tools will be widespread and, hopefully, taken for granted by the end of the century.

References

Becker, Franklin. 1990. *The total workplace, facility management and the elastic organization.* New York: Van Nostrand Reinhold.

Brill, Michael, with Stephen Margolis and BOSTI. 1985. *Using office design to increase productivity.* Buffalo, NY: Workplace Design and Productivity, Inc., 2 vols.

Hamer, Jeffrey. 1988. *Facility management systems.* New York: Van Nostrand Reinhold.

Harris, Lou & Associates. 1978-81. *Steelcase office environment index.* Grand Rapids, MI: Steelcase, 6 vols.

Muther, Richard, and Lee Hales. 1979. *Systematic planning of industrial facilities — S.P.I.F.* Kansas City: Management & Industrial Research Publications.

Palmer, Mickey A. 1981. *The architect's guide to facility programming.* New York: The American Institute of Architects and Architectural Record Books.

Tompkins, James A., and John A. White. 1984. *Facility planning.* New York: John Wiley & Sons, Inc.

EMPLOYEES

List every position in your group(s) that requires a work station at DATES 1, 2, and 3.

Check the "General Instruction" page for the specific dates represented by DATES 1, 2, and 3.

Detailed instructions follow:

DESCRIPTIVE JOB TITLE—Enter your job title, the job title of each person for whom you are answering, and the job title of any position(s) that will be added to your group(s) by DATE 3. Please use job titles consistent with those in your personnel records and abbreviate only if necessary. Examples are: Supervisor, Secretary, Acct. Pay Clerk, Keypunch Opr., Tax Attorney, etc.

If your organization uses grade designations for different categories of employees, use the last four boxes in this column to record each person's grade. The word "(grade)" occurs directly above those four spaces.

DATE 1, DATE 2, DATE 3—For each job position listed in the first column, mark the date(s) at which that job position will exist and require a work station. For example:

7 One year ago at this time, what was the TOTAL number of employees in the group(s) for which you are answering?

#	(grade)	DESCRIPTIVE JOB TITLE	DATE 1	DATE 2	DATE 3	
1	B	ASST VP	X	X	X	
2	C	SR ACCT	X	X	X	X
3	C	SR ACCT	X	X	X	Y
4	D	INT ACCT	X	X	X	X
5	D	INT ACCT	X	X	X	Y
6	E	JR ACCT	X	X	X	Y
7	E	JR ACCT	X	X	X	X
8	36	CASHIER	X	X	X	
9	E	JR ACCT			X	X
10						
11						
12						
13						
14						
15						

REMARKS

8 NEEDS AN ENCLOSED SPACE AND A CASHIERS BOX

— If the position exists now, and will continue to exist indefinitely, mark all three dates: X X X.
— If the position exists now, but will be changed to another type of work or abolished by DATE 3, mark it this way: X X __.
— If the position won't be created until DATE 2 and will continue indefinitely, mark it this way: __ X X.
— Should a position be needed temporarily, for instance, created at or about DATE 2, but changed or abolished by DATE 3, it should be marked: __ X __.

EMPLOYEE'S NAME—Fill in the name (last name, initials) of the person who fills each position. For those to be hired in the future, enter "TBH".

Use the last four boxes in this column to record the employee's PHONE EXTENSION.

LOCATION—Enter the floor number and room number of the work station each employee is currently occupying.

EMPLOYEE'S NAME (ph. ext.)	LOCATION floor	room
GOMEZ C	3	
NAKAMURA H	3	
COLEMAN B	3	
PETERSON D	3	
SMITH B	3	
LIPSEY W	3	
OBRIEN C	3	
JACOBS A	1	
TBH		

FIGURE 5-1. Two Pages from a Typical Survey Form

(courtesy Morganelli-Heumann and Associates)

HISTORICAL DATA FOR FINANCE GROUP

Year	1985	1986	1987	1988	1989	1990
Area (SF)	3750	4050	4700	4525	5500	5620
Headcount	25	27	31	30	37	38

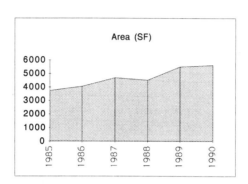

FORECASTED GROWTH

By simple rate

	1991	1992	1993	1994	1995
Rate	5%	3%	3%	20%	15%
Area (SF)	5901	6078	6260	7512	8639
Headcount	39.9	41.1	42.33	50.8	58.42

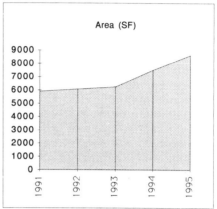

By regression analysis

	1991	1992	1993	1994	1995
Rate	8%	6%	6%	6%	5%
Area (SF)	6043	6430	6816	7203	7589
Headcount	40.86	43.48	46.09	48.7	51.31

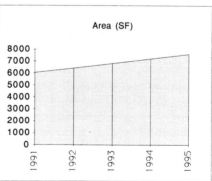

PREPARED BY CHED REEDER
FACILITY ASSETS COMPUTER TOOLS

FIGURE 5-2.   Historical Trend Analysis

(courtesy Reeder Consulting Group)

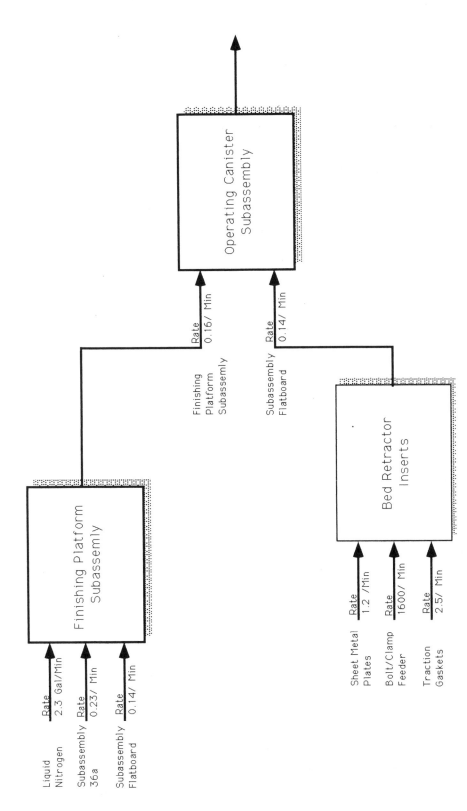

FIGURE 5-3. Manufacturing Flow Analysis

(courtesy Reeder Consulting Group)

121

AMI Corporation   09/17/91
                                                               Page 1
Staff & Area Forecast   Project Code:DEMO

ADMIN   Administration

Job/Space Std Description	Space Std Area(SF)	Staff			Rqd Area(SF)		
		01/91	01/92	01/94	01/91	01/92	01/94
PRES President	225	1	1		225	225	
VP Vice President	120	1	1		120	120	
EX-SEC Executive Secretary	150	1	1		150	150	
MGR Manager	150	1	1		150	150	
DIR Director	200	1	1		200	200	
RCPT Receptionist	80	1	1		80	80	
SEC Secretary	64	5	6		320	384	
CLERK2 Clerk 2	64	3	3		192	192	
TC-ANLST Technical Analyst	64	5	6		320	384	
C2 Medium Conference Rm	250	0	0		250	500	
CP1 Small Copy Room	80	0	0		160	160	
FI1 File Room	120	0	0		240	240	
STOR1 Storage Closet	200	2	0		600	400	
Subtotal		21	21		3,007	3,185	
Access Circulation					357	367	
Forecast by Percentage Growth Rate				4%			
				22			3,694
Subtotal Net Usable Area					3,364	3,552	3,694
Circulation Factor		34%	34%	35%	1,144	1,208	1,293
Subtotal Usable Area					4,508	4,760	4,987
Core Factor		12%	12%	14%	541	571	698
Total Staff and Rentable Area		21	21	22	5,049	5,331	5,685

FIGURE 5-4.   Projection Based on Current Status and Standards

(courtesy FM:Systems)

715 RIVER STREET SUMMARY

GROUP/UNIT	REQ'D PERSONNEL			EXISTING AREA (USF)	REQUIRED AREA (USF)		
	YE1990	YE1992	YE1995		YE1990	YE1992	YE1995
MLC	292	304	309	41,472	41,472	43,107	43,513
SPECIAL MARKETS GROUP	123	142	149	29,830	23,625	22,026	22,119
REGIONAL GROUP	48	53	72	7,694	7,694	8,304	10,315
CREDIT POLICY & ADMIN. GROUP	54	54	58	12,549	12,549	12,477	13,342
REGIONAL MARKETS GROUP	49	39	37	5,275	5,275	8,590	8,308
COMMUNITY GROUP	23	30	34	6,047	6,047	7,125	7,809
TECHNOLOGY &PROCESSING GROUP	31	37	43	7,920	7,920	10,562	11,274
FINANCIAL MANAGEMENT GROUP	189	202	222	26,731	26,731	29,852	32,239
ADMINISTRATION GROUP	81	86	91	13,575	13,575	14,852	15,788
HUMAN RESOURCES GROUP	22	22	22	6,502	6,502	6,502	6,502
NORTHEAST CREDIT CORP.	25	26	30	4,284	4,284	4,512	4,867
SYSTEMS LIAISON	5	7	9	600	600	799	998
CORPORATE FINANCE GROUP	32	38	43	incl. above	4,964	5,894	6,383
INDUSTRY & PRODUCT DIVISION	8	12	16	incl. above	1,241	1,861	2,375
TOTALS	982	1,052	1,135	162,479	162,478	176,463	185,833
FORECASTED CHANGE	-	+70	+153		-	+13,985	+23,355
DENSITY (USF/EMPLOYEE)					165	168	164

FIGURE 5-5. Master Plan Program — High-Level Summary by Group

(courtesy Whidden•Silver)

CORPORATE ORGANIZATION
FACILITY MASTER PLAN

SPACE NEEDS REPORT
25 MARCH 1991

CORPORATE TAX DIVISION

ID NO	FUNCTION	NAME/DESCRIPTION	SPACE CODE	REQ'D QUANTITY			ADD'L AREA REQUIRED		
				YE1990	YE1992	YE1995	YE1990	YE1992	YE1995
A. PERSONNEL									
1	SVP & Tax Counselor	R.J. Wall	A	1	1	1		0	0
2	VP & Tax Mgr.	V. Boniello	B	1	1	1		0	0
3	VP Tax Audits	A. Matero	B	1	1	1		0	0
4	AVP Tax Research	T. Sigismonti	C	1	1	1		0	0
5	AVP Computer Application	J. Rincon	C	1	1	1		0	0
6	AVP Tax Compliance		C	0	1	1		80	80
7	Secretary/Clerk		G	2	2	2		0	0
8	2 Additions to Staff		E	0	0	2		0	128
B. SUPPORT SPACES									
1	Library	new requirement	150	0	1	1		150	150
2	Auditors Room for IRS, etc...	new requirement	150	0	1	1		150	150
3	New gen'l office equipment	Allowance						50	50

CORPORATE TAX DIVISION TOTALS:							
PERSONNEL REQUIREMENTS		7	8	10			
	AREA SUBTOTALS					+430	+558
	CIRCULATION @ 30%					129	167
CHANGE (BASE=YE'90)		-	+1	+3		+559	+725
EXISTING AREA OCCUPIED (715 RIVER ST/22ND FL)					926	926	926
NET AREA REQUIREMENT (USF)					926	1,485	1,651

FIGURE 5-6.   Portion of Architectural Program—Mix of Head Count and Support Space Data

(courtesy Whidden•Silver)

| | LOAN OPERATIONS | | | | | | | | |

ID NO	FUNCTION	NAME/DESCRIPTION	ADJ REF	SPACE CODE	YE1990	YE1992	YE1995	YE1990	YE1992	YE1995
					+---REQ'D QUANTITY---+			+--------REQUIRED AREA--------+		

G. DEPARTMENTAL SHARED SPACE

ID NO	FUNCTION	NAME/DESCRIPTION	ADJ REF	SPACE CODE	YE1990	YE1992	YE1995	YE1990	YE1992	YE1995
1	LG. CONFERENCE ROOM	SEATING FOR 10 x 2 *subdividable into two rooms, pulldown screen, white board, service counter w/lockable cabinets under.*		300	2	2	2	600	600	600
2	SUPPLY ROOM *Relocate microfilm eqpt.to Copy Room, replace with shelving*				1	1	1	150	150	150
3	COPY & MAIL ROOM							0	0	0
	—COPY MACHINE			COPY	1	1	1	25	25	25
	—MAIL COUNTER/12 SORTING PIGEONHOLES (8 LF)			40	1	1	1	40	40	40
	—MINOLTA FICHE RDR. #RP-502	*On Counter*		T30	1	1	1	10	10	10
	—PANAFAX MACHINE	*On Counter*		T30	3	3	5	30	30	50
	—MINOLTA FILMER #DAR2800	*50X30"*		T	1	1	1	25	25	25
	—BESS TERMINAL			PC	1	1	1	60	60	60
	—BESS PRINTER			PTR	1	1	1	15	15	15
	Internal circulation							43	43	45
	TOTAL COPY & MAIL ROOM							248	248	270
6	STORAGE ROOM - Add 5 shelving units for boxes now on floor - Case file, 24x24" - relocate printer and fiche reader	*For boxed records*			1	1	1	120	120	120
7	FICHE READER, MINOLTA # RP-101 DL			T	1	1	1	25	25	25

CORPORATE ORGANIZATION
CBSD

SPACE NEEDS REPORT
25 APRIL 1990

| | LOAN OPERATIONS | | | | | | | | |

ID NO	FUNCTION	NAME/DESCRIPTION	ADJ REF	SPACE CODE	YE1990	YE1992	YE1995	YE1990	YE1992	YE1995
					+---REQ'D QUANTITY---+			+--------REQUIRED AREA--------+		
9	COAT STORAGE			COATS	79	79	98	119	119	146
10	DEPT. PANTRY/COFFEE AREA	*counter, microwave, refrig., coffee machine*		40	1	1	1	40	40	40

DEPT. SHARED SPACE (G) TOTALS				0	0	0	1,550	1,550	1,621
			Area with Circulation-->				2,015	2,015	2,108

LOAN OPERATIONS TOTALS: PERSONNEL REQUIREMENTS		61	61	75			
	AREA SUBTOTALS				9,370	9,370	10,797
	CIRCULATION @30%				2,811	2,811	3,239
NET AREA REQUIREMENTS (USF)					12,181	12,181	14,036
	FORECASTED CHANGE		+0	+14		+0	+1,856
	DENSITY (USF/PERSON)					200	187

FIGURE 5-7.   Portion of Interior/Space Planning Program—Highest Degree of Detail

(courtesy Whidden•Silver)

Adjacency Diagram

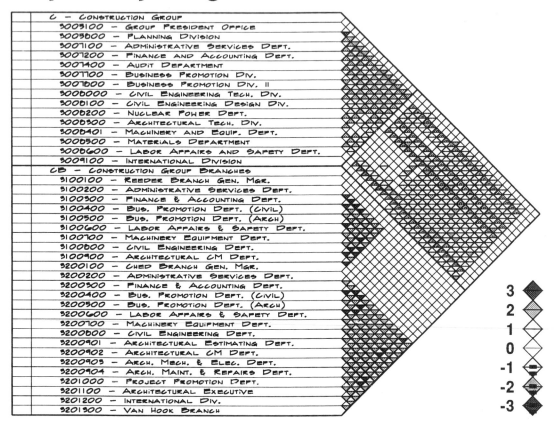

FIGURE 5-8.   Adjacency Matrix

(courtesy HOK)

```
PROJECT NO:      82206.00
21-DEC-82

                                             PERSONNEL-EQUIPMENT-SUPPORT SPACE PROJECTIONS
****************************************************************************************************
GROUP ID: 3800
GROUP   : NAD-PERSONNEL
MANAGER : OPEN
                             QTY              AREA
 SHARED BY GROUP        ID#  83  85  87        1/83    1/85    1/87   CODE     REMARKS
+----------------------+---+ --- --- ---  +-------+-------+-------+ -------  +--------------------------+
  PERSONNEL MANAGER      1    1   1   1        180.    180.    180.  MGR-B
  EOP MANAGER            2    1   1   1        140.    140.    140.  MGR-C
  STAFF                  3    3   3   4        420.    420.    560.  STF-A
  SECRETARY              4    3   3   4        225.    225.    300.  SEC-A
  TERMIN WKSTA           5    4   4   4        300.    300.    300.  TERM-B
                             --- --- ---  +-------+-------+-------+
                              12  12  14      1265.   1265.   1480.

 STORAGE                 1    2   2   2        220.    220.    220.  STO A
 TERMIN ROOM             2    1   1   1        200.    200.    200.  TER C
                             --- --- ---  +-------+-------+-------+
                               3   3   3       420.    420.    420.

                                              1685.   1685.   1900.  NET ASSIGNABLE
```

FIGURE 5-9. Early Batch Program Output

(courtesy Mitchell, Reeder, Hamer—The Computer-Aided Design Group)

Owned Facility: **Current Appraised Value: $140 Million**

Leases	Floors	RSF	$000/Yr	Expiration
Misc. Retail	Ground	5,200	240	various
CFGI	4,5,15	62,200	2,155	12/31/95
Allied	6–8	62,200	2,393	10/31/94
Strothers	9,10,11	72,600	2,929	7/94-8/95
PDC	12 part.	77,896	425	6/30/99
Universal Finance		77,896	2,804	1/31/99
Other 1990 income			2,371	
		357,992	13,317	

Capacity: Corporate floors   357,000 rsf on 18 floors
                 Tenant floors   235,000 rsf on 12 floors

Vacant Space: Corporate floors   part. 23rd: 2,300 rsf
                    Tenant floors   14th fl.: 20,700 rsf
                                       Ground fl. (retail): 1,200 rsf

Occupancy Cost: Total: $22.50/rsf ($13.342 million)

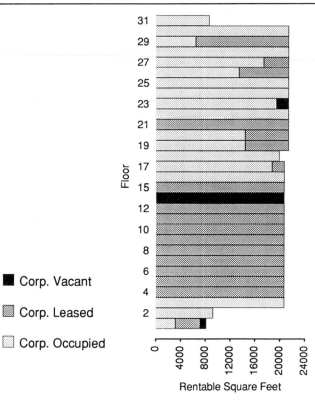

Corp. Vacant

Corp. Leased

Corp. Occupied

FIGURE 5-10.   Custom Spreadsheet Output

(courtesy Whidden•Silver)

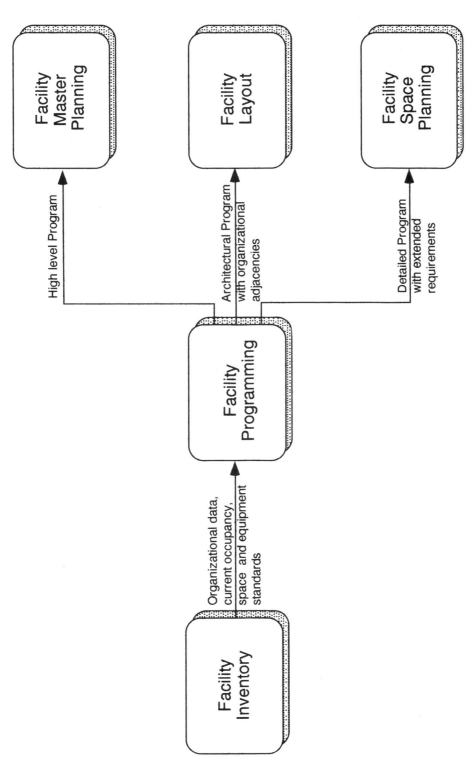

FIGURE 5-11. Key Data Flow Relationships for Facility Programming Data

(courtesy Reeder Consulting Group)

CHAPTER 6

Participatory Programming of Campus Child-Care Facilities

Henry Sanoff

INTRODUCTION

This chapter describes the way in which research findings can be integrated into design decision processes. The techniques described here are based on the results of personal experiences in the designing and programming of child-care facilities. Earlier experience suggests the need for a new approach that can engage the architect and the client/user group in a process that links children's developmental needs to facility requirements. Strategies are described that engage parents, teachers, and administrators in collaboration with the architect during the initial stages of design. This process has produced teachers with new capabilities in playroom planning and organization, as well as with an understanding of the way in which architects make decisions. Although the examples described here are campus child-care facilities, the same techniques can be generalized for noninstitutional groups as well. Integral to the process is the concept of the *nonpaying client*. For programming purposes, people who use the building are the clients of the architect, whether or not they pay for services. Reference to the user as the nonpaying client, then, attaches greater significance to the importance of user contributions, and to a nontraditional relationship between the paying and nonpaying client.

It is widely accepted that a developmentally appropriate environment—one with well-trained and consistent staff in sufficient numbers, moderately sized groupings of children, and proper equipment and activities—will lead to good

131

child care (Whitebrook, Howes, and Phillips, 1989). In all types of environments, working conditions affect services provided. Measures of quality child care have been discussed in several ways. Researchers have attempted to examine the *structural* aspects of child care, such as group composition and staff qualifications; *dynamic* aspects of child care, which pertain to children's daily experiences; and the *contextual* aspects of child care, which are concerned with the type of setting and staff stability. One approach for obtaining a quality assessment relies on a rating scale. The Early Childhood Environmental Rating Scale, referred to as ECERS (Harms and Clifford, 1980), examines seven dimensions of quality:

1. personal care
2. creative activities
3. language/reasoning activities
4. furnishings/display
5. fine/gross motor activities
6. social development
7. adult facilities and opportunities

Adding the scores across the seven factors provides an overall quality rating. The results of such assessments have shown that children in higher-quality centers showed more advanced communication skills and verbal intelligence and more positive social behavior and task orientation (Phillips, Scarr, and McCartney, 1989). It is apparent from the literature related to quality that classroom quality, child-care setting, and contextual features are measures of social interaction, and not measures of the physical features of the environment. Consequently, there is a general lack of understanding in the early learning field of the role of the physical environment in contributing to quality child care.

In recent years there has been a surge in the construction of child-care facilities. Each is approached in a unique way, with very little programmatic knowledge transferred or recorded. From the limited research related to children's environments, it is becoming evident that new facilities are meeting health and safety standards, but are not providing the physical conditions for the developmental needs of young children (Moore, 1987).

This chapter represents a synthesis of numerous consulting efforts with colleges and universities that are planning to construct a child-care facility. The results of these experiences consist of a process and techniques that can be used by architects and teachers to facilitate a constructive dialogue about facility needs. The diagram in Figure 6-1 describes the integration of three major components of the collaborative design process: *design research, design participation,* and *design development.* These components precede production, construction, and evaluation. In this model, programming represents the synthesis between design research and design participation. This collaborative design process is a departure from traditional programming approaches, since the client, the nonpaying client, and the architect are directly involved in all decision-making stages. Furthermore, the stages described as design research and design participation subsume what is normally referred to as facility programming. This distinction enables the identification of discrete activities for each stage as well as clarification of the difference between information received from secondary sources—such as surveys and databases—and from primary sources—such as direct, face-to-face involvement.

Typically, institutional client groups planning the child-care center initiate a formal needs assessment that includes the following steps:

1. campus survey of student child-care needs
2. survey of campus child-care centers
3. site visits to child-care facilities
4. consultation with child-care experts
5. departmental planning

The above steps constitute the design research phase of the collaborative design process. Although this phase is typically initiated by the client, the architect can often provide guidelines for more systematic fact-finding procedures. Surveys and visits to existing facilities, if properly organized, can reveal valuable insights into their functions, since casual visits often render only obvious results.

RESEARCH FINDINGS

Since needs assessment studies often yield conclusions far in excess of what is practical or feasible, the more important planning decision for the child-care center is the number of children to be served. Research studies (Kritchevsky, Prescott, and Walling, 1969) have shown that the developmental quality of child-care services drops sharply with increases in the number of children served in one building. Prescott, Jones, Kritchevsky, Milich, and Haselhoef (1975) found that center size was a reliable predictor of program quality. In centers that served over sixty children, major emphasis tended to be placed on rules and routine guidance. Conversely, teacher emphasis on these concerns was found to be significantly lower in smaller centers. Prescott et al. (1975) also found that large centers rarely offered children the experience of participating in wide age-range groups. These findings were also supported by Gump (1978). Mixing of ages in smaller centers offered opportunities for older children to serve as models and to enrich overall play possibilities (Moore, Lane, Hill, Cohen, and McGinty, 1979).

The age groups generally served by most centers are infants (six weeks to twelve months), toddlers (twelve months to two years), and preschoolers (three to five years). In order to achieve the needed critical number in each age group, a target number of sixty to seventy-five children is recommended (Moore, Lane, Hill, Cohen, and McGinty, 1979) as a basic planning module. As the institutional needs increase, the number of children should then be increased in multiples of sixty to seventy-five administratively independent units, to keep the scale of the facility within the child's grasp.

In addition to the number of children in a center, an adequate amount of space for children's activities is necessary to ensure a quality developmentally oriented program. In a commission study for the federal government, based on a review of cases of density and behavior in child-care settings, Prescott and David (1976) recommended a minimum of 42 square feet of usable floor space per child. Cohen, Moore, and McGinty (1978), in conducting interviews as part of their national research, suggested that 42 square feet per child permits a much more flexible program, allowing simultaneous options in active and quiet pursuits without children disturbing each other. This is in contrast to the average minimum requirement of 35 square feet that is stipulated in most states. A study by Rohe and Nuffer (1977) showed that while increasing spatial density by reducing space tended to increase aggressive behavior, sheltering activity areas by inserting partitions increased cooperative behavior. Both density and partitioning affected children's activity choices (Rohe and Nuffer, 1977). In a review of studies, Moore et al. (1979) concluded that the most desirable social environment occurs at a density of 42 to 50 square feet of usable activity space per child. These research findings provide the basis for facility size and classroom organization criteria.

DESIGN PARTICIPATION

During this stage of the process, background research findings are integrated into the activity analysis. Accompanying the area requirement for usable activity space for each child is the need for well-defined areas limited to one learning activity, with clear boundaries from circulation space and from other activity areas (Moore, 1986). Well-defined activity areas or centers may be created with surrounding partitions, storage cabinets, changes in floor levels and surface materials, or other visual elements that suggest boundaries. Spatially well-defined areas support social interaction, cooperative behavior, and exploratory behavior (Moore, 1986; Smith and Connolly, 1980). Well-defined areas also prevent ongoing play from being disrupted by intruders (Field, 1980).

A process in which the architect and teaching staff link behavioral objectives to spatial requirements corrects an inadequacy in the traditional practice of architecture in recognizing the behavioral requirements of the children in making design decisions. Decisions about classroom organization are usually delegated to the teachers, who attempt to create learning or activity centers but are often hampered by lack of knowledge of how to shape the centers physically. Consequently, running and chasing activities are common in classrooms where boundaries are not well defined (Smith and Connolly, 1980). Conversely, well-defined activity centers, with clear boundaries from circulation space and from other activity areas, and with some visual or acoustic separation, decrease classroom interruptions and contribute to longer attention spans (Moore et al., 1979). This implies that activity centers within the classroom require a high degree of spatial definition. The design task, then, requires the development of a building program that can spatially respond to the developmental goals of the teachers of young children as well as to the literature on child development and behavior.

CLIENT AWARENESS TECHNIQUES

The Walk-through

Early in the planning process, it is desirable for representatives of the user/client group to embark on a program of visits to other child-care centers. The visiting team "walks through" (Preiser, Rabinowitz, and White, 1988) each facility and reports on their basic features. The walk-throughs consist of a briefing session, open-ended interviews with teachers, and observations of plan layout patterns of different facilities. Visitors should note positive and negative features of the facilities. Unless the visits are organized to include an interview schedule and specific features to be observed, the results can produce only obvious and superficial results. The visits help to familiarize client groups with the issues they will encounter during the facility development process. They also provide nonprofessional visitors with the direct experience of observing a child-care center in action.

Modeling the Playroom

Since the playroom is the basic spatial unit of a children's center, prior familiarity with its constituent elements can enable teachers to enter into a productive dialogue with the architect. Modeling the playroom is an activity developed for a teachers' workshop that allows participants to manipulate fixed and movable playroom elements in order to achieve the desired developmental objectives. Working in teams of three people each, teachers are assigned a design task to create a playroom for a specific age group, such as infants, toddlers, or preschoolers. Found materials, including cardboard, wood blocks, styrofoam, construction paper, and plastic, are provided along with instructions to the teachers for measuring and cutting the materials needed to construct a three-dimensional model.

The model making is preceded by an exercise in which developmental objectives and corresponding activity areas for specific age groups are discussed and agreed upon by each team. Model results are discussed by participants, then playrooms are joined together to resemble a building for different age groups. At this juncture, issues of playroom adjacencies, building flow, and location of services are discussed by participants (Figure 6-2) in an exercise of four hours in duration.

Walk-throughs and playroom modeling are effective methods for preparing the client group to actively and constructively participate in the planning stages of a child development center.

CASE STUDY

Programming and design consultation were requested by the planning group of a proposed seventy-five-child facility and training center for Wake Community College's Child Development Program, in North Carolina. They contacted the Community Development Group at North Carolina State University for design assistance. Since this facility was intended as a demonstration site for the county, the department head and client representative, the teaching staff, and the educational consultants to the program were anxious to follow a planning process in which research findings, their expertise, and educational philosophy would be linked to design decisions. The design research phase included a needs assessment, visits to other child-care centers, and the establishment of educational goals, which included desired staff-child ratios and other factors inherent in a high-quality center.

Recording Activity Data

Planning began with focusing on the child as the basic unit of development. Next, the design participation phase involved the collection of behavioral data relating to each activity in which infants, toddlers, and preschoolers would be engaged. The conceptual framework used for the design of the facility was the activity center (Sanoff and Sanoff, 1981). The teaching staff of the child development training program identified the developmental objectives for each activity by age group and also the "molecular" activities that would occur in the activity center (Figure 6-3). The objectives of the water play area, for example, would include sensory and perceptual acuity, concept formation, and eye-hand coordination (Sanoff, 1982; Weinstein, 1987), and would include such molecular activities as pouring, measuring, mixing, and floating objects, all of which are related to the primary activity. Activity data sheets were used to record the relevant activity information, which served as a program and resource for future decisions. The data sheets provided a format in which specific equipment needs could also be identified for future purchasing.

Spatial Planning

Since the planning of a child-care facility also reflects a particular ideology about child development, a space planning exercise was developed to engage the teaching staff in decisions related to playroom layout. Since a planning guide of 50 square feet of usable space per child limited the number of activity centers that could be included in a playroom, scenarios were written by teachers about a typical child's day. The constraints encouraged the teaching staff to use "trade-offs" effectively, since they were required to decide which activity centers were most important for various age groups. Graphic symbols corresponding to each activity center (Figure 6-4) enabled the manipulation of children's movement patterns in the classroom. This was the first step in providing environmental information to foster mental image development (Hunt, 1985). Spatially organizing activity centers on a "game board" corresponding to a playroom permitted the determination of which centers were to be fixed and which flexible. The spatial layout process required teachers to consider planning concepts, adjacency requirements, circulation, and visual and acoustic privacy between activity centers. Most of all, the process reinforced the concept of activity centers.

The teachers worked through a playroom layout by manipulating activity symbols for each age group. They outlined the flow process—from entering the facility, greeting the staff, disrobing in the cubby area, and moving to various activity centers. When planning the infant room, the teachers identified the diaper change as the focal point, providing surveillance to all other activity areas. To avoid the clustering of unsightly cribs, the teachers proposed decentralizing the sleeping activity into several crib alcoves. This process entailed small group discussions that required consensus in all decisions. When agreement was reached, the symbols were fastened to the base to constitute a record of the group's decisions (Figure 6-5). Cardboard scale models of each playroom, with movable walls and furniture, were then constructed by the designer, and corresponded with the flow patterns in the diagrams developed by the teachers (Figure 6-6). This stage of the process permitted the teaching staff to visualize the three-dimensional implications of their decisions. Simplified schematic models of the playrooms limited the amount of information presented at one time, conveying only the most significant issues in order to minimize information overload (Milgram, 1970; Hunt, 1985). Teachers could reconsider earlier decisions, particularly when they saw conflicts arise that were not easily predicted in the two-dimensional diagrams. Although circulation between activity centers was considered in the development of the activity symbol diagrams, the scale model conveyed the need to establish clear boundaries between centers to prevent distraction, while permitting the teacher an unobstructed view of all children's play areas. The scale models included information not shown on the activity diagrams, such as furniture and equipment, but the movable pieces were easily manipulated by the teachers as they referred to the activity data sheets.

After the teachers had reached agreement about the best playroom arrangement, the designer developed form diagrams that elaborated on their spatial decisions (Figure 6-7). These diagrams combined activity centers into playrooms for different age groups. Although abstract in nature, the diagrams allowed teachers to gain an understanding of "conceptual relationships." Teachers were better able to clarify their intentions regarding the way in which the educational program would be enhanced in the design of the classrooms. This exercise also provided the participants with the tools to evaluate plan alternatives and, most important, a procedure for further playroom modification after the building was in use.

Design Criteria

The results of the participatory exercises helped to generate design criteria, as well as to modify the requirements of the building program. Several statements were developed to describe the fundamental environmental characteristics of an effective child development center. They are as follows:

The environment must be comfortable and inviting for children and adults. It should reflect an atmosphere conducive to children's growth. Materials and equipment should be easily accessible to children in order to encourage independence and self-esteem.

An effective means of organizing the environment is to develop interest centers where the playroom is divided into areas that focus on specific activities. It is advisable that quieter activity areas be placed in close proximity in order to promote a quiet atmosphere. Activity areas demand visual clarity and well-defined limits if children are expected to interpret cues on appropriate areas for certain types of play. A quality playroom would include the following activity areas:

creative expression/art	cooking
literature/language art	water play
dramatic play/housekeeping	carpentry
block building	manipulative
self-image, personal hygiene	music and movement
science and exploration	personal space

More specific guidelines that influenced the final solution included the following:

protected outdoor play area adjacent to each playroom
south orientation for playroom and adjacent outdoor area
daylight to be provided by rooftop glazing and glazing orientation

Facility Design

The teaching staff was involved in organizing all the building components into a facility design by using graphic symbols that corresponded to the major building parts, such as playrooms, kitchen, offices, corridors, and lobby area. Age group adjacencies were considered to provide opportunities for different age groups to have visual contact with each other. This was ultimately achieved in many ways, including low windows in each playroom for children to be able to see into the adjacent room. The parents' "drop-off" point was the initial step in the flow process, which also examined connections between indoor and outdoor activities. The planning concept that emerged from the discussion was that of a "central spine" to which playrooms would be connected. The spine would be more than a corridor; rather, it would be similar to a street, where parents, teachers, and visitors could see into the playrooms and observe children's activities (Figures 6-8 and 6-9). To emphasize the street concept, it was necessary to fill the area with daylight through the use of skylights (Figure 6-10). Each of the playrooms, too, would have a central spine leading to a covered outdoor play area. Spatially well-defined activity centers were located on either side of the playroom spine. These playrooms included fixed areas for art and water play and centers that could change their focus at the discretion of the teacher. The concept of "spatially well-defined centers" implies the need to be distinctly different from adjacent centers. This differentiation was characterized by physical features, such as partially surrounded dividers or storage units, implied boundaries through the use of columns, changes in floor level or ceiling heights, changes in floor covering, and changes in light levels. Learning materials, furniture, and equipment also contribute to the distinctiveness of the activity centers. The infant playroom is shown here with the central diaper change area and observation from the central spine of the building (Figure 6-11).

PLANNING OUTDOOR PLAY

Planning for outdoor play is an integral part of the design process and was a vital component of the North Carolina child-care center. Typically perceived as a staging area for large muscle development, the outdoor play area is not only important for the child's health but contributes to the child's learning experiences as well (Threlfall, 1986). Outdoor play space offers opportunities for adventure, challenge, and wonder in the natural environment (Frost and Klein, 1983). The only substantial difference between indoor and outdoor activity is that one has a roof over it. Both, however, need architectural and landscape definition, and both need to provide for the multiplicity of children's developmental needs. For example, a play yard with twelve tricycles, a rocking boat, a tumble tub, a jungle gym, a dirt area, and a sand table with water has seventeen separate play units but only four different kinds of things to do (Kritchevsky, Prescott, and Walling, 1974). Variety can be an important measure of interest. Also, complexity, or the number of subparts of a piece of equipment (such as a sandbox with play materials, water, climbing boards, and crates), can add to a child's interest.

The process of creating outdoor play spaces is age group-oriented and began with developmental objectives that help to generate the activities in which children engage (Sanoff, 1982). The teaching staff and design team worked together to establish linkages between objectives for outdoor play, the related children's activities, and the play settings required (Figure 6-12). To complement the indoor environment, the outdoors provides play settings that stress muscle development as well as natural settings that provide experience in the life cycle of plants and animals. The props used to enable the teachers to make spatial decisions included drawings of different play settings as well as statements of objectives and lists of activities. The planning group moved through a series of collaborative stages in which all members reached consensual agreement. Finally, the activities and play settings were organized into play zones, which ranged from passive to active play, and from private to group activities (Sanoff, 1982). This part of the planning process helped to generate discussions about the purpose of outdoor play, usually dispelling many of the myths surrounding large muscle development as the primary purpose of children's outdoor activities.

Learning objectives for outdoor play are discussed in a similar way to those in the planning of the playrooms. Objectives such as problem solving, concept development, and social development were key concerns of the teachers. Supporting activities, such as role playing, climbing, feeling and handling, balancing, sliding, and construction, constitute the array of choices most frequently made. As a result of making these linkages, the subsequent choices of play equipment and play areas were based on a clear understanding of the developmental needs that the outdoor play area should serve. Other types of individual or quiet activities, group games, and opportunities for exercising imagination were also identified for outdoor use, but did not necessarily require the construction of special equipment.

An analysis of the building site and its topography influenced the location and options for various play settings. A site map was used as the basis for planning areas where play settings would be clustered according to similarity of requirements. Play zones include areas for drama, nature, adventure, and large muscle development. Equipment and zone choices were then related to specific site requirements, such as solar orientation.

TEACHERS' RESPONSE TO THE PROCESS

The diagrams and scale models provided a clear, sequential procedure where all decisions could be traced and subsequently modified. The teachers, however, found difficulty in comprehending the consequences of many spatial decisions. While they were able to follow the process of playroom organization, they had difficulty in visualizing the implications of alternative playroom arrangements. A continual reference to scale models and perspective drawings aided the teachers substantially in contributing their expertise to the design of the building. The teachers remarked that this process provided them with a better understanding of the principles of spatial planning and the role of the architect. They experienced the "ripple effect," where minor changes in adjacency relationships manifest themselves in major revisions in the spatial layout of the playroom, or even of the building. This diagnostic procedure of examining flow processes and linking objectives to activity centers enables teachers to develop a conceptual understanding of playroom and building layout principles.

CONCLUSION

The interaction between teachers and the designer described in this project is clearly a departure from the traditional approach to facility development. Conventional practice usually denies the expertise of the users (nonpaying client) and their involvement in design decision making. Traditional designers also focus on the formal and visual issues and give less attention to the behavioral factors that may equally influence the form of the building. This tradition could be carefully guarded, since the design of a child-care facility is normally developed at the floorplan level, defining relationships between classrooms and other areas and disadvantaging the teaching staff because of their inability to comprehend floor plans. The teachers' expertise lies at the level of behavioral interactions within the playroom, but their concerns are typically ignored by architects and left to the teachers to resolve after occupancy of the facility.

In the project discussed, a structured process was provided to enable child development professionals to lend their expertise to the initial programming stages of the design process. Use of activity data sheets, activity symbols, and form diagrams permitted the architect to integrate knowledge about children's behavior and their requirements into a format that was conducive to making space planning decisions. Integrating the expertise of the staff in this guided process established clear linkages between child development goals and the types of places where these goals could be fulfilled. The teaching staff's continual involvement in the building design process encouraged the exchange of ideas and concepts with the architect, which increased the staff's ability to act as effective design team members. The active part of the process usually terminated with the schematic design of the children's center, which is the result of the team's involvement.

It has been shown that people who participate in design decisions have greater satisfaction with the product as a result of their involvement (Schwartz, 1978). It is evident from these experiences that the dynamics of a participatory process and product are different from the results of a more traditional design process. Not only is there a shared sense of ownership in the product, but participants are empowered by an understanding of the decisions that led to the physical form decisions. This approach has the further promise of enabling teaching staff to make spatial modifications after occupancy.

The effectiveness of a collaborative process is contingent upon the involvement of the architect from the inception of the project. When the architect is an integral part of the process, the building design proposals are clearly understood by the user/client group of teaching staff, parents, and administrators. On those occasions when the programming document was completed prior to the architect being commissioned for the project, significant communication problems can occur between the user group and the architect. In this instance, the architect-of-record, Haskins, Rice, Savage & Pearce, PA, was appointed by the college administration after the program and preliminary design had been completed by the consulting design team. Although considerable effort was made by the design team and teaching staff to explain the rationale for the programming and design decisions, the architect had great difficulty in grasping many of the nuances of the proposed design solution. The architect viewed collaboration in the programming and preliminary design stages initiated by the college as *typical client input,* and as a result modified several important design recommendations. The basic concept and building organization, however, was faithfully adhered to. Similarly, the architect's drawings were not understood by the teaching staff, since they were prepared for construction purposes. This created difficulty in the working relations with the client, because the architect often urged quick approval to expedite the production process. Construction of this facility was completed in 1991, with occupancy to take place thereafter.

The language of the program should reflect the concepts developed by the teaching staff and conveyed in terms of educational goals and children's activities. The language of the architect—the floor plans and elevations—are the interpretation of verbal concepts, and are often unintelligible to the user group, especially if they are not developed simultaneously with the program. The implications of these experiences is that ownership in the design process, achieved through active involvement in design decisions, permits the user/nonpaying client to exercise free and informed choice. The separation of the programming and design stages not only limits participation of a wide range of experts but jeopardizes the ability of the product to fulfill the expectations of the program.

ACKNOWLEDGMENTS

The success of this project is largely owing to Joan Sanoff, Department Head, Early Childhood Development, Wake Technical Community College, who participated in the programming and design development, and urged the college administration and architect-of-record to produce a high-quality building. A note of thanks is also due to James Utley, Community Development Group member, for his thoughtful design work.

An earlier version of this chapter appeared in *Children's Environments Quarterly,* Vol. 6, No. 4, Winter 1989.

References

Cohen, U., A.B. Hill, C.G. Lane, T. McGinty, and G.T. Moore. 1979. *Recommendations for child play areas.* Milwaukee: University of Wisconsin-Milwaukee, Center for Architecture and Urban Planning Research, Report. R79-1.

Cohen, U., G.T. Moore, and T. McGinty. 1978. *Case studies of child play areas and support facilities.* Milwaukee: University of Wisconsin-Milwaukee, Center for Architecture and Urban Planning Research, Report R78-2.

Frost, J.L., and B.L. Klein. 1983. *Children's play and playgrounds.* Austin, Texas: Playscapes.

Field, T.M. 1980. Preschool play: Effects of teacher/child ratios and organization of classroom space. *Child Study Journal* 10:3, pp. 191-205.

Gump, P.V. 1978. School environments. In *Children and the environment,* ed. I. Altman and J.F. Wolwhill. New York: Plenum.

Harms, T., and R.M. Clifford. 1980. *Early childhood environmental rating scales.* New York: Teachers College Press, Columbia University.

Hunt, M.E. 1985. Enhancing a building's imageability. *Journal of Architectural and Planning Research* 2, pp. 151-68.

Kritchevsky, S., E. Prescott, and L. Walling. 1974. Planning environments for young children: Physical space. In *Alternative learning environments*, ed. G. Coates. Stroudsburg, Pa.: Hutchinson and Ross.

Milgram, S. 1970. The experience of living in cities. *Ekistics*, August, pp. 145-50.

Moore, G.T., C.G. Lane, A.H. Hill, U. Cohen, and T. McGinty. 1979. *Recommendations for child care centers*. Milwaukee: University of Wisconsin-Milwaukee, Center for Architecture and Urban Planning Research.

Moore, G.T. 1986. Effects of the spatial definition behavior settings on children's behavior: A quasi-experimental field study. *Journal of Environmental Psychology* 6, pp. 205-31.

Moore, G.T. 1987. The physical environment and cognitive development in child care centers. In *Spaces for children: The built environment and child development*, ed. C.S. Weinstein and T.G. David. New York and London: Plenum.

Osmon, F.L. 1971. *Patterns for designing children's centers*. New York: Educational Facilities Laboratory.

Phillips, D., S. Scarr, and K. McCartney. 1987. Child care quality and children's social development. *Developmental Psychology* 23, pp. 537-43.

Preiser, W.F.E., H.Z. Rabinowitz, and E.T. White, eds. 1988. *Post-occupancy evaluation*. New York: Van Nostrand Reinhold.

Prescott, E., E. Jones, C. Kritchevsky, C. Milich, and E. Haselhoef. 1976. *Assessments of child rearing environments: An ecological approach*. Pasadena, Calif.: Pacific Oaks College.

Prescott, E., and T.G. David. 1976. *The effects of the physical environment in child care systems*. Concept paper. Pasadena, Calif.: Pacific Oaks College.

Rohe, W., and E. Nuffer. 1977. *The effects of density and partitioning on children's behavior*. Paper presented at the 85th annual meeting, American Psychological Association, San Francisco, Calif.

Sanoff, H., and J. Sanoff. 1981. *Learning environments for children*. Atlanta: Humanics.

Sanoff, H. 1983. *Planning outdoor play*. Atlanta: Humanics.

Schwartz, S. 1978. User participation in environmental change. In *Priorities in environmental design research*, ed. R. Brauer. Washington, D.C.: Environmental Design Research Association.

Smith, P.K., and K.J. Connnolly. 1980. *The ecology of preschool behaviour*. Cambridge: Cambridge University Press.

Threlfall, M. 1986. Inside/outside: The school environment. *Children's Environment Quarterly* 3:3, pp. 30-39.

Weinstein, C.S. 1987. Designing preschool classrooms to support development. In *Spaces for children: The built environment and child development*, ed. C.S. Weinstein and T.G. David. New York and London: Plenum.

Whitebrook, M., C. Howes, and D. Phillips. 1989. *Who cares? Child care teachers and the quality of care in America*. Oakland, Calif.: Child Care Employee Project.

144

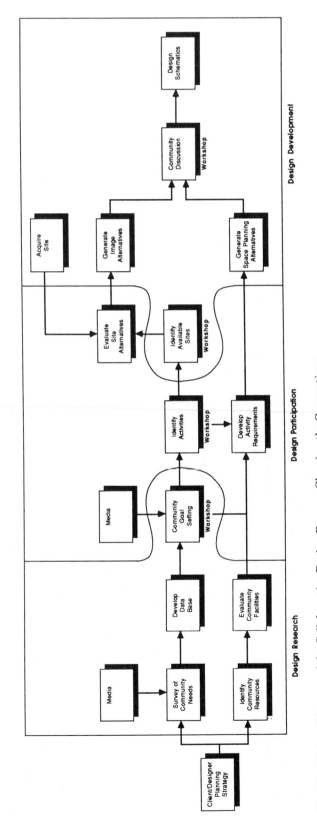

FIGURE 6-1. Diagram of the Collaborative Design Process, Showing the Connections Between Design Research, Design Participation, and Design Development

FIGURE 6-2.   Teachers Involved in Modeling a Classroom for Different Age Groups

Preschool

Water Play
Sand

Water and sand are both flexible materials and offer a wide variety of learning experiences for preschool children. Pouring, measuring, and coloring are just a few ways these can be used for tools of learning. Floating toys, blowing bubbles and mixing water with other mediums to create objects all develop hand-eye coordination. Building in wet sand teaches children about its unique qualities. The area is designed specifically for this type of particular activity and able to accommodate up to four children comfortably with provisions for individual play.

Objectives
Sensory and concept development
Opportunity for soothing/active play
Socialization, Visual-motor skill
development

Equipment
Water table with drain and cover
Water play toys and manipulatives
Water proof smocks
Towels and floor protection
Vertical display for concept development
Container for sand

Storage
Open   Closed
•
•
•
•

100 square feet

Notes
Natural lighting
Well ventilated

Acoustical level-Moderate
Visual access to other areas

FIGURE 6-3.   Typical Data Sheet Developed for Each Activity Center, Showing Molecular Activities

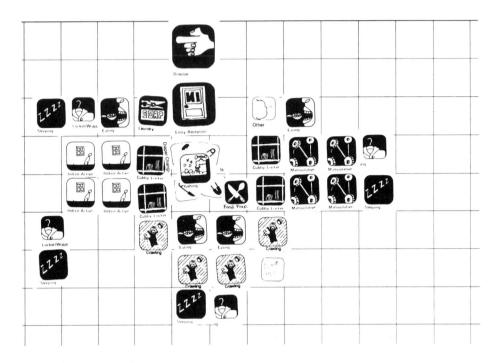

FIGURE 6-4.   Graphic Symbols Corresponding to Each Activity Center Are Used to Study Movement Patterns in the Classroom or in the Building

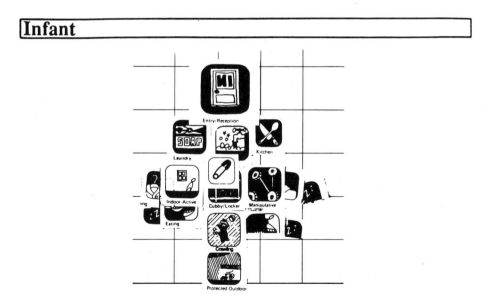

FIGURE 6-5.   Graphic Symbols Recording the Group Decision for Organizing the Infant Playroom

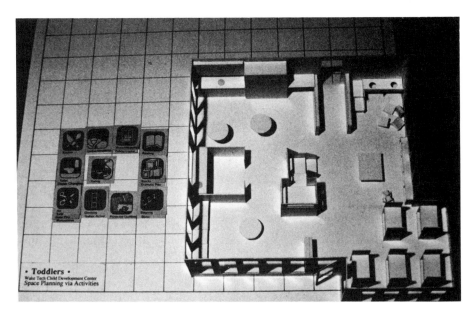

FIGURE 6-6. Cardboard Scale Model Corresponding to the Flow Pattern Diagram

(model by James Utley)

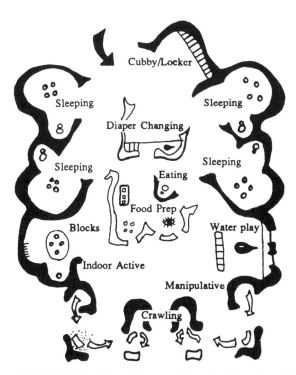

FIGURE 6-7. Form Diagram, Showing More Detail About the Infant Playroom

(drawings by James Utley)

147

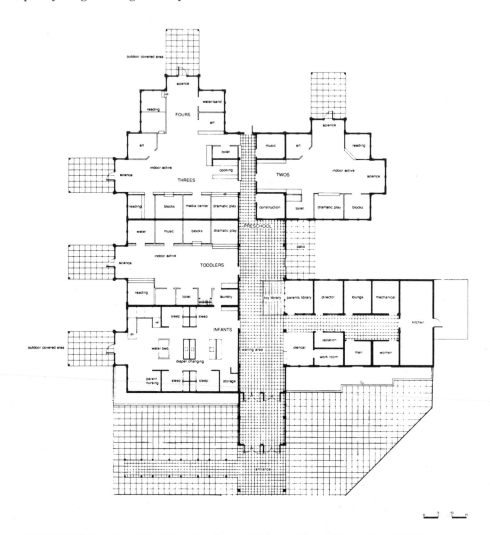

FIGURE 6-8.   Floor Plan Showing Central Spine or Street Connecting All Playrooms

(drawing by James Utley)

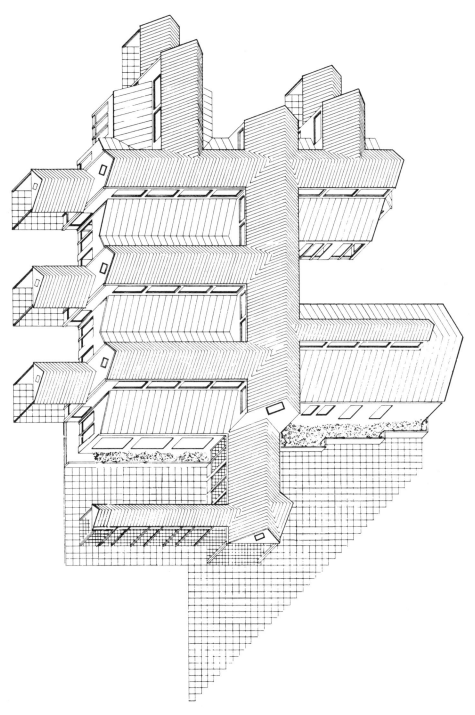

FIGURE 6-9. Axonometric Drawing of Building Emphasizing Daylight Entering the Playrooms in Central Spine

(drawing by James Utley)

FIGURE 6-10.   Interior Spine with Observation to Each Classroom and Overhead Daylight

(architect: Haskins, Rice, Savage & Pearce, PA; photo: Henry Sanoff)

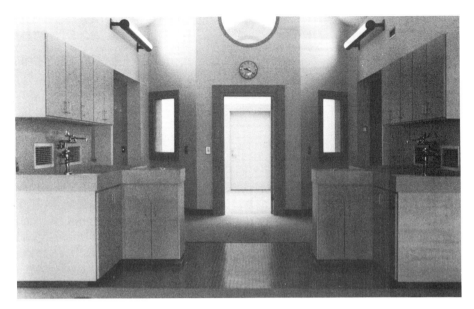

FIGURE 6-11. Infant Playroom, Showing Central Diaper Change Area and Observation from the Central Spine of the Building

(photo: Henry Sanoff)

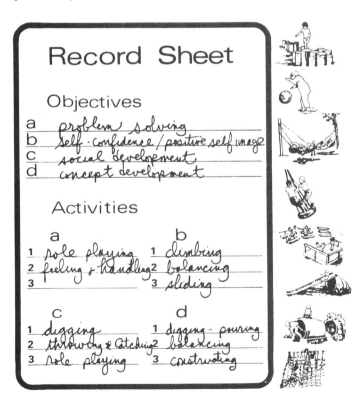

Record Sheet

Objectives

a _problem solving_
b _self-confidence / positive self image_
c _social development_
d _concept development_

Activities

a
1 _role playing_
2 _feeling & handling_
3

b
1 _climbing_
2 _balancing_
3 _sliding_

c
1 _digging_
2 _throwing & catching_
3 _role playing_

d
1 _digging - pouring_
2 _balancing_
3 _constructing_

FIGURE 6-12. An Example of Outdoor Play Objectives, Activities, and Drawings of the Activities

151

CHAPTER 7

Programming Office Space: Adaptive Re-use of the H-E-B Arsenal Headquarters

John Zeisel and Marc A. Maxwell

INTRODUCTION: PROGRAM OVERVIEW

In 1982, the H-E-B Food and Drug Company operated 148 supermarkets throughout South Texas. In that year H-E-B purchased an eleven-acre site in downtown San Antonio from the U.S. government for a new corporate headquarters (Figure 7-1). On the site, located along the as yet unfinished portion of the historic River Walk, were nine utilitarian buildings, two of which—a horse stable and a munitions arsenal—date back to the 1860s. Originally constructed as a U.S. military supply depot, these two oldest buildings were put into use as a replacement for the inadequate Alamo just prior to the onset of the Civil War. The site is surrounded by the remainder of the original twenty-acre "U.S. Arsenal District" (still owned by the federal government) to the west, a transitional residential neighborhood to the south, the San Antonio River to the east, and an undeveloped edge of downtown San Antonio to the north.

A detailed planning and programming effort began on parallel tracks once the property was secured. The project was roughly defined as 160,000 square feet of high-quality office space to house the headquarters and administrative functions of H-E-B. A program for a new, 500-person corporate headquarters facility was developed. The architects first presented a number of scenarios for selective demolition, renovation, and new construction, respectful of this historic yet run-down site. The final project created a central courtyard surrounded by three existing buildings and a single new building, achieved by renovating 60 percent of the space, using 40 percent new construction, and removing several dilapidated storage buildings.

Programming the H-E-B headquarters complex in San Antonio was an ideal experience. The client and the designers fully participated in the programming effort and incorporated the program findings and analysis into every aspect of the master plan for the complex, its architecture, and the space planning. Design inquiry—employing diagrams, sketches, models, and plans—and programming research—employing observation, focused interviews, questionnaires, and measurement—progressed hand in hand.

In the eight years since the corporate headquarters complex was programmed, built, and put to use in San Antonio, it has accommodated major organizational shifts, undergone changes in managerial personnel, and been the physical center for managing 100 percent growth in corporate sales. During the same eight-year period, a 40 percent growth in headquarters staff has been accommodated in only 10 percent additional occupied area without compromising the overall quality or design of the headquarters facility.

Project Definition and Scope

Programming for the headquarters complex was one part of a larger project, which began with a decision by H-E-B to relocate its headquarters from Corpus Christi, a Texas city on the Gulf of Mexico, to San Antonio, the geographic center of H-E-B's market area. This move met three corporate goals. First, the move co-located H-E-B's two business centers. A supermarket chain business has two related, yet independent, business centers—an administrative management center for the company, and a center for distributing goods to individual stores. The H-E-B distribution center was already located in San Antonio, so the corporate relocation joined these two essential activities—management and distribution—in the same city.

A second goal met by the move to San Antonio was to locate the headquarters of H-E-B so that it was physically and symbolically more accessible to its employees. At the time of relocation, H-E-B employed 21,000 people in its stores, warehouses, transportation centers, distribution centers, and headquarters throughout central and south Texas. In 1990, the number of personnel had grown to nearly 40,000. For these Texans, as for so many others, San Antonio is a cultural and tourist mecca. The Alamo is located downtown, as are the historic River Walk, HemisFair Plaza, La Vitta, the convention center, and the home court for the San Antonio Spurs basketball franchise (Figure 7-2).

Before relocating, and as a result of gradual, incremental growth, H-E-B's diverse headquarters divisions and departments were located in several adjacent, nearby, and not so nearby buildings in Corpus Christi. The relocation enabled H-E-B to meet its third goal; namely, to consolidate all its headquarters functions on a single multibuilding campus, providing all headquarters personnel with a single sense of corporate focus and identity.

The programming effort was charged with the following problem: Develop a facilities program for a unified corporate headquarters of diverse tasks and services in a new city, to accommodate headquarters employees administering a company of 150 stores statewide with 21,000 company employees working outside the headquarters complex. The program was to determine the number of employees to be housed, their organization in the complex, their needs, and spatial requirements, space planning guidelines, and accommodations for growth. The program was to augment and be a central component of the corporate decision-making and architectural design process for the headquarters (Figure 7-3).

Architect Selection

To design the headquarters, H-E-B selected the Washington, D.C., firm of Hartman-Cox Architects, with Warren Cox as partner-in-charge. Jonathan Barnett, FAIA, of New York City helped in the selection process by generating a list of architects who met the client's desire for "an individual, not just a firm, who could lead us through the process, beginning with site selection" (Freeman, 1986). Four sites were then under consideration: three "suburban" sites on the north edge of San Antonio, and the Arsenal, more central in location and containing nine almost unrelated buildings. By leading H-E-B through design alternatives, Cox won their support for the transformation of the urban Arsenal site into the new headquarters facility. Cox's verbal descriptions have remained fixed in the client's mind and were recalled during our later efforts in 1990. The San Antonio firm of Chumney/Urrutia served as local associated architects.

The Architect's Experience with Programming

Warren Cox's direct experience with programming was essential to the integral part that facilities programming played in the H-E-B corporate headquarters planning and design process. His contact began in 1973, when his partner, George Hartman, participated in an intensive weekend seminar on design and program communication organized by Don Conway, AIA, Director of Research Programs. Invited participants included four university-based environment-behavior specialists—Robert Sommer, Ph.D., University of California, Davis; Edward Ostrander, Ph.D., Cornell University; Robert Bechtel, Ph.D., University of Arizona; and John Zeisel, Ph.D., Harvard University—and four architects representing large and small design firms: George Agron of Stone, Marracini and Patterson, San Francisco, the largest firm; and then, in descending order of size, Shelton Peed, AIA, of I.M. Pei Associates, New York; George Hartman, AIA, of Hartman-Cox, Washington; and Louis Sauer, FAIA, of Louis Sauer Associates in Philadelphia.

Based on the discussion of the nature and process of programming and design between these professionals committed to both intellectual and practical problem solving, the American Institute of Architects published the report

Social Science and Design: A Process Model for Architects and Social Science Collaboration (Conway, 1973). At the same time, Hartman-Cox Architects began to formally incorporate facilities programming into several of their design projects through a consulting relationship with Walter Moleski of ERG-Environmental Research Group in Philadelphia. Ten years later, faced with a complex corporate headquarters design problem, Warren Cox would tell the client that he would not undertake such a design project without a thorough facilities design program being developed first.

Selecting the Programmer

H-E-B executives in charge of the corporate relocation project decided to hire the programming consultant directly, rather than ask the architect to engage a programmer as a subconsultant. This reflects a corporate style of managing consultants laterally rather than horizontally for all its operations; H-E-B likes direct contact with consultants working on H-E-B projects. This form of engagement was also critical to the programming effort being integrated thoroughly into the design process. H-E-B's president, Charles Butt, interviewed the programming team himself because he wanted to be sure that the programming consultant's style fit well with H-E-B's corporate style, as well as with the style that H-E-B wanted the design team and the design process to foster.

Connecting Programming and Design

H-E-B decided that a single team planning, programming, and designing its corporate headquarters—carrying out these activities simultaneously, sequentially, or overlapping one another, as the tasks demanded—would create the best results. H-E-B also employed coordinated meetings, interdisciplinary task review, and centralized project management to achieve this end. The approach mirrors H-E-B's corporate culture, reflecting a commitment to thoughtfulness in decision making generally. Linking these efforts provided H-E-B decision makers a built-in structure for analysis of the consequences of decisions and eventual action. The linked planning, programming, and design process engenders continual interaction and feedback between disciplines so that occasion for reflection and review are guaranteed.

A Sophisticated Client

The tenor and success of this programming effort resulted in large part from the sophistication, philosophy, and complexity of the client. H-E-B is a remarkable client to work with, and other programmers would be lucky to find such a partner every time out. H-E-B is an organization that values quality—in business, in personnel, in customer service, and in the products it sells in its stores. H-E-B therefore understood how to effectively employ the quality control aspects of programming.

With its many stores and shopping centers, H-E-B is also a sophisticated building owner and consultants' client. The organization includes a real estate department, a store planning and design department, and a construction arm among its divisions and departments. Thus, H-E-B knows buildings. H-E-B's complex and varied organizational structure includes accounting, advertising, publicity, printing, human resources, purchasing, marketing, planning and design, and real estate, all under one roof and one leadership structure. And this list does not include all the employees in its stores.

H-E-B has a history of moving the organization's center of operations as the company grows. H-E-B was started in a one-room country store in the small Texas town of Kerrville in 1905 by Howard E. Butt, Sr. After locating major operations along the Rio Grande, H-E-B moved its headquarters to Brownsville, on the Mexican border. There it grew to include 100 stores, and then moved headquarters to the Gulf Coast city of Corpus Christi, Texas. As operations further expanded north toward Dallas and Houston, and as Charles Butt, Howard's younger son, became president, H-E-B built a 1 million square foot distribution center in San Antonio, the geographic center of H-E-B's market area. Finally, H-E-B decided to move the corporate headquarters to San Antonio as well.

The programming and design team included participants from H-E-B's established organization. The real estate division, skillful at finding and negotiating the acquisition of retail locations, was able to transfer these skills to searching out alternative sites for the corporate headquarters. Charles Blackburn, a real estate attorney, managed the procurement and approvals process for H-E-B, while Ralph Mehringer, vice president for the company's in-house store planning, design, and construction division, oversaw the contracting and construction phases of the project.

The president and chairman of family-owned H-E-B remains an enthusiastic participant in the shaping and stewardship of the Arsenal facility. He instilled his own personal style of restrained elegance into the project through his involvement in all phases of planning, programming, and design. "H-E-B executives made it clear . . . that the company was not interested in making brash architectural statements. They wanted instead a headquarters with presence and style, yet one that appears to have been in place for decades" (Dillion, 1986). The majority of upper management was included in the programming process. Vice presidents served as experts for their particular department during programming, and the controller was intimately involved in the generation of accurate staffing counts and projections that served as the basis for large-scale space programming and allocations.

The Programmers

John Zeisel was selected as the programmer because of his previous involvement in buildings of similar scale and complexity and because of the way he fit into the team. He had recently completed a *Technical Programming Guidebook* (Zeisel, 1982) for large U.S. government office buildings and was carrying out Post-Occupancy Evaluation Methodology of complex, multipurpose office buildings for the Canadian equivalent to the General Services Administration, Public Works Canada (Zeisel and Harvey, 1988). He had also recently completed the facilities program for the administrative headquarters of Lucasfilm Ltd. in Marin County, California, with architect Ed Woll. Eight years after the project's inception, when the H-E-B headquarters complex had achieved its initial programmed performance and the building program needed to be refined and updated, Marc A. Maxwell, AIA, joined the team to work on the reprogramming as well as to implement the space planning and renovation changes.

The Team in Place

By 1983, the full design team included Warren Cox, of Hartman-Cox of Washington, D.C., in association with local architects Chumney/Urrutia. Pat Chumney served as local architect, and Judy Urrutia led the interior design team. James Keeter, a local landscape architect, designed the courtyard scheme, landscaping, and plantings throughout the campus. John Zeisel was selected to program the facility.

In sum, establishing the team and defining the planning, programming, and design problems took considerable effort. The effort yielded a three-part team of client, programmer, and architect that maintained a dynamic tension during the entire process—through implementation—that led to efficient, effective, and quality decisions. This effort also yielded a team that worked extremely well together and that, once in place, was able to tackle the relocation project with efficiency, effectiveness, and good will. With this dynamic, and with architect and programmer selected, H-E-B began the corporate relocation effort that included the programming effort described next. The process we describe here is founded on a belief that the firmest basis for building planning and design is a tripod structure, with client, architect, and programmer as the three legs supporting the project, process, and building that results (Figure 7-4).

PROGRAMMING METHODOLOGY

The programming methodology employed at H-E-B comprised three related approaches. First, programming was carried out on a "fast track," with master planning and design starting at the same time. Design and programming were undertaken simultaneously, yet they were related to each other as required by the project and decisions that had to be made. Second, the data-gathering methods employed were basic, established techniques used together as a multiple-method approach. Third, programming data were turned into design and project information through a phased approach in five discrete reports, the last of which was a full facilities design program. The program was translated into design employing a set of rules of thumb, presented at the end of this chapter.

Fast-Track Programming and Design

Using one type of logic, programming must precede design to be effective. You need to know what the project requires in order to design to meet its needs; as a concept, that seems to make sense. Most projects in practice, however, require that design begin when programming begins. In fact, when carried out in tandem, design and programming can be more robust and mutually beneficial than when they are carried out sequentially. Our H-E-B programming effort was carried out as an iterative spiral of research, reports, and decision, as represented in Figure 7-5, which is adapted from *Inquiry by Design* (Zeisel, 1983).

Because design is carried out in the same iterative way, the H-E-B program-design process resulted in two interlocking spirals, a sort of double helix (Figure 7-6), in which programming and design decisions that needed to draw on each other were carried out at the same time, and both processes moved forward without interruption.

Initial Independent Planning and Design Decisions

The existing buildings on the site constituted the immediate context for the adaptive re-use design of the H-E-B headquarters, just as the existing H-E-B organization was the context for the programming effort. These buildings required immediate attention, independent of anything the program might uncover and recommend.

Certification as historic buildings and approvals for specific exterior facade renovations were all necessary. Lead time was needed to meet with local as well as national groups, such as the River Walk Advisory Commission, the King William neighborhood design review group, the Historical Commission of San Antonio, and the National Register in Denver. The architects also had to make the buildings habitable; new roofs, a thorough cleaning, and demolition of a number of temporary quonset huts were necessary.

The buildings presented the architects with spatial and formal design challenges and opportunities that needed to be solved during feasibility studies and master planning, independent of programming. These problems included creating a courtyard in the complex, demolishing the quonset huts, and restoring the historic stables and arsenal buildings. The architects also decided to complete the courtyard by adding what was later called the "north" building; the new building had a facade that fit into the historic context in which it was set. And the architects brought light and views into the large nonoffice buildings by selectively cutting out portions and creating atria within the buildings.

All this was carried out at the same time the program was being created, resulting in an elegant master plan framing the buildings and the program that fed them (Figure 7-7).

In sum, the H-E-B program-design process comprised three related simultaneous streams. The architects in the design stream determined the overall direction for planning and design—the *parti*, as architects call it—namely, the courtyard scheme for the new complex. The programming stream focused on defining the planning and design problem; namely, how to consolidate a complex and disparate group of departments into a cohesive organizational whole, and at the right size for H-E-B. And the third stream was the client's management and decision making; namely, organizing the relocation from Corpus Christi, managing all the consultants involved in the project, making the financial and development decisions needed to keep the project moving, and determining the number of employees who would eventually move into the new headquarters.

Program Organization and Methods

The second component of the program methodology comprises the data-gathering methods employed in programming; the third is the organization and presentation of the information from the program to the client and architects. The organizational principles of the programming effort reflect principles established and validated in previous work.

Data collection was based on a multiple-method approach used throughout environment-behavior research and described in *Inquiry by Design* (Zeisel, 1983). These methods, adapted to focus on the needs of the H-E-B project, included the following:

- physical environmental observation
- behavioral observations
- photographic documentation
- questionnaires
- interviews
- archives review

The phases and reports for the H-E-B project were these:

1. *Briefing Report*, documenting existing conditions in the Corpus Christi offices of H-E-B and presenting the departmental and work group organization of the company.
2. *Goals and Objectives Report*, clarifying precisely the goals of the executives of H-E-B for the new headquarters and suggestions they had for actions that might be taken to achieve those goals.
3. *Space Standards Report*, developing space requirements and layout alternatives for all the various staff positions at H-E-B.
4. *Diagnostic Program Staffing Report*, laying out growth projections and right-sizing trade-offs for executive decision.
5. *Facilities Design Program*, summarizing program analysis and executive decisions to effectively inform the master planning, architectural, and space planning decisions to be made.

APPLICATION OF METHODOLOGY
TO PROGRAM

Briefing Report

The *Briefing Report* serves to consolidate and generate consensus among members of the programming team so that each team member starts on the same foot. This report, through descriptive materials, presents an image of the organization and present conditions that the client can edit, negotiate, and eventually agree with—thus forming bonds with the larger team. Architects find this report useful because although they may informally brief themselves on the situation, they seldom do it with the same depth and thoroughness as do programmers expressly assigned the task and employing systematic methods.

To gather data for the briefing report, we *observed every space* in use in the present offices, *photographing* each one for documentation. We handed out *questionnaires* to department and work group managers, analyzing the results to develop a preliminary understanding of the mission of each work group—its tasks, purposes, and functions.

Goals and Objectives Report

The second report, the *Goals and Objectives Report*, is based on two related methods: *focused interviews* and a *focused group interview* linked by a *modified Delphi-technique* consensus analysis. Focused interviews were conducted with all the vice presidents of H-E-B and with the company's president to determine what each individual wanted to see as outcomes of moving to and working in the new San Antonio headquarters. Specifically, we asked two questions. To determine *goals*, we asked: "If you look back at the new headquarters *five years after you move in*, and you judge it to be a success, what will you be looking at?" To determine *objectives*, we asked: "What do you think might be done *today* in planning and designing the new headquarters in order to achieve the goals you have set for the project?"

A summary of all the answers we received was then shared with all the executives, without attribution, and the whole group was queried with *focused interviewing* methods to arrive at a set of *consensus goals and objectives*. Throughout the design of the project, and again when we revisited the buildings five years later, the *Goals and Objectives Report* served as the reference guide for making significant decisions and trade-offs between alternatives.

Space Standards Report

The *Space Standards Report* represents the first set of programming decisions to reflect corporate goals for a new facility. One of H-E-B's stated goals and related objectives was to support H-E-B employees by standardizing work spaces and minimizing the differences in square foot space allocation between the highest and lowest employees. The space standards developed for H-E-B responded to this goal by allocating only 190 more square feet in offices for executives than for data entry personnel—both groups considered "partners" at H-E-B. (All H-E-B employees are referred to as "partners" and in fact share in the profits of the company through a program that distributes bonuses each quarter to work groups that exceed their work production goals throughout the company.)

The methods we employed to develop space standards were *observation of employees at work*, analysis of *documents* describing work group missions and individual positions, and *interviews* with partners to understand particular work tasks. This not only yielded a set of minimum requirements, but also gave us an appreciation of how employees at the same job level or rank carried out varied jobs with different work tasks. On the basis of these data, we generated a set of seven basic *rank-based space allocations within which there was variation*—additional space allocated to meet the requirements of specific job tasks. These included extra work surfaces for accountants who needed to review large printouts from stores, extra space for chairs in buyers' offices for product salespersons, and space for a drawing table in store planning architects' and engineers' offices.

We mitigated the small rank-based space differential by developing a space scheme that included many small office-sized *conference rooms*. Although their basic offices were not ostentatiously large, the higher the executives in rank, the more likely they were to have an adjacent or nearby shared conference space. Their staff also had responsibility for scheduling these conference rooms for meetings by personnel from their own or other departments.

The *Space Standards Report* was the guiding document for space planning and for work space and work group layout throughout both the initial and follow-up programming and design efforts.

Diagnostic Program Staffing Report

The *Diagnostic Program Staffing Report* dealt with what emerged as the most critical programming element in the project—*right-sizing the headquarters organization* in terms of move-in and projected one- and five-year populations. This programming focus came to light when we analyzed the "wish list" staffing and square footage requests in the initial questionnaires returned by department managers. Added together, these data showed a straight-line projection of growth for the company over time. H-E-B decided that it wanted to plan proactively for growth rather than to use past trends or department managers' expectations.

The method employed to gather data for this report was a *questionnaire*, distributed to all work group managers, reviewed by the programming team, and then used *in its filled-out form as an interview guide* for *in-person interviews*. The initial questionnaire requested *general growth projections;* follow-up interviews requested *specific personnel projections* for each staff level. The more detailed follow-up yielded more realistic figures. After all the data were collected, an H-E-B *management team* reviewed every specific projection, *deciding* on the growth that would most benefit the *organization as a whole.*

Facilities Design Program

The full *Facilities Design Program* represents an independent statement and record of the goals, objectives, and needs of the organization to be met in a new headquarters building. The facilities design program for H-E-B comprised all earlier report data on goals, objectives, space standards, and staffing projections, translating all this into design directives for master planning, architectural, and space planning decisions.

In sum, the *facilities design program* served as a useful decision-making tool for both client and architects. How this report was applied in designing the H-E-B Arsenal Headquarters building is the subject of the next section.

APPLYING THE PROGRAM TO DESIGN

The team applied the facilities program to the H-E-B project in master planning and space planning. In master planning, the program was used to select among building-plan scenarios, to determine the intent of the visual image of the entire project, and to decide which building to allocate to which corporate uses. In space planning, the program was employed to determine work space allocations, work group needs, work group adjacencies, departmental groupings, and accurate growth expectations.

Master Planning Applications

Following the project management policy of simultaneous and intersecting design and programming, the architects carried out their feasibility study while the initial programming efforts were underway. The architects' *Feasibility Study Report* ends with four alternative renovation scenarios for the Arsenal—for 250, 500, 750, and 1,000 employees. In each scenario a different mix of demolition, renovation, building adaptation, and new construction is proposed to meet four different headquarters personnel counts. The smallest scenario included minimum demolition and no new construction. The larger staffing scenarios included construction of new parking structures on the site of the present parking lot. The 500-person alternative, the one finally selected on the basis of programming research and client decision making, included demolition of all the temporary buildings and construction of a single new building to create a central courtyard.

A second major planning decision that the program brought to light and helped to specify was the question of the Arsenal complex's visual image. The choices were constrained by the existing buildings on the site, with their mid-1800s and early 1900s utilitarian look, but renovations to these buildings, the exterior of the new North Building, and all interior design decisions were affected by the program. Programming interviews with senior management led to a goal related to image: *to be a success, the building needs to be elegant but not ostentatious.* The reasons for this were that the H-E-B is a customer-oriented company selling food and other consumer goods in its stores to nearly half of the people living in South Texas. The company wanted to convey to these customers that H-E-B is competent and efficient, yet also that the company is neither making outrageous profits nor using its profits recklessly on lavish offices for executives at the corporate headquarters. With over 21,000 employees working throughout their market area, senior management similarly did not want the headquarters to ostentatiously point up the difference between that setting and the stockrooms and distribution warehouses where many partners work.

The third major master planning influence of the program was in the allocation of uses to the different buildings on the campus. The programmatic analysis of the H-E-B organization was based on a model of such analysis developed by the sociologist Talcot Parsons (1951). This model—summarized by the acronym AGIP—identifies four major functions for organizations:

1. adapting to the outside business environment
2. getting the job of the organization done
3. integrating the people who work in the organization
4. privacy for employees to deal with their personal lives, away from the organization

In programming the headquarters complex for H-E-B, we applied the AGIP model as follows, resulting in a loose fit between the AGIP activities and the spaces and buildings on campus:

A: The outside world for H-E-B is represented by product salespersons coming to the headquarters to meet with buyers, material being delivered to the print shop and being sent out from there, data communicated from store facilities to the central computer, job applicants and recruits coming for interviews, and so on. These activities were focused in the building closest to a busy street adjacent to the site.

G: The job being carried out at the H-E-B headquarters is a complex one. A major part of the work is accounting and financial management for the entire company, but the job also includes advertising, marketing strategy development, corporate management, and systems development. One building was essentially dedicated to the accounting and financial functions of H-E-B and another to the corporate and executive planning activities.

I: Integrating the employees of this complex organization, who are located in different buildings—by physically bringing them together as well as by giving them the sense that they are working in the same environment—was a major task of the planning effort. To accomplish this aim, the building with the best access to and views of the historic San Antonio River Walk was dedicated to employee-related activities. The cafeteria, a shaded patio, an exercise room, and human relations offices and conference rooms are located here. For the same reason, the complex includes a central courtyard surrounded by a covered walkway that connects all the buildings to each other and to the River Walk building (Figure 7-8). All employees coming and going, as well as moving between buildings, use this space and its walkways.

P: The privacy needed for personal affairs is dealt with by allotting personal territory to every partner throughout the facility, by making available public phones in the facility, and by providing easy access between the exercise facility and the River Walk for joggers and walkers who want this type of exercise at lunchtime or before and after work. But the major planning decision to accommodate these types of activities was the decision to locate the headquarters within minutes of downtown San Antonio, where personal errands can be carried out easily on foot or by car without interruption to work.

Using this organizational model, together with the basic programming data gathered and analyzed on H-E-B activities, opinions, and work groups, enabled us to locate work groups in such a way that the spatial organization augments and supports the operations and larger corporate goals of the company as a whole.

SPACE PLANNING PROGRAM APPLICATIONS

Space planning at the Arsenal was driven by individual employee space allocations developed in the program; work group space allocations based on questionnaire results indicating number of employees, tasks carried out, and approved growth in personnel; and shared space and facility needs. These were applied in the context and within the physical constraints of the existing buildings to which the master plan assigned work groups.

The first step in this application was to locate work groups in the different buildings both to meet their specific needs for physical adjacencies to other work groups and to reflect their functional similarity in the AGIP model of the master plan. *Questionnaire and interview* responses to questions about number of daily, weekly, and monthly face-to-face contacts with employees in other work groups were used to develop certain work group adjacency needs. Work group location thus reflected both the work group's and the organization's needs. This step, carried out in block diagrams representing general work group size needs, was undertaken systematically, building by building, floor by floor, department by department, and work group by work group. This merging of the master plan, the existing buildings, and the spatial needs of work groups also tested each building's ability to serve as the home for the organizational tasks assigned to it. Where the buildings did not fit precisely, the lowest-priority adjacencies were sacrificed, substituting other adjacency possibilities instead. For example, a human relations financial accounting group was located with other financial work groups, rather than in the human relations building, because of space limitations and organizational trade-offs (Figure 7-9).

REPROGRAMMING

In December 1988, we were asked to revisit the Arsenal. The company had doubled its sales in the six years since initial planning and programming, while the physical facility had undergone very few changes and no expansion. After five years of rapid corporate sales growth, during which no additional office space or major reconfiguration was required or made, many groups had put off filling approved staff positions because they had no place to locate another work station. After a series of on-site meetings with various executives, it became clear that H-E-B had successfully used the facility during this period. Groups had more or less grown in place to fill the available space, and many amenities, especially conference rooms, had been absorbed into work space for expanding groups. The maintenance department was preparing a number of interventions to add even more work stations. One particular change included building new closed offices along an interior sunlit atrium that brought daylight into a very dense, open office area. While this seemed like a reasonable solution to the immediate need for more manager-level offices, it would have diminished the quality of the entire surrounding area occupied by a number of work groups. H-E-B was concerned that quickly planned interventions would compromise the original programming, planning, and design parti of the complex.

We conducted an informal post-occupancy evaluation, including a *structured walk-through,* in conjunction with a series of *interviews* with officers and directors. It was clear that at the end of five years of H-E-B's occupying the Arsenal, the buildings had performed extremely well in supporting the activities required of this headquarters facility-in-use. The overall high quality of the planning, design, and ultimate building had endured, but was now being squeezed by the success and growth of the organization. Several new organizational priorities and relationships had developed, and the physical complex was not fully synchronized with the evolving corporate structure. In the initial planning and programming effort, much energy had been expended to match the needs of the corporation to the needs of work groups within the building complex. In the 1988 reprogram, H-E-B was committed to reiterating the original good fit between corporate priorities, organizational structure, the buildings and space plan, and individual work group allocations.

Reprogramming included evaluation of the entire facility. Several areas were identified for major refitting to better support and reinforce new organizational philosophies and priorities. The *post-occupancy evaluation* process included revisiting the original program goals and objectives for the Arsenal in focused interviews with H-E-B's senior management who continued to support them. But organizational alignments had shifted to keep H-E-B current and competitive within the marketplace, and required physical reorganization to support new groups, reporting structures, and office automation.

After a systematic post-occupancy evaluation *walk-through* of the entire complex, we *interviewed* vice presidents about organizational shifts and expected changes within their departments. We then conducted a *detailed visual survey* throughout the Arsenal with *informal interviews* of department managers and work group supervisors. The programming and space planning issues uncovered in this way were systemic to the entire facility. A new staffing projections *questionnaire* was developed and distributed to every department at the Arsenal. It asked respondents to identify present and future staffing needs for 1990, 1992, and 1994, by level within a simplified hierarchy. Each work group received a *space evaluation questionnaire,* which asked additional questions concerning support needs, special functional requirements, storage, meeting space, work space, special access, ambient conditions, and successes and deficiencies in their current work space. With some prodding, 100 percent of the questionnaires were returned. The information was tabulated on present staffing levels, anticipated 1990 levels, and 1992 projections. Again, as in the original programming effort, these projected staffing levels were reviewed with senior management. Our experience on this and other programming projects was borne out, in that department managers tended to overestimate their future staffing needs and departmental growth, while senior management is more conservative. Senior management is also in a better position to control staffing and growth than are managers and work group supervisors.

Through *observation of the campus in use,* several areas were identified as more in need of new space planning, refurbishing, and preventive maintenance work. Based on these observations, the interview data, and questionnaire responses, the reprogramming team developed new scenarios for renovation, personnel moves, and space planning. To fine-tune programming and space planning priorities and needs for each group, we reviewed the new scenarios with senior management, department heads, and in several cases with entire work groups. The product of this phase of programming was a *New Diagnostic Program Staffing Report.*

This report formed the basis for developing a set of organizational priorities for reprogramming and several alternative master space plans. Accommodation of organizational changes became a driving force, particularly in the case of the formerly single "marketing" division, which had recently been divided into separate buying (procurement) and selling (marketing) groups for greater effectiveness. The master plan scenarios, communicated through block diagrams, allocated "chunks" of buildings and floors to various departments. The final format, a stacking diagram, indicated allocations by building and floor on a single 8½″ by 11″ page, which represented 200,000 square feet. The reprogram suggested adding 30,000 square feet on four floors of the partially occupied South Building. Through a series of negotiations, new space allocations, and cost estimating, the eventual building project included 15,000 square feet, with extensive reconfiguration of the existing 150,000-square-foot complex (Figure 7-10).

To allocate the newly renovated and the reconfigured space, we returned to the original goals and objectives established for the 1984 project. Through *focused interviews,* we verified the validity and changes in corporate goals, and used this information as a tool to negotiate between work group wants, desires, and absolute needs. Groups who could not have additional space were reconfigured to alleviate the growing pains they were experiencing. Relocation of some groups to the new space allowed many other groups to expand "in place," absorbing adjacent space vacated by these groups. In many cases, work groups swapped places, ultimately being positioned in more functional locations, reinforcing organizational structures while meeting current and projected space needs.

After the new master plan for the complex was established, we employed a computer-based *project management and scheduling package* to investigate alternatives for sequencing the actual renovation and departmental moves. We created and analyzed scenarios to alleviate as many of the immediate space needs as possible while following a logical sequence of relocations, construction, and final occupancy throughout the entire complex and master plan. The goal was set and maintained to relocate each group no more than once, prior to moving them back to their final location. Ultimately, only one or two groups had to be relocated off campus during reconfiguration of their areas.

The 1990 reprogramming effort resulted in immediate shifts reinforcing changes in organizational structure through new space allocations and new adjacencies or separations of work groups and departments. A new five-year plan was developed to accommodate continued growth in several divisions of the company as well as selective streamlining and departmental downsizing anticipated by more efficiency in automated systems. Basic planning principles from the original programming effort were revisited, confirmed, altered, and integrated into new space allocation and planning.

RULES OF THUMB

In order to translate a facilities design program into a physical environment for a workplace, designers need more than numbers and diagrams. They need planning and design principles that respond to the organization's style—its culture. During programming of the H-E-B Arsenal Headquarters, we therefore generated the planning and design *rules of thumb* shown in Table 7-1.

TABLE 7-1   **Rules of Thumb**

Planning Principles

- Facility purposes from goals and objectives
- Gross space locations from functional analysis
- Gross space allocations include growth

Individual Work Space Planning

- Work spaces reflect both rank and tasks
- Minimize work space area differentials

Work Group Planning

- Work group as basic planning unit
- Work groups sized to minimize growth disruption
- Dedicated work group circulation
- Shared daylight/environmental quality for lower-rank employees

Common Amenities

- Conference space proximity/control for higher-rank employees
- Conference areas for growth and expansion
- Conference room allocation by work group task need
- Common amenities allocated for work group tasks

Planning Principles

Design Purposes from Goals and Objectives

The more facilities planners and designers know what a building's owner wants that building to achieve, the more effective their trade-off decisions about the building can be. Designers need to know a building's purpose. Some dimensions of purpose are derived from the type of building it is: post office, store, headquarters. Other dimensions of purpose are more specific to a client, owner, manager, or user group. Their goals and objectives for the building—how they will eventually judge the building's success or failure—determine its purposes.

At H-E-B, the goals for the Arsenal Headquarters fell into the following categories: corporate morale, employee unification, employee satisfaction, office efficiency, growth planning, neighbor relations, general public relations, and economy. These goals served as a subjective test of planning, design, and reprogramming decisions as they were made. The judgment that was made for each design decision was how well it furthered any particular goal or objective without diminishing any other.

The Functional Basis for Planning Decisions

Headquarters programming is organizational analysis. The more the program and the buildings that follow reflect a thoughtful theory of organizational structure and function, the more the buildings will support the organization's operations. The organizational approach employed at H-E-B aimed to support four areas of the organization: dealing with the outside world, getting the job done, integrating departments and personnel, and recognizing the employees' need to maintain contact with other parts of their own lives.

Gross Space Allocation for Growth

The more gross square footage allocated per person in planning reflects the organization's growth and expansion plans, the longer the period will be before the facility must be reprogrammed and redesigned.

To accommodate growth without leaving large spaces empty within each work space, an additional allocation of 12 percent was built into the space allocation at H-E-B, creating a spatial generosity within work groups. This number is derived from design inquiry that indicates that work group space planned for seven people will seem neither overly spacious with 12 percent too much space, nor crowded when an eighth employee, a 12 percent increase in staffing, is added.

In initial feasibility planning, a figure of 300 square feet per person was used for calculating the population that could be reasonably contained within the new and renovated buildings. Three hundred square feet per person includes this 12 percent factor for growth, or 36 square feet per person, as well as all common circulation and shared amenities, such as cafeteria, exercise, mail, and break rooms. Once the decision was made that the number of employees to be housed within the Arsenal was 500, simple multiplication indicated that 150,000 square feet would be required. The various master plan alternatives generated by the planning team were then evaluated against this number. The actual square footage per person for this project was 275 square feet per person, with the growth, or expansion space, programmed and built into conference rooms, storage areas, and a generousness throughout the entire facility.

Individual Work Space Planning

Work Space Allocation by Both Rank and Task

When the individual employee work space allocation reflects both rank and task needs, space use will be most efficient and support both the individual's and the organization's work goals.

Each employee's space at H-E-B reflects both the employee's managerial level within the organization—clerical, supervisor, manager, on up to president— and any additional space needs by virtue of specific tasks each employee carries out.

Precise work space allocation—as opposed to gross space allocations per employee—was most critical during the space planning phases of the project. Square footage assignments were made based on the needs of particular employees—considering the tasks, furniture, equipment, and storage required to perform the functions associated with each position.

Through this system of space allocation, staff members at the same "level," but with different functions, may have different-sized and -enclosed work spaces, while equivalence between rank, task, and work space is maintained. To meet the basic needs of approximately 500 employees, we generated nineteen work space types, based on seven basic types, plus optional support space that includes file cabinets, display space required for the function, drafting/ paste-up tables, storage space, guest chairs, and work tables. For example, a clerk required to correlate data from several books simultaneously receives reference space that an equivalent receptionist might not.

Minimizing Work Space Differentials

The quantitative difference in work space allocation between the lowest-rank employee and the highest-rank employee of an organization reflects the organization's attitude toward its own hierarchy.

The difference between the smallest and largest work space in the H-E-B complex is kept to a minimum; actually, a difference of 190 square feet. As with work space allocations, additional square footage was assigned as required by the tasks assigned to the work group or individual.

Work Group Planning

Work Group as Basic Planning Unit

When work group areas are used as the basic planning and design unit, space use is both most efficient and most effective from the individual employee's as well as the organization's perspective.

Work groups provide the basis for territorial privacy, without requiring totally enclosed work spaces for each employee. Within each work group, as few as six and as many as fourteen individuals perform similar or closely related tasks, and their proximity is essential for the proper functioning of the group's organizational mission.

Work Groups Sized to Minimize Disruption for Growth

Work groups of six to fourteen employees planned as cohesive areas give the greatest opportunity for incremental growth without major design shifts, and reduce the negative spiral impact of such growth throughout the organization. The work group planning unit is most adaptable to small-scale incremental growth.

Dedicated Work Group Circulation

If circulation within a work group is planned primarily for employees in the work group or others doing business with them, work group efficiency and effectiveness will be greatest, noise and traffic disturbances will be minimized, and employees will be able to concentrate better. This can be accomplished if separate shared circulation is provided for others to get from their work group area to such places as toilets, elevators, cafeterias, and other work groups. Foot traffic—circulation—within a work group is thereby dedicated to that work group.

Shared Daylight/Environmental Quality for the Lowest-Rank Employees

When clerical and other low-rank employees can see windows and daylight when seated at their work spaces, this offsets some of the negative effects of their having less space than others to work in. As a planning principle, shared access to daylight often requires trade-offs. At H-E-B, lower-level employees were given access to daylight at the expense of private enclosed offices with windows.

Common Amenities

Conference Space Proximity/Control for Higher-Rank Employees

Although work spaces are often close in size between employees of different rank, people in more managerial positions are located nearer to conference rooms and have greater control over their use. If conference spaces are located near the work space of higher-rank employees, and if these employees or their staff schedule their use, higher-rank employees have greater *effective territory.*

Conference Rooms to Absorb Expansion and Growth

If conference rooms are sized the same as enclosed offices, work group growth can take place by judicious conversion of these rooms to individual work spaces. This use can be either temporary or permanent as the needs of the organization dictate. This allows quicker realignments of space within work groups as the organization's staff grows, making less renovation and new construction necessary during periods of growth.

Conference Room Allocation by Work Group Task Need

When conference rooms are allocated by work group need, overall work space can be saved. The different ways conference rooms can be located include being dedicated to a work group, located within a work group but used by more than one work group, or being in a neutral area shared by several work groups, as well as for meetings by nonheadquarters personnel.

Common Amenities Allocated for Work Group Tasks

By virtue of the tasks they need to perform, different work groups have different needs for shared amenities. When these amenities are allocated to work groups by virtue of task need rather than by right, space efficiency and use of shared amenities is greatest.

Shared amenities include such things as copiers, computer terminals, high-speed printers, mail rooms, break areas, storage rooms, restrooms, and conference facilities. At H-E-B these amenities were distributed throughout the facility, located near work groups and departments that had an identified need for them. Not every work group that requested a particular amenity received it within their work group, but all were located within convenient proximity of the facilities necessary to the efficient fulfillment of their assigned tasks.

Rules of Thumb Postscript:
In Search of Excellence

During the programming at H-E-B we compared these planning principles or rules of thumb to Peters and Waterman's description of how successful companies are run—*In Search of Excellence* (1980). We found some remarkable parallels. The following memo, describing these parallels, was sent to the client and design team.

Physical Design Implications from *In Search of Excellence*

To: Charles Butt and Arsenal Design Team
From: John Zeisel
Date: August 15, 1983

In Search of Excellence represents a set of descriptive and explanatory stories about successful large companies. Some of these stories are about the role that physical settings play in such companies, particularly ways in which space planning and design can reinforce "excellent" management strategies. Some of the physical elements discussed in the book are:

1. **Small work group territory and control**: Areas of eight to ten employees who work together need a physical space which is theirs—through which others do not naturally walk when going from their work group to another place in the building. In other words, they need a space that is not intersected by a public hallway. In such an area, groups of employees have a sense of control and can see each other's contribution to the common effort. The authors of *Excellence* stress that "People can be themselves only in small, comprehensible groups." (pp. 126, 127, 274-77)

2. **Places for informal communication**: Such places include employee rooms, same floor location of related groups, escalators, small conference rooms with blackboards, and lunch rooms where employees rub elbows at large tables. According to our research, such communication is also fostered by locating rooms that represent frequent destinations in places that increase the chance that employees will cross each other's paths getting there—such as break rooms, conference rooms, and toilets. (pp. 122, 131-32, 219-20, 262, 290)

3. **Employee support areas and programs**: These contribute directly to employee satisfaction and enjoyment, and show how the company feels about its employees. They include provisions for physical fitness with showers, cafeterias with subsidized good meals, entertainment, clubs, library, and outdoor areas. This might include a day-care center run by the company, although *Excellence* does not mention this example. (p. 259)

There are also three items related to physical design that are mentioned in the book, but with less emphasis: (1) Providing a single space large enough for the head of the company to talk with all employees at one time (p. 251); (2) Involving employees in making certain decisions, i.e., listening to employees (p. 255); and (3) Places that bring together employees from different disciplines to solve common problems (p. 223).

What have we done so far and what directions can we take from now on? The Arsenal has already incorporated these principles to a certain degree in the program, space allocation, and site design. As we progress further into schematics, design development, working drawings, space planning, and interior design, H-E-B has the opportunity to decide the impact it wants the principles summarized above to have. If selected as objectives, their impact can be great.

For example, space allocation on the executive floors represents *design for the work group territory and control.* The grouping of related executives, the concentration of executives in a single building, and the linking of the two floors by an open stairway all reflect this approach. Planning for work group territories throughout the complex as a space planning principle, however, means developing a systematic approach that takes into account the unique attributes of the various Arsenal buildings as well as the planning principle. It can mean involving, to some degree, the work groups themselves during this design phase. Finally, work group territory and control will influence engineering decisions regarding the zoning and controls specified for the electrical, lighting, data, heating, ventilating, and air conditioning systems.

A decision to reinforce work group territories would greatly influence space planning. This approach is being implemented in Europe, to some degree, in opposition to the ill effects of open plan offices. In our own research we found that an eight- to ten-person space maximizes staffing flexibility, minimizes crowding, and can respond to lighting and temperature controlled locally. In reading *Excellence* I was struck by the recurrence of this eight- to ten-person theme from a management perspective. I think it might be useful to discuss this issue at our next design team meeting.

Places for *informal communication,* and in particular paths that cross, have been planned in the single front entry to the complex, in the single cafeteria, in the courtyard space, in the physical fitness and cafeteria location, and on the executive floors. Having an "Employee Building" alone reinforces this objective. At the smaller scale of space planning, informal communications can be fostered by carefully locating and integrating into the buildings break rooms, toilets, conference rooms, and photocopying equipment. Such decisions also have implications for building systems engineering.

Employee supports have been included: cafeteria, outside deck, courtyard, parking, River Walk access, van pool and car pool programs, physical fitness, and visitors program. Careful consideration now needs to be given to administering these areas appropriately, outfitting them well, and possibly planing an off-site day-care program.

The three minor design implications have also been addressed. First, the cafeteria and central courtyard represent indoor and outdoor places for the heads of H-E-B to *meet all employees at once.* Originally we expected the two special smaller dining/training rooms to be linked to the cafeteria to add to this large space. I don't think this is presently the case because those rooms are located on the second floor of the River Building. Nevertheless, this objective needs to be kept in mind during further space planning. The cafeteria planner we use for this area must understand this objective clearly.

Second, executives were *involved* in the programming effort, and will soon get involved with space allocation. By "involved," I mean both being informed of previous decisions and listened to for further ones. The degree to and manner in which such staff involvement filters down to other employees during space planning needs to be carefully considered.

Third, the "transdivisional" conference room located visibly in the Stable serves as a symbol of the *interrelationships between the various groupings* at H-E-B. Making it work as a true linking place is an organizational and administrative issue.

SUMMARY

In sum, the H-E-B headquarters programming project carried out between 1981 and 1983 demonstrated the powerful positive influence a thorough facilities design program can have in a well-conceived and -managed planning and design project. The side effects on cost savings for building maintenance and facilities management can be measured. The beneficial side effects on the organization and its business goals are more difficult to document, but are easy to see. Reprogramming and replanning the facility in 1989 reset the stage for this cycle to begin again.

The rules of thumb planning principles, applied throughout the Arsenal during planning, architecture, and space planning, resulted in five years of successful operations and staff growth of 40 percent within the facility with a minimum of spatial reallocation. During this same time period, corporate sales grew by 300 percent.

References

Conway, Donald. 1973. *Social Science and design: A process model for architect and social scientist collaboration.* Washington, D.C.: American Institute of Architects.

Dillion, David. 1985. The Alamo and other battles. *Architecture Magazine,* March 1985, pp. 62-69.

Freeman, Allen. 1986. Complex regional character. *Architecture Magazine,* May 1986, pp. 119-125.

Parsons, Talcot. 1951. *The social systems.* Glencoe, Ill.: Free Press.

Peters, Thomas J., and Robert H. Waterman, Jr. 1982. *In search of excellence: Lessons from America's best-run companies.* New York: Harper & Row.

Zeisel, John. 1982. *Technical programming handbook, GSA, design management series.* Washington, D.C.: U.S. General Services Administration.

Zeisel, John. 1983. *Energy & occupancy: Functional analysis of the Harry Hayes Building, Calgary.* Ottawa: Public Works Canada.

Zeisel, John. 1983. *Inquiry by design: Tools for environment-behavior research.* New York: Cambridge University Press.

Zeisel, John, and Joan Harvey. 1988. *Hospital post-occupancy evaluation methodology.* Ottawa: Health and Welfare Canada.

FIGURE 7-1. The Arsenal Campus as Abandoned by the U.S. Government

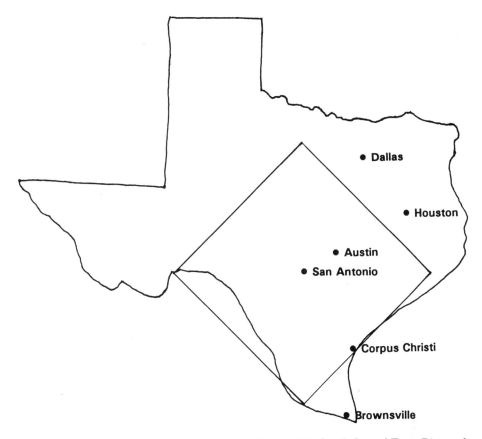

FIGURE 7-2.   San Antonio Is Located in the Center of the South Central Texas Diamond

HEADQUARTERS STAFF

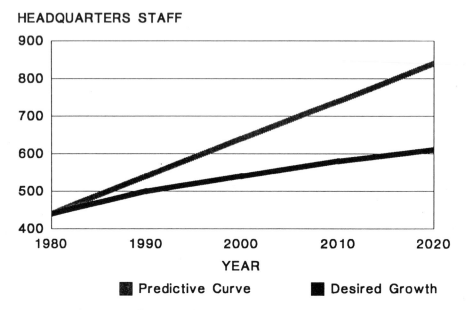

FIGURE 7-3.   H-E-B Corporate Growth Over the Life of the San Antonio Headquarters

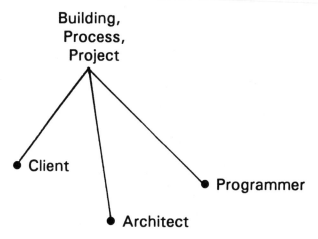

FIGURE 7-4.   The Design Team Tripod

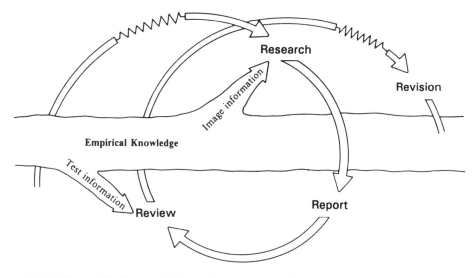

FIGURE 7-5.   The Research, Report, Revision Spiral

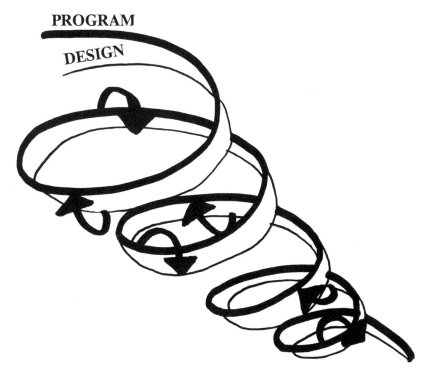

FIGURE 7-6.   The Program-Design Double Helix

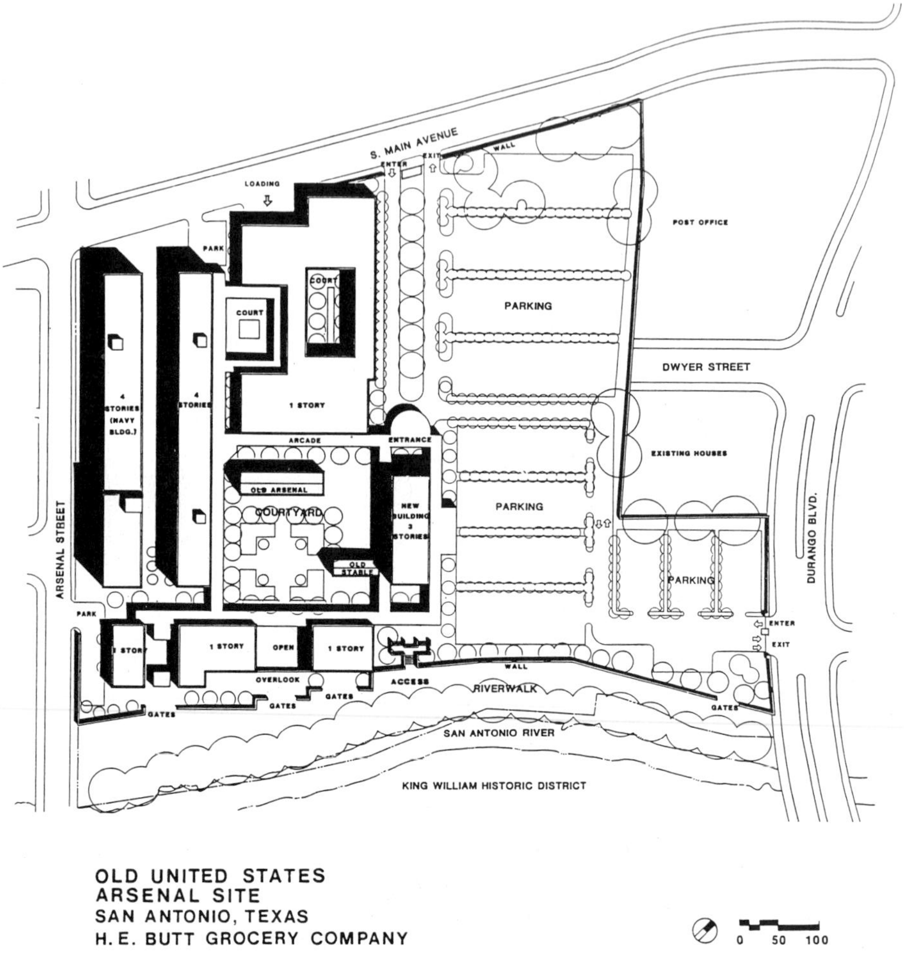

OLD UNITED STATES
ARSENAL SITE
SAN ANTONIO, TEXAS
H. E. BUTT GROCERY COMPANY

FIGURE 7-7.   The Final Selected Campus Plan Alternative

FIGURE 7-8.   The H-E-B Arsenal Courtyard Provides a Focus for the Complex

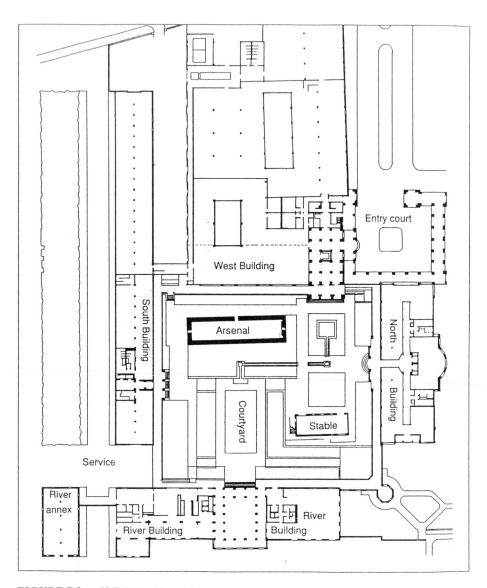

FIGURE 7-9. H-E-B Building Diagram

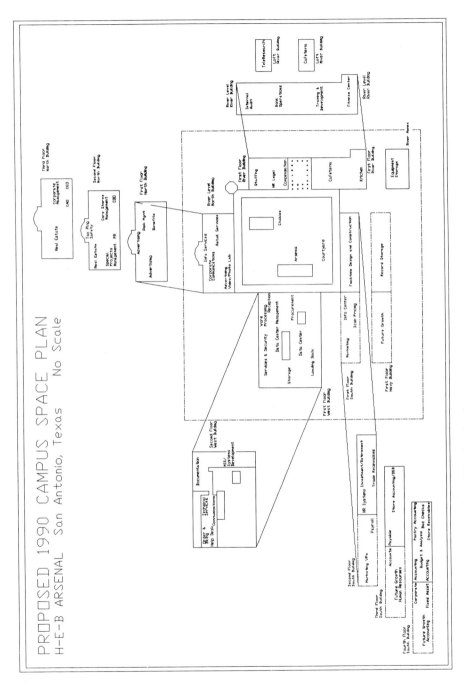

FIGURE 7-10.   1990 New Stacking Plan for the Campus

PART II

Programming Case Studies

CHAPTER 8

Interior Programming, Stacking, and Blocking for Society National Bank

Richard C. Maxwell and David J. Wyckoff

INTRODUCTION

The firm of Gensler and Associates was retained by Society National Bank early in 1988 as interior architects for their new headquarters facility in Cleveland, Ohio. The client anticipated a 1992 relocation to fourteen floors within Society Center, which was being designed by Caesar Pelli. Society Center would include a historically significant building that had been designed by Burnham and Root late in the nineteenth century. The historical building would be gutted above the banking hall level, leaving the stone exterior intact. New floors would be built into the gutted space that would match the elevation level of the adjacent floors in the new fifty-five-story building. The floors of the two buildings would meet, creating large floor plates for use by Society Bank.

The historical building had been the headquarters for Society Bank for many years. But, as Society Bank continued to grow, they relocated to a site several blocks away. The new facility would allow the bank to reoccupy its expanded historical headquarters on Public Square in the heart of downtown Cleveland.

The following chapter outlines the preferred method of producing a program for a project of this size. Comments are included that explain how certain portions of the Society Bank programming process actually occurred.

CONFIRMATION OF THE
PROGRAM OBJECTIVES

One of the first things that must occur once the programming phase begins is the establishment of the program objectives. Facility programs can be prepared for one of several purposes. Two, what we are concerned with here are strategic long-range planning and detailed planning for a specific project.

A program for use in strategic planning would not include as much detail as one oriented to a specific design project. However, strategic planning requires a broader view of the total needs of a specific company. Therefore, the program prepared for use in developing a strategic plan should encompass all areas of the company. Development of a project-oriented program would require much more attention to detail regarding space needs for the various work groups. The intent would be to begin space layouts soon after establishing the program.

Development of a program can lead to unforeseen problems within the company if confidentiality, protocol, and office politics are overlooked. Program information could be used unscrupulously by others to analyze and predict future business directions to their advantage. Internally, premature disclosure of anticipated organizational changes could become the catalyst for political maneuvering, thereby complicating timely implementation. Senior executives are often reluctant to make immediate decisions at meetings attended by employees several levels down. In some cases, senior management will want to meet only with the principal of the programming firm. The process of determining space needs can also lead to heightened rumor activity among workers, as well as among real estate brokers. Knowledge of accurate square footage needs by the brokerage community can lead to less favorable lease negotiation positions.

Society Bank had committed to be the lead tenant within Society Center prior to retaining Gensler and Associates. The nature of the programming was to be project-oriented. However, executives of Society Bank knew that they had a greater space requirement than could be accommodated within the set number of floors at Society Center. In the downtown area, they occupied space at 800 Superior, the Bohn Tower, and their Corporate Services Center. While certain departments were not candidates for occupancy at the new facility, the space needs of the remainder of the departments were to be analyzed.

TEAM

The programming team should include persons other than those specifically charged with developing the program. Ideally, it should include persons who are familiar with subsequent processes once the program is accepted. The architect's team should also involve the project manager, project designer, and space planner. This makeup avoids situations wherein a program is simply handed to another group, which must then repeat many of the familiarization steps prior to developing solutions to programmatic needs. The client's team should include persons who are very familiar with their company. This knowledge will help in sorting real needs versus stated needs that are not consistent with the business goals of the company. There may also be a need to include specialists in certain areas such as business management, records management, communications, information management, and real estate. Roles and responsibilities should be firmly established.

Responsibility for the success of the project had been given to the senior vice president of the Corporate Facilities Division. The senior vice president was assisted by a vice president with over twenty-five years of experience at Society Bank. This person had extensive insight into how Society Bank functioned and had recently been through the process of renovating and replanning their Corporate Services Center. Society Bank also retained an expert in the banking and construction industries to assist Society Bank in the overall process of timely acquisition and outfitting of suitable space for the headquarters of their major financial institution. In many respects, each Society Bank person who provided information, whether executive, department head, or assistant, was also a part of the programming team.

The Gensler team included many people, although not all at the same time. The managing principal of the Gensler Houston office was involved during the early meetings, in which project directives were established by senior management of Society Bank. Since the project was not on a fast track, Society Bank elected to establish the first draft of their detailed program during the last quarter of 1988, well after initially retaining Gensler. The effort was led by a senior programmer who had a ten-year history of producing programs and space utilization studies for major clients in the banking industry, and by the project principal, who also had a strong programming background. Also involved during certain interviews that had the potential to affect base building construction or general design philosophy were the project manager and project designer, both of whom had extensive bank design and construction experience.

PROJECT DIRECTIVES

Major goals to be achieved by going forward with the project must be discussed with senior management. General directives should be sought regarding such issues as corporate image, space utilization, work environment, quality level, budget, expansion, growth, flexibility, space standardization, furnishings, circulation, amenities, corporate policies, automation, security, lighting, good and bad aspects of current facilities, location, work force, government regulations, organization/reorganization, merger, acquisition, and time constraints.

Responses can be solicited via a questionnaire with a follow-up interview. Alternatively, a group meeting can be held to bring all of the issues and responses to the table with all of the senior management present. A conference room wall might become a tack board on which to place significant comments made during meetings. Summation should occur at the end of a series of meetings or interviews. Some goals may not be achievable and should be discarded or refined to be more realistic.

The senior vice president and vice president for Society, along with the managing principal and project manager for Gensler, conducted a series of interviews with Society senior executives during the middle of 1988 to obtain their views of what should be accomplished as direct and side benefits of the relocation. Significant comments included these:

- "Society National Bank is to have a world-class facility" and ". . . among the top ten interiors."
- "Ongoing facility management costs after initial occupancy are to be kept as low as possible."
- "Easier flow of information is needed."
- "Customers should feel welcome in the office areas."
- "A major food facility and training facility was to be included."
- "Society Bank will become more of a full-service financial services player."
- "Give the right impression at the front door."
- "Plan for universal workplaces."
- "Anticipate continual refinement of the organization."
- "Accommodate matrix management."

Key issues that surfaced included the need to organize the space such that all staff have access to daylight, and the need to be able to tap into the data communications systems. All workplaces will eventually have computing equipment. Interchangeable cubicles and offices were desired. Post-occupancy movement of people will be much more desirable than reconstruction of walls to accommodate inevitable changes in organization and related requirements. Traffic patterns that allow quick, orderly circulation to other departments, services, and exits were mandatory. To conserve space, persons at very high levels within the organization were to be in cubicles rather than private offices. This necessitated an increase in the number of adjacent small meeting rooms for times when acoustical privacy was important.

Opinions of Society Bank executives were solicited regarding the following topics:

work groups	universal workplaces
interactive video	customer service
security	dining
training	teleconferencing
health facilities	child care
reception spaces	trading
business goals	department locations
corporate communications	marketing
future office environments	growth
flexibility	image
branch services	customers
reorganizations	centralization

SCHEDULE

In effect, the facility programming process never fully ends, considering the dynamic nature of most corporations. Changes in business, management, and organization do not stop in the interim between initial program approval and occupancy. However, there are periods when the level of programming efforts is more intense. The initial program may be fairly loose, with only a broad-brush approach to detail. This would satisfy the needs of planners doing feasibility studies. As the project progresses, the level of detail necessary for planning purposes increases. The first intense programming effort investigates space requirements that are based upon current and projected head counts, adjacencies, support spaces, and other factors that will affect departmental sizes, locations, and layouts. Near the point of preparing construction documents, the detail level should increase to include specifics of such items as equipment types, power outlet locations, and cabling requirements.

The programming schedule, as well as the rest of the schedule, should clearly define the time frames in which the work will be accomplished. A critical path schedule helps define periods for tasks and reviews, approval dates, individual responsibilities, and the sequencing of the work (Figure 8-1). Some executives are more comfortable with a bar graph version of the schedule (Figure 8-2). Ideally, the software used to maintain the schedule would be capable of quickly converting from one format to the other.

Once established, the schedule should be maintained or modified quickly as change becomes necessary. Senior executives may have filled calendars for months ahead. It is, therefore, prudent to request meeting times well in advance. The impact of a slipped date could cause the final product to be delivered late.

Society Bank felt that the initial detailed programming tasks should occur late in 1988 after departmental preparation of the 1989 budget. Kick-off, first set for October 1, was later reset to November 1. At the outset, the schedule was intended to have an annual update process in order to keep the space requirements database current. Results of the first program, however, would confirm the prior decision to initially occupy fourteen floors and would identify those departments for which other space must be obtained, it was hoped.

CURRENT LAYOUTS AND POTENTIAL LOCATIONS

Where possible, furnishings layouts of the current spaces should be obtained. Some companies may have layouts that have been updated to reflect current conditions. However, more frequently, there may be nothing available but a reduced photocopy of an out-of-date plan. These plans should be copied and brought to the interview, where they will be used to help identify current locations of departments and analyze the current use of space. They can also be useful during the analysis and establishment of space standards.

Society Bank had maintained good plans of all current spaces. Some plans required splicing of remodeling drawings to achieve a correct full floor layout.

Society Center was still in the planning stages. However, floor plates had been sufficiently developed to allow calculations of available square footage and to prepare hypothetical layouts.

SPACE STANDARDS

The establishment of space standards can expedite the process of determining the amount of space that will be required by a company. Some companies have pre-established space standards; other companies may lack standards, have unenforced standards, or have standards that require further refinement. Often, there is some latitude (real or perceived) given to the user groups within large organizations. Standards should be set for all space users. This includes personal workplaces, shared support spaces, and miscellaneous dispersed equipment, such as convenience copiers or multiuser computer work stations. Once established and implemented in the programming process, these standards can be compared to ascertain the validity of abnormal space requests.

The process of establishing space standards for personnel, if it is not pre-established, does not have to delay the gathering of information regarding the various departments. Corporate titles can be misleading. However, peer groups can be established. These may be based on job function, grade level, title, or a combination of these. The department heads can then be asked to assign each staff position to one of these groups. The issue, often emotional, of cubicle or office—small, medium, or large—can thus be avoided during the completion of a survey form and the subsequent interview.

The separate task of reviewing personal workplace needs can be done concurrent to forms completion, interviews, and data entry. This allows time to analyze current workplace conditions, to prepare recommended improvements, and to have the recommendations approved prior to the initial issuance of space requirements reports. Physical configurations of the workplaces, which may need to incorporate the inventory of existing furnishings, do not need to be established at this point. They can be tested and finalized during the space planning phase.

Shortly after being retained, Gensler promoted the concept of universal floor layouts and universal workplaces that would be suitable for a wide range of employees. This would be different from the more typical approach of elaborate customizing of the space for each department and a long menu of possible cubicle and office footprints. The major rationale was that implementation of this concept would accommodate ongoing growth and organizational change by allowing Society Bank to move people without perpetual demolition, reconstruction, modification to furnishings, and revisions to communications cabling and HVAC. Society Bank approved the concept for the general office areas. Much testing of the floor plates versus potential cubicle sizes occurred. In the approved scheme, the majority of the staff would be given cubicles approximately 7'0" by 7'6". Cubicles for vice presidents would be approximately 10'0" by 11'6". Senior vice presidents would be in offices of 196 square feet. Executive vice presidents would also have offices of 196 square feet, but they would also have an adjacent conference room reserved for their use. Society Bank executives higher than executive vice president would be located on a separate floor. Space standards for that floor were not an issue (Figure 8-3).

SPACE REQUIREMENTS SURVEY FORMS

Completion of a space requirements survey form by each department head greatly expedites the interview process. While appearing simple—the listing of space needs for people and support areas—the determination of adjacencies and the discussion of other related topics can be fairly complicated and time consuming. Forecasting for the future can seem impossible. Completing the survey form forces department heads to consider issues and to quantify specific needs. The form also provides a vehicle for in-house reviews and approvals prior to discussions with the programming team.

The form also provides a uniform communication system for conveying requirements information. Without such a system, each department head would be free to explain needs in their own way. Information would then be more difficult to interpret and, almost certainly, needs would be overlooked.

The survey form should be tailored to the specific client and at the level of detail necessary for the program. Certain questions may be inappropriate, and certain words have different meanings within different companies or subcultures. For instance, one company may have "departments" within "groups," while another may have "groups" within "departments." Often, a term such as "division" can be confusing, since it can refer to a large body of people that may include some at other sites. "Work station" refers to a stand-alone computer system within energy companies, while it may mean a "cubicle" to a space planner.

Issues as basic as client name, contact phone numbers, and page sequencing should also be addressed and modified as necessary. Several basic topics should be covered. These include the following:

- name of the department that is being discussed
- a statement about function
- the name of the person who completed the form
- the current location of the department
- the rationale that supports future needs
- a list of the peer groups and their role in the process
- current and projected positions (including contract staff)
- assignment of positions to peer groups
- current and projected support space needs
- internal adjacency requirements
- external adjacency requirements
- security

- industry trends
- amenities
- good and bad features of current locations

During the 1970s, it was not uncommon to work with companies that believed that space needs could be projected out ten, fifteen, twenty, and even twenty-five years. The rapidly changing business environment has proved otherwise. Some of those companies have gone out of business or have been merged into others. Today, projections in the three- to five-year range are still very difficult to make.

A survey form for Society Bank was developed based on experience with similar bank headquarters projects designed by Gensler and Associates. Society Bank realized that specific long-range projections made by department heads would not be meaningful if the target dates were too extreme. Therefore, the survey form targeted dates out only four years, which coincided with the intended relocation in 1992. There would be a planned update of the information, also out four years, on an annual basis.

Another feature was built in to avoid problems with resolving actual current head count. Since there are often unfilled positions within the various departments, a decision was made to request the base figures for "actual head count" and for "authorized head count." The two totals could then be compared as necessary with official figures from the human resources department.

Management reports were required, listing the areas of Society Bank that were under individual senior executives. Use of matrix management by the bank complicated determination of the true reporting structures, since several key staff reported to more than one superior. Quarterly financial statements issued for public use showed the organization. It turned out, however, that some liberties had been taken and that there had been some reorganization after the printing of the statements. In fact, because of a regional structure, Society Bank stretched throughout Ohio and into portions of adjacent states.

Peer groupings were not mentioned directly on the form. However, as in many other U.S. banks, Society Bank has an official title hierarchy, as follows:

- senior executives (chief executive officer, vice chairman, president, etc.)
- senior executive vice president
- executive vice president
- senior vice president
- vice president
- assistant vice president
- officer
- non-titled (exempt status)
- non-titled (non-exempt status)

Society's existing method of assigning workplaces had evolved in an unregulated manner. It was known that Society Bank wished to limit the menu of workplace footprints for the majority of the employees. This included persons up through the executive vice president level. Information was requested on the survey form regarding the need for visual and acoustic privacy, visitors, and storage in order to form a basis for developing alternatives for cubicles and offices. By requesting an official title, as well as a functional title, there was enough information to later assign a workplace from the evolving menu.

As with any form, individual respondents will take liberties with questions and will interpret requests in ways that the creator of the form had not intended. Therefore, a sample filled-in form was also reviewed with the department heads during the pre-completion kick-off presentation. This handwritten set of sample answers indicated how to handle typical situations that otherwise would require a lengthy and complicated set of instructions.

A copy of the original Society National Bank Space Requirements Survey form can be found in the appendix to this chapter.

ORGANIZATION

Current organization charts are helpful in determining who should receive survey forms and who should be interviewed. They also help to develop the organization of the computerized database. Keep in mind that the organization chart represents the intangible personnel reporting structure within the company; it does not address space or adjacencies (Figure 8-4). Therefore, the programming staff should use it only as a general guide when organizing the gathered information. Summary reports indicating the needs of many departments are more readable if spaces for executive groups, to which subordinate groups report, are considered as peer spaces that, along with the spaces for the reporting groups, make up the larger whole (Figure 8-5).

Often, common support spaces are assigned, by default, to a facilities or support department within the official organization. If they are not separated into individual units, it becomes difficult to stack them onto the various floors. Therefore, the programming team should create "nondepartmental units," such as cafeterias, conference centers, and other spaces for services shared by all departments on a floor or in a given zone. These services could include beverage bars, copying, facsimile transmission, meeting rooms, reception areas, and supply storage. There may be other groups that should be split into smaller pieces in the program. For example, a bank may have all tellers under one official cost center number, but it may require several locations for them. Another company may have support liaison staff accounted for under one cost center, but may need to locate them individually within the departments that they support.

Official identification numbers, if any, most likely will have been assigned for financial accounting purposes and may not follow any humanly logical sequence. Therefore, it is wise to determine and assign identification codes based on a system that is readily understandable by the programming team. To follow the client organization too literally implies that the planning firm will constantly update the space needs database to reflect the never-ending series of minor reorganizations. However, major organizational change is inevitable.

Therefore, when necessary, the software that tracks requirements must allow rapid reorganization of the data.

Once determined, the Society Bank database organization did not vary from that typically used for Gensler projects. Newer software has resolved the difficulties that were encountered when the first major reorganization occurred soon after initial reports were issued for review.

KICK-OFF PRESENTATION

There is a fair amount of work that will be requested of the various department heads. It is preferable to invite them to a presentation rather than to simply send them a form (from a consultant, no less) via interoffice mail. The invitation should carry the highest signature possible in order to properly convey the importance of their role. The purpose of the presentation is to build enthusiasm for the project and to review their immediate and specific role in the process. There should be some discussion of why their input is so important at such an early stage. Visuals are helpful. The survey form should be distributed and reviewed in detail. A sample completed form can be used to indicate typical responses. Usually, a period of one or two weeks is allotted for preparation of the requested information prior to the interview. The programming staff should be accessible during that period to assist with questions.

The Society Bank kick-off presentation occurred early in November 1988. Due to scheduling and room size limitations, three separate presentations were given. Department heads were invited by the chief executive officer to attend the meeting, during which they would be given a status of the project, an update on the schedule, some overviews of the planning, an introduction to Gensler and Associates (along with some examples of completed work), as well as many copies of the form. Each page of the sample form was reviewed in detail, allowing time for questions about individual situations.

FORMS COMPLETION AND
INTERVIEW SCHEDULING

As the forms are completed, they should be reviewed by the senior executives of the company. Head count projections, reorganization, and relocations are sensitive issues. An in-house review process ensures that there is a greater degree of control over the forecasts. Forms should be funnelled back to the day-to-day client contact and cataloged before being turned over to the architect. There will almost always be stragglers. It would not be unlikely to receive a form or two as interviews begin. Filling out the forms during the interviews, however, will require much more time than if the forms are completed in advance.

The interview schedule should be established concurrent with forms completion. The interview team should first estimate the amount of time needed for each interview. Scheduling should be done by someone within the company who is familiar with personalities and who is good at expediting those unwilling to be interviewed within the requested time frame.

Because of the nearness of Thanksgiving, the Society Bank interviews were set to occur during the two-week period just after the holiday. During the interim, the forms were completed by the majority of the department heads. However, as expected, there were a few that needed special prompting.

INTERVIEWS

The purpose of the interview is threefold: to review the information on the survey form; to use existing plans to indicate the current boundaries of the department; and to physically walk through the current layout of the area in question. As the interviews progress, development of the computer database can begin.

While there may be two or three persons from the programming team at the interview, it is best to have one person act as the lead when going through the form. There are times when a particular question track is leading to clarification of a complicated or sensitive issue. Side track questions from other people are not helpful, since it may be difficult to get back to the original issue and because it gives the interviewee a chance to escape a difficult decision. Other members of the interview team should hold their questions until the lead interviewer opens the discussion to all.

Colored pencils can be used to coordinate forms to annotate bubble diagrams drawn on existing layouts during the interview. There may be overlooked space outside the main bubble, possibly on another floor or even in another building, or there may be space that is claimed by more than one department. Coloring the plans is a good way to see that space requests are not duplicated and that all existing space is counted, even if it is only considered "spare."

Conducting the interview at the department location allows the team to take a quick tour to see the character and flavor of the space. Missed requirements can be found. It also helps to break the uniformity of the room in which the interviews are conducted. Otherwise, after the first day the interviews tend to become blurred in the team members' memories.

One person, the lead interviewer, must attend all of the interviews. Responses in one interview may contradict or further clarify those received regarding the same topic from a previous interview. Relationships between the various departments and other issues will become clearer as the interviews progress. Not having at least one person present at all interviews will allow a degree of uncertainty to creep in—the old adage of the left hand not knowing what the right hand is doing becomes evident.

The core interview team included the senior programmer and project architect from Gensler and the vice president from the Corporate Facilities Division of Society Bank. Certain interviews were also attended by or conducted separately by the project manager. Those conducted separately regarded special areas of consideration such as food (a major cafeteria was required) and training (there was to be a major training function).

Interviews occurred at the departmental locations. While this did mean a good deal of movement throughout floors and between the buildings, a good overview was obtained of the extremely crowded and dissimilar conditions of Society Bank spaces. Some departments had adequate space, while others were extremely overcrowded. Space standards were virtually nonexistent. Some department heads preferred cubicles for professionals while others, such as the head of the Trust Department, felt that an open-desk platform area was more suitable because of the one-on-one nature of their business.

During the interviews, reduced plans of the current spaces were reviewed and color-coded (to match an arbitrary color that was also applied to notes and the original survey form) to indicate locations of all spaces in use by each department. For some departments, areas were found that had been overlooked on the survey forms. The use of the colors was helpful when analyzing the information prior to later entry into the computerized database.

COMPUTER DATABASE

As the interviews occur, information can be entered into a computer. Software to track quantitative information is essential. The system to be used should allow organization of the information in a user-defined manner. Usually, this will loosely follow the organization charts of the client. Since companies reorganize faster than rabbits multiply, the ability to easily reorganize the database is also critical.

For detailed programming, the system should allow use of space standards to specify current and future space needs per department on a line item-by-line item basis. The ability to add contextual annotations per line item and per department is a handy feature. Calculations should show extended totals of net square footage per line item at the current and future forecast date. Department totals should allow addition of factors that are often used to raise net square feet to usable, rentable, and gross square feet.

Other methods of calculating future square footage include square footage per head count, lump sum, and percentage change. With the "square footage per head count" method, the programming team must make assumptions regarding average figures per department. Total head count is then multiplied by the averages to obtain forecast totals. "Lump sum" is merely the entry of predetermined amounts that have been calculated by some other method. "Percentage change" requires anticipation of the percentage growth or shrinkage of each department from the previous forecast date. A base figure must first be established.

The Society Bank project was out of town for Gensler and Associates. The computer technology in 1988 required use of a central processing unit within the Gensler offices in Houston. Therefore, data entry did not begin until the end of the interview phase. All forms, plans, notes, and other materials were reviewed by the programming team and further annotated as necessary. Annotations were then highlighted for entry to the computer system. Coding conventions were used to identify departments, line items per department, and space standards. Square footages for personnel were not yet developed. However, the use of a coding system allowed later application of test sizes prior to running reports.

ADD-ON FACTOR

Space standards include an allocation of net square feet (NSF). This is the amount of square footage that the area described by the space standard uses in practice. For larger spaces, such as an office enclosed by drywall, the NSF is the result of multiplying the footprint dimensions. The office may, in fact, also include portions of the column system, window wall, or other architectural aspects of the base building. For smaller space users, such as a file cabinet, the NSF must also include some space for a person to access the file, open the drawers, and retrieve materials. For a rectilinear open-plan cubicle, the NSF must also include some space outside the cubicle, for two reasons: one, to account for the inability of the cubicle to absorb the base building architecture; and two, to account for the extra circulation space that will be necessary to access smaller spaces in greater multiples off the main circulation paths.

Once the base is established by summing the NSF of all the spaces required at a given date, the total must then be multiplied by add-on factors to arrive at usable square feet (USF), rentable square feet (RSF), and gross square feet (GSF). For a full-floor tenant, USF is all space available to a tenant for office needs. The additional amount to arrive at RSF includes all other space on the floor that directly supports the same tenant. GSF would also include the vertical penetrations, such as elevator shafts. Individual leases spell out specific methods of measurement and may include factors for spaces on other floors that also support the tenant.

The add-on factor required to arrive at USF was tested for Society Bank. While the building was still in the planning stages, available square footages per floor were determined. Preliminary paths of major circulation were also determined and deducted to arrive at USF. Hypothetical space plans were prepared. Take-offs were tallied to determine programmatic NSF from the hypothetical plans. At that point, the add-on factor could be determined to reach the available USF (Figure 8-6).

REPORTS

Various space requirements reports should be available to the programming staff. Commonly used ones include detail reports, square footage (SF) summary reports, and stacking reports. Other types of reports also exist.

Detail Report

Detail reports would be used when calculating detailed space needs. Basic information should include identification of the project, department name, program identification code for the department, line-item listing of space users, assigned space standards by code and net square footage, quantities required at projection dates, extended head counts and net square footages, add-on factors, totals for head count, and totals for square footages that include the add-on factors (Figure 8-7).

SF Summary

The SF summary report should be available with any of the methods of calculating space needs. Basic information should include identification of the project, statement as to the nature of the add-on factor being reported, listing of the department codes and names, department totals for head counts and square footages at each of the projection dates, and grand totals for head counts and square footages (Figure 8-8).

Stacking Report

The stacking report also should be available with any of the calculation methods. Basic information should include identification of the project and a separate section for each floor within each building. Each of the sections should include identification of the building and floor, available square footage on the floor (with a note as to the type—net, assignable, usable, rentable, or gross), departments assigned to this floor (by code and name), current and projected head count per department (all dates), current and projected required square footage (same type as available), totals for each summable column, and the differences per projection date between required square footage and the amount available (Figure 8-9).

Other Reports

Other types of reports may be written to help analyze the input. These include reports on space standards descriptions and quantities per department, square footages per head count per department, etc. Report formats should be written by the software company to allow some flexibility regarding dates to be shown and the inclusion or exclusion of certain columns of data as the programming team sees fit.

Once the reports are run and proofed, they should be presented and discussed with the client. Explanations of how to read the reports are helpful. Since data have been collected from various sources within their company, it is not unusual for the client to find that their estimation of head counts and square footages differs from those submitted from the department heads. At this point, in-house reconsideration of future head counts usually intensifies and new figures are edited into the database. It is important to have executive agreement that space requirements figures accurately reflect the needs of the company. Otherwise, future work on stacking and blocking will not result in workable plans.

Test space standards and add-on factors were developed for Society Bank as the data were entered into the computer. Initial reports were run, submitted for review and edited; the database was refined; and secondary reports were subsequently run. Several sets of space standards were tested. Initial figures, anticipated to include more space need than would fit within the intended floors, were higher than expected. Departments that were candidates for location elsewhere were determined. However, Society Bank decided to include one additional floor in the initial occupancy lease in order to accommodate all necessary headquarters departments.

STACKING

Stacking is the process of test-locating the various departments on the target floors within a facility or series of facilities. Even a single-story building must be stacked, since not all departments may fit onto the floor.

Ideally, the database used to generate space requirements reports should also be able to test various stacking options, both numerically and graphically. There are software programs available that create stack alternatives automatically by using a mathematical value to weigh the adjacency needs between the departments. The stack with the highest score, per the computer, represents the best stack. In practice, however, they do not produce realistic solutions. Learning the subtleties of assigning values to achieve a good stack for a set of departments within a specific range of floors, which have varying amounts of available square footage, is not what the programming staff has been hired to do. Often, too, the most significant factors in determining a final stack are strictly political—something computers are still not capable of understanding. A simple written or bubble-diagramed statement of adjacency needs, coupled with a rapid numerical and graphic "what if" software program, expedites the process of producing workable stacking alternatives.

Once generated, stacking alternatives must be discussed with senior management in order to select the best option. Often these executives wish to participate in the process or, at least, make changes just prior to approving the final direction. Use of a computer with these executives is risky, since things tend to go wrong at the worst time. Having an expensive meeting in which the graphics are suddenly lost because of a power failure or a balky computer chip would be embarrassing. A reliable method is to use the computer tools to produce paper stacking diagrams that can be cut into strips per floor. Department names would be annotated within the strips and color-coded according to organization. Several alternatives can be produced and discussed during a work session presentation with executives. During the work session, the effect of changes to floor assignments, accelerated growth, departmental reductions, and increased expansion space can be viewed rapidly. Major political maneuvering can be minimized by having the chief executive officer and direct reporting executives of the company together for the final workout/approval of the stack. Being able to smoothly conduct such a work session can greatly expedite the entire stacking process.

Initial stacking of Society Bank indicated that several more floors would be needed than Society Bank cared to lease. One additional initial occupancy floor was added to the lease. Final stacking would not begin until the program requirements were refined and the first update occurred one year later. By that time, there had been a major reorganization of Society Bank and a refocusing of the business goals in general.

As the master schedule pressed, the stacking plan had to be finalized and approved. Society Bank required that detailed stacking information be distributed to the senior executives for their comment prior to approval. Color drawings were prepared, indicating major business groups along with the identification codes and names of each department (Figures 8-10 and 8-11).

BLOCKING

Once a stack has been established, block layouts can be prepared. Although this begins the process of schematic design, it is important to test whether the various floor plates will allow the necessary adjacencies to occur. One of the fastest methods excludes the use of a computer. Instead, rough visual estimates of the percentage of the floor that each department will take can be made. Bubbles representing approximate department sizes and locations can then be drawn over base building floor plans. The resulting plans can be referred to more accurately as "amoeba plans" rather than blocking plans. The amoebas can be pinched-off or flow around other departments as the layouts and design progress, as workplace configurations are finalized, and as the company continues to refine its organization. The use of loose bubbles versus hard-edge blocks also implies a certain degree of being preliminary and, therefore, not totally binding to the space planners and designers as their concepts develop.

Blocking plans were developed on the heels of the approval of the stacking plan. As with the stacking plan, senior executives were to review the blocking plan of each floor prior to final approval. Color block plans were thus prepared, indicating the general location of all departments (Figure 8-12).

CONCLUSIONS

In most detailed facility projects, the programming process never really stops. Organizational change, acquisition and divestiture, realignment of corporate goals, revised corporate policies, and personnel changes at senior management levels are some of the major influences that should initiate a reassessment of the validity of the current program.

Late in the third quarter of 1991, Society Bank acquired one of their competitors—AmeriTrust. The facility plans—program, stacking, and blocking—for the Society Bank space were all affected by this merger. Because of the generic nature of the typical floor layouts, modifications necessary to accommodate this major reorganization were not extreme (Figure 8-13). At the outset of the programming and planning process several years earlier, Society Bank had made a decision to "move people, not walls." There was success with the first real test of this state-of-the-art planning concept. Major replanning, expense, and delays were not necessary.

The preliminary Society Bank design process ran concurrently with the establishment of the initial program. Early hypothetical planning concepts were tested against real requirements as the program developed. The interactive process of refining the planning concepts and the program continued to unfold and, subsequently, space plans were prepared and presented to department managers as well as senior management. As anticipated, some of the approved planning concepts were altered slightly upon review of these plans with the line managers. These changes occurred because of specific needs for increased security, for higher degrees of privacy, and for special functions that could not be adequately accommodated by a generic floor plan. For the most part, however, the generic and interchangeable nature of the planning concepts for the individual floors, as outlined in the original program, remained intact (Figure 8-14).

ACKNOWLEDGMENTS

Society Bank Team:

> Dave Edmonds, Senior Vice President, Corporate Facilities Division
> Rose Mary Blessing, Vice President, Corporate Facilities Division
> Al Kageler, Independent Banking and Construction Consultant

Gensler and Associates Team:

> Antony Harbour, Vice President—Managing Principal
> Richard C. Maxwell, Vice President—Project Principal
> David J. Wyckoff, Senior Associate—Programmer
> Anne R. Burton, Programming Assistant
> Lori Cummings, Project Assistant
> Charles Kifer, Vice President—Project Designer
> Bill Livingston, Senior Associate—Project Manager

Database Software

> FM:Space-Management, FM:Systems, Raleigh, North Carolina

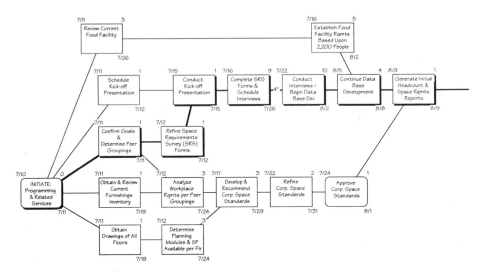

FIGURE 8-1.   Portion of a CPM Schedule

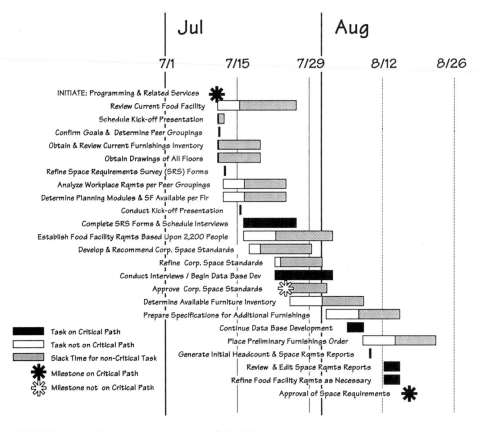

FIGURE 8-2.   Portion of a Bar Graph Schedule

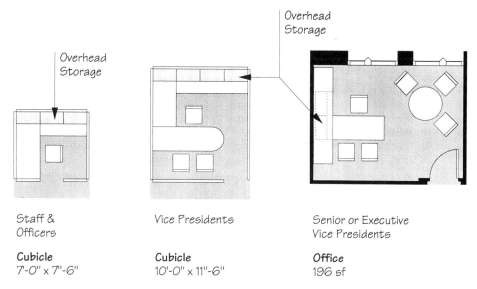

Overhead Storage

Overhead Storage

Staff & Officers

Cubicle
7'-0" x 7'-6"

Vice Presidents

Cubicle
10'-0" x 11"-6"

Senior or Executive Vice Presidents

Office
196 sf

FIGURE 8-3.   Society Bank Space Standards

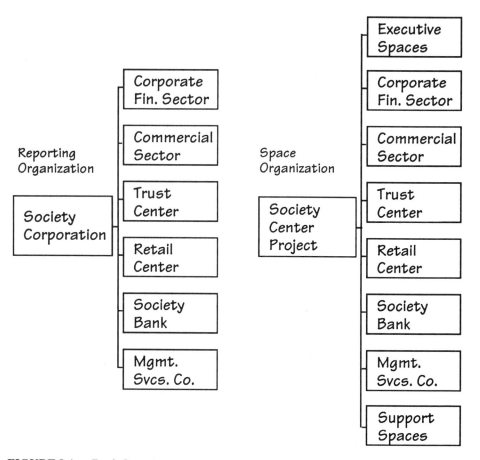

Reporting Organization

Society Corporation

- Corporate Fin. Sector
- Commercial Sector
- Trust Center
- Retail Center
- Society Bank
- Mgmt. Svcs. Co.

Space Organization

Society Center Project

- Executive Spaces
- Corporate Fin. Sector
- Commercial Sector
- Trust Center
- Retail Center
- Society Bank
- Mgmt. Svcs. Co.
- Support Spaces

FIGURE 8-4.   Bank Organization versus Space Organization

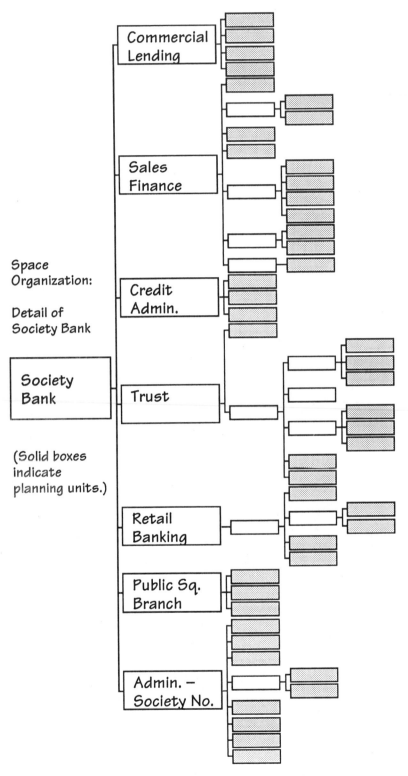

Space
Organization:

Detail of
Society Bank

Society
Bank

(Solid boxes
indicate
planning units.)

Commercial
Lending

Sales
Finance

Credit
Admin.

Trust

Retail
Banking

Public Sq.
Branch

Admin. –
Society No.

FIGURE 8-5. Space Organization Detail—Society Bank

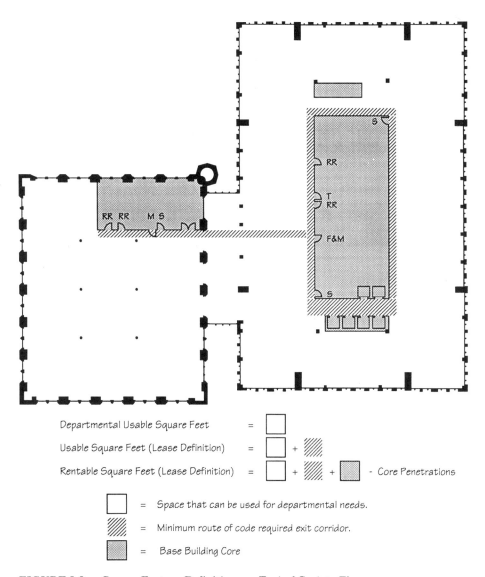

Departmental Usable Square Feet   =   ☐

Usable Square Feet (Lease Definition)   =   ☐ + ▨

Rentable Square Feet (Lease Definition)   =   ☐ + ▨ + ▦ - Core Penetrations

☐ =   Space that can be used for departmental needs.

▨ =   Minimum route of code required exit corridor.

▦ =   Base Building Core

FIGURE 8-6.   Square Footage Definitions on Typical Society Floor

31500 COMM CENTER ADMIN
        Head/Info By: LEN BARKER
        Cost Center: 3027

ID #	Space User	Space Std	Space Std Description	Space Std Area(SF)	Qty 11/91	Qty 11/92	Qty 11/94	Rqd Areas(SF) 11/91	Rqd Areas(SF) 11/92	Rqd Areas(SF) 11/94
Personnel Space										
2.01	CC ADMIN MGR	SVP	OFFICE: 192sf plan	192	1	1	1	192	192	192
2.02	MARKET MGR	VP	CUBICLE: 120sf plan	150	2	3	5	300	450	750
2.03	MARKET RES MGR	AVP	CUBICLE: 52sf plan	65	1	1	1	65	65	65
	Should be located near CC ADMIN MGR.									
2.04	SECRETARY	STAFF	CUBICLE: 52sf plan	65	2	2	2	130	130	130
	Doubles as area receptionist.									
Subtotal					6	7	9	687	837	1,137
Support Space										
3.01	STORAGE ROOM	STO120	STORAGE ROOM	120	1	1	1	120	120	120
	For brochures.									
Subtotal								120	120	120
Misc. Equipment Space										
4.01	FILE	MF	MISC FILE	12	4	4	4	48	48	48
4.02	FAX MACHINE	FAX	FACSIMILE MACHINE	15	1	1	1	15	15	15
	Confidential materials; must be dedicated to this department.									
4.03	TYPEWRITER	TYPE	AUX TYPEWRITER	25	1	1	1	25	25	25
	Near Secretary.									
4.04	PRINTER/LASER	PRINT	PRINTER	15	2	2	2	30	30	30
	Near Secretary.									
Subtotal								118	118	118
SUBTOTAL NET SF								925	1,075	1,375
Dept Circulation Markup					38%	38%	38%	352	409	523
TOTAL DEPT USABLE SF								1,277	1,484	1,898

This department must be located adjacent to
31600 COMM CENTER STAFF GROUP.

FIGURE 8-7.   Sample Report Page: Detail

| | | Staff | | | Rqd Areas(SF) | | |
		11/91	11/92	11/94	11/91	11/92	11/94
30000	COMMERCIAL CENTER						
31000	COMMERCIAL CENTER						
31100	PRODUCT MANAGEMENT	3	5	6	758	1,172	1,379
31200	COMM CENTER SALES MGMT	2	4	4	414	711	711
31300	RELATIONSHIP MGR WRKSTN	3	3	3	464	464	464
31400	CORP BANKING ADMIN	3	3	3	322	322	322
31500	COMM CENTER ADMIN	6	7	9	1,277	1,484	1,898
31600	COMM CENTER STAFF GROUP	5	7	10	683	863	1,249
32000	SPECIALTY LENDING						
32100	ASSET-BASED LENDING	19	21	21	2,761	3,091	3,058
32200	COMMERCIAL REAL ESTATE	15	18	18	2,728	3,115	3,148
32300	INTERNATIONAL ADMIN	12	12	12	1,856	1,973	1,990
32400	INTERNATIONAL OPS	20	21	23	3,874	4,099	4,278
32500	COMMS LENDING	7	7	7	1,245	1,245	1,212
32600	SELC ADMIN	5	5	6	978	978	1,185
32700	CASH MANAGEMENT SALES	10	10	10	2,570	2,570	2,570
32800	SPEC LENDING GROUP ADMIN	2	2	2	727	727	727
33000	CAPITAL MARKETS GROUP						
33100	CAPL MkTS GROUP ADMIN	2	2	2	658	658	658
33200	SECURITIES						
33210	TRADING SUITE				12,023	12,023	12,023
33220	INSTITUTIONAL SEC	9	10	13			
33230	BROKERAGE SEC	3	4	4			
33240	RETAIL SEC	6	6	6			
33250	SEC ADMIN	2	2	2			
33300	VENTURE CAP	6	7	7	1,455	1,544	1,710
33400	INVESTMENT BANKING						
33410	INVEST BANKING ADMIN	2	2	2	393	393	393
33420	PUBLIC FINANCE	8	8	10	1,260	1,260	1,674
33430	CORPORATE FINANCE	12	14	14	2,162	2,480	2,519
30000	SUBTOTAL - DEPT USABLE SF	162	180	194	38,608	41,172	43,168

FIGURE 8-8.   Sample Report Page: SF Summary

| Floor | Available Dept USF | Planning Unit | | Qty | | | Rqd Areas(SF) | | |
		ID	Name	11/91	11/92	11/94	11/91	11/92	11/94
04	35,882	22000	STRATEGIC FINANCE	5	5	5	987	987	987
		23100	FUNDS MANAGEMENT	2	2	2	733	733	733
		23200	ECONOMICS	3	3	3	650	691	708
		23300	TREASURY	11	11	11	(Within Trading Suite)		
		23400	BOND TRADING	6	6	6	(Within Trading Suite)		
		23500	FOREIGN EXCHANGE	8	8	8	(Within Trading Suite)		
		23600	TREASURY SERVICES ADMIN	2	2	2	355	355	355
		23700	TREASURY SERVICES	6	8	8	788	967	967
		23800	INVESTOR RELATIONS	1	1	1	373	373	373
		23900	FUNDS MGMT ADMIN (TRDG)	1	1	1	(Within Trading Suite)		
		23A00	BALANCE SHEET ANALYSIS	6	8	9	864	1,043	1,133
		33100	CAP MKTS GROUP ADMIN	2	2	2	658	658	658
		33210	TRADING SUITE				12,033	12,033	12,033
		33220	INSTITUTIONAL SECURITIES	9	10	13	(Within Trading Suite)		
		33230	BROKERAGE SECURITIES	3	4	4	(Within Trading Suite)		
		33240	RETAIL SECURITIES	6	6	6	(Within Trading Suite)		
		33250	SECURITIES ADMIN	2	2	2	(Within Trading Suite)		
		33300	VENTURE CAPITAL	6	7	7	1,455	1,544	1,710
		33410	INVESTMENT BANKING ADMIN	2	2	2	393	393	393
		33420	PUBLIC FINANCE	8	8	10	1,260	1,260	1,674
		33430	CORPORATE FINANCE	12	14	14	2,162	2,480	2,519
		73000	CORPORATE PLANNING	5	5	5	952	1,042	1,042
		78000	CORPORATE DEVELOPMENT	5	6	6	1,605	1,784	1,823
		81300	LEVEL 4 SUPPORT SPACES				5,741	5,741	5,741
				111	121	127	31,009	32,084	32,849

Dept USF: Available less Required   4,873   3,798   3,033

FIGURE 8-9.   Sample Report Page: Stacking

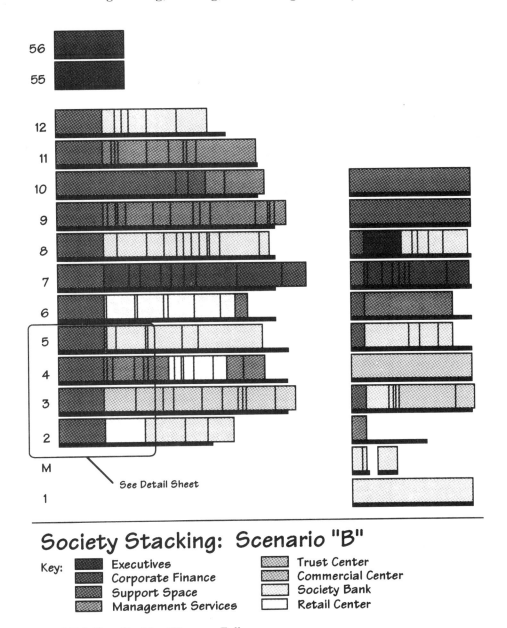

FIGURE 8-10.   Stacking Diagram: Full

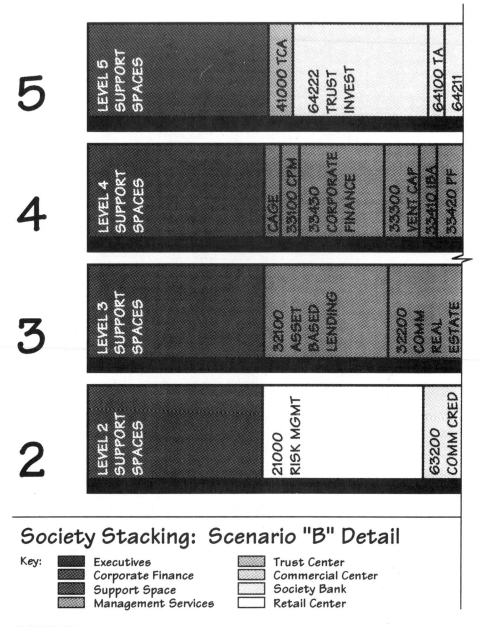

Society Stacking: Scenario "B" Detail

Key:
- Executives
- Corporate Finance
- Support Space
- Management Services
- Trust Center
- Commercial Center
- Society Bank
- Retail Center

FIGURE 8-11.   Stacking Diagram: Detail

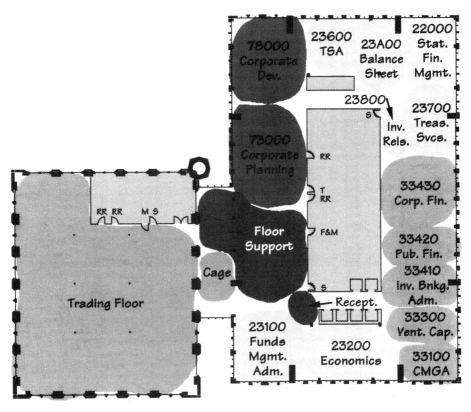

Society Blocking: Scenario "B"   Floor 4

Key:
- ■ Executives
- ■ Corporate Finance
- ■ Support Space
- ■ Management Services

- ▨ Trust Center
- ▨ Commercial Center
- ▨ Society Bank
- ▢ Retail Center

FIGURE 8-12.   Portion of a Blocking Diagram

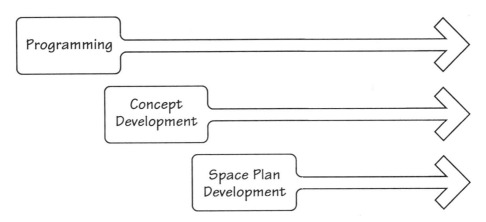

Programming

Concept Development

Space Plan Development

FIGURE 8-13.   Schematic of Overlaps in the Planning Process

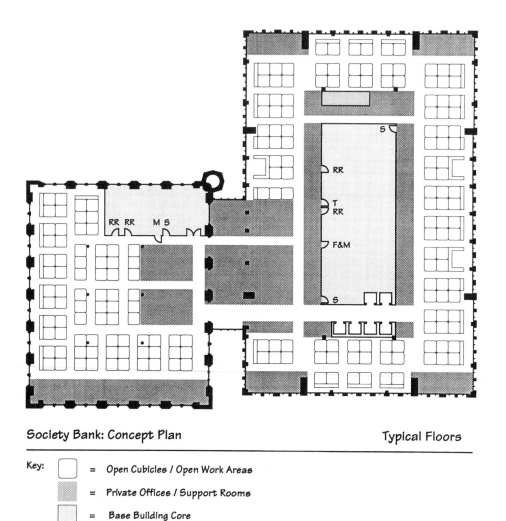

Society Bank: Concept Plan   Typical Floors

Key: ☐ = Open Cubicles / Open Work Areas

      ▓ = Private Offices / Support Rooms

      ☐ = Base Building Core

FIGURE 8-14.   Space Planning Concept

APPENDIX

Space Requirements Survey

SOCIETY NATIONAL BANK

General Instructions:

1. **Please read through this entire survey form before starting to complete it.**

2. Printed responses will be appreciated. We realize that some of you may have lengthier responses than will fit the spaces provided. If this occurs, please feel free to attach additional pages as necessary. A completed copy of this form, together with your related work papers, should be retained for your records.

3. You should **not** include (a) positions at other locations (unless they will be transferred to this Unit) or (b) other Units at the same location which report separately.

4. We want to avoid overlooking any requirements and we also want to ensure that requirements are not double counted. A few of you may have to contact representatives of other Units to resolve any uncertainty as to which Unit will include certain **Staff**, **Support Spaces**, or **Common Equipment** which are shared between Units.

5. When providing quantities for **Staff**, **Support Spaces**, and **Common Equipment** (pages 2a and 3a) each entry should represent **cumulative totals** as follows:

Under	**BDGT**:	Indicate **authorized** quantities per the BUDGET as of **November 1, 1988.**
Under	**ACTL**:	Indicate quantities you ACTUALLY HAD as of **November 1, 1988.**
Under	11/1/**89**:	Indicate quantities **estimated** for **November 1, 1989.**
Under	11/1/**90**:	Indicate quantities **estimated** for **November 1, 1990.**
Under	11/1/**91**:	Indicate quantities **estimated** for **November 1, 1991.**
Under	11/1/**92**:	Indicate quantities **estimated** for **November 1, 1992.**

6. We realize that estimating for four years into the future is very difficult. However, we do ask that you make the best assessment of future needs as possible.

7. Your responses to the issues raised during this survey are very important to the acquisition and management of space for this Unit as well as for each of the other Units. The information you provide is preliminary and it may be discussed in an interview.

8. If you need any further assistance in understanding the nature of the expected responses, the following persons will be able to help you:

Bill Livingston	Gensler and Associates	(713) 228-8050
David Wyckoff	Gensler and Associates	(713) 228-8050
Rose Mary Blessing	Society	(216) 344-5221

Gensler and Associates / Architects

SOCIETY NATIONAL BANK

Space Requirements Survey (Unit Name: ....) **1**

General Information:

1. Please provide the **Proper Name** and **Cost Center Number** of this Unit:

   Organization: ....
                         (If other than SOCIETY NATIONAL BANK)

   Division: ....

   Department: ....

   Sub-Department: ....

   Cost Center Number: ....

2. It is possible that these pages may become separated. To avoid confusion please put the name of this Unit at the top of each page.

3. Provide the following about the **Head** of this Unit:

   Name: ....

   Functional Title: ....

   Telephone: Local # ....

4. Provide the following about the person **who completed this form**:

   Name: ....

   Functional Title: ....

   Date Completed: ....

   Telephone: Local # ....

5. Provide the following regarding the **11/1/88 location** of this Unit:

   Building Name: .... Floor(s): ....

6. List the current working hours of this Unit: (If there are other shifts, please list them individually.)

   ❏ **Shift 1:**   .... am/pm - .... am/pm. (Number of Employees: ....)
   ❏ **Shift 2:**   .... am/pm - .... am/pm. (Number of Employees: ....)
   ❏ **Shift 3:**   .... am/pm - .... am/pm. (Number of Employees: ....)
   Please check the appropriate box above to indicate the **Main Shift.**

7. What is the reasoning that supports the estimation of future requirements for this Unit?

   ....
   ....
   ....
   ....
   ....
   ....
   ....

Gensler and Associates/Architects

SOCIETY NATIONAL BANK

Space Requirements Survey (Unit Name: ....)   **2**

Staff Information:

The instructions on this page should be followed when completing **page 2a.**

1. Under **POSITION**, list **all** positions within this Unit by both **CORPORATE TITLE** and **FUNCTIONAL TITLE**. **Include** any **vacant budgeted positions** as well as any **anticipated new positions**. Also, be sure to include **part-time staff, contracts,** and **non-Society staff**. Don't forget to include **your own position** where appropriate.

2. The shaded column should be left blank.

3. Under **HEADCOUNT**, list the **BUDGETED** and **ACTUAL** quantities of people per position for this Unit as of **11/1/88**. Also provide **estimated** quantities for each position at each of the **four future dates**.

4. Under **PRIVACY**, indicate whether **VISUAL** or **ACOUSTICAL** privacy is a **major concern** for each position. Please state the reasons if privacy is required.

5. Under **VIS** (Visitors), state how many persons **average** (other than the occupant) must be accommodated with guest seating per position.

6. Under **STORAGE**, indicate the **average Total Lineal Feet** required for each type of stored material. If the **OTHER** column is used, please describe the stored material type in the **REMARKS** column.

   Please note that this storage is only that which is considered part of the position's **normal individual workplace**. Shared filing and storage will be described on **page 3a.**

7. Under **REMARKS**, please provide any additional clarifying information or other comments that you feel would be helpful.

Gensler and Associates/Architects

2a

POSITION		HEADCOUNT						PRIVACY			VIS	STORAGE (Total Lin. Feet)						REMARKS
CORP TITLE	FUNCTIONAL TITLE	BDGT 11/1 88	ACTL 11/1 88	11/1 89	11/1 90	11/1 91	11/1 92	VISUAL	ACOUSTIC	IF YES, WHY . . . ?	VISITORS Qty Seated	LETTER	LEGAL	COMP'TR RUNS	MANUALS/ BOOKS	OTHER Describe	
1																	
2																	
3																	
4																	
5																	
6																	
7																	
8																	
9																	
10																	

(Use Additional Sheets and Revise the Sequence Numbers as Necessary)

SOCIETY NATIONAL BANK

Space Requirements Survey (Unit Name: ....)   **3**

Support Spaces and Common Equipment:

The instructions on this page should be followed when completing **page 3a**.

1. Under **SPACE OR ITEM TYPE**, describe each type of Support Space or item of Common Equipment required by this Unit. Include rooms or areas for **file cabinets, storage, meetings, terminals, telecopiers, shredders, printers, etc.**

   Certain types of cabinets are often required. **Standard Codes** for these cabinets are listed on **page 3b**. Please use these codes when possible.

   Under **SQ. FT.**, indicate the **Actual Square Footage (or size)** required for each listed space or item as of **11/1/88**.

   Please note that requirements considered to be part of an individual's personal workplace should be described on **page 2a**. Also note that Society has elected to configure all personal workplaces to uniformly accommodate personal computer systems.

2. Under **QUANTITIES**, list the **BUDGET** and **ACTUAL** quantities for each described space or item as of **11/1/88**. Then, provide estimated quantities (or percentage increases/decreases) for each of the **four future dates**.

3. Under **THIS SPACE OR ITEM IS SHARED WITH . . . ?**, indicate situations in which described items or spaces are **shared with other Units**. Proper names of the other Units should be provided. Also, to avoid double-counting requirements, please try to ensure that there is no duplicaton of described items or spaces.

4. Under **CONTENTS (and Quantities) AS OF 11/1/88**, list the **actual contents** of spaces as of **11/1/88**. Examples include tables, chairs, cabinets (by type and number of drawers), shelving units, equipment, printers, etc. Also indicate how many there were of each.

5. Under **CONTENTS (and Quantities) AS OF 11/1/92**, list the anticipated increases and/or decreases by **11/1/92**.

6. Under **REMARKS**, please provide any additional clarifying information or other comments that you feel would be helpful.

SPACE OR ITEM TYPE:		SQ. FT.	QUANTITIES						THIS SPACE OR ITEM SHOULD BE SHARED WITH . . . ?	CONTENTS (and Quantities of Each) AS OF 11/1 88	Estimated Additional (and/or deleted) CONTENTS AS OF 11/1 92	REMARKS
CODE	DESCRIPTION	(or Size) ACTUAL 11/1 88	BDGT 11/1 88	ACTL 11/1 88	11/1 89	11/1 90	11/1 91	11/1 92				
1												
2												
3												
4												
5												
6												
7												
8												
9												
10												

(Use Additional Sheets and Revise the Sequence Numbers as Necessary)

3a

SOCIETY NATIONAL BANK

Space Requirements Survey (Unit Name: ....)   **3b**

Standard Codes:

Please use the **standard codes** shown on this page whenever possible to describe items on **page 3a.**

LETTER FILE
CODE: LT(# of Dwrs)
Example: **LT4**
= 4-DWR LETTER FILE

SHELF FILE
CODE: TF(# of Tiers)
Example: **TF4**
= 4-TIER SHELF FILE

LEGAL FILE
CODE: LG(# of Dwrs)
Example: **LG4**
= 4-DWR LEGAL FILE

STORAGE CABINET
CODE: SC(# of Shelves)
Example: **SC4**
= 4-SHELF STOR CABINET

LATERAL FILE
CODE: LA(# of Dwrs)
Example: **LA4**
= 4-DWR LATERAL FILE

BOOKCASE
CODE: BC(# of Shelves)
Example: **BC4**
= 4-SHELF BOOKCASE

Gensler and Associates/Architects

SOCIETY NATIONAL BANK

Space Requirements Survey (Unit Name: ....) **4**

Internal Adjacencies:

Information requested on this page refers only to adjacencies required within this Unit as described on page 1 of this form.

1. Indicate the **nature of the work** performed by this Unit as one of the following types:

    ❑ **Individual Oriented:**   Tasks/assignments performed essentially to completion by individuals.

    ❑ **Team Oriented:**   Tasks/assignments performed essentially to completion by small groups of individuals.

    ❑ **Work-flow Oriented:**   Tasks/assignments performed to partial completion prior to additional work with the same materials by others (either within this Unit or within another Unit).

    ❑ **Other:**   Please describe: ....
    ....
    ....
    ....

2. Describe (and/or diagram on a separate sheet) the manner in which the nature of the work performed by this Unit affects the required layout of Positions, Support Spaces, and Miscellaneous Spaces.
    ....
    ....
    ....
    ....
    ....

3. Describe or diagram the **flow of work** through this Unit. (This may not apply to some Units).
    ....
    ....
    ....

4. Could (or should) some of this Unit work separately (i.e., on another floor or in another building)? If so, is distance a factor? Please indicate on pages 2 and 3 which Positions, Support Spaces, and Miscellaneous Spaces would be involved.
    ....
    ....
    ....
    ....
    ....

5. Please attach an **Organization Chart** of this Unit as of **11/1/88 ACTUAL**.

    It should include all Positions as listed on **page 2**.   This chart should also indicate the upward reporting structure of this Unit to the level of **Society Corporation**.

Gensler and Associates/Architects

SOCIETY NATIONAL BANK

Space Requirements Survey (Unit Name: ....) **5**

External Adjacencies:

Information requested on this page refers only to the relationship of this Unit to other Units and visitors.

1. Under UNIT list the **other** Units with which **this** Unit has an adjacency need. Please use the proper Name and Cost Center Number for each Unit listed. Under ADJACENCY REQUIRED check the **highest** required degree of adjacency for each Unit listed. Under NATURE check whether the adjacency is Essential or merely Convenient. And under NOW state whether the adjacency requirement had been met as of November 1, 1988.

UNIT:		ADJACENCY REQUIRED:			NATURE:		NOW:
Name	CC Number	Adjoin-ing	Same Floor	Next Floor	Essen-tial	Conven-ient	(Y or N)
....		....			....		....
....		....			....		....
....		....			....		....
....		....			....		....
....		....			....		....
....		....			....		....

2. For each adjacency listed above as **Essential** please state the specific reason:

   ....

   ....

3. If there is any Unit or group of Units which should specifically **not be adjacent** to this Unit, please indicate the proper Name, Cost Center Number, and reason:

   ....

   ....

4. How many **visitors** does this Unit have per **average week**?

   SOCIETY Employees: ....   Vendors & Contractors: ....   Customers: ....

5. Further describe the visitor **types** and **interaction** that normally occurs.

   SOCIETY Employees: ....

   Vendors & Contractors: ....

   ....

   Customers: ....

   ....

6. If there are any **non-SOCIETY** entities (such as a "department" consisting of outside audit staff) which this Unit must be nearby (or must not be nearby), please name them, indicate the required degree of adjacencies, and state the reasons:

   ....

   ....

SOCIETY NATIONAL BANK

Space Requirements Survey (Unit Name: ....)   6

Other Considerations:

1. Should **access** be **restricted** to any areas of this Unit? .... If yes, please describe the circumstances:
   ....
   ....
   ....

2. Discuss any **business factors** or **industry trends** that may impact office space needs for this Unit:
   ....
   ....
   ....

3. Attributes of this Unit's **current space** that are:

   Good: ....   **Bad:** ....
   ....
   ....
   ....
   ....
   ....
   ....

4. List any **special facilities** such as non-office space, auditoriums, training facilities, dead storage, etc., which this Unit requires (or will require) that are not considered as "owned" by this Unit. Please indicate the Unit which you feel is (or should be) the actual owner.

FACILITY TYPE:	CAPACITY:		OWNED BY... :	AVAILABLE NOW?
	Qty :	of each item (i.e., people, tables, etc.)	Which other Unit is/should be in charge of this facility?	Yes or No?
1.	....	....	....	....
	....	....		
	....	....		
	....	....		
2.	....	....	....	....
	....	....		
	....	....		
	....	....		
3.	....	....	....	....
	....	....		
	....	....		
	....	....		

SOCIETY NATIONAL BANK

Space Requirements Survey (Unit Name: ....)   **7**

General Comments:

Please provide any additional comments which you feel would clarify the requirements for this Unit.

CHAPTER 9

Programming: The Third Dimension

Wilbur H. Tusler, Frank Zilm, James T. Hannon, and Mary Ann Newman

INTRODUCTION

Quality architecture originates from a synthesis of quality programming and visionary design. This chapter will explore the nature of the interrelationships between programming and design in health care planning. Examples will be drawn from a recently completed programming and concept design project at the University of Texas M.D. Anderson Cancer Center, one of the premier health care institutions in the United States.

Expenditures for health care have risen at a rapid pace over the past two decades, and currently exceed 12 percent of the gross national product. The aging of the population, new medical technologies, reconfiguration of economic incentive systems, and changing consumer expectations, coupled with obsolescence of existing structures, point to a continued need for new health care architecture and renovation of existing buildings.

Although the 1980s saw a proliferation of ambulatory care facilities of various types, the hospital remains the focus for a great portion of the sophisticated medical care provided today. Hospitals can be viewed as a model of the "high-tech," "high-touch" organizations that have emerged during the twentieth century. For large teaching hospitals, the information and technical skill necessary to make the organization work are beyond the control of a centralized administration. Among the characteristics of these organizations are the division of information and technologies into subunits (departments), with significant decision-making authority and control delegated to these components.

Large teaching hospitals only *look* like hierarchical organizations; in reality, they are closer to symbiotic organisms, dependent on maintaining a functional and political balance among components. To some degree, all hospitals today reflect these characteristics, a challenge the health care programmer must recognize and accommodate.

Managing a creative building project becomes particularly challenging in this environment. Responding to departmental goals and the complex balance of power can limit the ability of an organization to seek new, bold visions for the future. Maintaining rigorous project budgets in response to severe economic pressures requires deciphering the "real" needs of each user group and balancing these needs against the overall organizational goals. This must be done while developing and maintaining a total building concept that seeks to integrate needs and express visionary solutions.

There are a series of complex and conflicting concerns that must be successfully resolved during every health care programming and design process:

- create a humane environment for patients, visitors, and staff
- provide a functional design that ensures efficient, safe, and appropriate work spaces
- accommodate technical requirements for highly sophisticated equipment
- provide an unambiguous path for arrival at and entry into the building
- create clear, segregated paths for movement of people and material within the building
- conform to a myriad of often conflicting building codes and regulations
- blend technical and functional requirements into a design that brings delight to those who use the building and those who pass by it
- develop building systems concepts that can accommodate rapid change
- facilitate incremental growth and replacement of facilities over time

INTEGRATION OF PROGRAMMING AND ARCHITECTURAL DESIGN

The complexity of programming health care facilities has led to specialization of programming skills and a fragmentation of the programming process from what traditionally were closely interrelated design activities. Forces that have resulted in the separation of programming from design include the following:

- focus on non-facility related strategic planning
- bias in architectural schools against specialization
- perceived conflict of interest between defining building scope and providing architectural services
- contemporary definitions of, and compensation for, basic architectural services
- requests for extensive technical justification required in certain states for certificate of need approvals

- increasing need to achieve new levels of operational efficiency
- limited education of architects in psychology, communications, finance, statistics, and other skills necessary for effective programming

Specialization has led to a situation where programs for health care facilities are often developed by professionals with no architectural training or experience, in isolation from architectural consideration. The major accounting firms that consult in the areas of market analysis, strategic planning, and financial analysis have in the last few years acquired planning firms and are now offering functional and space programming, and often master planning, for health facilities.

The dividing line between programming and design is very inhibiting. Great buildings rarely result from a sequential process of programming and architectural design. They result from a symbiosis of form giving and user insight, a collaboration of design and programming skills. Splintering of the processes for user decision and design presents one of the major challenges to the creation of quality architecture. Effective programming requires specific technical knowledge and interpersonal skills to help users define needs, identify relationships, and visualize future opportunities. The programming process is ultimately the translation of external opportunities, the users' needs, available resources, and institutional values into a *viable building concept*. This requires an interactive collaboration between client, programmers, and architectural designers. Programming is the first step in the design process.

The fallacy of segregating programming from architectural design is that traditional programming builds from the inside out and is *two-dimensional in nature*. It is valuable in that it is sensitive to the needs of users; it is limited in that it deals with physical relationships and square footage in the abstract. That is, programs are developed in isolation from building and site realities and potential. Sequential programming is a two-dimensional approach. It assumes that complete building requirements and operational systems can be established without testing context-sensitive site and building concepts and without addressing building form and mass.

Traditional architecture, on the other hand, is "outside in." It tends to derive the form of the building with only a cursory understanding of the program and the total square footage required. It is three-dimensional in that it deals with the reality of the building, but often it is insensitive to user requirements. For example, the building may be conceived in a formalistic sense, with symmetry around a grand entrance and atrium lobby or two triangles with points touching, independent of the actual needs of those for whom the building is intended. The needed space is later stuffed into the building form in the best way possible.

Great architecture requires interaction between programming and design. That is, a *third dimension* is needed in programming. The program must be derived from the concept and at the same time define the concept. It must speak about the building as a piece of architecture as well as a place to house users. It must define and establish the aesthetic goals for the building. It must also establish in the collective client's mind the possibilities that a well-designed building can reveal.

Imagine the parts of a grand piano scattered separately in one place. While all the makings of a great instrument are there, a talented craftsman would be at a loss as to what to do with the pieces, unless he or she had a concept: first, the idea of music; and second, the idea of a piano. Only then could the skill of the craftsman be applied to make a truly great instrument. Architecture is similar. The programmer produces the parts, and the architectural designer must visualize the great instrument. Throughout the planning process, the client also must be able to visualize the end product in order to fulfill his or her role in making appropriate decisions. Thus, the programmer and the designer must collaborate and work simultaneously, not sequentially as at present, with the client as an integral part of this collaboration. A shared vision—the music—must exist between all three.

SERVING CLIENT NEEDS

Health care architecture needs to mirror subspecialization in a way that reflects the clients we serve. Clients are looking for a high degree of skill and expertise in architects. At the same time, there is renewed interest in humanizing the health care environment and an acknowledgment that health care buildings are major works of architecture that have impact as buildings, both on the community and on those who use them. In selecting a planning team, enlightened hospital clients increasingly are looking for a blend of specialization and design leadership. These forces reflect basic market-driven economics. Clients will select firms that are perceived to have an effective blend of specialization and architectural design commitment. Firms, or combinations of firms that routinely work closely together, that offer a successful blend of these skills probably will continue to increase market share by providing a unique understanding of health care and architecture that can be applied interactively during the programming and design process.

M.D. ANDERSON CANCER CENTER: SIMULTANEOUS PROGRAMMING AND DESIGN

M.D. Anderson Cancer Center is an example of a large teaching institution that chose to define program needs through an interactive programming and design process. A recently completed programming and concept design effort for M.D. Anderson illustrates the advantages of this approach and the complexities of programming in today's technological, political, and economic climate.

M.D. Anderson Cancer Center marked its fiftieth anniversary in 1991, having been established by the Texas legislature in 1941 as the cancer resource for the state. It has large clinical and basic science components, with nearly 600 physicians and scientists on staff and more than 7,000 total employees.

M.D. Anderson has a strong sense of mission and an institutional philosophy of being on the "leading edge," emphasizing a multidisciplinary approach toward eliminating the cancer problem. The institution has a tripartite mission of patient care, research, and education, with prevention recently added as a fourth mission element. The organization structure centers around these mission elements, with a vice president for each reporting to the president. The clinical and research divisions and departments are matrixed to the respective mission vice presidents. Each of the vice presidents has authority over a pool of resources that include staff and space positions. No one office in the institution has overall authority in planning facilities; each vice president manages his or her own space.

The hospital has 518 inpatient beds and houses one of the largest ambulatory functions dedicated to cancer patients in the nation. The main building complex contains 1.8 million square feet of space, nearly half of which was constructed in the 1950s and 1960s. Figure 9-1 illustrates the existing site plan for M.D. Anderson Cancer Center. Prior to the programming and concept design effort discussed here, there were four separate points of patient entrance, six for staff, and four points of access for service entry. All of these were linked with a complex, conflicting, and sometimes disconnected circulation system.

The planning process started with the development of an internal strategic plan. While discussions concerning the need to upgrade and improve existing departments had been ongoing for many years, it was the institutional strategic planning process that prioritized the upgrading of existing facilities as a key strategic issue if the institution was to continue its "leading edge" patient care and research. A faculty attitude survey conducted during the strategic planning effort identified state-of-the-art facilities as the most important factor in faculty recruitment and retention. Strategic planning sparked a focused and targeted facility planning effort.

From this effort, a ten-year, $400 million capital improvement plan was identified, including $270 million of new construction, renovations, and upgrades of existing buildings. Most projects listed in the capital improvement plan were not thoroughly evaluated or programmed initially by the in-house planning team.

Because of the complexity and size of M.D. Anderson's proposed project, the institution requested special permission from the University of Texas Board of Regents to conduct a functional and space programming and planning effort, prior to final confirmation of the budget and selection of a firm for architectural basic services. Once approval had been obtained, a request for proposal was sent to architectual/engineering firms.

A selection committee, made up of institutional and University of Texas system personnel, identified the criteria for the selection process. Key criteria included experience in large health care and research projects, with an equal emphasis on programming and facility master planning; a demonstrated understanding of hospital organization and function; comprehensiveness and depth of the consulting team in terms of experience and specialty areas, including engineering; the reputation of the firms; and compatibility with the institution.

Fourteen firms/teams submitted qualifications, twelve were selected for first-round interviews, and three teams were selected for final interviews with the key institutional decision makers. The selected team demonstrated an understanding of the complexity of the project and presented a strong consulting team with the diversity of skills to address *all elements* of the project.

The institution viewed this major facility planning effort as an opportunity to identify and correct operational deficiencies that could be attributed to space or physical layout. Facility development goals were defined early in the process. "Improving operating efficiencies and the sharing of valuable resources" was a goal that required the programming and planning team to have a firm grasp on the operational, organizational, and system requirements of complex health care centers.

In addition to the operational issues, the facility planning issues at M.D. Anderson Cancer Center were formidable. The hospital is located on an impacted site in the Texas Medical Center, a mega-complex of health care providers in Houston. Any prior planning for future expansion or replacement of obsolete facilities was not apparent. Parking and entrances to the hospital were ambiguous and confusing. Circulation inside the building was equally confusing and inefficient. The facility badly needed additional space—750,000 square feet of new space was proposed—and mechanical and electrical systems needed upgrading. The ground floor plan shown in Figure 9-2 will illustrate the complexity of the existing facility.

PROGRAMMING IN THE THIRD DIMENSION

An integrated programming/design process has many of the components of traditional, sequential programming and design. The following will describe the challenges of developing a major building program for a complex teaching hospital using an integrated and highly interactive programming/design approach.

Establishing an Organizational Concept

Elegance is defined by the *American Heritage Dictionary* as "refinement and grace in movement, appearance, or manner." This term is frequently used to describe a design solution that creates a unique, effective, and pleasing solution to a problem. The creation of an elegant design solution needs to begin in the programming phase, through identifying user needs and instilling in users the possibilities and opportunities that exist in creating new space or using existing space in new and interesting ways.

Exploration of traditional and innovative space concepts is part of the language of architecture and should be part of the programming process. This is a reflective process, as described by Donald Schön: exploring, evaluating, and redefining a problem.[1] This process does not follow the scientific model of knowledge and can therefore be confusing to health professionals and health care consultants alike.

The political nature of space (territory), status, and control in hospitals presents a major barrier to the type of open communications necessary for identifying needs and opportunities for design solutions, particularly as these cross traditional departmental boundaries. Space is a critical resource and is also a symbol of the success and strength of an administrative program or medical discipline. Realignment, sharing, or reduction of functions or space can be perceived as a threat to departmental goals and long-term status. Programming within this context must encompass several simple, but frequently overlooked, fundamentals to ensure success:

- effective communication of the proposed process to all involved
- resolution of institutional goals with goals of each subcomponent
- application of methods for defining space and functional needs that do not lock in preconceived solutions
- maintenance of subcomponent needs in perspective with overall organizational goals and resources as the process proceeds
- provision of opportunities for frequent testing and review of architectural design concepts as functional and space models are explored during the programming process

Preparing an institution to plan and program complex and diverse spaces, such as those in hospital and research facilities, requires a dedicated staff that is positioned to transcend the organization, one that understands and incorporates the organization's decision-making subtleties. A programming process such as this requires considerable attention to defining the scope and approach to the project. A team approach on the part of the institution and consulting firm is called for, beginning with careful selection of a consulting firm that is compatible with the institutional culture and that has the skills and knowledge to work with diverse, often highly specialized, technical individuals. The process requires the dedication and attention of the institution's top management to quickly resolve conflicts and make required decisions so that planning and programming can progress. Most importantly, it requires a clear definition and understanding of the goals and priorities of the institution.

Effective programming for contemporary health care facilities calls for a careful integration of group process leadership skills with planning and data analysis techniques. If user needs are to be properly identified and analyzed, the planning/design team must include programmers and designers who can guide and facilitate a clear decision-making process. These skills are essential resources in helping the client's leadership to set project priorities and make difficult choices regarding user needs — needs that are often inconsistent and contradictory.

---

[1]Schön, Donald. 1983. *The Reflective Practitioner.* New York: Basic Books, Inc.

At M.D. Anderson Cancer Center, positioning the institution for such a major capital expansion was one of the first tasks. The assistant vice president for planning was appointed as the interim project manager, bringing to the project the element of a centralized and dedicated office. A decision-making structure for facilities planning was defined and articulated. A Facility Steering Committee (president and vice presidents) was established to define the vision for the capital expansion and to serve as the final decision-making and conflict-resolution body. Another key group established for the facility effort was the Facility Focus Group (FfoG), composed of the direct line facility managers for each of the vice presidents. The assistant vice president for planning served as the chair of this group. The FfoG provided day-to-day guidance to the consulting team.

At the departmental level, many of the user groups were established and began meeting prior to retaining the programming and planning team. In total, the individuals from M.D. Anderson involved in the pre-architectural planning numbered in the hundreds. The programming and planning process involved over 400 meetings with users and key decision makers. The first charge given to these user groups was to examine current operational and organizational patterns to identify ways in which redesign might improve efficiencies and promote the sharing of resources. Figure 9-3 provides an example of the complexity of planning group relations necessary in a large health care institution today.

The programming/planning consulting team included programming specialists (such as nurses and equipment planners), programming generalists with an understanding of long-term health care trends and economics, functional planners, and building design specialists. Both health care and research disciplines were represented. Team members included individuals with knowledge of local building conditions, codes, and construction costs. Structural, mechanical, and electrical engineering disciplines also played an active role from the beginning of the programming process.

An essential ingredient in making the M.D. Anderson Cancer Center planning experience a success was the development of a comprehensive, detailed schedule for all planning activities. A portion of the schedule is illustrated in Figure 9-4.

Providing the Right Tools and Techniques

A methodology for health care facility programming was elaborated in the chapter "Health Care Facility Programming" in *Programming the Built Environment* published in 1985.[2] This methodology remains pertinent for

---

[2]Tusler, Wilbur H., Jr., Richard T. Schraishuhn, and Eve R. Meyer, 1985. Health-care facility programming. In *Programming the built environment*, ed. Wolfgang F.E. Preiser. New York: Van Nostrand Reinhold Company Inc.

today's health care environment. This chapter addresses experience gained in the intervening years in dealing with an increasingly pressurized economic and political environment.

The design team must know how to manage user group interviews to avoid two common tendencies that lead to collecting user "wish lists" based on a limited frame of reference. First, user groups sometimes encourage inexperienced design teams to jump prematurely into discussions of precise space requirements and detailed design issues before departmental goals are established and there is a clear understanding of these goals. Second, it is difficult for many users to visualize or consider future requirements and opportunities, as opposed to present activities, and the facility implications they represent.

Traditionally, facility programming has examined various key functional parameters to derive space requirements and planning criteria. For instance, space allocations for clinical and other technical departments should be based in part upon a careful examination of present and projected future workload. Depending on the department, workload is measured in terms of the future projected volume of procedures, tests, daily deliveries, or similar indicators; equipment; staff; functional systems; and hours of operation. For less technical areas such as offices, the primary drivers of space needs are indicators such as staffing projections, forecast changes in technology, and the expected volume of specialized activities such as conferences, training classes, records processing, document reproduction, and so forth.

A variety of statistical techniques and related data analysis tools are commonly used to project expected daily requirements for key rooms around which a specific department is organized. For instance, given the projection of expected daily and weekly surgical procedures by type and associated equipment requirements for specialized rooms, simulation and queuing modeling are often employed to infer an optimal number of operating rooms in surgery. Similar techniques are used to determine medical center educational conference and training rooms by size and type, given historical and projected data on meeting schedules and staffing.

The most important value of such analyses is not precise mechanical estimates of room requirements as the end point in the programming process. Rather, it is the opportunity such estimates provide to inform a user group as to reasonable boundaries for space needs. The technique of grounding user group discussions in a rigorous examination of workload-based functional activities can be essential in sorting out true space needs from unsupported wish lists. The data from technical analyses can be employed to keep the process objective and, along with the application of appropriate group leadership skills, to balance competing departmental power group interests. Finally, workload and space projections also provide a familiar vehicle that users can understand and apply to address the future and free themselves from focusing only on current physical building requirements. Workload-based programming is one of the more valuable techniques to keep all participants oriented to an appropriate planning horizon and future needs.

Interdepartmental Collaboration

A common pitfall of traditional programming has been to overly emphasize functional and space needs assessment techniques that sequentially examine individual departments or organizational units in isolation from other issues. This leads to architectural space programs that are simply an amalgamation of individual department programs with little sense of how the total building is to work functionally or physically. It is a typification of the "inside-out" approach to building programming and design.

One of the most dramatic examples at the M.D. Anderson Cancer Center of cross-departmental collaboration in the redefinition of operational policies and structure was in the critical care area. A multidisciplinary user group composed of surgeons, internal medicine physicians, pediatricians, anesthesiologists, nurses, and hospital administrators was formed to discuss common programs and issues. Radiologists, pharmacists, infection control staff, and laboratory medicine staff met with the user group on an ad hoc basis. It became apparent that a physical adjacency of the intensive care units could be beneficial from a quality of care and a resource perspective. In addition, there was concern about the growing number of patients with extraordinarily long lengths of stay in the intensive care units and the emotional burden this situation places on the patient's family. The need for a pediatric intensive care unit was identified, because of new leadership and a change in treatment philosophy of the pediatrics department. The critical care model developed by this cross-departmental user group included medical, surgical, and pediatric units and a supportive care unit that would permit increased visitation by family members, all physically adjacent to one another and sharing important resources such as special procedure rooms, treatment areas, and staff support functions.

The programming and planning team worked with the user group to identify space needs and shared support space and to develop and test possible layouts that would accomplish the stated goals. It was also recommended by the user group that a critical care division be established with the primary responsibility for managing the care of patients in all the units. While this new division structure had not yet been implemented at the time this chapter was written, the concept met with general approval by the staff.

In groups where individuals represent different organizational reporting lines, building consensus is often difficult because of conflicting goals and priorities. The critical care group effectively overcame these obstacles because of initially well-defined and consensual objectives. Among these objectives was the goal to establish physically adjacent critical care units, which would improve quality of care and avoid a duplication of support services caused by organizational reporting lines. The user group recommended that the critical care units be adjacent to the surgery suite (because of the close association between surgical intensive care and the ORs); the planning team determined that this was not physically possible on the same floor level. However, the priorities established by the user group prevailed and the comprehensive critical care adjacency remained intact, with the units located on a different level than surgery. Working together, the user group and the planning team developed a feasible solution that retained the comprehensive critical care structure, while maintaining a dedicated vertical link to the operating rooms.

A related issue was the feasibility of creating a floor plate big enough to accommodate all the critical care beds on one level. The site was limited and major issues of allocation of site footprint to research or to clinical space surfaced early in the planning process. The testing of floor plate size was necessary to feed into the critical care committee discussions. Had it not been possible to locate all of these beds on one level, further complex discussions would have ensued to set new program priorities.

The critical care example illustrates the importance not only of crossing traditional departmental boundaries in structuring programming focus groups, but also of testing physical solutions as programming discussions proceed, so that unobtainable objectives can be recognized early and alternative solutions can be found.

Hospitals and related health care facilities are knit together by numerous cross-facility logistical and technological systems. These are the sinews and arteries that connect functions into a coherent whole. The most important of these systems include intradepartmental circulation routes and horizontal and vertical transport systems (elevators, escalators, conveying devices, stairs) for staff, patients, visitors, and materials; cross-departmental systems, procedures, and technologies; and telecommunications and information systems. These systems dramatically affect interdepartmental adjacency needs, specific space allocation within departments, and overall building support space size, type, and location.

Often, intradepartmental issues are addressed only superficially in conventional programming. This is a serious omission. An integrated programming/design process mandates that these issues be addressed. In order to do so, cross-disciplinary user groups must be formed and the realities of adjacencies and building organization must be the basis for planning. For many systems—information transfer, for example—spatial organization is not an issue. The programming of these systems, however, is closely interrelated to departmental function and should be addressed with other programming issues.

Visualizing Alternatives

Finally, it is important that the user and the building owner fully understand the building that is proposed. Most users have never been exposed to the possibilities that architecture can offer; they have never seen an excellent building. Most users have difficulty visualizing a room of 200 square feet, or a space about 12 feet by 18 feet. For M.D. Anderson, the planning team was able to present plans of typical rooms from other architectural projects with equipment layouts to assist in visualization. This was also true of overall building concepts, which would have remained abstractions if concept plans had not been developed simultaneously.

Hard data-derived estimates of space allocations should be supplemented with techniques to help users visualize the impact of alternate systems, procedures, and approaches to patient care. Taking user groups on tours of different new facilities can provide valuable perspectives on the implementation and relative success of new design concepts in a "live" situation. Specific functional systems and design details need to be fully clarified and evaluated in user meetings after each field visit. For instance, in programming critical care patient rooms, the effect of providing a service column system instead of a conventional bed headwall system for medical gases and utilities is best visualized on field trips with users. Systems such as these can significantly affect options for space in the room, the position of the bed, and the accessibility for the medical team in the room during routine procedures or a major resuscitation situation. In the absence of a field visit, a graphic presentation, a dynamic computer-aided design modeled directly in a user meeting, or, in some cases, a full-sized mock-up may be effective in exploring options and for assisting users to come to a decision.

Techniques such as an analytical approach to workload forecasts and utilization patterns, computer simulation of operations, and cross-departmental focus groups are useful tools for programming when applied in the right circumstances. So are tests of physical possibilities during programming discussions, examination of cross-departmental systems early in the programming process, and the identification of ways to assist users to visualize new solutions. These techniques will provide a scope and depth of information that is far greater than the traditional space listing. A program must also contain design data, which can be derived and tested most effectively if programming and design occur in tandem. Rarely is this done in traditional programming.

Programming/Design Interrelationships

The programming and planning effort at M.D. Anderson Cancer Center included many examples illustrating the essential nature and benefit of simultaneous programming and designing; that is, bringing the program "out of the paper." As has been stated, great buildings are born of great concepts, a higher level of exploring the "third dimension." Rarely are great buildings conceived exclusively from the programming process. Functional and space programming is an activity of inquiry and information seeking. It evaluates what is and builds on a body of ideas that have been evolved over a period of trial and error at other institutions, hopefully with new ideas added in the process. The program remains, however, a series of aspirations and ideas that do not express a total building reality; it is without life, without the third dimension.

Great concepts are derived from knowledge and understanding, the ability to grasp the essence of the whole. A planning effort that has as a goal innovation and new insights must have both client and architect who are willing to take an intellectual leap, to go beyond what any one individual user or the collective user conceives. This is why the programming process is the essential first step in the design process and must be interactive with exploration of physical solutions. Both client and programmer/planner must collaborate closely in combining creative energies to visualize the whole as well as the parts, simultaneously throughout the programming and planning process. Fully realized, programming is a creative act of the highest order and essential to great architecture. The following discussions illustrate further areas where this process proved invaluable in the M.D. Anderson planning effort.

Stacking and Relationship Issues

At M.D. Anderson, a great many of the programmatic issues centered around the ability to achieve certain adjacencies or proximities. The critical care example has already been mentioned. There was also an issue of the location of surgery. The ability to align the new surgery on the same floor as the existing surgery meant that overflow from surgery could be accommodated in existing space. This was established by testing building the concept organization during the programming phase. Adjacency meant a reduction in the amount of new surgical space constructed initially. Another example was the ability to evaluate the cost trade-off of consolidating radiation therapy treatment areas on one level rather than two levels, which significantly changed the support spaces required for both the patient care areas and staff and administrative components. Location of ambulatory surgery staging areas on the same level as diagnostic imaging functions provided opportunities for operational and space savings through shared waiting, recovery, and support spaces.

In the existing facility, floor-to-floor heights were less than 12′. Despite the strong desire to achieve horizontal adjacencies, matching existing floor-to-floor heights would have resulted in building an obsolete facility. After careful consideration, the medical center decided to use an integrated building systems approach for highly technical functions that required interstitial space. Although this approach would achieve much greater long-term flexibility, it further limited the ability to match existing floors without extensive ramping. Again, careful study of building concept options, balanced with programmatic requirements, resulted in a solution that was finally endorsed by senior management. Figure 9-5 illustrates the final building section and horizontal relationships that were achieved.

A critical factor in establishing relationships between functions was the need to stack floors. Functions located on upper floors could not be larger than those on lower floors without incurring additional construction cost. The ultimate proposal for the new addition had eight floors. Matching square footage floor to floor became a juggling act, one that materially affected many programmatic issues and desired relationships.

Building Re-use

In today's health care environment, capital must be conserved wherever possible. Therefore, in many programmatic situations, existing buildings must be renovated and re-used. Where programming for re-use is done without testing architectural design, traditional ratios of net to gross space often are invalid. Existing space cannot be used with the same level of efficiency. Likewise, building costs cannot be accurately forecast without a thorough assessment of mechanical, electrical, and plumbing cost implications. The configuration of existing building wings or elements may also be a limiting factor in deciding the proper re-use of a given space. All of these considerations require an experienced architectural assessment and testing of design solutions. The proposed construction for M.D. Anderson Cancer Center included 200,000 square feet of retrofit space that needed to be incorporated in the planning and budgeting process.

Expansion Strategies

There are many ways of ensuring that a facility can accommodate growth and change. Use of an integrated building systems approach is one that has been mentioned. Another commonly used technique is to locate highly complex space, which would be expensive to relocate, adjacent to "soft" space, which can be moved with little disruption or cost. This technique provides a built-in area for expansion. Knowledge of expansion capabilities affects program area; if a zone for expansion is available, less internal expansion needs to be programmed in the initial configuration. These strategies also affect the amount of initial space to be provided, the building footprint, and horizontal adjacencies. Expansion strategies are almost never considered in programming unless architectural concepts are developed simultaneously.

Budgetary Control

At M.D. Anderson Cancer Center the budget was absolute. Increasingly, this is the case with hospitals: There is no margin for error. While the traditional program defines the net and gross square footage required, there are many other factors that affect construction cost. Space determinations at early stages of planning are far from precise. Room net square footage is generally reasonably accurate, but the translation to departmental gross and building gross square footage is increasingly problematical. Building design has a particularly significant effect on building gross square footage. Two designs may vary by 10 percent or more in this translation. The ability to develop a building concept that is known to satisfy programmatic needs and is tested in a three-dimensional sense provides additional assurance that construction budgets established at this stage are achievable.

Circulation and Movement Systems

One of the greatest challenges at M.D. Anderson was to conceptualize and evaluate the major circulation paths along which patients, visitors, supplies, research animals, and waste material moved. The existing hospital had grown over time and circulation systems defied logic. Although the planning team's assignment was to address the specifics of the new addition and proposed backfill, circulation and points of arrival and discharge could not be avoided as an issue. The proposed solution was to create a major new arrival point for patients and visitors, a secondary arrival point for radiation therapy patients, a greatly expanded loading dock to be served by a major new hospital "street" sized for automated vehicles, and new entry and discharge points for animals. This solution affected such criteria as departmental relationships, building cost, and priorities for construction. Had the programming proceeded without a study of building organizational issues, none of these criteria would have been considered until much later in the design process and, as a consequence, the budget would have required a readjustment that would have been destructive to the original project intent.

Building Character and Amenities

Buildings are for people. Traditionally, hospitals are thought of as the doctor's workshop and have been built for technology, not for people—least of all the patient. The result is that user groups relate to what they have experienced—the workshop—and become advocates for more of the same. Programmers reflect what the users tell them, and this often means that no one is the advocate for patients and others who use the building. The architectural designer is trained to act as the advocate for people, including patients, unrepresented in normal user discussions.

The building must be a good neighbor; it must fit in the context of the community and neighborhood in which it is located. It must offer delight. In the case of a hospital, it must provide a sense of reassurance and well-being to those who are frightened or confused. The building is a statement of institutional culture. The building is a work place. There must be consideration of natural light and air, energy consumption, colors, and art. Most of all, there must be a unifying concept to the building, a sense of organization and clarity of structure to it.

At M.D. Anderson, there was a great need to humanize the building. Cancer patients are perhaps the most apprehensive of all who use a hospital. The existing building did nothing to reassure patients or even to simplify the processes to which patients were subject. Early on, the architectural designers on the team became advocates for creating a social gathering place, one that would provide rest and respite for patients and staff alike. This space would also serve as a means of orientation, a place to relate to. Despite rigid budgetary limitations, the president of M.D. Anderson, Dr. Charles A. Le Maistre, embraced the idea and defended the expenditure of money for this amenity throughout the many budgetary battles that ensued. He understood the true purpose of the new building: to create a caring environment.

Concepts of human needs and responses must become an integral part of the program and the project budgeting process for every building. This rarely happens in today's traditional, sequential (two-dimensional) programming process.

A NEW DIRECTION

A tradition has developed that programming should be completed before an architect is hired to develop building concepts. The programmer may be trained as an architect, a hospital administrator, an accountant, or a health planner/statistician. The discipline doesn't matter, as long as the assessments of need are objective and not influenced by an "edifice complex"; that is, a bias to build too much. In health care architecture, the tradition of programming in isolation from building design is misguided. It may be misguided for other building types as well.

There clearly is a specialty of health care programming. The best programmers do not necessarily emerge from the architectural professions, although many of them do. A programmer is not a generalist; it is unlikely that many could design a good hospital without assistance. Architectural design is also a specialty. Most architectural designers are poor programmers. For the M.D. Anderson Cancer Center, collaboration was based on mutual respect. If a traditional, sequential programming process had been used, the results would have been an abstraction with greatly diminished value for the owner. In this case, both programmers and designers came from the same firm, supplemented by an independent programmer. It is not necessary for health care architects to develop in-house programming capability. What is necessary is for both disciplines, design and programming, to be involved simultaneously in the very early, formative stages of project conception. There also needs to be mutual respect for each other's specialization and a close working relationship as an integrated team.

Great buildings come from a collaboration of individuals, each of whom can subordinate their preconceptions and together capture a new vision. The client must be an equal partner in this collaboration. The new possibilities that grow out of this fusion of thoughtful and innovative minds, each with a different perspective, if widely adopted, would quickly elevate health care architecture in the United States to a new level.

ACKNOWLEDGMENTS

Owner:	Charles A. LeMaistre, M.D., President
	Mary Ann Newman, R.N., M.P.H., Project Manager
Architects:	Morris Architects, Houston, Texas
	Stone Marraccini and Patterson, San Francisco, California
Consultants:	Frank Zilm & Associates, Inc., Programming Consultant
	Earl Walls Associates, Research Consultant
	Mulhauser/McCleary Associates, Inc., Food Consultant
	Burns DeLatte & McCoy, Inc., Mechanical and Electrical Consultant
	Busby Denny International, Inc., Cost Estimating
	Walter P. Moore & Associates, Inc., Structural Engineer

References

Arora, Rajeev, Charles Goldsmith, Janet Kraegsl, and Virginia Mousseau. 1974. *Patient care systems*. Philadelphia. J.B. Lippincott Company.

Building Systems Development, Inc., Stone Marraccini Patterson. 1972. *VA hospital building system*. Washington, D.C.: Department of Veterans Affairs.

Carpman, Janet Reizenstein, Myron A. Grant, and Deborah A. Simmons. 1986. *Design that cares: Planning health facilities for patients and visitors*. Chicago: American Hospital Publishing, Inc.

Chi Systems Inc. 1978. Canadian Department of National Health and Welfare, Ottawa: Space Programming Methodology Series.

Fischer, Harry W., M.D. 1982. *Radiology departments: Planning, operation, and management*. Ann Arbor: Edwards Brothers, Inc.

James, W. Paul, and William Tatton-Brown. 1986. *Hospitals design and development*. New York: Van Nostrand Reinhold Company, Inc.

Porter, David R. 1982. *Hospital Architecture: Guidelines for design and renovation*. Ann Arbor: Regents of the University of Michigan.

Tusler, Wilbur. May 1987. "The architecture of future hospitals," *California hospitals*.

Zilm, Frank, and Dennis Brimhall. August 18, 1976. "Ambulatory care survey paves way to the future," *Hospitals*.

Zilm, Frank, and Brooke Hollis. Oct. 1981. "An application of simulation modeling to surgical intensive care bed needs at a university hospital," *The Journal of the Foundation of the American College of Hospital Administrators*, Vol. 28, No. 3.

Zilm, Frank, and Lucy Calderraro. August 16, 1976. "Computer simulation model provides design framework," *Hospitals*.

Zilm, Frank. May, 1991. "Four key decisions in the evolution of a critical care unit," *Critical Care Nursing*, Issue 14, No. 1, pp 9-20.

Zilm, Frank, and Paul Jorgensen. August 1986. "Planning and programming of emergency facilities," *Emergency Medical Services*, Volume 15, Number 7, pp 22B-22H.

Zilm, Frank. Oct. 1981. "Simulation and surgery: Planning a complex service," *Health Care Planning & Marketing*, Vol. 1, No. 3.

Zilm, Frank, and Marie Brown. June 1984. "Simulation of SICU and step down beds," *Healthcare Finance*, Vol. 38, No. 6, pp 26-34.

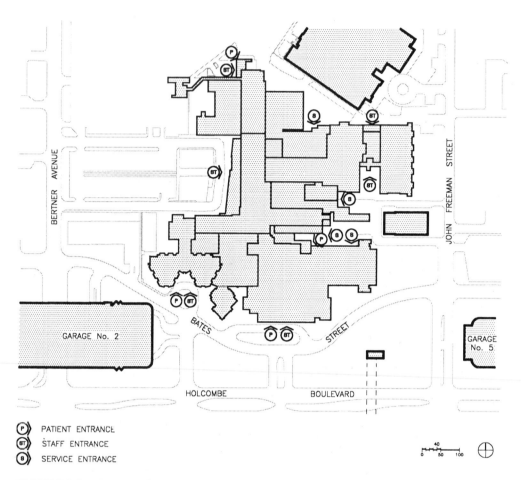

P) PATIENT ENTRANCE
ST) STAFF ENTRANCE
S) SERVICE ENTRANCE

FIGURE 9-1.   Existing Site Plan

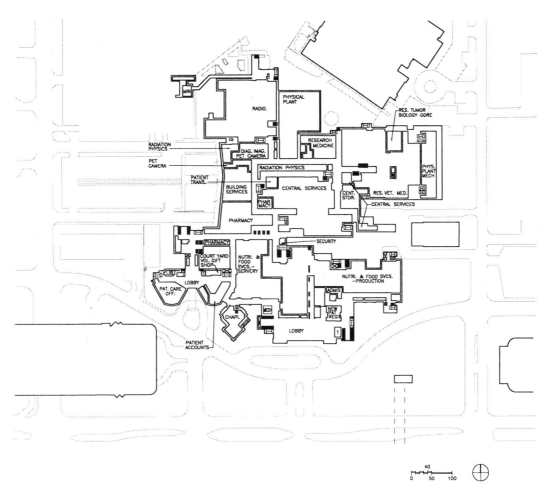

FIGURE 9-2.   Ground Floor Plan

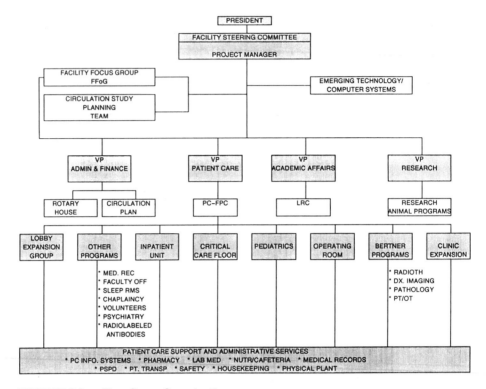

FIGURE 9-3.   User Group Organization

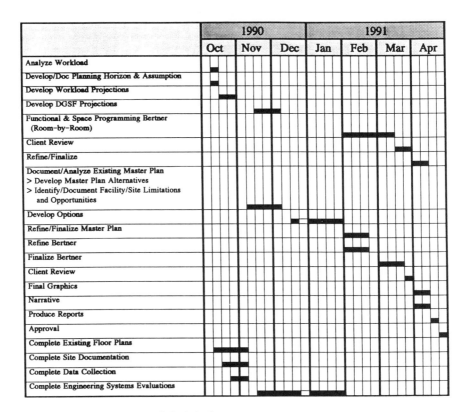

FIGURE 9-4.   Planning Schedule Summary

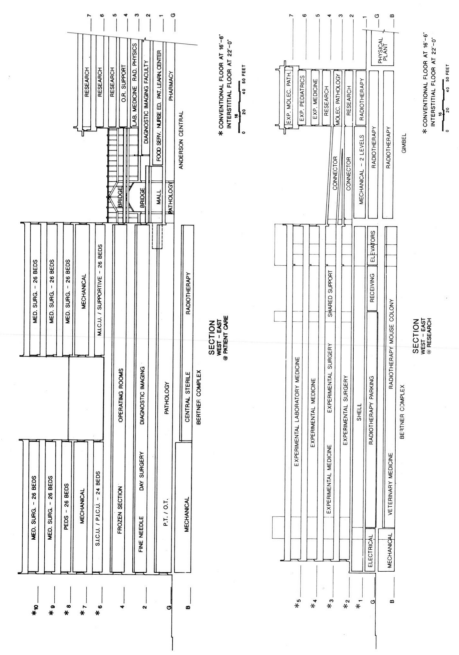

FIGURE 9-5. Building Sections

CHAPTER 10

Programming Processes for Military Health Care Facilities[1]

Clarence E. Maxwell
Dale R. Brown

The U.S. Army has a long, proud history of contributions to health care. From Major Walter Reed's discoveries in controlling yellow fever (1900) to current breakthroughs in AIDS vaccine research, the Army Medical Department has always sought to push the envelope of health research (Haggard, 1989). Likewise, in its contributions to health facility architecture military medicine has also proved influential—from the Roman Legion's military hospitals (*valetudinarium*) in the first century A.D., to Surgeon General James Tilton's "Indian hut" hospital designs during the American Revolutionary War (1777-1781), and Brevet-Lieutenant Colonel John Shaw Billings' (1875-1889) central role in designing the new Johns Hopkins Hospital (Wylie, 1877; Thompson and Goldin, 1975). Although this long tradition of designing health facilities appropriate to the soldier's needs remains a constant, military health facility's project management recently experienced an exhaustive strategic and operational realignment.

A significant and fundamental change in facility planning and management philosophies ensued with the establishment of the U.S. Army Health Facility Planning Agency (HFPA) in 1965. The mandate to establish a dedicated health facility project management command sprang principally from mounting concerns over increases in project cost growth—reaching 15 to 17 percent

---

[1]This chapter reflects the personal opinions of the authors and not the official opinion of the U.S. Army.

per project by the mid-1960s—and from recognition of the design complexities inherent in an exploding health care delivery environment. With its primary mission to counter these challenges, the HFPA assumed both strategic and operational responsibility for the Army's health facilities modernization program. Today, the HFPA oversees a capital investment program for health facility design and construction totaling approximately $1 billion annually, and a facility modernization program encompassing over fifty medical centers and hospitals plus hundreds of health and dental clinics worldwide.

The Army's health facility planning environment may best be compared with that found in a large, civilian hospital management system or health maintenance organization (HMO)—one responsible for operating numerous hospitals and clinics. A key similarity among many of these larger systems is their centralization of health facility planning within the corporate structure. Centralized planning can return substantial benefits in improved designing flexibility, rapid incorporation of new technologies, adaptable financing options, and economies of scale in services and materials procurement. Centralized systems planning also enables programmers to embrace an integrated, life-cycle management approach, which fosters a learning organization and promotes swift implementation of lessons learned from previous and ongoing planning efforts.

However, the military's health planning environment also differs considerably from that of its civilian counterparts. These health planning differences ultimately translate into distinctive military programming and design issue emphases. One major planning and design issue difference relates to the patient types treated in military facilities. For the most part, the Army operates an acute care delivery system wherein patients are younger and healthier and patient stays are generally shorter than in nonmilitary hospitals. Therefore, Army hospital planning and space programming reflects an emphasis on rapid bed turnovers and outpatient, ambulatory care. Military hospitals also differ in their consolidation of medical services. The military physician's office, clinic, and all diagnostic and treatment facilities are available in one location. For this reason the military hospital's ratio of gross square footage to bed averages over four times that of a similar civilian hospital. Further, the Army allocates only one hospital per installation. This single hospital may support a community of soldiers, dependents, and military retirees equal to a medium-sized city. By comparison, the city would typically have more than one hospital, several physicians' office buildings, many outpatient treatment centers, and assorted pharmacies distributed throughout its environs. Additionally, since military health care facilities are located worldwide, their designs must be aesthetically sensitive to the diverse cultural requirements of host nations, as well as structurally responsive to climatic variations ranging from the Arctic Circle to the equatorial belt.

Finally, and most importantly, the Army's health facility management system contrasts with civilian systems in the types and training of personnel on their planning and programming staffs. Since its inception, the Army's Health

Facility Planning Agency has assiduously cultivated a small career field of officers who have become expert in all facets of health facility planning—from programming, design, and construction to health facility operations. By combining a formal education in design with extensive health facility work experiences, the military programmer learns to appreciate unique health facility designing needs. This "people" difference presents a primary strength in the Army's planning approach.

PROGRAMMING METHODOLOGY

Within the Army's system, health facility programming describes a broader scope of activities and emphases than normally found in the civilian architectural community. While military programming similarly results in a tangible product and conforms to a definable timeline, neither the process nor the product stands alone as simply a "pre-design activity." Viewed from the vantage point of a total health delivery management system, programming seems to be a fluid process influencing planning and designing activities across the life-cycle continuum. At the level of the individual project, even though programming appears more an identifiable single stage in the project planning effort, it is not—nor should ever be—an isolated process. Programming's importance cannot be understated. Programming provides a fundamental structure for designing, and effectively defines the users' image of their health care delivery environment. Yet, just as facility programming must respond to practical exigencies in the overall health planning environment, so too health planning processes remain an integral component of the greater military environment—comprising both medical and nonmedical needs and plans (see Figure 10-1). Within the U.S. Army, as with any civilian corporation, plans abound and change endures. Orchestrating individual health facility plans so that they mesh smoothly within an extremely fluid planning environment presents endless challenges for planners and programmers. In order to better explicate military programming processes, the following discussion will briefly examine the effects of programming within life-cycle systems planning, programming's influence on designing, and the impacts of the methods and tools employed by programmers to manage these processes.

Programming Within Life-Cycle Systems Planning

Within the concept of life-cycle systems planning, programming plays a critical role in influencing and supporting all facets of health facility project management. As programming needs realistically manifest—both formally and informally—throughout a facility's operational life, recognizing and proactively managing this phenomenon improves the quality of the designed care-giving environment and garners significant economic savings. In order to exploit these potential returns, however, program management must begin with initial planning efforts and continue throughout the health facility's practical life cycle—from inception through its many renovation and replacement projects. Life-cycle project management provides one of the keys critical to effectively anticipating and efficiently responding in a volatile planning context.

Tracing the various stages in military facility planning may help to clarify the benefits of life-cycle management, and the essential role programming plays at each stage (see Figure 10-2). For a typical Army health facility project, the following planning stages occur (for an expanded discussion, see Brown, 1989):

1. *Monitor and sense project requirements:* Because of a health facility's condition (a function of life safety upgrade requirements, age of the building's systems, and maintenance record), changing health services and technologies, and backlog of designing/programming demands, the local hospital staff, with HFPA assistance, officially requests a construction project.

2. *Conceptually define project:* Based upon the priority of the hospital's needs within the larger health and military planning systems context, a conceptual, or notional, project develops that practically bounds initial programming efforts.

3. *Gather data:* A project manager assumes responsibility for shepherding the project through programming and for overseeing the design effort. The program manager and programmers gather initial project information, to include basic data on workload, staffing, population supported, and alternative sources of health care in the local area. Additionally, every Army hospital operates under the authority of a "mission template." This template details the services mix that the hospital is authorized to provide, and thus those services that the programmer may resource in the design program.

4. *Perform an economic analysis:* The economic analysis assists in formulating project decisions by quantifying the fiscal implications of alternative planning and design solutions. Importantly, economic analyses are conducted at two levels. The first level is an assessment of "should we really do this project," which focuses on the scope of medical services required and the availability of alternate care providers in the hospital's region. The second level, "if we do a project, what is the most cost-effective means," targets comparing strategies such as building new, renovating, adding on, and sharing resources. Programming objectives are further refined in accordance with economic analysis findings.

5. *Develop space program:* The space program evolves from a synthesis of many information sources, including standardized space guidelines, facility-specific operational information, and numerous on-site surveys. For any Department of Defense health facility, the resulting collation of project space requirements becomes identified as the facility's "Program for Design" (PFD).

6. *Design the project:* Following initial programming efforts, the government contracts with a civilian architectural firm to provide concept and working designs. The programming guidance furnished to the architectural firm comprises far more than merely the space program (a discussion of programming documents appears in the next section). From this guidance the architect completes six phased submittals during project development. These submittals increasingly define the project and refine the costs. The hospital staff and their consultants track design formulation, recommending necessary adjustments to the working PFD.

7. *Document the designer's concept of operation:* Throughout the planning process, myriad decisions have been made concerning anticipated hospital operations and their impacts on design, and vice versa. The architects' contract includes a requirement to document their as-designed "concept of operation." In essence this document becomes a users' manual, narrating the architects' design response to programming requirements. This narration proves invaluable, both in terms of integrating hospital operations and in resolving change impacts during construction.

8. *Construct facility:* Throughout the construction period an HFPA health facility planning team remains on-site to continuously review and update plans with the hospital staff. These construction reviews identify new, and missed, needs that directly influence the current program and/or future projects.

9. *Develop users' concept of operation and transition plans:* The on-site facility planning team also initiates user concept of operations and transition planning—both important adjuncts to overall planning and programming processes. The users' concept of operations (C-O) plan details all proposed operational aspects for the hospital in its new facility. Concepts planning begins with the hospital's lowest working levels and progressively broadens to link each level of operations into a network of interdependent relationships. The hospital's transition plan provides directions both for activating the new facility and deactivating the old, to include such obvious requirements as training on new procedures and technologies, moving patients from old to new, and cleaning up at the former facility, and less immediately obvious demands such as formulating new hospital evacuation and mass casualty procedures. In developing C-O and transition plans, myriad problems with working programs and designs may be uncovered.

10. *Occupy and operate the new facility:* Project completion and occupancy mark the beginning of a major adjustment period for hospital operators. The hospital's staff must learn not only to navigate and function efficiently within their new facility, but also to manage the facility's complex environmental and medical support systems. To assist the staff during this normally traumatic transition period, the health facility

planning team remains on-site for approximately six months following opening day. This team not only helps the hospital staff learn to operate within their new facility, it also provides a form of interactive post-occupancy evaluation by assessing building functions during operations and resolving design deficiencies.

11. *Conduct a formal post-occupancy survey:* After at least one year of hospital operations, the HFPA conducts a comprehensive post-occupancy survey. This survey includes observing daily operations, conducting questionnaires and interviews with hospital staff and patients, assessing design functions in accordance with a post-occupancy checklist, analyzing maintenance requirements, and reviewing additional design requests. All successes and failures noted are incorporated as changed planning and programming guidance for future and ongoing projects.

12. *Monitor the facility's condition:* The hospital's operational characteristics and maintenance pattern systematically feed back into the military's life-cycle management system. This final stage in facility planning closes the loop in life-cycle planning—becoming the information resource and catalyst for the first step. Information gathered on each facility's "health" influences specific future projects and the health delivery system in general. Finally, health facility planners assigned to administrative positions in various hospitals are provided with a learning, working experience that further affects the programming process.

Throughout the extended life cycle and project management process, pertinent lessons learned and experiences from other projects—either completed or in design—are expeditiously incorporated. Rather than targeting planning and programming efforts for a single project, the HFPA focuses on improving the quality of individual projects by managing these projects within a life-cycle systems environment. Figure 10-3 illustrates how lessons from individual health facility projects are networked throughout the facility's system managed by the Army Medical Department. Life-cycle management emerges from the belief that a medical facility's design quality acts to empower, or limit, operators in the accomplishment of their health care mission. The programmer interprets the evolving image of the users' environment, and in so doing defines an image that alternately aids or detracts from quality health care delivery. Therefore, programming processes must never be conceptually or operationally isolated from the care-giving environment. Programming forms the first link and affects all subsequent links in designing. There may be no more important component in facility life-cycle planning.

Programming's Influence on Designing

The programmer's fundamental goal remains "simply" to provide the building designer with a document containing comprehensible information regarding the users' needs and desires. Obviously, the more complex the building, the more challenging this effort. A formal definition supporting this conventional depiction of a *program* reads as follows:

> *Program:* a statement prepared by or for an owner, with or without an architect's assistance, setting forth the conditions and objectives for a building project including its general purpose and detailed requirements, such as a complete listing of the rooms required, their size, special facilities. . . . (Harris, 1975)

Unfortunately, while this lexicographer's interpretation objectively details the various elements in a program it misses the more important operations. Programs are purposeful products that function principally as communications tools, translating the users' associational requirements into a language comprehensible by designers. Merely "setting forth the conditions and objectives" discounts the challenges inherent in identifying those requirements and creating reliable translations. The health facility's program must clearly delineate all the conditions intrinsic to a complex health care organization. Quality programming must reflect how an organization will operate, the extent of commitment to competing opportunities, and the constraints that will be imposed on future operations. Reconciling the health care delivery team's skills, as well as patients' needs and expectations, must underlie the programming effort. Additionally, as military health facilities operate within the context of a much larger health care system, the program must reflect the role the individual facility component plays in this larger system. While architects and their consultants may be capable of independently synthesizing sufficient information to produce a generalized design program, no one can better define critical operational relationships than the hospital's staff. However, neither the architect nor the hospital operator possesses the experience necessary to incorporate these diverse operational demands within the health system's strategic context. The scope and types of involvement necessary to produce quality programs, which consolidate all these need levels, requires employment of "in-house" programmers with specialized training and experiences, programmers who can practically coordinate and facilitate the essential dialogue between users and designers that must carry through all phases of design and construction.

Programming Methods and Tools

Methods and tools employed in military health facility planning may be separated into two functional categories—those having to do with people, and those supporting systematic assessment. People tools and methods are basically those learned and inherited skills that enable individuals to perform certain expert, tool-like functions in a specific setting. Assessment tools and methods are the many technologies that act to strengthen expert functioning; for example, user surveys and guideplates. Clearly, people tools are inefficient without assessment, and assessment tools are useless without people. However, a management philosophy that recognizes the fundamental differences and similarities of the two enhances effective, normative interventions.

The one ingredient crucial to producing and managing reliable health facility programs remains the selective acquisition and training of people. For people to function as expert programming tools, they must thoroughly understand a health facility's needs and possess the skills essential to produce operational as well as facility design solutions. In designing single-family dwellings, some architects advocate moving in with the client in order to gain a more thorough understanding of how the client lives and what they need from their home. The HFPA exercises a similar yet expanded philosophy. Individuals selected to become health facility planners are chosen initially based on their personal preference for such work and their having an educational background closely aligned with facility planning and construction (architecture, engineering, construction management). With these core skills, planners are then assigned to diverse administrative positions in health facilities throughout the Army's system.

Army officers move—worldwide—every four years or less. During these moves, planners rotate through increasingly responsible positions: within health care facilities, on health facility construction projects, and into programming and project management positions. These deliberate rotations are intended to furnish planners with the type of intimate insights into health care operations that will refine their health facility planning skills, and develop those leadership traits essential in all military officers. Additionally, military health facility planners are also afforded opportunities to obtain graduate-level education. Often planners elect to pursue graduate degrees in hospital or business administration. Combining graduate-level administration with an architecture or engineering background provides an excellent educational foundation for facility planners. Education and work experience, however, must complement one another. Quality programming and designing requires a corporate commitment to providing planners with diverse job exposures: Operate it, plan it, build it, and then operate or plan another.

By the very nature of his or her professional exposure, the military health facility planner/programmer becomes a health care system integrator. The facility planner's expertise with health systems' operations provides the Army with additional critical analysis skills. The commitment to an internal development of health facility planners provides the Army's Medical Department with dedicated people equipped to recognize and manage the system's effects intrinsic to complex health planning decisions. The health facility planner learns to perceive the interrelationship of departments, services, support functions, and circulation within the hospital by experiencing firsthand such everyday hospital routines as patient flow, the resupply of clinics and wards, committee meetings, and staff and patient complaints. Having been immersed in hospital operations, military planners also recognize how programming decisions influence the extended health care planning system. Trained programmers learn the impacts of widely divergent issues, and while they are never able to resolve them all, their programming efforts will be superior because of their appreciation of these crucial relationships.

Another key element in crafting reliable people tools is the facility's users. Because planners involve users in every facet of programming activities, and since users furnish the program's developmental environment, realistically users must be integrated into our kit of people tools. This philosophy may appear discordant, since by definition people tools are intended to bridge the perceptual gap between users and designers. However, during program formulation users not only provide necessary contextual data, but they begin to distinguish and express those data as designing information—they learn to program. Initial programming activities are typically characterized by their strict tripartite arrangement of players—users, programmers, and designers, with programmers squarely in the middle. By exploiting participatory designing processes, however, programmers begin to negate these early divisions. Programming efforts coalesce into an enhanced team approach wherein users assist designers in identifying design alternatives, and designers suggest operational changes based on specific design options. Users become adept at better analyzing their own needs, and thus perform as people tools.

Finally, functional area consultants serve as a critical force-multiplier in the Army's health facility planning management system. Although facility planners and programmers strive to perfect a broad understanding of health care operations, there remains a continuing demand for expert insights into specific health care needs and operations. Functional area consultants assist military programmers in meeting these demands. The most qualified specialists in the Army Medical Department—from logistics to nuclear medicine—are assigned the additional, and prestigious, duty of being a consultant to the Surgeon General. These experts are available to support Army programmers on an as-needed basis. Planners and programmers involve consultants in the development of initial project criteria, program documents, equipment selection, and in architectural plan review. While not members of the HFPA, users and consultants offer a unique opportunity to augment our kit of people tools.

Assessment tools are those standardized technologies that not only support programming environment assessment but also translate identified requirements into useful designer information. Educating the designer must be both a comprehensive and an interactive venture. In order to make informed decisions, the designer must have access to all pertinent information, and an open means of communicating concerns about this information. While the HFPA promotes open and timely communications through its emphasis on integrating people tools, programming comprehensiveness results from our employing a broad-brush approach in supporting programming guidance with numerous, diverse assessment tools. The following list provides brief descriptions of the principal assessment-communications tools used in defining programming requirements. Notably, while every tool underwent extensive development and testing prior to being implemented, each remains flexible, adapting in response to evaluative feedback. Effectively and efficiently bonding people and assessment tools defines the basic methodology employed in military health facility programming.

- *The Project Summary:* describes the project in macro terms using a narrative and programmed dollar amounts. This concise document also defines the scope of congressional authorization and appropriation for the project.
- *The Program for Design (PFD):* lists each space to be designed, as well as the equipment, and numbers and types of personnel that will occupy the space (Figure 10-4, Space Planning Criteria, and Figure 10-5, sample PFD).
- *The Medical Design Guide (U.S. Army Technical Manual 5-838-2):* documents both general and specific guidance, to include a departmental relationship matrix, minimum noise and illumination standards, HVAC requirements, and room finish data (Figure 10-6, generic Relationship Matrix).
- *The Guide Plates Set:* provides plans for 101 typical room types found in a military hospital. This set furnishes exemplars for most space requirements documented in the PFD. While the architect's design for each room does not have to equal the guide plate, it must support the functional intent (Figure 10-7, sample Guide Plate Plan, and Figure 10-8, Guide Plate Matrix Data).
- *The Equipment List:* includes data on all medical and nonmedical equipment to be installed into the facility, to include identification of utility requirements for each item.
- *Technical Manuals (TMs) and Engineer Technical Letters (ETLs):* contain detailed information concerning diverse building systems' designs. For example, one such manual details various ways to design a dental oral evacuation system.
- *The Installation's Design Guide:* delineates the project installation's aesthetic goals, and provides performance data on finishes, exterior signage, landscaping, building massing, etc.
- *The Installation's Master Plan:* supplies information on near- and long-term changes in the installation's facility and infrastructure planning. From this, the architect may discern future changes having impacts on the proposed hospital.
- *Guidance on Issue Resolution:* informs the architect about mechanisms for timely resolution of those problem issues inherent in complex health projects.

CASE STUDY OVERVIEW

In the military design environment, as with other multihospital management groups, programming activities continue uninterrupted. Programming teams, at any given moment, are initiating, formulating, and concluding diverse programs for health care projects worldwide. Within the Army's health planning environment, even though each hospital retains its site-specific uniqueness, all projects are managed as interdependent components in a synoptic health care delivery system. Managing individual projects as a system's component facilitates efficient use of designing resources, and ensures that failures and triumphs of the one can be swiftly exploited to aid the many. Given this interconnectedness of programming processes, a credible case study must look across the system to compare and contrast projects in various stages of execution. The following truncated analysis assumes this approach by examining programming activities for three separate medical center projects. When gathering data on these projects, we first reviewed all the available documentation concerning their development, and, where possible, consulted with those programmers, designers, and hospital personnel involved in the projects. Then, through discussions with other programmers, we compared our case study data with observations from their broader experiences. In analyzing the data, we were most interested in exposing qualitative knowledge; with understanding realistic trends and commonalities rather than creating statistical contrivances. Our research goals went beyond merely substantiating what we knew "worked" to focus on probing the foundation of our programming processes. Therefore, when examining project data, we primarily sought new insights into such questions of process and flow as "What is programming?"; "How, and where, does programming fit within the greater design environment?"; and, "What makes a 'good' program?" By examining these types of questions, we tried to construct a descriptive model of our planning environment that would provide directions for resolving "wicked" programming problems, and would practically support normative, instrumental improvements to our methods (Rittel, 1970; Rittel, 1973).

The first programming case study examined a major renovation and addition project to modernize the 500-bed Tripler Army Medical Center (originally constructed in 1948) located on the island of Oahu, Hawaii (Figure 10-9). Although planning for the Hawaii project began in 1975, final dedication and occupancy of Phase III renovations did not occur until the spring of 1991. This extended design and construction schedule resulted from numerous mission-oriented scope changes, and from both medical and economic demands that necessitated maintaining complete health care delivery services during construction. The second project considered provides a 450-bed replacement facility for the San Antonio, Texas, Brooke Army Medical Center (whose last major renovation occurred in the 1930s and 1940s) (Figure 10-10). Design planning for the Texas hospital began in 1980. However, similar to the Hawaii project, initial programming was not concluded until 1985. Furthermore, in response to compelling economic considerations, programming and design activities were extended through 1991. Project completion and occupancy for the Texas facility are now scheduled for 1995 and 1996. The third case study project will provide a 323-bed medical center upgrade to replace Womack Community Hospital (1958 York and Sawyer plan) at Fort Bragg, North Carolina (Figure 10-11). Programming for the North Carolina project was initiated in 1988, but, because of dramatically changed strategic and operational requirements following political upheavals in Eastern Europe, major program revisions continued through 1991. Design completion and construction award for this final project are now expected in 1993, with a beneficial occupancy in 1997.

Although all three projects are comparable in scope—each being a large, tertiary care and medical teaching facility—they remain distinct in both site characteristics and programming stage. Additionally, all have an interesting, yet decidedly not unique, similarity: Throughout project development, each was significantly affected by national and international policy changes. These policy shifts caused planners to redefine operational missions and economic priorities, which resulted in iterative programming efforts. While these external changes had perceived "negative" impacts, they provide worthwhile exemplars of the necessity for exploiting flexible programming methodologies and design management systems—systems that can keep pace with meteoric sociopolitical, economic, and technological changes.

CASE STUDY ANALYSIS

What is Programming?

From our previous discussion, *programming* may be described "simply" as the processes employed in formulating the program, while the *program* comprises the collated and translated needs and desires of the user-client population presented as a narrative and/or graphic exposition. However, from our observations, the program also effectively functions as the programmer's extended memory, as a delimiting communications tool that informs designers about user requirements, and as a "transcribed image" resulting from shared "sense making" (Boulding, 1956; Forester, 1985; and Cuff, 1991). This "pre-design" documentation incorporates fundamental contextual information critical to guiding the diverse activities of numerous design disciplines. Thus, for the program to practically communicate the user's full range of requirements, the *programmer* must be expert at implementing processes similar to those required of the "knowledge engineer." The programmer must be expert not only at synthesizing disparate—and often seemingly unrelated—user data, but also at translating these data into practical, "designer-friendly" information. Data synthesis and translation, however, often prove remarkably challenging, especially for health care facility programmers. While health care providers (one level of facility user) have a conceptual image of what they need, they typically realize, and communicate, this image in associational terms, such as: "I must be able to transport emergency room patients quickly and safely to radiology" and, "My exam room must be large enough to comfortably position all my medical equipment around the patient." Designers, on the other hand, structure their mental image in perceptual terms, wherein gross versus net square footage, vertical versus horizontal transportation systems, and massing relations have meaning (Rapoport, 1982). The programmer supplies the critical requirements translation between the two—here, "Top priority on the adjacency matrix for emergency room and radiology," and "Emergency exam rooms will be minimum 100 sq/ft., with minimum 4'0''-clear circulation space around exam tables." Like the design program, drawings and specifications act to communicate the designer's perceptual image of the user's associational needs. These designer communication tools also furnish evaluative findings regarding programming effectiveness. The quality of the programming effort may be measured not only by the programmer's ability to integrate and translate the objective substance, but also by the subjective nuance of the user's image into a language commensurate with the designer's processes and professional vocabulary (Kuhn, 1970).

How, and Where, Does Programming *Fit* Within the Greater Design Environment?

We evaluated this question in two stages; first by analyzing data related to the life cycle of the three case study hospitals, and then by comparing those findings with standards of practice in the design community. From our previous description of programming, whenever users experience change—altered mission, expanding staff, new procedures and/or technologies—that necessitates modifications to their physical environment, then programming must occur. Regardless of whether the resultant program consists of a crude, handwritten sheet or a 100-page formal document, someone must intercede as a "programmer" to record and translate the users' associational descriptions into practical design programs. Figure 10-12 depicts a composite trend graph of potential programming requirements and representative change influences extant during one portion of a health care facility's life cycle. Although a number of interesting observations may be made concerning this graph, because of space constraints, only two will be presented here. First, the hospital's functional life cycle obviously exceeds that of any portion of its physical plant. In other words, the hospital "lives on" in various physical forms from its inception, through minor repairs, major renovations, and replacements, until the day the "hospital" ceases to function. Second, at no time during the hospital's life cycle have all the requirements for physical change been met. For example, even at a replacement facility's dedication, additional design projects are being considered and executed to modify the new space—justifiably, a hospital's designing demands are never satisfied.

What conclusions may be drawn from these basic observations specific to programming's "fit"? Clearly, throughout the hospital's functional life cycle, designing requirements, and thus programming activities, never cease. Practically, programming, designing, and constructing continue apace; each augments and flows through the other without any "natural" interruptions. Therefore, programming fits and has an impact everywhere within the processes encompassed by the greater design environment. Yet, when comparing the hospital's diachronic flow of physical change requirements to the synchronic interventions of modern design praxis, there appears a disjoint. Even though the hospital "evolves" ceaselessly we typically pursue design interventions by slicing across the hospital's growth continuum with artificially compartmentalized processes.[2] Basically, we perform like the surgeon who undertakes a radical invasive procedure with little regard for the patient's history or future—this is both irresponsible and potentially dangerous. Perhaps, in order to "efficiently" identify physical requirements and create a cost-effective product, programmers and designers realistically must check the flow of change; they must arbitrarily determine a point at which program changes cease. In doing so, however, they ensure that their final products—programs, designs, and facilities—will never fully satisfy, or even *satisfice,* the user's needs (March and Simon, 1958).

Programming must be more than merely some stand-alone "pre-design" activity. As change continues unabated, so too programming must proceed uninterrupted. Every program issue reacts as an interdependent node within the greater programming environment, and each synergistically affects other issue nodes throughout the design decision network. Therefore, programming efforts, and designing decisions, must realistically be managed as temporal, typically impermanent constructs rather than artificially controlled end products. The numerous ad hoc programming requirements developed throughout the hospital's life cycle—including those following the programmer's "efficient" change deadline—represent the hospital's rational response to a relentlessly evolving operational environment. From the hospital staff's viewpoint, any isolated design intervention attempting to provide for all their needs must appear to be simply some designer's fantasy. The staff "knows" that in an explosive health care environment, programming and designing needs cannot practically be partitioned into neat, insulated packages without negatively affecting quality patient care. Thus, any model purporting to be descriptive of health care programming processes must account for the dynamics of change. Unfortunately, *change*—normally equated with cost overruns and delayed projects—remains the antithesis of efficient, economically sound designing.

What Makes a "Good" Program?

From the previous discussion, a "good" program seems to be one that recognizes change as inevitable, and incorporates flexible methods to transmute negative aspects such that change facilitates, rather than inhibits, responsible designing. Our next question then becomes, "Do the case study data identify

---

[2]The architectural profession typically segments the phases of *designing* into discrete, artificial categories. For example, the American Institute of Architects clearly separates programming from other designing activities, such as design, construction, and post-occupancy evaluation, in their published definitions of functional relationships and payment schedules, and in references to professional prestige—all other than *design* being alternate careers for architects (AIA *Profile* 1989-90; Readers Poll, *Progressive Architecture,* October 1990).

means to support practical, normative procedures that would promote *good* change-oriented programming?" Change was a major factor in all three case study projects—change caused by diverse influences such as political pressures, fluctuating strategic and operational missions, evolving medical technologies, economic uncertainties, and numerous other internal and external factors. In fact, the most consistent trait in every project's programming environment was that change was certain. Figure 10-13 illustrates some of the effects various change types had on project development. Please note that those depicted represent only a small sampling of the myriad changes—both minor and major—that directly influenced programming. In analyzing the case study data, and from extensive discussions with other programmers, three programming techniques appear to have had the greatest positive impacts on "good" program management in a change-intensive environment: integrated life-cycle management (discussed earlier), participatory decision preparing, and the concept of operations planning.

First, effective programming and designing cannot be realized in a conceptual vacuum. *Participatory decision preparing*, like participatory design, acts as a catalyst transforming conceptual vacuums into ideation generators. Realistically, a "symmetry of ignorance" exists between the many necessary "experts" on a design team, to include the hospital's staff and patients (Rittel, 1989). While none knows everything, all know something. Given this "symmetry," designing processes must begin with the "Principle of Idoniety"—wherein designers follow "a method of intellectual inquiry through dialogue" (Protzen, 1981). Programmers who understood and exercised these underlying principles reaped significant benefits in dynamic change environments. On those projects where participatory programming and designing processes were promoted, change was more often anticipated, and negative effects ameliorated. Involving as many experts as practical in programming improved every phase of problem formulation, analysis, and evaluation. User experts not only provided critical design information, but they also foresaw likely change, and proposed reliable designing alternatives. Further, resulting from their involvement, users voluntarily shared accountability for both programming processes and decision formulation. Within the military's programming environment, participatory decision preparing remains a strength.[3] On each of the case study projects, programming teams worked extensively with users using surveys, interviews, and countless small-group sessions to inform and assist users in understanding and developing their program requirements. These efforts established a solid working rapport, which—even when stressed by a seemingly capricious environment—allowed programmers and users to swiftly respond to volatile changes.

---

[3]Contrary to popular perceptions, the military system encourages broad-based participation in the decision-preparing phase of decision-making processes. Although, typically, the final decision may be rendered by an individual or small group of leaders—similar to most civilian corporate structures—decision-preparing involves many levels of worker participation.

The second effective change management technique involved an emphasis on establishing and integrating the user's *concept of operations (C-O) plan*. Even though during initial planning hospitals typically have prepared "standard operating procedures" for current functions, they normally have none for their new facility. Promoting reliable C-O planning should be a top programming priority. However, before programmers can persuade the users to creatively plan new operational procedures, they must overcome considerable organizational inertia. Most users envision their new facility as merely some reasonable facsimile of the old one—with new paint. Instead of planning innovative ways to improve current operations, users often assume that they will simply transfer their old procedures into new spaces. Effective C-O planning induces users to consider entirely new operational alternatives, and to practically integrate these with other hospital operations. The C-O plans that users create are comprehensive documents that exhaustively record and interconnect every conceivable issue related to the hospital's proposed operations in its new environment. C-O planning begins at the lowest working level and expands upward, with each supervisory layer above collating and cross-referencing their group's C-Os until a consolidated hospitalwide plan emerges that addresses and links all aspects of daily operations. This consolidated plan may be used by the hospital to ensure that anticipated operations are consistent with strategic goals and missions, assess impact relationships across working groups, determine new supply-level requirements, orient incoming personnel, and address a multitude of other purposes. Notably, C-Os are never static; they remain a living document. In order to remain credible, operational concepts must be constantly reviewed and modified to coincide with current and anticipated standards of practice. Equally important, C-O planning provides the programmer with specific "directions" concerning future operations. These directions expedite identifying design-specific data, and significantly enhance program translation efforts. Furthermore, when change occurs—whether as a result of internal demands or external pressures—not only can the programmer and user then differentiate specific impacts caused by the change, but they can also rapidly assess modifications required to bring the system back into dynamic equilibrium.

In summary, where change remains inevitable, and the price of change—realized in both dollars and design team and user frustration—can cause significant problems, finding effective methods to mitigate negative aspects can provide appreciable returns. Figure 10-14 graphically illustrates how exploiting both participatory decision preparing and user concept of operations planning modulates the negative impacts of change. Advantages for programming processes may include greater, and more reliable, problem formulation; decision preparation based on multiple heuristic and empirical analyses; enhanced impacts tracking within the network of linked project issues; realistic assessments of proposed design alternatives; designers and users "buying in" to process functions and outcomes; and swift response to time-sensitive changes.

Potential disadvantages include a steep learning curve for all participants, initial expense in time and design team resources, and a fundamental reluctance within the professional community toward participatory designing. Each of these advantages and disadvantages was evidenced in the case study data.

While programmers and design managers on every hospital project pursued comprehensive participatory processes, all procedures could have been improved. For example, even though programmers involved users in all designing stages, preliminary program questionnaires and design concept drawings were too often simply mailed to the hospital staff for their response. While seeming to involve users, surveys and drawings that are forwarded without the benefit of an on-site interpreter serve only to confuse and frustrate processing. The answers received are typically partial responses that may or may not address the programmer's intent. The resources saved in sending unaccompanied design materials are expended many times over when attempting to translate the users' enigmatic responses into recognizable design information. Surveys and drawings are already once-removed facsimiles of their originator's image. Survey responses merely add another level of distortion. Finally, while at each case study project initiating and integrating C-O plans was a priority, their timing within design processes missed the mark. C-Os for each project were begun too late in the design cycle. In order to fully profit from the extensive, necessary information available in the C-O plan, the plan's inauguration should precede programming. Users—with programmer and designer assistance—should develop a thoroughly integrated operations plan that addresses their anticipated needs *before* the programmer begins asking design-oriented questions.

CONCLUSIONS

The U.S. Army enjoys a volume of work that supports a permanent planning staff as well as the development and maintenance of a rigorous, synoptic planning methodology. Notably, the volume of work and the methodology provide for a corporate environment that continuously learns. Open communication channels and available expertise foster product and process improvements. Centralized planning promotes appropriate standardization and systems analysis while allowing the individual hospital's charter and needs to be reflected in unique designs. A planning staff possessing both facility operation and construction project experience improves communication and translation efforts between health care clinicians, architects, and the construction disciplines. A multiple-health facility system permits comparative analysis of programming activities. Additionally, and most importantly, because a single planning staff manages the project from inception through post-occupancy inspection, lessons learned can be expeditiously transferred between programming efforts.

When analyzing the case study projects, we tried to address qualitative questions of process and flow. Exploiting these analyses, we devised a practical, descriptive model of our programming environment. This model emphasizes the interminable nature of programming requirements and the practical melding of programming and design processes, and incorporates change as a realistic consequence of a dynamic health care delivery setting. However, we also strove to distinguish tenable, normative adjustments that could improve programming processes. The three process variables identified as affording the most potential for improved programming were participatory decision preparing, user concept of operations planning, and facility life-cycle programming. Fully formulating definitive modifications to exercise these normative opportunities exceeds the scope of this chapter. Nevertheless, briefly, our proposed adjustments shall include the following: programmers and designers will receive additional, formal training in methods for anticipating and managing change requirements through enhanced participatory decision preparing; user concept of operations planning will be elaborated and, more critical, repositioned at the start of our design cycle to ensure optimizing beneficial effects; and we shall develop new programming, and designing philosophies and methods that fully address the hospital's entire functional life cycle, such that our design interventions practically augment—rather than artificially constrain—the hospital's rational change pattern.

References

American Institute of Architects. 1989-90. *Profile.* Washington, D.C.: American Institute of Architects.

Boulding, Kenneth. 1956. *The image.* Ann Arbor: University of Michigan Press.

Brown, Dale R. 1989. *Health facility project officer's manual: Guidelines and procedures for managing the design and construction of health care facilities.* Washington, D.C.: Office of the Surgeon General.

Cuff, Dana. 1991. *Architecture: The story of practice.* Cambridge: The MIT Press.

DOD 4270.1-M: Construction criteria manual. 1983. Washington, D.C.: Department of Defense.

Forester, John. 1985. Designing: Making sense together in practical conversations. *Journal of architectural education* 38:3, pp. 14-20.

Haggard, Howard W. 1989. *The doctor in history.* New York: Dorset Press.

Harris, Cyril M. (ed). 1975. *Dictionary of architecture and construction.* New York: McGraw-Hill.

Kuhn, Thomas. 1970. *The structure of scientific revolutions,* 2d ed. Chicago: University of Chicago Press.

March, James G., and Herbert A. Simon. 1958. *Organizations.* New York: John Wiley & Sons.

MIL-STD-1691C: Construction and material schedule for military medical and dental facilities. 1986. Washington, D.C.: Department of Defense.

Protzen, Jean-Pierre. 1981. Reflections on the fable of the caliph, the ten architects and the philosopher. *Journal of architectural education* 34:No. 4, pp. 3-8.

Rapoport, Amos. 1982. *The meaning of the built environment.* London: Sage Publications.

Readers poll: Alternatives to traditional practice. 1990. *Progressive architecture* 10:90, pp. 59-61.

Rittel, Horst W.J. 1970. On the planning crisis: Systems analysis of the first and second generations. In *Bedriftsokonomen* 8, pp. 35-41; republished by the Institut für Grundlagen der Planung, Universität Stuttgart, 1977.

Rittel, Horst W.J. 1989. Personal notes from a lecture delivered at the Department of Architecture, University of California, Berkeley.

Rittel, Horst W.J., and Melvin Weber. 1973. Planning problems are wicked problems. In *Policy sciences* 4, pp. 155-69; reprinted in Nigel Cross (ed). 1984. *Developments in design methodology.* New York: John Wiley & Sons.

Thompson, John D., and Grace Goldin. 1975. *The hospital: A social and architectural history.* New Haven, Conn.: Yale University Press.

U.S. Army technical manual 5-838-2: Army health facility design. 1990. Washington, D.C.: Headquarters, Department of the Army.

Wylie, Gill W., M.D. 1877. *Hospitals: Their history, organization, and construction.* New York: D. Appleton and Company.

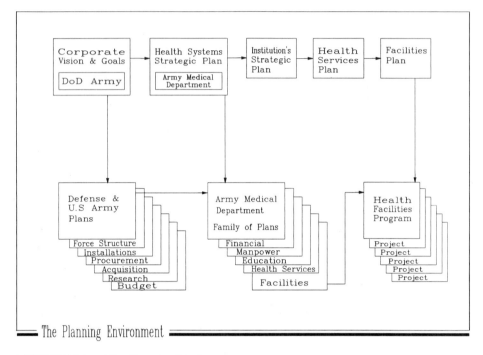

FIGURE 10-1. The Planning Environment

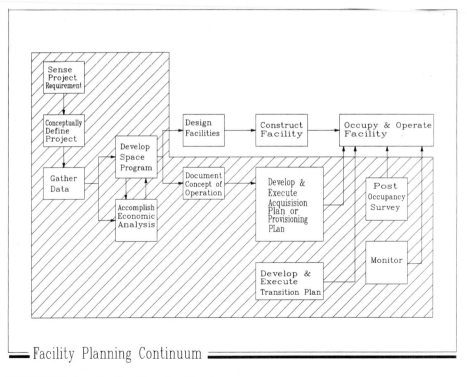

FIGURE 10-2. Facility Planning Continuum

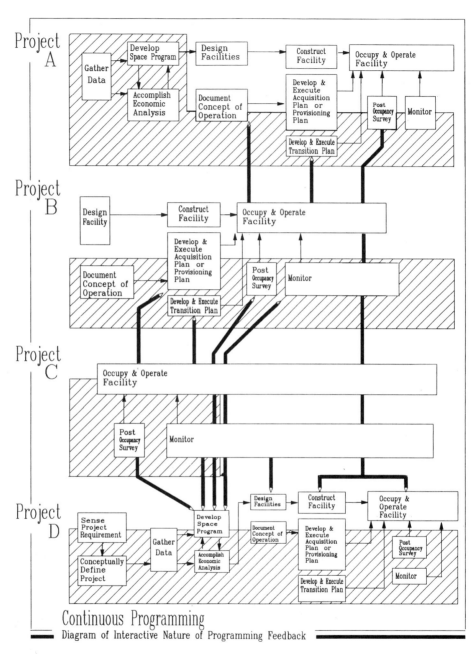

FIGURE 10-3.   Continuous Programming—The Interactive Nature of Programming Feedback

```
FUNCTIONAL   CRITERIA - OUTPATIENT   CLINICAL   SERVICES
Function                              NSF              Planning Range
Pediatric Clinic                      Authorized       Comments

a. Adolescent -      A separate adolescent clinic will be
                     programmed when justified by work load.

        Doctor's Office   100       1 per doctor programmed

        Exam Room         100       2 per doctor programmed

b. Pediatric -

        Waiting/Play       16       per space
        Area               25       per handicapped space
                                     4.3 spaces per exam or
                                     treatment room 5% of total
                                     space dedicated to
                                     handicapped

        Toy Storage       100       1 per clinic

        Patient Toilet
            Male           50        20 NSF per fixture and 10
                                     NSF for counter w/sink for
            Female         50        diaper change

        Isolation Suite
        Isolation Waiting 100       1 per clinic

        Isolation Toilet   50        20 NSF per fixture and 10
                                     NSF for counter w/sink for
                                     diaper change
                                     1 per clinic

        Isolation Exam    100       1 per clinic

        Treatment Room    150       1 per 8 doctors

        Nurse Pract. Off  100       1 per nurse

        Exam Room         100       2 per practitioner
                                     programmed

        Weights and       200       1 per clinic
        Measures Room

        Vision & Hearing/  80       1 per clinic
        Screening Room
```

Space Planning Criteria
(Example)

FIGURE 10-4.   Space Planning Criteria

```
280100 ADMINISTRATION
                              NO OF   UNIT    NET     GROSS # OF
LN NO   RM NO SPACE           SPACES  AREA    AREA    AREA PERS    REMARKS
280101  OFC06 CH DEPT OF PEDS   1     140.0   140.0    1 70,000 ANNUAL VISITS PROJECTED        EA 67,175
                                                                     FY84    FY85    FY86    FY88    FY89
                                                         PEDS       51858   52628   41168   38924   46000
                                                         WELL BABY   5051    6119    5771    7451    7400
                                                         EFMP                        3691   10665   11600
                                                         TOTAL      56909   58747   50630   57040   64000
                                                       CHAMPUS RECOVERY FROM 2100 BIRTHS TO 2900 BIRTHS
                                                       IMMUNIZATIONS FROM 37000 TO 40000
280102  SECTY SECRETARY/WAITING  1    120.0   120.0    1
280104  OFF01 NCOIC'S OFFICE     1    100.0   100.0    1
280107  OFF01 ADMIN OFFICE       1    160.0   160.0    2
280109  OFF01 NURSE'S OFFICE     1    100.0   100.0    1
-------------------------------------------------------------------------------
280100  ADMINISTRATION   TOTAL   5            620.0   1045    6


280200 TREATMENT
                              NO OF   UNIT    NET     GROSS # OF
LN NO   RM NO SPACE           SPACES  AREA    AREA    AREA PERS    REMARKS
280201  EXR09 EXAM ROOM         24    100.0  2400.0    0 INCLUDES SPACE FOR FAM PRAC RESIDENT/NURSE PRACTIONERS
                                                         LOCATE 2 EXAM ROOMS ADJACENT TO RECEPTION FOR TRIAGE PHYSICIAN.
280203  OFFD1 DOCTOR'S OFFICE    9    100.0   900.0    9
280205  OFFNC PED NURSE PRACT    3    100.0   300.0    3
-------------------------------------------------------------------------------
280200  TREATMENT        TOTAL  36           3600.0   6069   12


280300 SUPPORT
                              NO OF   UNIT    NET     GROSS # OF
LN NO   RM NO SPACE           SPACES  AREA    AREA    AREA PERS    REMARKS
280301  CR200 CONFERENCE ROOM    1    300.0   300.0    0 SUPPORTS PATIENT/RESIDENT TEACHING
280303  CU120 Clean Utility Rm   1    150.0   150.0    0
280305  JANCL Janitor's Closet   1     40.0    40.0    0
280307  LR015 STAFF LOCKERS      1     80.0    80.0    0 12 LOCKERS AT 6.5 NSF EACH
280311  LM060 Lit/Whlchr Strg    1     40.0    40.0    0
280313  SL200 Staff Lounge       1    200.0   200.0    0
280315  SR100 Equipment Storage  1    100.0   100.0    0
280317  SUCLI Soiled Utl/Trash   1    120.0   120.0    0
280319  TH110 STAFF TOILET, F    1     50.0    50.0    0 1 LAV 1 WC
280321  TH11M STAFF TOILET, M    1     50.0    50.0    0 1 LAV 1 WC
280323  TC211 TOILET PUBLIC, M   1    130.0   130.0    0 2 LAV 1 WC 1 URINAL PLUS A DIAPER CHANGING AREA
280325  TC220 TOILET PUBLIC, F   1    130.0   130.0    0 2 LAV 2 WC PLUS A DIAPER CHANGING AREA
280329  REC01 RECEPTION          1    150.0   150.0    0
-------------------------------------------------------------------------------
280300  SUPPORT          TOTAL  13           1540.0   2631    0


280500 PEDIATRIC
                              NO OF   UNIT    NET     GROSS # OF
LN NO   RM NO SPACE           SPACES  AREA    AREA    AREA PERS    REMARKS
280501  SPC22 WAITING/PLAY AREA  1   1090.0  1090.0    0 60 SEATS AT 16 NSF PLUS 2 SPACES AT 25 NSF FOR HANDICAP
                                                         AND 80 NSF FOR PLAY AREA
280503  SR100 Toy Storage        1    100.0   100.0    0
280509  HR007 Isol Suite/Wait    1    100.0   100.0    0
280511  TC110 ISOLATION TOILET   1     60.0    60.0    0 INCLUDES DIAPER CHANGING AREA
280513  EXR09 Isolation Exam Rm  1    100.0   100.0    0
280515  TRT06 Treatment Room     1    150.0   150.0    0
280517  SPC15 HEIGHT & MEAS RM   1    200.0   200.0    0
280519  SPT34 Vision & Hear Scr  1     80.0    80.0    0
280523  SPT01 IMMUNIZATION AREA  1    200.0   200.0    0 40,000 ANNUAL IMMUNIZATIONS PROJECTED
280524  SPC06 IMMUN HOLDING      1    100.0   100.0    0
-------------------------------------------------------------------------------
280500  PEDIATRIC        TOTAL  10           2180.0   3674    2


280900 WELL BABY
                              NO OF   UNIT    NET     GROSS # OF
LN NO   RM NO SPACE           SPACES  AREA    AREA    AREA PERS    REMARKS
280901  REC01 SUB-CONTROL        1    100.0   100.0    0
280903  WR019 WAITING ROOM       1    400.0   400.0    0 25 SEATS
280905  NUS11 FEEDING ROOM       1    100.0   100.0    0
280907  TC110 TOILET M           1     60.0    60.0    0 1 LAV 1 WC 1 DIAPER CHANGING AREA
280909  TC110 TOILET F           1     60.0    60.0    0 1 LAV 1 WC 1 DIAPER CHANGING AREA
-------------------------------------------------------------------------------
280900  WELL BABY        TOTAL   5            720.0   1214    0


281100 EFMP
                              NO OF   UNIT    NET     GROSS # OF
LN NO   RM NO SPACE           SPACES  AREA    AREA    AREA PERS    REMARKS
281109  ///// OFFICE SCREENING   3    100.0   300.0    3
281111  ///// WAITING            1    208.0   208.0    0 13 SEATS
-------------------------------------------------------------------------------
281100  EFMP             TOTAL   4            506.0    856    7


-------------------------------------------------------------------------------
        TOTAL                   73           9186.0  15489   27
```

Program For Design
Pediatrics Clinic

FIGURE 10-5.   Program for Design—Pediatrics Clinic

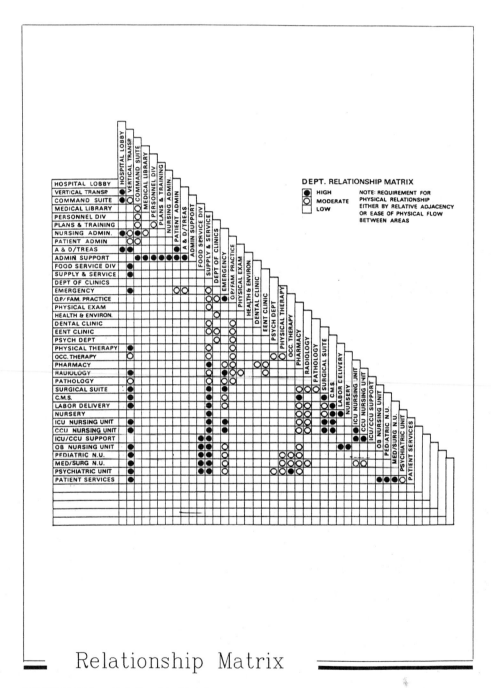

Relationship Matrix

FIGURE 10-6.   Relationship Matrix

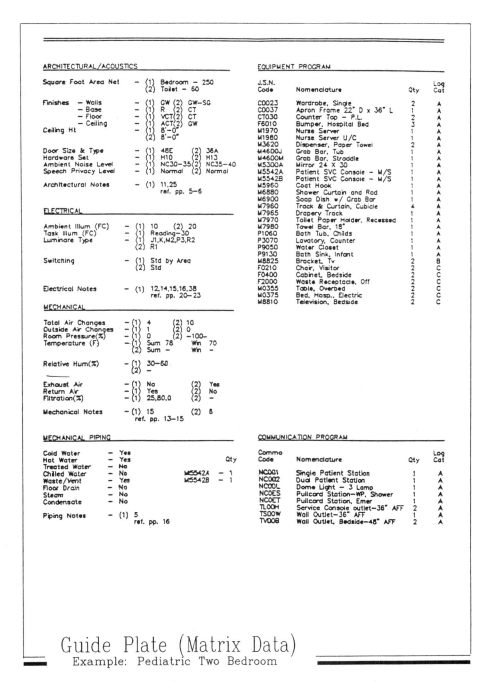

FIGURE 10-7.   Guide Plate (Matrix Data—Pediatric Two-Bedroom)

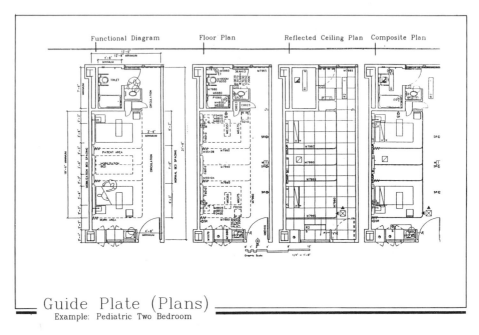

Guide Plate (Plans)
Example: Pediatric Two Bedroom

FIGURE 10-8.   Guide Plate (Plans—Pediatric Two-Bedroom)

FIGURE 10-9.   Model View of Tripler Army Medical Center

FIGURE 10-10.   Artist's Rendering of Brooke Army Medical Center, San Antonio, Texas

FIGURE 10-11.   Womack Army Hospital, Fort Bragg, North Carolina

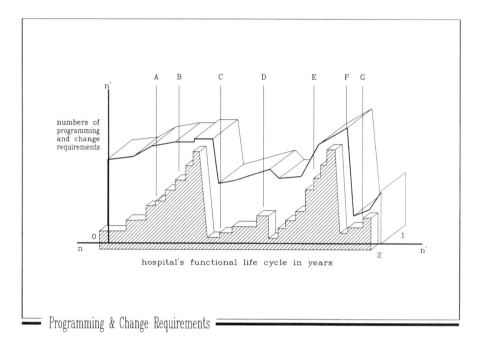

Programming & Change Requirements

FIGURE 10-12.   Programming and Change Requirements

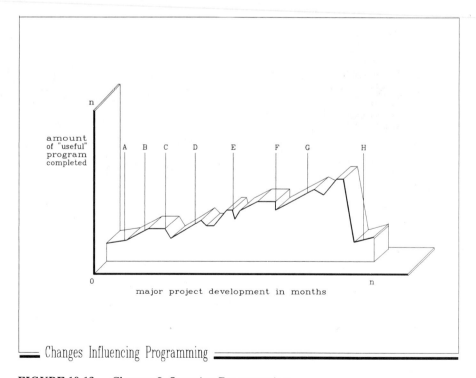

Changes Influencing Programming

FIGURE 10-13.   Changes Influencing Programming

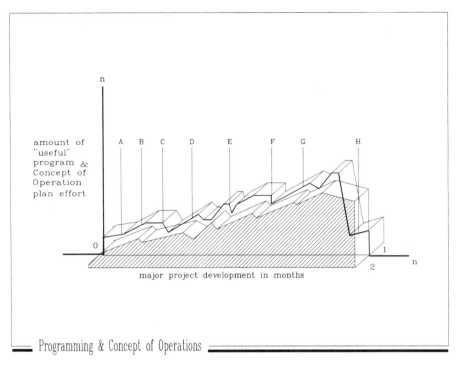

FIGURE 10-14.   Programming and Concept of Operations

CHAPTER 11

The Fit-Up for the World Headquarters of British Petroleum Company plc

Gary A. Miciunas

We trust our buildings
To make us feel better about ourselves;
"If I just lived in a decent place,"
We say, "I could get work done."

We put pressure on foundations
That foundations were never designed
To bear; we try to make
Steel, concrete, and glass do

What the human heart cannot.
We carry our belongings, ourselves,
From building to building,
Looking for one that fits.

—D.S. Lawson
L'Architettura

INTRODUCTION

British Petroleum Company plc (BP), one of the top three oil companies in the world, has taken significant steps to reshape the ways in which its employees communicate and collaborate. Organizational changes were initiated concurrently with the company's decision to move back into its original headquarters building, which was being renovated to meet the demands of today's commercial real estate market. BP took advantage of the office relocation to foster desired cultural changes and create a physical environment supportive of new ways of working. This chapter documents the planning process, which simultaneously encompassed both BP's corporate restructuring and its office relocation. The portion of the BP organization involved in the project is known as its Group Head Office (GHO), and the building, located at 1 Finsbury Circus in London, is officially known as Britannic House.

Britannic House was originally designed by Sir Edwin Lutyens and opened in 1924. The neoclassical structure was built to house the Anglo Persian Oil Company, the founding company of today's British Petroleum Company plc. The initial purpose of the office building was distinct from that of its contemporaries:

> It has been loosely said that Britannic House is the last of its type: that Adelaide House is the truer line of development for the office architecture of a modern city. But it would seem to be better criticism to say that the programme differed in the case of all the three buildings. Bush House is an office building, but it is also a dedication to the "friendship of the English-speaking peoples." Adelaide House frankly acknowledges itself as the home of a number of separate businesses. Britannic House is the headquarters of a great industrial corporation, to which additional prestige is given by its connection with His Majesty's Government. (*Architectural Review*, 1924, p. 185)

The architectural renovation of Britannic House and the corporate reorganization of BP created a unique opportunity for their reunion.

The Architectural Renovation of Britannic House

BP's decision to return to Britannic House was not the initial reason for the renovation of the building. By the mid-1980s, Britannic House was listed as a historically significant building. However, its economic life as an office building was obsolete. The purpose of its renovation was to extend its commercial life with new building systems and an internal reconfiguration more accepting of today's private offices and open plan work stations. The renovation was carried out as a speculative venture by Greycoat plc, owner of the property since 1986.

Advised by the English Heritage Commission and the Lutyens Trust, the developer commissioned architects Inskip & Jenkins and William Nimmo & Partners to renovate the entire property. Listed spaces on ground, first, and fourth floors were authentically restored and respected Lutyens' original design intent. However, the new scheme boldly introduced an atrium giving natural light to deep interior spaces. The design was inspired by one of Lutyens' preliminary drawings for Britannic House, which showed a circular court that was not executed (*Architecture Today*, 1990). The new atrium features gallery

TABLE 11-1   Schedule of Net Lettable Floor Areas

Floor	Square Feet	Square Meters
Eighth	10,120	1,005
Seventh	18,020	1,674
Sixth	21,170	1,966
Fifth	20,540	1,908
Fourth	19,470	1,809
Third	19,710	1,831
Second	20,670	1,920
First	23,080	2,144
Ground	12,530	1,164
Lower Ground	16,330	1,517
Basement	1,520	141
TOTAL	183,860	17,080

circulation paths to and from the elevator lobby on each floor. High-speed elevators and new mechanical and electrical systems were installed along with raised flooring throughout the building (Figure 11-1). An increase in rentable area was achieved by creating an additional floor within the volume of the original mansard roof (Table 11-1).

Relocation Planning

In August 1988, BP delegated a task force, Project Phoenix, to make recommendations for accommodating its future office needs. Project Phoenix considered 137 properties in Central London. Moving outside of the capital city or to the London Docklands or redeveloping its present high-rise complex were also considered. The selection criteria weighed heavily on a few key factors:

- international communications capabilities
- close linkage with governmental, financial, industrial, and commercial institutions
- minimizing staff disruption

In April 1989, Project Phoenix had reduced its search to a short list of seven eligible properties and recommended Britannic House, which was being renovated at the time.

In July 1989, the announcement that BP's corporate core would be moving from a twenty-nine-story high-rise into an eight-story midrise dramatized the underlying restructuring of the headquarters staff. Because of the reorganization, the determination of which groups would be moving into Britannic House would not be made for months. It was clear, however, that there was a strategic direction to disperse BP's main businesses, thereby reducing the need for a large central building.

The Corporate Reorganization of British Petroleum Company plc

In August 1989, BP delegated an in-house team of seven, known as Project 1990. The intention of Project 1990 was to understand the corporation and how the world and business were changing. The brief to the task force included the following objectives:

- to reduce complexity throughout the corporation
- to redesign the central organization
- to reposition the corporation in approach and style for the 1990s

The work of the task force involved over 500 interviews and 6,000 questionnaires in a survey of BP employees.

The recommendations of Project 1990 were not formally announced until March 1990, upon the inauguration of a new chairman. The recommendations of the task force were based on the following proposals:

- a simpler, more flexible organization designed to ensure that corporate strengths are maximized
- working processes built upon teamwork and better use of networked technologies, and complemented by rapid planning, control, and decision making
- development of a corporate culture characterized by team spirit, trust, cooperation, confidence, and innovation

The resulting organization would be a slimmer, flatter, more efficient, and flexible Corporate Center.

The structure of this new organization was depicted in the shape of an egg deliberately to avoid any connotations of status implied by hierarchical reporting relationships. The Corporate Center would be composed of about twenty small policy and strategy teams ranging in size from two to twenty. In addition, an almost equal number of larger teams for support services was identified. The new organization design focused attention on the regional dimension of global business and the need to act in an integrated manner. This emphasis eliminated bureaucratic barriers and identities, which operated against the interests of the corporation as a whole (Figure 11-2).

PROCESS AND METHODS

There are slight differences between American and British architectural practice with regard to facility programming. In American practice, "programming" is the distinct task of reaching a preliminary understanding between architect and client about project parameters and overall design requirements. Documentation of this understanding, known as a "program," serves as a reference tool and fulfills its purpose once a satisfactory design direction or solution is established and accepted. However, in British practice, "programmes" and "programming" imply what Americans know as schedules and scheduling, mostly involving matters of timing or phasing of a project. In England, a "schedule of accommodation" approximates what Americans look for in a program as a listing of spaces and their respective sizes.

An alternative term in British practice is "briefing" and is almost identical to American programming. Briefing differs slightly in that more of the responsibility for the "brief" (or "program") is often assumed by British clients. Once the architect is "briefed" by the client, preliminary design may commence and the architect's responsibility to document or restate the brief in a formal manner may be elective. In either case, neither the Royal Institute of British Architects (RIBA) nor the American Institute of Architects (AIA) clearly includes briefing or programming as part of the architect's basic services. In practice, fees allocated to pre-design services are generally inadequate to cover the scope of work, unless the client is convinced of the importance of such services. Contractual matters aside, as projects and building types continue to increase in complexity, the mutual agreement between architect and client about their preliminary understanding of the project is crucial for successful management of quality, time, and budget.

However, mutual agreement about detailed requirements is not always possible or necessary in order to proceed with planning and design. Agreement about the appropriate course of action, given what is known and unknown at the time, is the critical issue. Dealing with uncertainty and evolving requirements requires flexibility in physical terms as well as flexibility in the project approach. White (1991) quotes an interviewee:

> . . . There is a real danger to extensive documentation. It gives the illusion that more has been worked out than really has. Things look more certain than they actually are. All concerned must constantly be prepared for change at any point in the design process. The projects must be managed to stop or change directions at any time. This makes many architects very uncomfortable who want the problem to be well defined and stable. Many times a building must be planned without knowing the schedule of accommodation. (p. 136).

Lack of certainty only defines a programmatic requirement for flexibility. Uncertainty is not a reason to postpone planning and design until the program or brief can spell out all details. In most cases, the time to act will have passed.

The Client's Brief to the Architect

In August 1989, BP issued a Request for Proposal (RFP) to the architecture firm of Hellmuth, Obata & Kassabaum (HOK), including a brief titled "Outline Statement of Requirements for the Fit-Out of Lutyens House for the BP GHO." The brief was a twenty-two-page document addressing the tenant's requirements for office accommodation, catering, communications, general/support services, interior components and finishes, mechanical and electrical services, sanitation, and security systems.

The brief was primarily an outline specification for purposes of budgeting and estimating. Although the brief was sufficient in detail to define the scope of work, the need for further definition was recognized:

> . . . This Statement of Requirements will need to be developed by an Architect and, where appropriate, a Designer into detailed Specifications and Drawings. BP anticipate that during that process, discussion with the Architect and Designer will be necessary to choose between alternative solutions and clarify any conflicting requirements. (p. 4)

Based on a proposal for professional services, HOK was awarded the commission and assumed the role of lead consultant.

In this role, HOK coordinated all planning and design activities of a multidisciplinary team including engineers and specialist consultants. These efforts were also coordinated with a management contractor responsible for execution of the project on site, including all procurement and sequencing of labor and materials. (Figure 11-3).

The project team met weekly to report on status and progress. BP was represented by two individuals: a project manager and a relocation manager. The responsibility of the project manager was to monitor programme (schedule) and budget, while the relocation manager acted as liaison between the design team and the Project 1990 task force to ensure that user needs were accommodated.

Client/User Interviews

HOK's primary method for collecting information about the evolving organization was client/user interviews: The early problem encountered in this effort was simply that the new teams had yet to be defined and the team leaders had yet to be identified.

In September 1989, HOK conducted a series of interviews with BP's executive management to gain an understanding of the direction of the corporation and the work of Project 1990. BP's management leaders endorsed HOK's need for advanced insights into likely organizational changes. General topics discussed in these interviews included the following: (1) organizational changes and business directions, (2) overall relationships among business units, (3) corporate image, (4) satisfaction with current facilities, and (5) facility improvements to support business functions. HOK conducted interviews with executive management accompanied by representatives of BP's in-house project team.

Project 1990 task force members advised the design team based on the following loose criteria for general office accommodation:

- accommodate about 500 people,
- support fewer and smaller flexible teams, and
- integrate new office technologies.

Discussions also emphasized the likelihood of two types of teams: policy-oriented staff functions and support-oriented service functions. The stacking concept of separating policy and service teams between the lower and upper halves of the building was introduced early and held its merit throughout the project.

The first draft of team size and composition was provided to HOK by Project 1990 at the end of February 1990. Prior to that time, between September 1989 and February 1990, the design team focused on the planning of special areas and functions, including a ground floor conference center, third floor boardroom functions, fourth floor directors suite, seventh floor food service, and eighth floor medical clinic. This strategy reserved the first, second, part of third, fifth, and sixth floors for general office accommodation. Detailed requirements for the special areas were developed in conjunction with specialist consultants and BP's project representatives through a series of interviews and work sessions.

During this period, HOK conducted base building studies of existing conditions to determine capacities of structural, electrical, and mechanical systems. Such studies involved the engineers in detailed evaluations of air velocities, including on-site full-scale mock-ups of the proposed office sizes. These evaluations determined the 3.0 meter by 4.5 meter nominal dimensions for typical private offices as well as the configuration of floor support spaces (such as conference, file, copy, and mail rooms). Open plan areas were developed on the basis of universal planning principles that imposed grid-like order on the odd geometry of the building. These concepts resulting from building studies were formally presented to the client, including presentations to an executive steering committee first in February and later in April of 1990. In other words, general planning principles were reviewed and approved by the executive steering committee prior to working directly with the end users or team representatives.

In March 1990, HOK conducted a series of thirty interviews, referred to as accommodation meetings, with representatives of the newly formed teams. The purpose of the interviews was to understand the mission, size, composition, and office needs of each team in more detail than the Project 1990 briefings offered. These interviews were conducted for information only. Interview topics addressed general office needs of teams and team members. These topics included (1) team work space, (2) personal work space, (3) working relationships, (4) storage and equipment needs, and (5) special requirements. Many interviews were conducted with small groups because teams were in their infancy stage and were only beginning to develop through participatory management.

In mid-April, HOK made a general presentation of design proposals to an assembly of team leaders. This presentation was followed by a full-scale furniture mock-up for review and comment by all team members (Figure 11-4). No formal feedback instrument was employed. Members of the HOK design team were available to explain features of the furniture system, including wire management, storage, work surface heights, seating, etc., and to address any questions. A handout explaining the proposed space and furniture standards was provided.

Space Planning Reviews

Beginning in May 1990, HOK conducted two to three space planning reviews with representatives of each new team. The first review incorporated information gained in the accommodation meetings on team size, composition, and ways of working. Such requirements were incorporated in a first draft of a space plan. The plan positioned each team in a particular location on a floor based on adjacency relationships suggested to HOK by BP's Project 1990 task force. The principles of the planning concept for general office areas were explained, and team representatives made suggestions for the detailed layouts of their team areas. Most team members took advantage of the opportunity to view the furniture mock-up prior to the first space plan reviews.

The suggestions offered by team representatives, including the choice of furniture standard for each individual, were incorporated in a second draft of space plans for all general office floors. If the second draft fulfilled all foreseen requirements, a sign-off was obtained for furniture procurement and construction drawings to proceed. If not, a third draft and subsequent review were necessary until all team layouts were satisfactory. All reviews took place over a period of about four weeks.

The facilitation of space plan reviews with end users was conducted by HOK design team members who initially worked with the Project 1990 task force. Since requirements for general office accommodation evolved over a period of about nine months, such continuity was critical to understanding overall parameters as well as specific needs of individual teams or team members.

ELEMENTS AND OUTCOMES

As mentioned previously, the scheduled separation of planning and design work between special areas and general office areas allowed time for detailed developments about the reorganization to unfold. During the first half of the planning and design effort, work on four key areas progressed into detailed design: (1) conference center, (2) boardroom functions, (3) directors suite, and (4) food service. Programmatic issues and design considerations for each of these areas are now briefly discussed.

Conference Center

The conference center was located on the ground floor, for three key reasons. First, the center was to be used after normal business hours for evening events as well as business meetings during the day. This posed a security requirement for controlled public access. Second, the space required adequate ceiling height for front-screen projection. Only the ground floor provided high structural bays with adequate height. Third, the space program identified need for one large assembly space divisible into three smaller rooms. In order to create functional room proportions, a clear span space of adequate length and width was necessary. Only the ground floor provided such unencumbered floor area. The conference center features a pre-function area and breakout area.

Boardroom Functions

Boardroom functions, including the boardroom and board dining room, were located on the third floor along the Finsbury Circus elevation. Initially, these functions were expected to fit on the same floor with the directors suite. A preliminary test-fit, however, determined that such an arrangement could not be accommodated because of the building geometry. Access to the boardroom from the directors suite on the fourth floor is possible either by the passenger elevators or by an original internal staircase connecting the first through fourth floors. A separate catering kitchen for the dining function is also provided with convenient access to the service elevator.

Directors Suite

The directors suite, located on the fourth floor, consists of seven executive offices including the chairman's office. In addition, the floor includes two conference rooms, video conference facilities, floor reception, and a private reception function in the original chairman's office, one of the listed spaces in the building restored to Lutyens' original design (Figure 11-5). The conference and video conference facilities were vertically aligned with those on other floors to allow for building services (i.e., HVAC systems). This was identified early on as a programmatic requirement for service grouping of such facilities.

Food Service

The food service function was located on the seventh floor. Programmatic requirements for shipping and receiving suggest a location closer to the building loading dock. The ground floor, however, could not accommodate the area requirement. Second, the additional floor created within the volume of the mansard roof provided natural daylight from skylights in the roof. The interesting character of the space proved to be very appropriate for dining functions. Early test-fits determined that the space was not as suitable for general office use. Third, ventilation through the roof was easily achieved. The seventh floor consists of kitchen and service areas located near the service elevator, servery located near the passenger elevators, staff dining for about 150 persons, four private dining rooms for ten persons each with separate service access, and guest dining for forty persons (Figure 11-6).

General Office Areas

Layouts for general office areas on the first, second, partial third, fifth, and sixth floors were based on universal planning concepts and adherence to furniture and space standards. Concepts and standards were developed in conjunction with Project 1990 briefings, which identified overall project objectives for building capacity, team settings, and user participation.

Standardization of individual area and furniture allocation resulted in only two different size footprints: (1) a nominal size 3.0 meters by 4.5 meters, or approximately 10 feet by 15 feet, private office, and (2) a nominal size 2.5 meters by 3.0 meters, or approximately 8 feet by 10 feet, open plan work station. Each standard included a limited number of options for furniture configuration based on individual work style and job tasks. Team representatives selected appropriate options during the space planning reviews (Figures 11-7 and 11-8). The options were devised such that if the occupant of a work station changed location, the change-out of the work station to suit the new occupant would not require a total reconfiguration of all components, nor would it affect neighboring work stations. This solution was based on the notion that people move, but furniture does not.

A typical general office floor includes private offices, open plan work stations, and a zone of common support spaces for the entire floor. Support spaces include two conference rooms with a conference reception room, copy and mail room including a document hoist, and central filing room (Figures 11-9 and 11-10).

User participation influenced the layout for each team. Team representatives offered suggestions for the orientation and configuration of each office or work space. Other plan elements, including shared files or equipment areas, were also addressed with team representatives. Needs for privacy, interaction, work flow, and communication patterns were accommodated for teams and individual members to the extent that overall parameters could still be achieved. For example, in most cases the needs of the team as a whole were given priority over needs of individuals. Individual team members were able to select among design options for their own work space; however, the physical orientation of each work space, depending on its clustering in one of the three basic configurations ("C," "T," or "F"), was determined on the basis of relationships among all team members. If there was no consensus, final say on layout was usually had by the team leader. Any conflicts between the needs of neighboring teams were worked out in group meetings of team leaders. The latter may have involved the proposed location on the floor, or the boundary conditions between two teams.

Discussion of Process and Methods

The success of proceeding with relocation planning while BP restructured its organization resulted from several conditions established early in the project: management leadership, project team assembly, and user participation.

BP's management leadership set strategic direction in the absence of detailed information. Executive management espoused the attitude that the new headquarters environment would be an important contributor toward realizing the proposals and recommendations of Project 1990. The new chairman recognized the need for the planning and design team to consult the Project 1990 task force and to obtain privileged, advanced insight into likely organizational change, albeit preliminary and subject to change. The early involvement of an executive steering committee on policy matters and design issues, especially during development of prototypical planning concepts, was critical to the successful administration of such concepts later with the identified teams.

Early commissioning and assembly of a project team, including project management, interior architecture, tenant engineering, and specialist consultants, allowed for interactive and iterative rather than sequential phases of work. Programming was not a phase of work, but rather more an activity from preliminary space planning through detailed design and furniture systems selection. In this case, programming needed to remain general in nature while exploring preliminary design concepts. Planning and design studies informed the continuing programming process about the relevance and timeliness of detailed requirements. Information progressed from the general to the specific in a deductive manner.

Design intent, building services, budget, and schedule were treated simultaneously, achieving balance among roles, perspectives, and interests of the entire project team. This required that all parties were "on board" from the beginning to the end, including, in some cases, subcontractors and suppliers who contributed valuable suggestions for availability of labor and materials as well as constructability. Such early vendor involvement was also effective in furniture procurement.

An emerging corporate culture that fosters teamwork, trust, and cooperation involves empowering employees and delegating decision making. A need for consistency and project standards may conflict with unique needs of individual situations. Increased employee participation need not jeopardize standardization as long as project parameters are clearly articulated. A disciplined planning framework emphasized a clear distinction between top management's endorsement of policies and end users' choice and selection among design options. By necessity, the programming effort defined an open-ended framework for user participation to affect final space plans based on flexible planning concepts and standards.

Management leadership, project team assembly, and user participation were keys to success and demonstrate the maxims espoused by Walton (1988, p. 26):

1. integrate multiple perspectives
2. emphasize casting
3. sift for relevant facts
4. manage pluralistic decision making

Conditions necessary to realize these maxims were established from the outset of the project.

CONCLUSION: THE CHANGING OFFICE

The office is a place for processing information. In the traditional office, the processing of information could be "seen" by observing work flow, primarily the movement of paper and people. Electronic processing and digital transmission have drastically changed our ability to "see" the processing of information. Today's electronic office is transforming the way work is performed well beyond yesterday's preconceptions of the "office of the future."

Traditional office planning and space needs forecasting are fairly straightforward in approach. Since office space is driven by the number of employees, the assumptions of one person, one space, eight hours per day, and centralized facilities allowed a simple recipe for space planning. It is possible to determine the number of people, multiply by a standardized allocation of floor area per person, factor in an allowance for circulation, add some common support facilities, and sum it up. For example, typical allowance for general office usable area may range between 225 and 250 square feet per person, including circulation, in American corporate headquarters. Long-range forecasting using such a model is based on a predictable future and static organizational structures. Although such approaches are still commonly used today, they no longer reflect realities of a changing corporate world.

Today's realities indicate new patterns, with implications for planning and design. Although some patterns are reflected in this chapter, broad trends are affecting the state of the art in office design more generally. These changes result from shifts in patterns of corporate organization and the nature of work, primarily because of new electronic capabilities. Such shifts are discussed in the following paragraphs.

A Shift Away from Hierarchical Management
Toward More Teamwork

Tall organizational structures characterized by many levels of vertical reporting relationships are being replaced by flatter organizational structures made up of more autonomous business units. This shift plays havoc with corporate standards programs for office space based on hierarchical status! Such standards programs, which aggregate individual offices in a contiguous layout, do not always satisfy team needs for people working together. Progressive approaches to office design and space standards must accommodate a variety of new forms of team organization.

Pava (1983, p. 123) advocates a contingency approach. He suggests a multimodal configuration of settings to embrace at least three forms of team organization: (1) work-group organization, (2) product-line/market-segment team organization, and (3) reticular organization. Each form of organization is characterized by varying degrees of routineness in task performance.

Work-group organization is based on one overall conversion process with a high degree of routine work. The work could be characterized by a series of tasks performed sequentially in assembly-line fashion yielding tangible work products. An example of this form may be a mail-order processing function that involves receiving, sorting, logging, coding, etc., in serial fashion. Job rotation is common.

Product-line/market-segment team organization is based on a mixture of routine and nonroutine tasks. This form may involve a team responsible for providing a complete range of services. Many companies are creating customer service teams to address all matters of customers' needs, including trouble-shooting unusual problems without need for referral to another department.

Reticular organization is based on nonroutine work. The distribution of information and authority is constantly shifting among team members. Communication is informal and depends more on lateral exchanges across formal lines of demarcation. This is the most complex and ambiguous form of organization and is characteristic of managerial and executive staff functions.

A Shift Toward Geographical Dispersion and Decentralization

New forms of organization coupled with new office technologies pose new temporal and spatial possibilities. Possibilities for configuring office settings of a corporation are no longer confined to central facilities. Pava (1983, p. 142) also suggests three scenarios for an end to the office as we have known it:

1. *Disaggregation of office-based services.* It may be preferable to disassemble central offices. A home- or community-based work force lessens the need for a large office complex. Purchasing outside services and contracting temporary help reduce the need to house as many employees under one roof.
2. *Dissolution of barriers that separate office and factory work.* Central offices may be distributed at local production sites. Production and administrative operations may be geographically integrated.
3. *Diminished administrative operations in the context of greater reliance on self-service.* Getting the customer to do some of the work reduces need for administrative staff. This is already evidenced by the popularity and acceptance of automatic teller machines and making travel reservations by using personal computers in the home.

The central office will not disappear, but it will most probably be smaller in the future.

A Shift Away from Employees Working During the Same Hours and Occupying the Same Premises

An increase in the number of people working at home and telecommuting is changing the boundary between home and office. An increase of women in the work force places new social demands on family lifestyles and community support systems. Regional work centers may complement a central office and be located closer to where employees live. Consequently, the purpose of the central office also changes.

Handy (1989) suggests a new concept of the central office as a club center; i.e., "a club being a place of privileged access to common facilities" (p. 110). This idea suggests that the central office be thought of more as a complex of amenities and shared facilities for employees to use video teleconferencing, or meet in person, or use other specialized equipment. Handy cautions that "the idea of a club center only works, however, if people have somewhere else to be. It is a perfect facility for a network of individuals linked into a small core . . ." (p. 111).

A Shift Toward More Balanced Emphases on Efficiency and Effectiveness in Attempts to Measure Productivity in Office Environments

Attempts to measure the impact of office design on employee productivity have focused on individual performance. Most studies of this sort base productivity measurement on traditional notions of efficiency; i.e., input versus output. Input is "labor" usually measured in units of time (hours worked). Output is measured by quantifying converted outcomes, such as claims or invoices processed. Pava (1983) points out that "this view assumes that there is a strong, direct correlation between the number of hours worked and the amount of output obtained . . ." (p. 139). It is also biased toward increased output and lowered cost, while viewing labor as a commodity. This view may not apply to today's workers using information technology. The number of hours worked may no longer correlate with output obtained. Distinctions between labor outputs and service outcomes may be more relevant; however, there are currently no measures to adequately compare the two. Service outcomes are based on effectiveness, not simply efficiency, and allow for consideration that a worker may add value to the product rather than merely producing more of the same more quickly, over and over again.

Pava (1983) argues that "efficiency and effectiveness are achieved under vastly different circumstances. Efficiency entails perfecting internal operations under conditions of stability. . . . Effectiveness entails bettering the match with one's surrounding environment under conditions of change" (p. 141). Both are necessary for organizations to be successful.

Office environments designed to support teamwork need to be evaluated on performance measures of organizational effectiveness at the unit level of the group, rather than aggregated measures of individual performance. Measures of design performance for the ambient environment, the work group environment, and the individual environment all need to be carefully considered.

There is reason for expanding the scope of this chapter to include issues raised in this conclusion. Projects such as the new British Petroleum world headquarters involve changes in dozens of variables at once: physical, organizational, cultural, and technical. To reiterate the objectives of BP's Project 1990 task force, they included the following:

- to reduce complexity throughout the corporation,
- to redesign the central organization, and
- to reposition the corporation in approach and style for the 1990s.

These are broad, long-term objectives consistent with the trends and shifts in corporate organization and relocation discussed earlier. Flexible teams, using integrated office technologies and discovering new ways of working, pose dynamic tenant requirements and require a flexible planning approach as well as flexible design solutions. The corporate restructuring and relocation described in this chapter is only a hint of the dramatic challenges ahead for office planning and design in the 1990s.

ACKNOWLEDGMENTS

On behalf of HOK, the author wishes to thank all representatives of British Petroleum Company plc, including the Project 1990 Task Force, the Relocation Team, the Executive Steering Committee, and team representatives for their valuable contributions and insights on this project.

References

Britannic House, London. 1925. *Architecture review* 57, May, pp. 185-201.

Handy, Charles. 1989. *The age of unreason.* Boston: Harvard Business School Press, pp. 109-13.

Monumental geometries: Learning from Lutyens. 1990. *Architecture today,* February, pp. 36-41.

Outline statement of requirements for the fit-out of Lutyens House for the BP GHO. 1989. London: British Petroleum Company plc, June, pp. 1-22.

Pava, Calvin. 1983. *Managing new office technology: An organizational strategy.* New York: The Free Press, pp. 122-44.

Project 1990 special report. 1990. London: British Petroleum Company plc, March, pp. 1-18.

Walton, Thomas. 1988. *Architecture and the corporation: The creative intersection.* New York: Macmillan, pp. 25-48.

White, Edward T. 1991. *Design briefing in England.* Tucson, Ariz.: Architectural Media Ltd.

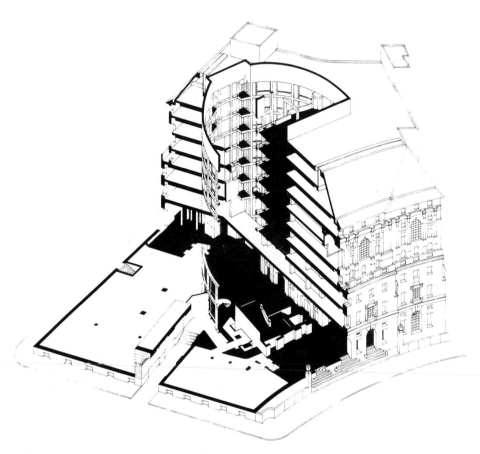

FIGURE 11-1.   Cut-Away View of the Renovation of Britannic House, Featuring New Atrium

(courtesy of Greycoat plc)

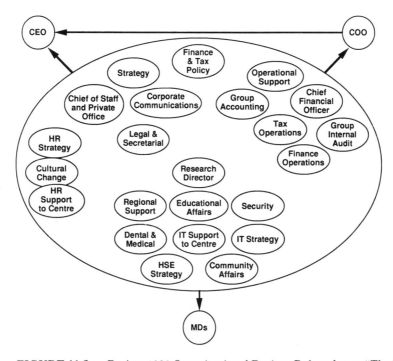

FIGURE 11-2.   Project 1990 Organizational Design, Referred to as "The Egg" Diagram

(courtesy of British Petroleum Company plc)

Project Team Working Relationships

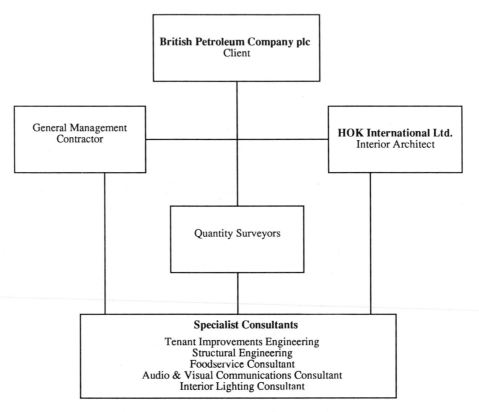

FIGURE 11-3.   Project Team Working Relationships, Including Client, Management Contractor, Interior Architect, and Consultants

FURNITURE AND SPACE STANDARDS
FOR
1 FINSBURY CIRCUS

MAY 1990

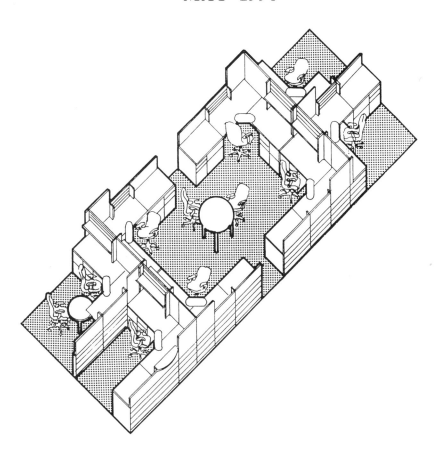

INTRODUCTION

This brochure introduces the furniture and space standards on display for the new fit out of 1 Finsbury Circus. The general office areas will be predominantly open plan with a complement of cellular offices. The furniture standards are similar for both. The space standards are based on two common "footprints": one universal size floor area for all cellular offices, and one universal size floor area for open plan work stations. This approach creates flexible and manageable layouts before, during, and after the move into the new facility. The illustrations inside explain the range of options to suit the needs of individuals and teams.

FIGURE 11-4.   Full-Scale Furniture Mock-Up Installed On-Site for Team Member Review

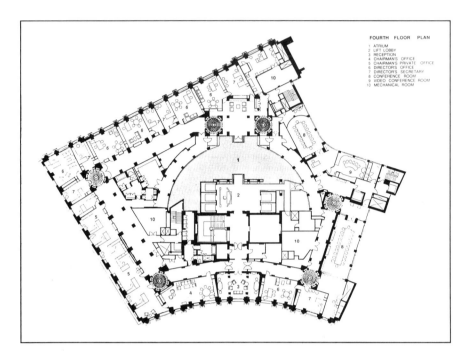

FIGURE 11-5.   Floor Plan of Directors Suite, Including Offices and Executive Support Functions

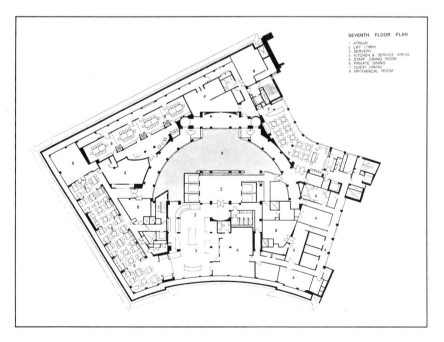

FIGURE 11-6.   Floor Plan of Food Service and Catering Function, Featuring Natural Daylight Above Employee Dining Areas

SUITING THE NEEDS OF INDIVIDUALS

The furniture and space standards are designed to accommodate a variety of fit out options for individuals and teams. Options for individuals are illustrated below. The plan to the left highlights the portion of the furniture mock up which is explained in more detail by the captions and three-dimensional drawings.

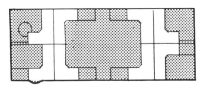

STANDARD CORNER UNIT

All workstations are based on a common L- shaped corner unit. This assembly provides a primary and secondary worksurface with options for storage above and below the desk top. Optional components may be easily added or changed at the side of this corner unit.

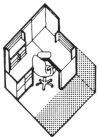

EXTENDED WORKSURFACE OPTION

The extended worksurface option allows additional desk top area for office equipment. The floor area beneath the desk top allows additional storage for filing.

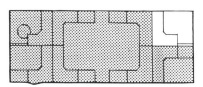

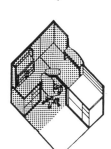

GUEST CHAIR OPTION

For individuals with less demand for storage and conferencing, the guest chair option accommodates frequent one-on-one meetings at the workstation.

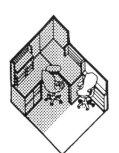

CONFERENCE EXTENSION OPTION

For individuals who interact more frequently, the conference extension provides a separate desk top to meet with two other persons.

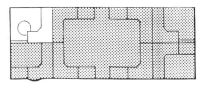

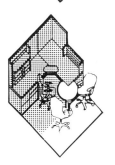

FIGURE 11-7.   Furniture Solution Options for Individual Team Members

CREATING TEAM SPACES

The thoughtful arrangement of individual workstations can greatly enhance the effectiveness of a team. Depending on the organisation and style of team work, clusters of workstations will be a combination of three basic configurations, the 'C', the 'T', and the 'F'. These configurations are included in the furniture mock up and highlighted below in each plan. Any of the options for individual workstations may be mixed or matched in the 'C', 'T' and 'F' configurations.

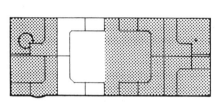

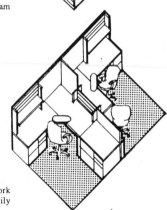

THE 'C' CONFIGURATION

The advantage of the 'C' configuration is that it allows the floor area of each individual footprint to create a common open area between team members for shared amenities like a conference table.

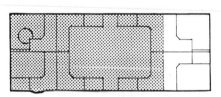

THE 'T' CONFIGURATION

The 'T' configuration is best suited to team members who do not work together as interactively, yet eye contact and the opportunity to easily pass documents between individuals may be useful.

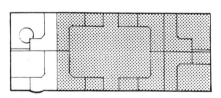

THE 'F' CONFIGURATION

The 'F' configuration affords individuals three sides of partial enclosure. This configuration may work best for team members who generally work independently of each other.

FIGURE 11-8.   Furniture Solution Options for Configuring Team Work Space

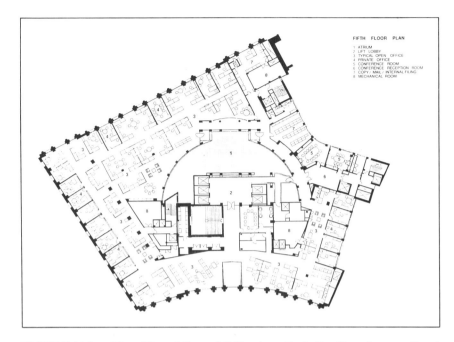

FIGURE 11-9.   Floor Plan of General Office Area, Including Team Layouts Developed With Employee Participation

FIGURE 11-10.   Interior View of General Office Area Along Finsbury Circus

(courtesy of British Petroleum Company plc; photo: Niall Clutton)

CHAPTER 12

Facility Master Plan for Mattel Toys Worldwide Headquarters

William T. Coleman and Branka V. Olson

INTRODUCTION

Mattel Toys, Inc. (MTI) engaged Sindik Olson Associates (SOA) to develop a facility master plan for its Worldwide Headquarters in July 1989. SOA assisted MTI in evaluating the feasibility of remodeling and/or rebuilding its existing site and developed a relocation master plan following MTI's decision to sell the facility, acquire an existing office building, and relocate the entire headquarters to a nearby location. The plan identified MTI's spatial, functional, and operational requirements and analyzed them in relation to the corporation's short- and long-term business and operational goals.

The relocation of this major U.S. designer, manufacturer, and marketer of toys required the development of planning data and facility occupancy alternatives for 460,000 net square feet (NSF) of office and industrial space, housing a work force consisting of 1,600 staff organized into seven divisions with more than 150 departments. Once the decision was made to relocate the facility, programming, planning, construction, and moving had to be accomplished within a condensed fourteen-month time frame.

Project with Pre-Design Focus

This chapter has a strong pre-design focus. At the inception of the planning process, MTI's facility executives determined that the company's needs would be best served if systematic program data and planning criteria were developed prior to the selection of a design firm, since it was not known whether MTI would redevelop its existing headquarters site or lease, purchase, or construct a new facility elsewhere.

MTI sought a consultant who could provide them with facility alternatives that supported their long-term business plan and financial objectives. As a consulting architect programmer, SOA provided MTI with an independent analysis of their unique functional and operational requirements, enabling MTI to make prudent decisions regarding the disposition of their valuable headquarters real estate assets.

Headquarters with Diverse Space Types

The MTI Worldwide Headquarters consists of corporate offices, a design and development (D & D) office (containing special office and industrial space), and facility support space. The special office is primarily a creative environment where new products are designed and developed. The industrial space includes shops, labs, studios, and a warehouse where new design prototypes are fabricated and tested. Facility support space includes a cafeteria, conference rooms, training rooms, company store, presentation rooms, and toy display areas.

Project Objectives and Elements

MTI engaged SOA to identify and evaluate both short- and long-term facility solutions. SOA analyzed MTI's staff and space requirements, their physical and environmental criteria, their functional adjacency/work flow relationships, and their use of existing space. The development of new work space standards and an evaluation of MTI's systems furniture requirements resulted in the establishment of efficient space planning concepts. Occupancy alternatives were developed to organize MTI's diverse functional components so as to improve the company's operating efficiency and productivity. The master plan included the following:

- staff and space requirements database
- stacking/blocking occupancy alternatives
- design and planning guidelines
- relocation phasing plan (ten-year)

The results of the master plan process will significantly affect MTI's bottom line for many years. Recommendations resulted in the following:

- reduction of space requirements by 28 percent over a five-year time frame
- assignment of departmental space supportive of MTI's business plan
- establishment of a stand-alone Design Center

The new Design Center, established in conjunction with the acquired office tower, consolidated all of the D & D office, industrial, and related support space under one roof, realigned the physical relationship between MTI's D & D and corporate marketing functions, and resulted in a more efficient product development environment for Mattel Toys.

CONTEXT

Evaluation of Existing Facility

At the inception of the planning process, MTI occupied 635,000 NSF of space in its headquarters of more than thirty years in Hawthorne, California. The total facility comprised some 835,000 NSF in a thirty-six-acre complex of owned buildings, with an outside tenant leasing 200,000 NSF from MTI. The space was inefficiently utilized and contained substantial blocks of vacant and underutilized space, the result of its manufacturing functions being decentralized to other worldwide locations during the 1980s.

Buildings included a six-story tower and a sprawling complex of interconnected one-story tilt-up buildings housing its industrial space, plus whatever office space would not fit in the tower. The low-rise buildings also accommodated much of the company's support space, including conference rooms, presentation theater, and cafeteria. Within walking distance were two leased buildings accommodating the company store and miscellaneous office, industrial, and support functions.

By 1989, MTI management was actively looking for ways to increase the return on investment from its headquarters real estate assets. Preliminary in-house studies indicated that MTI could operate more efficiently with less space. MTI began negotiations to sell its buildings and land to a developer who would redevelop the site into a multitenant office park and provide MTI with a new, "right-sized" headquarters via design/build contract.

To evaluate the developer's work letter, plans, and renderings, MTI first engaged SOA to prepare a building performance specification in the spring of 1989. The specification codified MTI's functional requirements for the site, parking garage, base building, tenant improvements, and mechanical, electrical, and plumbing systems. The developer's subsequent analysis revealed a 25 percent cost differential between MTI's expected end result and the developer's proposal. MTI subsequently sold the Hawthorne facility and purchased a new office tower in nearby El Segundo. The combination of a pre-existing building, an attractive price, and a desirable location proved irresistible to MTI management.

Evaluation of New Building and Alternative Uses

From July through December of 1989, SOA developed a space requirements database, evaluated the building, and made recommendations as to how the building could be organized and improved to meet MTI's requirements. The new fourteen-story tower caused MTI to rethink basic proximity/work flow relationships (vertical instead of horizontal), to adopt new work space standards based on the building's structural module, and to consider off-loading either "nonessential" office staff or industrial space to other locations in order to fit their organization into the building.

SOA developed alternative occupancy scenarios to determine the optimum utilization of the new building. At issue was the need to satisfy a diverse range of users representing various types of office and industrial space. Solutions were developed that tested adjacency requirements, code occupancy limitations, and functional splits between office and industrial activities. An analysis of functional, physical, and environmental criteria resulted in a recommendation to establish a separate Design Center in a nearby industrial building.

Implementation

Concurrent with SOA's master planning activities in the fall of 1989, MTI engaged the services of a design firm to develop the detailed space requirements program necessary for space planning and construction documents. This space requirements program included all freestanding furniture and equipment. SOA's ongoing involvement during the design and construction document phases included space planning and design review, industrial space programming and planning, relocation phasing planning, systems furniture bidding, and negotiations. SOA subsequently updated the design firm's space requirements program to incorporate adjustments made during the space planning process and to provide MTI with an accurate database for ongoing facility management following move-in. SOA assisted MTI through occupancy on the last day of 1990.

METHODOLOGY

SOA's methodology encompassed four phases, described shortly. The tasks necessary to develop a facility master plan for Mattel Toys are summarized in Figure 12-1. The four phases are:

- familiarization
- evaluation
- recommendations
- implementation

Phase 1: Familiarization

The purpose of this phase was to establish a clear image of the MTI corporate headquarters that responded to the strategic needs of executive management and the operational needs of departmental users. SOA sought to relate MTI's near- and long-term business plans to concepts of facility planning and to identify those factors that would affect the amount, type, and quality of space required during the next five years. This phase included the development of the following tasks:

- base data gathering,
- decision schedule,
- executive management interviews,
- management goals and objectives, and
- questionnaire and information package.

Base Data Gathering
At the inception of the project development process, milestones and objectives were outlined at a kick-off meeting with the MTI project team. SOA toured the existing headquarters space to gain an understanding of the type and quality of the space then occupied. Existing in-house planning documents, space projections, work space standards, space plans, and furniture procurement data were analyzed to ensure a proper understanding of existing baseline information. Organizational charts were assembled for all headquarters departments.

Decision Schedule
A schedule was developed to identify the decisions executive management had to make through the course of the planning process. SOA worked closely with MTI in-house staff to identify fixed conditions, given assumptions, and other important planning parameters not requiring further review, as well as those decisions that would need to be made in order to keep the project on track.

Executive Management Interviews
Key MTI executives, including the CEO and heads of the seven major operating divisions, provided macro-level direction for the study. Interview questions were directed toward gaining an understanding of management's priorities, planning strategy, functional requirements, operational issues, growth rates, and planning objectives. MTI executives provided insight into new business areas, organizational changes, workload indicators, space utilization, work space standards, facility amenities, locational issues, and desired environmental conditions.

Management Goals and Objectives Definition
Following the interviews, a statement of facility goals and objectives was developed and distributed to executive management for review and confirmation.

Questionnaire and Information Package
A questionnaire and information package was developed and distributed to 150 department heads. The information package provided guidelines approved by executive management so that each department head could initiate growth projections from a common baseline. The questionnaire elicited information regarding staff levels, existing and probable future conditions, proximity relationships, and special area and equipment requirements. (The questionnaire is reproduced in the appendix to this chapter.)

Phase 2: Evaluation

The purpose of this phase was to gather the data necessary to project future staff and space requirements. This phase included the development of the following tasks:

- space utilization analysis
- space standards
- operations analysis
- interviews
- support area requirements
- staff and space requirements database

Space Utilization Analysis

Existing departmental space allocations were tabulated using MTI's base occupancy drawings. Net area factors (net square feet per person) were calculated and opportunities to improve space utilization on a departmental basis were documented.

Space Standards

Existing space allocation standards for private offices, open office work stations, conference rooms, and special areas were reviewed. The standards were modified to work with the new building's structural module, to minimize the number of work station footprints, and to establish equitable space assignments based on MTI job descriptions, titles, and work requirements (Figure 12-2).

Operations Analysis

Operational procedures were reviewed to gain an understanding of MTI's design and development process. The review included product flow through the design studio, development laboratories and warehouse, and paper flow through the office. Flow diagrams depicted existing conditions as well as opportunities to improve material handling, communication, and intradepartmental travel times. Figure 12-3 summarizes divisional operational requirements by location.

Interviews

Departmental interviews were conducted to view and discuss each department's space with a representative who was knowledgeable as to its functional and operational requirements. Approximately 150 interviews were conducted with department managers. Each department's needs for storage, filing, copying, reception, conferencing, and other unique activities were quantified.

Support Area Requirements

Centralized facility support for such shared services as the display area, lobby, reception, print ship, cafeteria, training, and meeting rooms were investigated.

Staff and Space Requirements Database
Database spreadsheets were developed for all headquarters office and Design Center space. An example of a division level summary is presented in Figure 12-4. The spreadsheets projected MTI's staff and space requirements from 1989 through 1995, with 1991 and 1993 as intermittent planning periods. Each department's staff and space needs were summarized. Macro-level data, suitable for stacking and blocking, included quantity and type of private offices and work stations, special rooms/areas, and building support space. (The internal contents of special rooms and areas would be developed by MTI's design firm during the space planning phase.)

Phase 3: Recommendations

The purpose of this phase was to analyze the database and develop occupancy alternatives based on efficient space allocation concepts, develop planning and design guildelines for use by the firm ultimately selected by MTI to perform interior design services, and develop furniture selection criteria. This phase included the development of the following tasks:

- decision criteria
- adjacency analysis
- special programmatic needs
- occupancy profiles
- planning and design guidelines
- concept space plans
- furniture procurement specification

Decision Criteria
Executive management meetings were conducted to identify each division's locational criteria. Criteria included departmental access, visibility, autonomy, ease of relocation, environmental conditions, and logistic and economic considerations.

Adjacency Analysis
Following the departmental interviews, the required or preferred adjacency relationships and specific material and work flow relationships were documented. Adjacency diagrams identified work and material flow, potential for shared use of equipment, and enhancements to departmental relationships.

Special Programmatic Needs
Special functional areas were analyzed, including the design studio, model shops, chemistry lab, plating/rotocast shop, reprographics shop, camera graphics, and reworking studio. Special needs were documented for electrical requirements, dust control levels, humidity and temperature requirements, clear ceiling

heights, floor loading, and the need for compressed air, water, oil, and waste treatment.

Occupancy Profiles

Alternative occupancy profiles were developed for the new facility. Stacking diagrams depicted each department's final occupancy in terms of a building and floor location (Figure 12-5). Spreadsheet summaries indicated each department's space requirements with resultant space surpluses (or shortfalls) when compared to overall space availability at a given time frame.

Planning and Design Guidelines

Executive management's goals for the project were translated into planning and design guidelines for interior space planning. The guidelines established circulation patterns; requirements for contiguous departmental space; location of core, service, and support modules; location of private offices; relationship of open office space to natural light; systems furniture power supply methods; construction time frames; standardization of build-out; and furniture. Aesthetic design directives were also developed for both tower and Design Center office space.

Concept Space Plans

For typical tower office areas, concept space plans established ratios of open to enclosed space, location of conference and office support amenities, relationship of private office to work stations, and alternate work station cluster configurations (Figure 12-6). The space plans enabled SOA to allocate and test appropriate database circulation and layout factors prior to the interior design phase. A block plan was developed for the Design Center based on test layouts of efficient work station cluster configurations, work flow, access, security, and code compliance requirements.

Furniture Procurement Specification

A procurement specification was developed to define specific price, function, and design criteria as well as MTI's business terms and conditions. The specifications were used to obtain competitive bids from pre-qualified furniture manufacturers.

Phase 4: Implementation

SOA provided MTI and its consultants with ongoing support during the design, construction, and move-in phases of the project. This phase included the development of the following tasks:

- phasing schedule
- plan and design review
- space planning (industrial space)
- database update

Phasing Schedule

A computerized phased timeline schedule was developed to ensure an orderly sequence of moves during the project time frame and beyond. The schedule documented each department's ultimate and interim locations, move date and duration, critical dependencies, and other pertinent information.

Plan and Design Review

The design firm's space plans were reviewed for conformance to MTI's goals and objectives, space requirement database, and operational requirements. SOA verified that functional and adjacency issues were satisfied and that omissions and inconsistencies were documented. SOA provided assistance in resolving program compliance issues early in the design process.

Space Planning (Industrial Space Only)

SOA developed space plans for all Design Center industrial space. Space plans illustrated the size and location of plan components, including systems furniture, freestanding furniture and equipment, and new interior construction.

Database Update

SOA made adjustments to the staff and space requirements database following approval of the design firm's space plans. This "as-built" database was to be used by MTI for ongoing facility management purposes.

ELEMENTS AND OUTCOMES

Space Requirements

Total space requirements decreased 28 percent from 635,000 NSF at the old Hawthorne facility to 460,000 NSF at the new tower and Design Center. The reduced space requirements included a five-year staff growth allocation. The magnitude of reduction can be attributed to programming methodology that included the employment of highly efficient space allocation and planning concepts, the relinquishment of underutilized space, and relocation of certain storage functions to an off-site location.

Mattel office staff now occupy approximately 180 NSF per person, down from over 200 NSF per person in the old facility. Overall, headquarters facility space requirements decreased from 260 to 244 net square feet per person when all industrial, support, and storage space was included. Space allocations and utilization indexes are expressed in terms of usable square feet and exclude base building core space.

Occupancy Alternatives

Organizational Split Between Buildings

SOA tested occupancy scenarios to determine the optimum use of the new tower. Building code occupancy restrictions caused SOA to look at logical ways of splitting the corporate office and design & development (D & D) functions. SOA accordingly developed a scheme that split the corporate office and D & D functions by creating an off-site Design Center, a scheme that put the D & D office space and limited product development facilities in the tower with hazardous occupancies in a nearby industrial building, and a scheme with design staff in the tower and their shops and labs in a nearby industrial building.

Each scheme was evaluated with regard to function, schedule, cost, and an assessment of MTI's short- and long-term objectives. The off-site Design Center scheme was preferable from a functional standpoint because it allowed D & D to consolidate all of its office and industrial space in one location. This scheme also provided D & D with large open floors that were deemed necessary for a creative work environment based on team interaction and were not available in the tower.

A significant impetus for the Design Center scheme was also the availability of a 180,000 NSF industrial building within walking distance of the new tower. This one-story structure had an 18′0″ clear ceiling height and large loading dock. The availability of this space meant that construction could be accelerated and planning could be faster by having two simultaneous projects. Executive management followed SOA's recommendation to secure this building for its D & D functions.

The Tower Stack

A typical tower office floor is approximately 19,000 NSF and accommodates 80 to 100 staff. Usable space on the lower three floors ranges from 21,500 NSF to 23,500 NSF. The second floor serves as the entry for most MTI visitors and staff via bridge connection to the parking garage. There is also a second-floor bridge connection to a cafeteria in an adjacent pavilion.

SOA organized the fourteen-story tower by placing the senior executives and legal staff on the top floor, operating divisions on contiguous floors four through thirteen, and facility support services on the lower three floors. Stacking diagrams included allocations for code-required corridors and toilets not part of the base building, and quantified each division's future space surplus (or shortfall) by floor location. Alternate stacks depicted adjustments to accommodate future growth and expected corporate reorganizations.

The Design Center Block Plan

The Design Center is a 180,000 NSF industrial building consisting of high bay warehouse and low bay office space. SOA developed block plans that located D & D office and industrial functions in the high bay warehouse (140,000 NSF) and located the remaining support functions in an adjacent low bay ground floor office (20,000 NSF) and mezzanine (20,000 NSF). An existing fire wall in the high bay structure provided the necessary occupancy separation between the D & D office and industrial space users.

Planning and Design Guidelines

Planning and design guidelines were developed for both the tower and Design Center. The primary planning criteria were to do the following:

- standardize space allocation and furniture inventory
- maximize space utilization
- maximize natural light penetration (tower)
- maximize design staff interaction (Design Center)
- establish cost-effective planning and implementation concepts

Standardize Space Allocation and Furniture Inventory

New work station standards were developed to fit the building module of the new tower (Figure 12-2). These standards were also used in the Design Center because of MTI's desire to standardize work stations throughout the new facility.

SOA derived two work station footprint sizes (with six internal component variations) following an analysis of MTI's job classifications, work functions, and a study of the new tower's floor plate configuration and structural module. A 7'6'' by 9'0'' work station accommodated the needs of supervisors, professionals, secretaries, and clerks. A 9'0'' by 11'0'' work station accommodated the needs of managers.

While the new professional work station consumes fewer usable square feet than MTI's old standards, it provides 45.4 square feet of work surface, compared with 20.5 square feet for a desk and return. The station also has a potential filing capacity of 10 lineal feet (equivalent to a 30-inch-wide, four-drawer lateral file) and nine lineal feet of overhead cabinet storage. The supervisor's work station can accommodate a guest chair, while the secretarial/ clerical station includes two 30-inch-wide, four-drawer lateral files in addition to a two-drawer pedestal file. One variation for the special needs of design staff can accommodate a drafting table, ironing board, sewing machine, power drill, or oversize storage unit.

Two private office sizes were developed for typical division use. Vice presidents were allocated 195 square feet—large enough to hold a desk, credenza, and conference table. Directors were allocated 130 square feet—for a desk, credenza, and two visitor chairs. A third size was developed for use by the chief executive officer and executive vice presidents on the executive floor.

Maximize Space Utilization

The typical tower floor is a rectangle with a central core and open triangular bays at either end. The dimension from the core to the window wall is only 37 feet deep, while the perimeter structural columns are spaced at 30-foot intervals. Perimeter column enclosures project into the usable space by almost 36 inches, resulting in a considerable loss of usable area between columns. In addition, the floors had to be divided into two 9,500-square-foot areas separated by demising walls and rated vestibules to comply with the building code of the City of El Segundo. Space utilization was also affected by a 27-inch-high typical window sill, below the height of a standard work surface.

SOA developed work station standards to allow for one-and-a-half clusters per 30-foot bay (Figure 12-6). This configuration maximized space utilization on the floors, and resulted in six or nine work stations per bay, depending on the necessity for core build-out. Work station standards also had to be modified (by eliminating one work surface in favor of a visitor chair or file) to accommodate the lower sill height at the exterior window wall.

Maximize Natural Light Penetration (Tower)
SOA recommended interior offices for MTI's directors to maximize the penetration of natural light on each floor. Directors' offices would be located along the core wall, as indicated in Figure 12-6, with vice presidents' offices located on the perimeter window wall in the triangular end bays. This locational criteria was modified during the interior design phase as the directors' desire for an exterior window were accommodated, resulting in all private offices being located in the triangular end bays of each floor.

Maximize Design Staff Interaction (Design Center)
SOA developed planning criteria for interaction hubs within the design and development office space (Figure 12-7). The work stations were to be configured so as to provide open space where teamwork and a regular exchange of ideas could occur between the staff of different product lines. These occurred at key circulation nodes to encourage impromptu discussions.

Establish Cost-Effective Planning and Implementation Concepts
In the tower, systems furniture clusters were located adjacent to perimeter columns, spandrel enclosures, and core walls to provide power to systems furniture panel raceways from pre-set junction boxes since floor core borings were not permitted. In the Design Center, SOA developed a planning concept whereby standard work stations would be attached to pony walls, eliminating the need for systems furniture panel spines. This concept was based on the assumption that drywall spines would be less costly than electrical systems panels. During the interior design phase, the pony walls were omitted in favor of electrical systems panels in order to accelerate the construction schedule and to allow for future reconfiguration flexibility.

Additional Design Directives

Additional SOA-developed design directives challenged MTI's design firm to satisfy the following aesthetic requirements:

- develop a "fun," "entertaining," and "light" interior environment appropriate to a creative toy company
- develop a professional interior environment appropriate to a Fortune 500 corporation

MTI's design firm was able to resolve these diverse requirements by developing distinct design strategies for each building. A sense of quiet and order was sought for the administrative, financial, legal, and marketing functions housed in the tower. On typical floors, a predominantly gray-and-white color scheme was selected as a backdrop for MTI's product line, displayed throughout the building, and to communicate a prudent business environment to clients, visitors, and vendors. Additional visual relief is provided by a single-color accent on the interior doors, window frames, and file cabinets.

The Design Center, in contrast, exudes a sense of fun (Figures 12-8 and 12-9). A vast skylight space boasts an 18'0'' clear ceiling height with exposed trusses and mechanical ducts painted in vibrant colors. Staff interaction nodes occur at the intersections of a street grid that organizes 350 work stations into departmental neighborhoods. Private offices, conference, project, and storage rooms appear as building-like elements with angled tops and vibrant supergraphics. Upon occupancy, MTI's toy designers responded with enthusiasm to their new environment by suspending prototype toys from the exposed structure and naming streets for such well-known Mattel product lines as Barbie and Hot Wheels.

Space Plan Review

Occupancy Densities

SOA reviewed the design firm's space plans for utilization efficiency. The tower office floor plans yielded densities of 180 net square feet per person, consistent with SOA's database and concept space plans. The Design Center office was space planned at 222 NSF per person, compared with 203 programmed by SOA. While the programmed density was achievable, MTI approved a 45 percent circulation factor during the design development phase (instead of the programmed 35 percent) to accommodate the designer's streetscape parti, based on generous circulation aisles and interaction nodes. If necessary, higher utilization densities can be achieved at a later date by reconfiguring the systems furniture panels.

Conclusion

This was a successful project. Four hundred sixty thousand square feet of office and industrial space was programmed, planned, and moved within 14 months. Mattel now occupies a highly productive facility that enables it to compete more effectively in the marketplace. The success of this project may be attributed to the actions that are outlined below.

Objective and Impartial Recommendations

As pre-design consultants, SOA was able to develop recommendations without preconceived solutions or alternate interests. Occupancy alternatives were investigated and analyzed prior to the development of costly preliminary design studies. SOA's recommendations enabled senior management to make informed and organized decisions regarding the disposition and development of their real estate assets, from pre-design through move-in.

Implementable Concepts

As architects, SOA principals tested circulation factors, assessed the impact of code requirements on space utilization and documented critical environmental criteria. This enabled the consultant to develop fully implementable design and planning standards. Planning data was written in spreadsheet formats familiar to Mattel's business-oriented staff and included architecture/engineering terminology useable to its other external consultants.

Efficient and Innovative Methodology

SOA's efficient and innovative planning methodology was readily adaptable to MTI's unique needs. SOA's top down approach ensured that the strategic needs of executive management as well as the operational needs of departmental users would both be met.

Database Development Process

SOA's database development process required a thorough understanding of MTI's corporate culture, business/marketing plan, management goals and objectives, organizational structure and operational issues. SOA's data collection, data analysis and recommendations were based on a clear understanding of MTI's current and future business directions.

Client Satisfaction

MTI's headquarters now supports its on-going business plan. The facility has been "right-sized" for the company's needs. Morale is improved. Productivity is up. Space efficiency has been substantially increased. Each department's functional and operational requirements have been considered with future flexibility in mind, to allow for a rapid response to changing conditions over time.

On-Going Facility Management Tools

SOA's database development process was so effective that senior management engaged SOA following the completion of the headquarters relocation project to maintain the database and tie it to an in-house facility management space tracking system. This on-going relationship has lead to other consulting assignments as MTI continues to grow and change over time.

ACKNOWLEDGMENTS

Client: Mattel Toys, Inc., El Segundo, California — Facility Planning & Design Department. Norman Vaughan (Vice President, Facilities); Ed Orrett (Project Manager); Jan Caparella, Margaret Jarc, Mandy Liggett, Oscar Opus (Planning Team).

Programming Consultant: Sindik Olson Associates (SOA), Santa Monica,

California — Branka V. Olson, AIA (Principal-in-Charge); William T. Coleman, AIA (Principal-Senior Programmer); Saeed Mohasseb (Senior Industrial Engineer); Tom Farrell (Programmer); Erika Epstein (Planner).

Sindik Olson Associates (SOA) is a facility programming and planning consulting firm based in Santa Monica, California.

SOA's pre-design specialization ensured that MTI's business plans and operational requirements were systematically gathered, analyzed, codified, and translated into architecture/engineering terminology useful to both in-house staff and the design firm.

SOA is known for its innovative Space Needs Analysis Program (SNAP), a proprietary dBase software program for projecting and summarizing an organization's staff and space requirements over an extended time frame.

APPENDIX

Questionnaire

MATTEL TOYS
HEADQUARTERS RELOCATION PROJECT
FACILITY PLANNING QUESTIONNAIRE

Please complete this questionnaire and return to Ed Orrett, Manager–Facilities Planning and Design, M/C 12–014–R04 by 5:00 PM on November 6, 1989.

I. GENERAL IDENTIFICATION

Division: _____

Department: _____

Your Name and Title: _____

Your Immediate Supervisor: _____

Your Location: _____

Your Telephone Number: _____

II. ORGANIZATION CHART

Please attach a current organization chart. Indicate staff quantities for each level. If a formal chart does not exist, please sketch one.

III. STAFF LEVELS

Do you have staff in buildings or on floors other than the location listed on the previous page? If so, please provide a total staff breakdown by location on the following table. (Note: Shaded line represents an example of type of response requested.)

Total Staff by Location:

Building/Floor	Code	Department	Exst'g Staff
Tower–6	DJRAD	Promotional Services	12
		Total	

Do you have part time staff not identified on the previous page? If so, please provide a staff breakdown by catagory on the following table.

Total Staff by Category:

Category	Description	Exst'g Staff
Full time	Permanent	
	Temporary	
	Consultant	
	Other	
Part time	Permanent	
	Temporary	
	Seasonal	
	Other	
	Total	

Staff Mix:
Please discuss any expected future variance to the current mix of full time and part time staff.

_____
_____
_____
_____

Seasonal Fluctuation:
Do your staff levels vary significantly during the year?
Please explain any seasonal variance, staff impact, time of year and duration.

_____
_____
_____
_____

How do you prefer to provide the necessary work space? Dedicated workstations versus shared tables?

_____
_____
_____
_____

Hours of Operation:
What are your department's operating hours? _____
How many days per week? _____
Do you have shifts? Hours per day? _____

Goals and Responsibilities:
Discuss potential changes in department goals or responsibilities that may affect future staff levels or space requirements.

_____
_____
_____
_____

Organizational Realignments:
Discuss potential organizational realignments, new operations or procedures that might impact the amount of space you need, your location and equipment requirements.

_____
_____
_____
_____

Please identify existing and projected staff levels and the type of work space they currently occupy on the following table. Future projections refer to year end staff levels and should show expected staff levels as opposed to minimum or maximum. Please provide your best guess for 1993 and 1995. Use the following codes to indicate existing workspace type: Private Office=PO, Cubicle=C, Open Desk=D, Special Room=SR, Field=F.

Total Staff by Classification:

Job Classification	Staff				Existing Work
	Today	1991	1993	1995	Space Type
Analyst (Example)	3	4	5	6	C
Total					

IV. WORKSPACE REQUIREMENTS
Please indicate private office and workspace requirements for the new location.

Individual Workspace Requirements:

Classification	Privacy			Equipment				Storage/Lin Ft		Other	
	Full Ht Wall	Panel	Open	PC	VDT	Printer	Type-writer	Shelf	File	Guest Chair	Conf Table
Analyst		X		X				12	6	1	
Consultants											
Visitors											
Other											

Networking:
Please discuss special networking or data communications requirements for your department.

_____
_____
_____

Telephone:
Which job classifications from the table above require multi-line telephones?

_____
_____
_____

V. LOCATIONAL REQUIREMENTS

In the table below, identify organizations within your own division that must be located close to you. Your proximity requirements should be due to significant material flow or need for extensive person to person (rather than telephone) interface. (Note: Shaded lines represents an example of the type of response requested).

Adjacency Requirements:

Division	Department	Code	Location		
			Adjacent On Floor	Same Floor	Same Building
Mattel USA	Traffic	DAFA		X	

Please indicate any areas that can be shared with another department now or in the future.

Shared Special Use Areas:

Common Use Area	Shared With			Comments
	Code	Division	Department	
File Room	DJF	Mattel USA	Marketing	Shared records
Reception Area				
Conference Room				
Training Room				
Presentation Room				
Project Room				
Sample Room				
Shop				
File/Supply Room				
Library				
Other				
Other				

Department Autonomy:

Please indicate how your division/department could be split onto separate floors if it is not possible to locate everyone together.

_____

_____

_____

Please identify departments within your division that are relatively autonomous and could be separately located. How many staff? _____

VI. SPECIAL ROOM/AREAS AND SUPPORT SPACE

Please indicate your square footage and quantity needs for space within your area.

Special Room/Area:

| Item | Description | Area (Estimated Sq. Ft.) | | | | Shared | Comments |
		Today	1991	1993	1995	Today	
Sample Room	Toys	120	150	150	150	X	Shared with Admin
Presentation Room							
Project Room							
Sample Room							
Shop							
File/Supply Room							
Storage Room							
Library							
Other							

Special Room/Quantity:

| Special Room/Area | Description | Quantity | | | | Shared | | Frequency of Use |
		Today	1991	1993	1995	Today	Future	
Conference Room	6–8 Person	1	2	2	2		X	3 hours daily
Conference Room	16 Person							
	10–12 Person							
	6–8 Person							
	Other							
Training Room	Persons							
Reception Area	Persons							
Visitor's Office								

VII. **FILING & STORAGE**

Please indicate your filing and storage storage requirements on the table below. Include open area (general office) and special room requirements only. Do not include items stored at individual workstations and those items which may be stored in a central storage area within the building or off site. Projected requirements should anticipate purging old files and consolidation into larger fewer/files if possible. Use the following codes to indicate space type: Enclosed Room = ER, Open Area = OA.

Items Not Found in Personal Workstations:

Item	Description	Quantities				Space	Location
		Today	1991	1993	1995	Type	
Lateral Files	3 dwr	4	5	6	7	ER	File Room
Lateral Files	2 dwr						
	3 dwr						
	4 dwr						
	Other						
Vertical Files	2 dwr						
	3 dwr						
	4 dwr						
	Other						
Storage Cabinets	36″w,72″h						
Open Shelving	36″w,72″h						
Bookcase	36″ h						
Other							
Other							

On the table below, provide an estimate of non-active records, samples and general storage that could be located in a central building storage area but is now located within your department. Also, provide an estimate of active records, samples storage that is now located outside your area (on another floor, warehouse or off-site) that should be relocated to your new space. Do not include cage items that will remain in a warehouse or bulk storage environment.

Filing and Storage:

Item	Description	Qty	Active	Non-Active	Move From	Move To
File Cabinets	4 dwr	35		X	Existing office	off-site records center
Shelves	36″w, 6 shlvs					
Storage Cabinet	36″w					
File Cabinets	4 dwr					

VIII. EQUIPMENT

Please list all required general office and special room equipment that will not be located at individual workstations in the new space.

Equipment:

Item	Description	Quantities				Table	Floor	Location
		Today	1991	1993	1995			
Photocopier	Large	1	1	1	1		X	File Room
Photocopier								
Microfiche	Reader/Printer							
Microfilm	Reader/Printer							
Terminal								
PC								
Printer								
Typewriter								
Fax								

IX. SPECIAL REQUIREMENTS

Unique/Custom Items:
Please identify specially designed and fabricated counters, pass–thru windows, workstations or other items that should be relocated with you.

_____
_____
_____

Special Construction:
Please identify areas requiring a raised floor, dedicated air conditioning, or special electrical, mechanical and/or plumbing and any heavy floor loading requirements.

_____
_____
_____

Security:
Please identify external and internal security requirements for all of your spaces.

_____
_____
_____

Do you require card key access to your department or a special room within your space?

_____
_____

Enclosed Versus Open Department:
Does your department require any full height wall separations from other division/department or occupants on the floor?

_____

_____

_____

Public Contact:
Does your department have significant public contact? What are the average number of visitor's per day?

_____

_____

_____

Move Date:
Please indicate months of the year that your department cannot move for functional reasons. State reasons.

_____

_____

_____

Do you need to move at the same time as another organization? Why?

_____

_____

_____

Other:
Please provide the consultant with any additional information necessary for an understanding of your staff and space requirements. Attach additional pages if necessary.

_____

_____

_____

END OF QUESTIONNAIRE

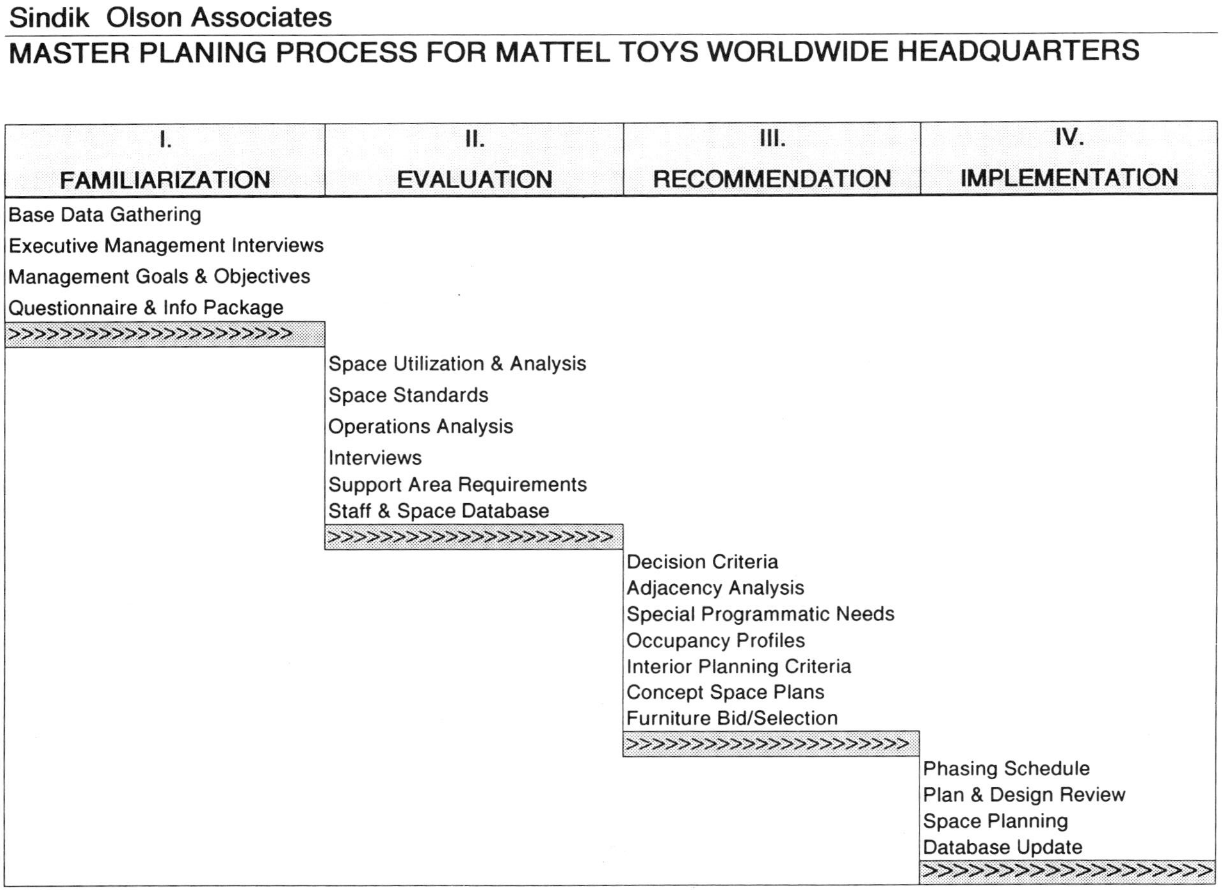

Sindik Olson Associates

MASTER PLANING PROCESS FOR MATTEL TOYS WORLDWIDE HEADQUARTERS

I. FAMILIARIZATION	II. EVALUATION	III. RECOMMENDATION	IV. IMPLEMENTATION
Base Data Gathering Executive Management Interviews Management Goals & Objectives Questionnaire & Info Package	Space Utilization & Analysis Space Standards Operations Analysis Interviews Support Area Requirements Staff & Space Database	Decision Criteria Adjacency Analysis Special Programmatic Needs Occupancy Profiles Interior Planning Criteria Concept Space Plans Furniture Bid/Selection	Phasing Schedule Plan & Design Review Space Planning Database Update

FIGURE 12-1.   Master Planning Process for Mattel Toys Worldwide Headquarters

MATTEL TOYS, INC.
HEADQUARTERS RELOCATION PROJECT
OPEN SYSTEMS WORKSTATION STANDARDS

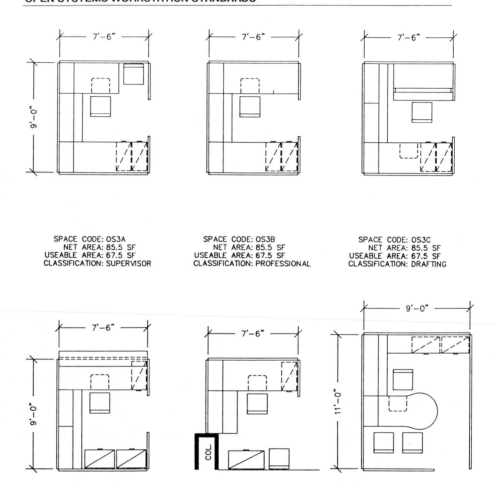

SPACE CODE: OS3A
NET AREA: 85.5 SF
USEABLE AREA: 67.5 SF
CLASSIFICATION: SUPERVISOR

SPACE CODE: OS3B
NET AREA: 85.5 SF
USEABLE AREA: 67.5 SF
CLASSIFICATION: PROFESSIONAL

SPACE CODE: OS3C
NET AREA: 85.5 SF
USEABLE AREA: 67.5 SF
CLASSIFICATION: DRAFTING

SPACE CODE: OS3D
NET AREA: 85.5 SF
USEABLE AREA: 67.5 SF
CLASSIFICATION: SECRETARIAL

SPACE CODE: OS3F
NET AREA: 85.5 SF
USEABLE AREA: 67.5 SF
CLASSIFICATION: (NON-SPECIFIC)
LOCATION: AT WINDOW

SPACE CODE: OS5A
NET AREA: 117 SF
USEABLE AREA: 99 SF
CLASSIFICATION: MANAGER

FIGURE 12-2.   Open Systems Work Station Standards

MATTEL TOYS, INC.
HEADQUARTERS RELOCATION PROJECT
OPERATIONAL CHART

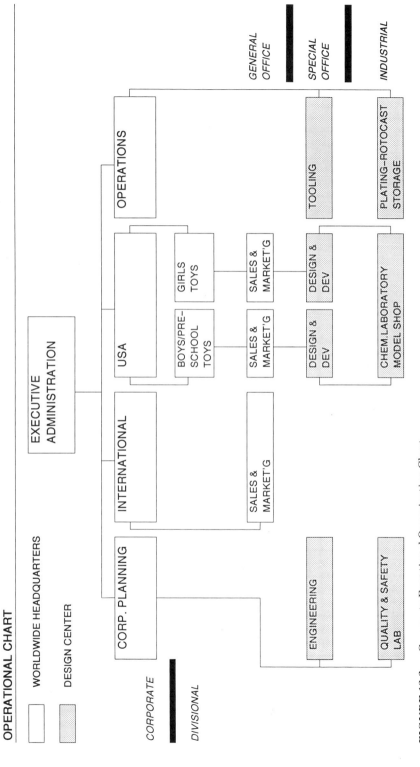

FIGURE 12-3. Corporate Functional Organization Chart

MATTEL TOYS
HEADQUARTERS RELOCATION
MACRO-DATABASE SPREADSHEET

TYPICAL DIVISION: STAFF & SPACE REQUIREMENTS

Code	DEPARTMENT	1989 LOC	1989 STAFF	EVP 260	VP 195	DIR 130	MGR 117	STAFF 86	CSLT 86	TOTAL STAFF	1991 NSF	CIRC %	SUBT'L NSF	CONF	STO	WS	OPEN	NSF	CIRC %	SUBT'L NSF	TOTAL SPACE (NSF)	NAF	RATE %	1993 TOTAL STAFF	1993 SPACE (NSF)	1995 TOTAL STAFF	1995 SPACE (NSF)
E	ADMINISTRATION	4	2		1		1			2	312	40%	437	225	250		60	535	35%	722	1,159	580	3%	2	1,230	2	1,305
EA	PERSONNEL	4	12			3	5	2	2	12	1,319	40%	1,847	150	80			230	35%	311	2,157	180	3%	13	2,288	14	2,428
EB	ADMIN SVCS	4	2			1		1		2	216	40%	302					0	35%	0	302	151	3%	2	321	2	340
EC	RECRUITMENT	4	4			1	1	3		5	505	40%	707	100		86	45	231	35%	312	1,019	204	3%	5	1,081	6	1,147
ED	SECURITY	5	30			1	1	6		30	763	40%	1,068	150	240		1,001	1,391	35%	1,878	2,946	98	3%	32	3,125	34	3,316
EDA	PURCHASING	2G	5				1	4		5	461	40%	645				210	210	35%	284	929	186	3%	5	985	6	1,045
EE	CORP AFFAIRS	4	5		1	2		3		6	713	40%	998	150	100			250	35%	338	1,336	223	3%	6	1,417	7	1,503
EF	CREDIT UNION	4	6			1		5		6	560	40%	784	225	250		328	803	35%	1,084	1,868	311	3%	6	1,982	7	2,103
EH	FACILITIES	4	2			1		1		2	216	40%	302	150				150	35%	203	505	252	3%	2	536	2	568
EHA	PLANNING	4	5				1	4		5	461	40%	645		112	258	48	418	35%	564	1,210	242	3%	5	1,283	6	1,362
EHB	OPERATIONS	4	3			1		2		3	302	40%	423					0	35%	0	423	141	3%	3	449	3	476
EJ	COMPENSATION	4	15			1	2	13		16	1,482	40%	2,075	225	375			600	35%	810	2,885	180	3%	17	3,060	18	3,247
	TOTAL		91	0	2	12	12	44	2	94	7,310	40%	10,234	1,375	1,407	344	1,692	4,818	35%	6,504	16,738	178	3%	100	17,758	106	18,839

FIGURE 12-4. Database Spreadsheet

MATTEL TOYS WORLDWIDE HEADQUARTERS STACK (1995)

TOWER	1995	Available
14 EXECUTIVE	7,853	
CORPORATE AFFAIRS	1,503	
LEGAL	6,715	
Ring Corridor	1,580	
Unassigned Space	1,323	18,974
13 FINANCE	14,827	
ARCO	3,600	
Unassigned Space	547	18,974
12 FINANCE	13,558	
LEGAL	3,297	
Unassigned Space	2,119	18,974
11 INTERNATIONAL	16,688	
Unassigned Space	2,286	18,974
10 USA	22,693	
Unassigned Space	(3,719)	18,974
9 USA	14,344	
Unassigned Space	4,630	18,974
8 USA	17,559	
Unassigned Space	1,415	18,974
7 USA	14,453	
Unassigned Space	4,521	18,974
6 USA	10,662	
CORPORATE PLANNING	9,700	
Unassigned Space	(1,388)	18,974
5 CORPORATE PLANNING	8,655	
OPERATIONS	8,817	
USA	553	
Unassigned Space	949	18,974
4 OPERATIONS	7,070	
FINANCE	9,561	
USA	1,077	
Unassigned Space	1,266	18,974
3 ADMINISTRATION	10,455	
SUPPORT & CORRIDOR	7,680	
Unassigned Space	5,438	23,573
2 ADMINISTRATION	4,303	
MESSAGE CENTER	1,562	
AUDIO VISUAL	713	
PRESENTATION ROOMS	5,000	
SUPPORT & CORRIDOR	11,695	
Unassigned Space	300	23,573
G COMPANY STORE	4,490	
CREDIT UNION	1,524	
CHILD TEST CENTER	2,317	
TRAVEL AGENCY	130	
REPROGRAPHICS/MAIL	5,852	
SUPPORT & CORRIDOR	7,009	
Unassigned Space	201	21,523
BUILDING TOTAL		277,383
ASSIGNED SPACE TOTAL	257,495	
UNASSIGNED SPACE TOTAL	19,888	

DESIGN CENTER	1995	Available
OFFICE		
USA	83,480	
OPERATIONS	4,861	
CORPORATE PLANNING	1,600	
Subtotal	89,941	
SHOP		
CHEMISTRY LAB	4,766	
MODEL & MOLD SHOP	25,978	
SAMPLE SHOP	6,312	
AUDIO VISUAL & PHOTO	8,963	
CAMERA GRAPHICS	2,962	
PRODUCT DESIGN SHOP	3,174	
ULTRASONIC LAB	864	
QUALITY & SAFETY LAB	4,766	
MAINTENANCE SHOP	666	
MAIL	140	
REPROGRAPHICS	3,503	
Subtotal	62,094	
SUPPORT	7,000	
STORAGE	20,800	
BUILDING TOTAL		180,000
ASSIGNED SPACE TOTAL	179,835	
UNASSIGNED SPACE TOTAL	165	

FIGURE 12-5.   Stacking Diagram

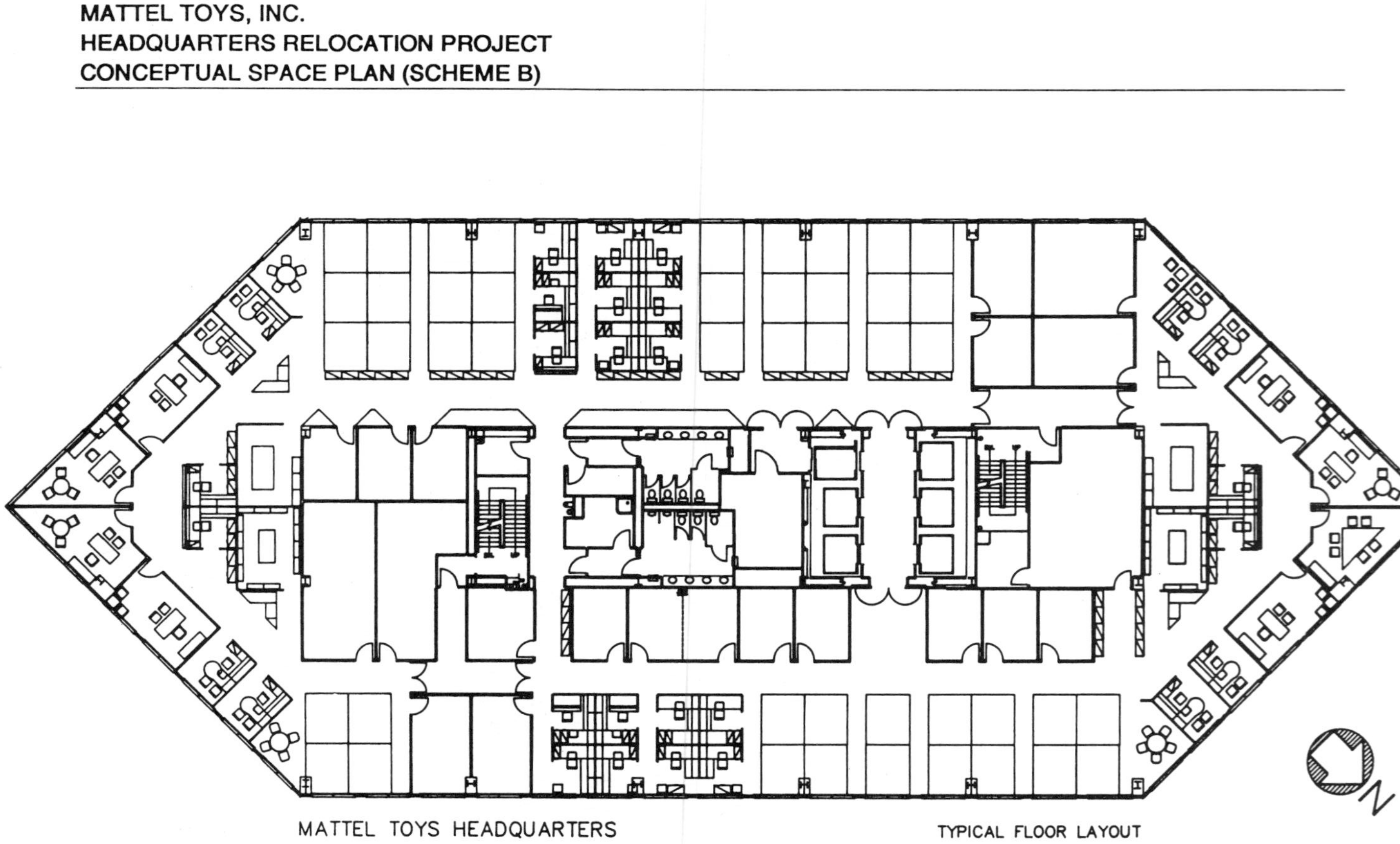

MATTEL TOYS, INC.
HEADQUARTERS RELOCATION PROJECT
CONCEPTUAL SPACE PLAN (SCHEME B)

TYPICAL FLOOR LAYOUT

MATTEL TOYS HEADQUARTERS

FIGURE 12-6. Concept Space Plan for Tower

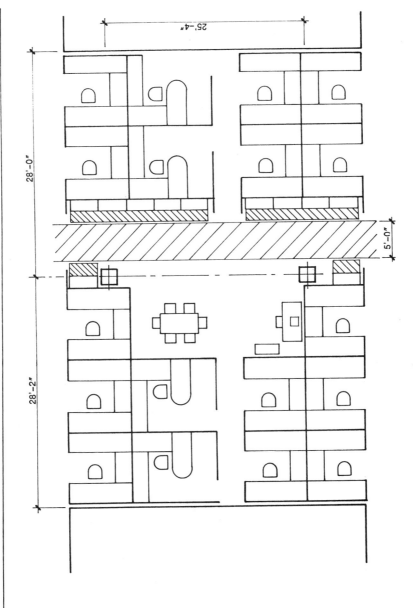

MATTEL TOYS, INC.
HEADQUARTERS RELOCATION PROJECT
DESIGN CENTER INTERACTION NODE (TYPICAL)

FIGURE 12-7. Staff Interaction Node for Design Center

333

FIGURE 12-8. Design Center: Toy Design and Development Studio

FIGURE 12-9.   Design Center: Toy Designer's Work Station

CHAPTER 13

A Facility Planning Framework for Programming the Office Environment

Peter McLennan

INTRODUCTION

The strategic brief integrates the quantitative business reality of the present (measured in dollars and cents) with the qualitative vision of the future (expressed in the corporate mission statement and culture) to guide office accommodation decisions. DEGW Ltd., an international design and consultancy practice headquartered in London, has been creating briefs for a variety of British, European, and multinational clients for twenty years. The focus of their work is the user, and DEGW continues to develop models for understanding and predicting the changing needs of office users.[1] This chapter describes an approach to strategic facility briefing using these models. The benefits of these models are the following:

- a user focus and research agenda
- visible and adaptable methods allowing comparison between cases
- a focus on supporting the organization's business goals and objectives

---

[1]DEGW Ltd. 1992. *The responsible workplace.* Publication pending. Oxford, United Kingdom: Butterworth Architecture.

DEGW Ltd. 1985. *Eleven contemporary office buildings: A comparative study.* London: DEGW.

Duffy, Francis, Franklin Becker, Gerald Davis, and William Sims. 1985. ORBIT 2. Norwalk, Conn.: Harbinger Group Inc.

Duffy, Francis, and Alex Henney. 1989. *The changing city.* London: Bulstrode Press.

These features provide benefits to clients through these means:

- solutions that are user-specific while drawing on comparable data
- systematic comparison and benchmarking of space use and building stock
- solutions that maximize the effective use of a building

The strategic facility models rely on data: The broad principles for the organization of these data are the subject of the next four sections. The sections are Facility Management Framework, Space Taxonomy and Measurement, Supply and Demand, and Space in Use: Identifying User Requirements. A case study of a strategic facility brief follows to illustrate how these methods are used in practice.

FACILITY MANAGEMENT FRAMEWORK

The Library of Congress defines facility management in this way:

> The practice of coordinating the physical workplace with the people and work of the organization; integrates the principles of business administration, architecture, and the behavioral and engineering sciences.[2]

The facility manager is at the center of the briefing process for the organization. The rising importance of facility staff in service organizations reflects the increasing complexity of the modern service organization. Businesses involving insurance, banking, accountancy, law, and financial services are undergoing changes similar to those of the early eighteenth and nineteenth century industrialists with the introduction of information technology.[3] This increasing complexity requires a briefing approach that recognizes not only the importance of the organization and its mission, but also the users, their requirements, and the need to prioritize key decisions related to office accommodation.

The strategic facility brief touches on all four functional areas of the typical facility department. It deals with real estate, general services, operations and maintenance, and facility planning. However, facility planning is the central focus of the briefing process. It is through the briefing process that the

---

[2]Binder, Stephen. 1989. *Corporate facility planning: An inside view for designers and managers.* New York: McGraw-Hill.

[3]Toffler, A. 1980. *The third wave.* New York: Bantam Books.

Davis, S. 1987. *Future perfect.* Reading, Mass.: Addison-Wesley.

Drucker, P. 1985. *Innovation and entrepreneurship.* New York: Harper & Row.

Forester, T., ed. 1989. *Computers in the human context: Information technology, productivity and people.* London: The MIT Press.

Sproull, L., and S. Kiesler. 1991. *Connections: New ways of working in the networked organization.* London: The MIT Press.

organizational goals and mission are developed within the context of a building. The strategic facility brief also allows the general objective of facility planning to be incorporated within the planning process. This objective can be stated as "the management of office accommodation, through time, in the most cost-effective way in order to achieve the organization's goals."[4]

DEGW's facility planning initiatives model provides the methodology for developing the strategic brief. The initiatives are a hierarchy of five key elements used to structure the client's accommodation requirements. (Figure 13-1). They provide a simple framework that clarifies the relationship between office accommodation and the organization, and help prioritize each organization's special accommodation requirements. It is thereby possible to establish the key needs relating to the project at hand. A brief definition of each initiative follows.

- *Space budget*: the quantitative and qualitative description of needs required to satisfy an organization's demand for space based on space guidelines.
- *Planning concepts*: the key organizing principles used to locate space and objects to ensure both efficient and effective use of space.
- *Furniture and equipment*: the objects of the planning concept tailored to satisfy an organization's operations.
- *Building performance*: environmental and servicing standards and strategies for the effective management and sustainability of the organization's working patterns.
- *Image and design*: the effective communication of the company's internal (culture) and external images through processes that use all the facility planning initiatives in combination with design flair and innovation.

These initiatives are a synthesis of DEGW's current thinking in the area of office accommodation, and they incorporate many current concepts on the analysis of the office environment.[5]

As the hierarchy shows, space is the core of the facility brief. The model uses

---

[4]Thomson, Tony. 1990. The essence of facility management. *Facilities* 8:8, pp. 8-12.

[5]Bordass, W. 1991. Building performance: The user perspective. *The responsible workplace*. Publication pending. Oxford, United Kingdom: Butterworth Architecture.

Bradman, G., ed. 1990. *Buildings and health: The Rosehaugh guide to the construction, use and maintenance of buildings.* London: RIBA.

Davis, G., and T. Ventre, eds. 1989. *Performance of buildings and serviceability of facilities.* Philadelphia: ASTM.

Hedge, A. 1990. Sick building syndrome correlated with complex array of factors. *Facility management journal* Jan./Feb., pp. 52-58.

Hedge, A. 1989. Environmental conditions and health in offices. *International review of ergonomics* 3, pp. 87-110.

Leaman, A. 1991. The responsible workplace: User expectations. *The responsible workplace*. Publication pending. Oxford, United Kingdom: Butterworth Architecture.

McLennan, P. 1990. Sick building syndrome: An alternate view. *Facilities* 8:4, pp. 21-23.
Preiser, W., ed. 1989. *Building evaluation.* New York: Plenum Press.

DEGW's space taxonomy for the measurement of space. The consistent measurement of space enables the data to be collected with a high degree of conformity, which allows comparative interpretation of the data. This measurement is further differentiated into the supply side—dealing with the building—and the demand side—dealing with the organization's requirements.

SPACE TAXONOMY AND MEASUREMENT

The taxonomy of space enables the space data to be clearly structured. The purpose of the measurement of space is to identify the net usable area (NUA). The NUA is used for establishing the amount of space an organization requires, the amount of space an organization uses, and the amount of space available in a building. Using the NUA as a measure of space allows for comparison and understanding of space requirements.

The following are definitions for the space categories illustrated in Figure 13-2:

- *Gross internal area (GIA):* total floor area of building, to internal face of external wall or atrium wall, including internal structure and core. It excludes roof plant and totally unlit areas.
- *Core area:* the area containing elevators, stairs, common lobbies, plant and service areas, ducts, rest rooms, and the area of internal structure.
- *Net internal area (NIA):* total floor area of building to internal face of external or atrium walls excluding core (GIA minus core).
- *Primary circulation:* major routes within the NIA that link fire escapes. Routes are arranged so that no point within the NIA is further than 9 meters from a primary circulation route.
- *Net usable area (NUA):* the usable area remaining after core and primary circulation have been subtracted from the GIA.
- *Work space:* the usable area given over to workplaces for individuals. This area is net of all ancillary space. Work space is divided into enclosed (separated by continuous, full-height walls) and open plans.
- *Ancillary space:* the usable area given over to functions that support an individual division, unit, or working group (local machine rooms, meeting rooms, storage areas, shared terminals).
- *Support space:* the usable area given over to functions that support the whole organization or building (mail room, telecommunications areas, central computer room, library).
- *Fit-factor:* an allowance for space to take account of the fact that fitting into actual buildings inevitably means some inefficiencies in occupation because of natural obstructions (columns, awkward angles, etc.) and the size of the floors (do not fit the size of divisions or units precisely). A fit factor of 5 percent is common in regular rectangular buildings.

SUPPLY AND DEMAND

The DEGW supply-demand model separates office space into two distinct areas for spatial analysis. Buildings are providers of space in which activities take place. This is called *supply*. The building (supply) categories of space are gross internal area (GIA), net internal area (NIA), and net usable area (NUA). These measurements depend on the design of the building and indicate the amount of space within a building. The evaluation of a building has two components:

- quantitative—the dimensional and measurable aspects of the building spatially, structurally, and mechanically
- qualitative—the level of services of the planning grid, internal components, and the fitness of the space for its intended purpose

On the other hand, the activities that take place within buildings can be thought of in terms of the amount of space that these activities require. This is called *demand*. The organizational (demand) categories of space are the net usable area (NUA), which is divided into work space, ancillary space, support space, and fit-factor. The areas are determined by the requirements of the organization. The organizational space need is also developed in two parts:

- quantitative—the space standards or space guidelines; the space budget using a classification of space into three areas: work space, ancillary space, and support space
- qualitative—an understanding of the organizational goals and mission, group structure, patterns of work, use of information technology, and points of change

SPACE IN USE: IDENTIFYING
USER REQUIREMENTS

The process of reviewing a client's present accommodation enables the client to understand where they are today. As business decision studies have noted, human judgment relies on particular heuristics for structuring and reviewing information.[6] It is important to understand and demonstrate how space is currently being used. The decision makers are "anchored" to the situation as it exists. Figure 13-3 illustrates the connection between supply and demand and the current space use. In an existing occupancy situation, the analysis will point out those areas in the building that are not working optimally and those areas of organizational demand that are changing and are therefore new requirements for the building to match.

---

[6]Bazerman, M. 1986. *Judgment in managerial decision making*. New York: John Wiley & Sons.

Kahneman, D., P. Slovic, and A. Tversky, eds. 1982. *Judgment under uncertainty: Heuristics and biases*. New York: Cambridge University Press.

THE FACILITY PLANNING
INITIATIVES IN USE: A CASE STUDY

Background

DEGW was asked by a service group within a large insurance company to review their current office accommodation in London's Chatham Place. The purpose was to consolidate their present use of space and recommend a facility planning approach for the ongoing use of Chatham Place. The primary focus of the strategic facility brief was the review of the work space. The service group has occupied the majority of the space within Chatham Place, an eight-story 1960s building in the City of London, for over two years. As an internal service department of an insurance company, the group has come under increasing pressure to be competitive with external service providers. An effective use of space can enable the group to reduce overhead and maintain a competitive pricing position. Space is a major contributor to the group's overhead, which is exaggerated by the fact that the City of London is one of the world's most expensive property markets. For example, a range of base city rental costs in 1990 were £20 to £70 ($38 to $134) per square foot (NIA), to which rates (taxes) and operating charges (electricity, insurance, and heating) are added, resulting in a net cost of £40 to £120 per square foot (NIA) ($75 to $220 per square foot). In addition, London is also an inflexible property market, since the twenty-five year lease with five-year upward-only rent reviews remains the traditional form of leasing contract. Given the present building of 39,000 square feet (NIA) (3,700 square meters NIA), the costs would range from £1.56 million per year to £4.68 million per year ($2.97 million to $8.93 million).

Strategic Facility Recommendations

The strategic brief outlines recommendations for the short-term and the long-term occupancy of Chatham Place. The short-term recommendations focus on two elements that would immediately affect the efficiency of space use within Chatham Place:

- Regularize the work space, ancillary space, and furniture layouts using space standards that complement the modularity of the building. This reflects current best practice among similar organizations and will lead to long-term operational savings as modifications to the layout occur.
- The strong organizational mission statement is not expressed in the interior fit-out and decoration of the present office environment. The recommendations are to:

    redecorate the core area from the basement to the sixth floor to create a consistent fit between the organizational goals and the visual environment, and

    add signage to the areas immediately off the core to reinforce departmental identity.

The long-term recommendations require management decisions regarding the need for current levels of ancillary space and support space, furniture, and building services. The specific priorities for further investigation follow:

- The storage and shared equipment provision (ancillary space) is comparatively higher than for other similar organizations and should be reviewed with a view toward a 30 to 40 percent reduction to yield long-term space gains. The use of electronic data storage is a potential option that should be considered.
- The cafeteria, conference rooms, and training room (support space) could be multiple-use facilities, which would increase utilization. This would release space to increase the overall building density.
- A review of the current furniture will be required to demonstrate compliance with EC directive 90/270 on video display unit use in the workplace (pending Parliamentary interpretation of this directive in 1992).[7]
- The natural ventilation system does not appear to be coping with the increase in heat gain from the high density of computer equipment. This has implications on both staff comfort and productivity. Careful planning can eliminate some of the problems, but a considered review of the possibility of adding limited mechanical ventilation is suggested.

Analysis of Chatham Place— Understanding the Supply

The analysis of Chatham Place reviews the quantitative aspects of the building. The quantitative analysis uses two efficiency ratios to assess the quantity of space in buildings: the landlord efficiency ratio and the tenant efficiency ratio. The landlord efficiency ratio is a measure of the amount of leasable space that is lost to the cores of the building (tenants do not pay for the core areas in the United Kingdom). This ratio is expressed as a percentage of net internal area/gross internal area (NIA/GIA), with three ranges: excellent, good, and poor. The tenant efficiency ratio is a measure of the amount of net internal area a tenant will lose because of the need for primary circulation routes. The pattern of these primary routes is determined by statutory requirements for fire exits. Tenant efficiency is expressed as a percentage of net usable area/net internal area (NUA/NIA), with four ranges: excellent, good, fair, and poor. These spatial ratios represent comparative, but not absolute, judgments on the relative success of a particular office building plan. The efficiencies reflect commercial practices and are used as a reference point that is considered a benchmark for comparative purposes. The process involves the measurement

---

[7]EC directive 90/270 concerns the minimum safety and health requirements for work with display screen equipment. It is very broadly conceived in that it deals with equipment, the working environment, the software interface, and the management of the work. The directive mandates membership compliance by December 31, 1992.

TABLE 13-1   Building Area Data

Chatham Place	Gross Internal Area (GIA)	Core	Net Internal Area (NIA)	NIA/GIA % Efficiency	Primary Circulation	Net Usable Area (NUA)	NUA/NIA % Efficiency
Total sq m	4523	875	3648	81%	478	3170	87%
Total sq ft	48686	9419	39267	81%	5145	34122	87%

of the gross internal area, the measurement of the core areas, and the establishment and measurement of the primary circulation routes. All areas are based on measurements from computer drawings and copies of existing plans. The important aspects of the quantitative and qualitative analysis are summarized below (see Figures 13-4 and 13-5 and Table 13-1).

Key Supply Findings
QUANTITATIVE
- 3,170 square meters is the estimate of net usable area available in the building
- 417 square meters NUA is the size of a typical floor
- good landlord efficiency ratio of 81 percent
- excellent tenant ratio of 87 percent
- 15 percent, or 475.5 square meters, of the NUA is difficult to plan primarily located on floors 1 through 5
- 3.6 meters by 6.0 meters is the principal grid for enclosure, a function of the column spacing, the operable windows, and the downstand beams in the ceiling

QUALITATIVE
- good data, telecommunications, and electrical supply and distribution through raised floor and structured wiring system
- good parking and goods delivery areas for city building
- floor loading could be a potential problem on the upper floors
- natural ventilation is the principal weakness of the building, owing to lack of cross-ventilation and acoustical problems with open windows

Analysis of the Building in Use—Identifying Opportunities and Constraints

An analysis of the building in use identifies the opportunities and constraints within the present layout of the building. The facility initiatives provide the framework for the review. The key items of space use, planning concept, furniture and equipment, building services, and image and design are outlined.

Space Use
NET USABLE AREA
The percentage of space used in each category follows (Figure 13-6):

- workspace is on the whole minimum with little scope for change; the enclosed offices, while large at 3.6 meters by 6 meters, are best left as is
- ancillary space, at 18 percent of the total NUA, is some 3 percent more than typically found in offices of this type
- support space, at 27 percent is not unusually high, given that there is a large catering facility on-site

DENSITY
- 15.21 square meters/staff is the average density of net usable area across the building for all departments (this figure excludes catering and maintenance staff); this figure is high in comparison to other organizations of this type
- 10.93 square meters/staff is the average density of work space and ancillary space across the building (this figure excludes the 882 square meters of support space); again, this figure is high
- 4.28 square meters/staff is the average density of support space for each staff member

Figure 13-7 illustrates the range of department densities against the average density figure represented by the horizontal line of the graph. The larger departments using open plan are under the average density figure and use the space effectively at present. The smaller departments with enclosed staff are over the density figure, with little scope for modification.

Current Planning Considerations
A review of the building diagram indicates the planning potential for the various areas of the building. This plan analysis will form the basis of the proposed planning concept, given the present requirements of the organization (Figure 13-8).
The key considerations for the existing planning follow:

- a review of the current stacking and blocking indicates the potential for consolidating the existing departments to free up at least half a floor
- 3.6 meters by 6.0 meters bay size is the current enclosed office module established by column spacing and the window mullion condition
- enclosed office locations need to be more clearly established
- building size is perceived by staff as a very positive quality
- corridor route edged with 2.2-meter-high storage cabinets and partitioning causes a dark tunnel effect along the primary corridor and inhibits cross-ventilation within the building
- the wing area adjacent to the core is more difficult to use owing to single-sided ventilation and separation from the rest of the building

Furniture and Equipment Issues

- Storage seems to be overprovided-for within departments and the tall (2.2-meter-high) cabinets inhibit cross-ventilation.
- Shared equipment could be rationalized within some areas and moved away from the primary corridor.
- Desks could benefit from the addition of screening, with paper flow and/or shelf attachments to help organize the paperwork.

Building Services Issues

Natural ventilation does not cope with the amount of information technology equipment currently in use within Chatham Place. Overheating occurs where computer printers and copiers are located along the corridor edge of the open land. This may contribute to a potential localized "sick building syndrome" problem for those staff seated near these areas (laser printers and copiers emit limited quantities of ozone, which is a known respiratory irritant).

Image and Design Issues

- Bland colors and finishes provide little differentiation between the open plan area and the public spaces, like the main stairwell-elevator shaft and the primary corridor.
- Signage is needed in two areas: a general building directory on the ground and each subsequent floor, more visible individual signage on each floor.

Organizational Demand—Identifying the Future User Requirements

Buildings have become more central to the business performance of service organizations. Improving the match between the building, the users' requirements, and company culture is adding to business success.[8] The user requirements of an organization begin with an understanding of the group's organizational goals; these goals provide a set of criteria and standards for a building to respond to and support. The service group's goals are clearly stated in their service charter and other organizational literature (Figure 13-9). They have stated a desire to be perceived as innovative, professional, and friendly. These organizational objectives can be translated into general planning and design objectives as follows:

- develop guidelines for space use that allow for individual expression while using the building effectively
- develop planning concepts to support staff in their work while reducing operational expense
- develop planning strategies that will adapt to changing economic conditions
- utilize the property to respect commercial value

---

[8]Cassels, S. 1990. Design in business. *Facilities* 8:9, pp. 10-11.

Space Use
SPACE STANDARDS
The proposed standards reflect the trend among international organizations of creating operational effectiveness through these means:

- using a small number of modular standards for different grades of staff
- using furniture to provide the basis of a work station standard that can be developed through the hierarchy of grades
- optimizing the provision of ancillary and support space

The four work space standards are recommended to complement the modularity of the primary building grid of 3.6 meters by 6 meters (Figure 13-10). There are two enclosed and two open plan work space standards (both standards will use existing furniture):

- 43 square meters for managing directors; includes meeting room
- 21.6 square meters for managers with enclosed offices
- 10.8 square meters for department managers in open plan
- 5.4 square meters for all open plan staff

NET USABLE AREA
Figure 13-11 illustrates the effect of the space standards on the total NUA required. There is a flat head count growth forecast for all departments, indicating no demand for additional space. The pie chart illustrates the space categories as a percentage of the existing NUA in order to demonstrate the space savings that can be achieved with the rationalization of the work space standards.

DENSITY
In rationalizing the work space standards, the density is increased slightly.

- 14.98 square meters NUA for each staff (10.69 productive space/staff) is the immediately achievable density
- any further reasonable increase in density requires a management review of the current ancillary and support space provision; additional equipment space should come from the existing provision

Planning Concepts
The proposed concept layout is intended to maximize the modularity of Chatham Place to provide a degree of adaptability for future changes within the organization. The concept layout supports the facility planning and design objectives (Figure 13-12).

Furniture and Equipment
There is a likely increase in the use of specialist information technology equipment. This will put additional pressure on the need for shared work space. The implications are that additional work surfaces are required and that

additional space is required. It is anticipated that any additional space requirements can be met with a rationalization of the existing ancillary space.

Building Performance

The increased use of information technology (computers, printers, and other peripherals) is likely to increase the need for mechanical ventilation, especially during the summer months.

Image and Design

Stronger design elements are needed to match the group's mission statement and management objectives.

CONCLUSIONS

Three conclusions can be drawn from the case study. First, it demonstrates that solutions to accommodation issues can be identified through the use of the models outlined. Attention was focused on the areas that required management decisions in creating a more responsive and effective office environment, specifically the generous ancillary space and support space provision and the need to review the building ventilation. This happened because there were quality data that could be codified into building-related information specific to the organization. The ability of the facility management staff to provide and verify complex data was critical—this saved time and reduced the cost of collecting the initial data. The facility manager is well placed to coordinate the complex design and organizational data to ensure that the company's vision of the future is supported through the office environment. This case study demonstrates the benefits of this collaboration through the quantitative benefits of improving the quality of the working environment for employees.

The second conclusion, within the larger context of facility planning, is the usefulness of the systematic application of the models for comparing buildings and for developing profiles of particular user types. The model for building (supply) appraisal is currently used in this fashion by developers looking to improve the quality of their building stock within a particular business sector—financial services, for example. The landlord and tenant ratios quoted are the result of DEGW's systematic appraisals of city building stock. In addition, the appraisal method can be applied by building users to assess a series of buildings for future occupancy. Developers and tenants can use comparative building information and user profiles to improve the effectiveness of both the creation and selection of buildings.

The last conclusion is the importance of establishing visible criteria that can be reviewed and evaluated as the organization changes over time. This provides a way toward providing a deeper understanding of the increasing complexity of the organization's requirements on the office environment. Understanding the pressures for change from the use of information technology to planning innovation demanded by matrix organizations is important.

Reviewing and evaluating facility information provides organizations with a business edge on their competition by providing an office environment that directly supports business goals.

References

Bazerman, M. 1986. *Judgment in managerial decision making.* New York: John Wiley & Sons.

Binder, Stephen. 1989. *Corporate facility planning: An inside view for designers and managers.* New York: McGraw-Hill.

Bordass, W. 1991. Building performance: the user perspective. *The responsible workplace.* Publication pending. Oxford, United Kingdom: Butterworth Architecture.

Bradman, G., ed. 1990. *Buildings and health: The Rosehaugh guide to the construction, use and maintenance of buildings.* London: RIBA.

Cassels, S. 1990. Design in business. *Facilities* 8:9, pp. 10-11.

Council Directive (EEC) 90/270 (OJ L156 21.6.90 p14) concerning the minimum safety and health requirements for work with display screen equipment (fifth individual Directive within the meaning of 89/391, art 16(1)).

Davis, G., and T. Ventre, eds. 1989. *Performance of buildings and serviceability of facilities.* Philadelphia: ASTM.

Davis, S. 1987. *Future perfect.* Reading, Mass.: Addison-Wesley.

DEGW Ltd. 1985. *Eleven contemporary office buildings: A comparative study.* London: DEGW.

DEGW, Ltd. 1991. *The responsible workplace.* Unpublished research report.

Drucker, P. 1985. *Innovation and Entrepreneurship.* New York: Harper & Row.

Duffy, Francis, and Alex Henney. 1989. *The changing city.* London: Bulstrode Press.

Duffy, Francis, Franklin Becker, Gerald Davis, and William Sims. 1985. *ORBIT 2.* Norwalk, Conn.: Harbinger Group Inc.

Forester, T., ed. 1989. *Computers in the human context: Information technology, productivity and people.* London: The MIT Press.

Hedge, A. 1989. Environmental conditions and health in offices. *International review of ergonomics* 3, pp. 87-110.

Hedge, A. 1990. Sick building syndrome correlated with complex array of factors. *Facility management journal,* Jan./Feb., pp. 52-58.

Kahneman, D., P. Slovic, and A. Tversky, eds. 1982. *Judgment under uncertainty: Heuristics and biases.* New York: Cambridge University Press.

Leaman, A. 1991. The responsible workplace: User expectations. *The responsible workplace.* Publication pending. Oxford, United Kingdom: Butterworth Architecture.

McLennan, P. 1990. Sick building syndrome: An alternate view. *Facilities* 8:4, pp. 21-23.

Preiser, W., ed. 1989. *Building evaluation.* New York: Plenum Press.

Sproull, L., and S. Kiesler. 1991. *Connections: New ways of working in the networked organization.* London: The MIT Press.

Thomson, Tony. 1990. The essence of facility management. *Facilities* 8:8, pp. 8-12.

Toffler, A. 1980. *The third wave.* New York: Bantam Books.

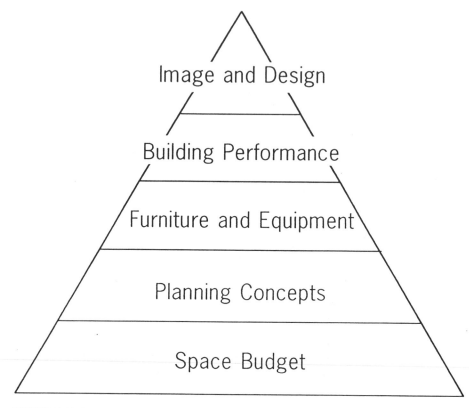

FIGURE 13-1.   Facility Planning Hierarchy

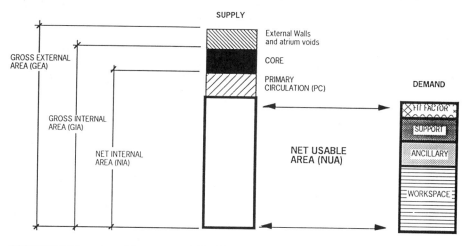

FIGURE 13-2.   Area Measurement Graph

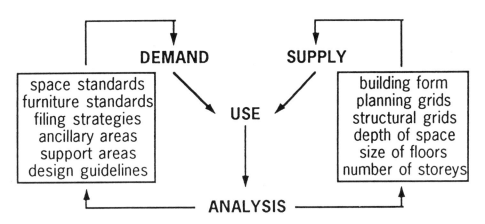

FIGURE 13-3. Model of User Analysis

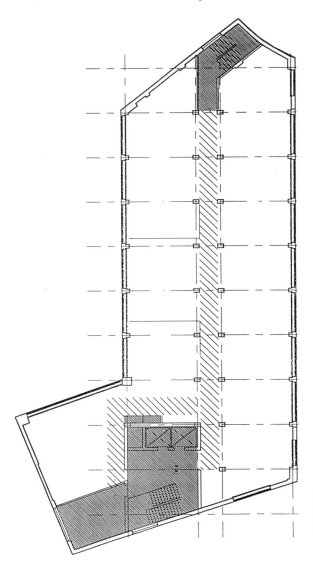

FIGURE 13-4. Building Diagram Illustrating the Core, Primary Circulation, and NVA for a Typical Floor

351

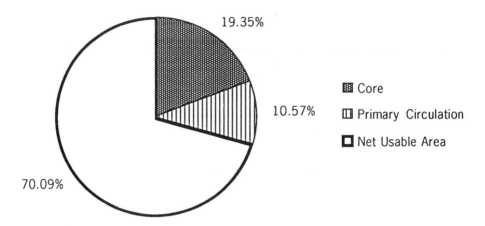

FIGURE 13-5.   Building Area Ratio Chart as a Percentage of Total GIA of 4,523 Square Meters from Area Data Table

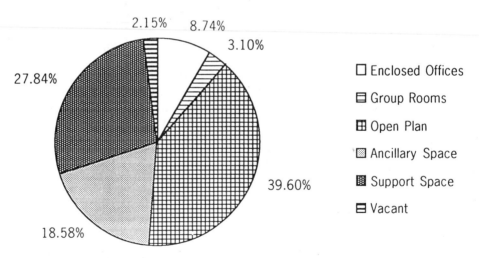

FIGURE 13-6.   Existing Space Category Ratios as a Percentage of the Total NVA Within Chatham Place

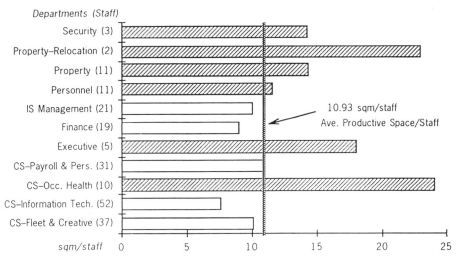

FIGURE 13-7. Average Density in Square Meters for Work Space and Ancillary Space (Productive Space) by Department Against the Total Average Density (Average Productive Space) of Chatham Place

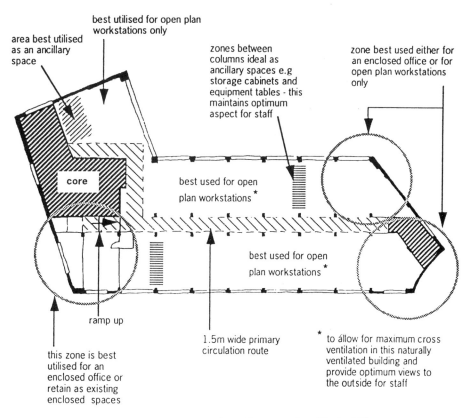

FIGURE 13-8. Concept Planning Analysis Diagram for a Typical Floor

Our Culture	Our Goals	Service Charter

We want to evolve a culture which:
 	
• recognises the needs of the individual
• awards on performance
• encourages innovation, participation,
  mutual trust and self esteem
• is informal, friendly and professional
• delivers service excellence
• is cost conscious
• communicates effectively.
	Understand
	  customer needs
	Respond
	  positively and timely
	Provide
	  quality service at
	  an appropriate price
	Obtain
	  customer feedback
	Add
	  value and make profits
		Know your customer
		
		Earn their respect
		
		Win their business
		
		Be part of their team
		
		Never forget
		the customer has a choice

FIGURE 13-9. Culture, Goals, and Service Charter

DIVISION / DEPARTMENT
Services Group

Grade/ Function	Proposed Space Standard sq metres	PROPOSED		
		Number	Net Usable Area sq metres	sq feet
WORKSPACE				
Enclosed Offices				
Managing Director	43.0	1	43.0	463
Middle Manager	21.6	11	237.6	2558
Location (existing)	4.8	1	4.8	52
Security (existing)	7.9	1	7.9	85
Group Room				
Departmental Manager	10.8	3	32.4	349
Secretary	5.4	2	10.8	116
Professional	5.4	10	54.0	581
Open Plan				
Middle Manager	10.8	1	10.8	116
Departmental Manager	10.8	14	151.2	1628
Professional	5.4	141	761.4	8196
Designer	5.4	8	43.2	465
Secretary	5.4	2	10.8	116
Clerical	5.4	1	5.4	58
Occupational Health	24.1	10	241.0	2594
Messenger		5		
Maintenance		8		
Catering		14		
ANCILLARY				
Filing	1	173	173.0	1862
Meeting	10	3	30.0	323
Shared Workspace	5.1	6	30.6	329
Shared Table/pc	3.6	24	86.4	930
Ancillary Equipment			101.0	1087
Ancillary Rooms(incl. inter. rm)		3	23.5	253
Other Ancillary			144.1	1551
SUPPORT			882.4	9498
VACANT			68.0	732
Total Headcount		233		
Total Enclosed Office		14	293.3	3157
Total Group Room		15	97.2	1046
Total Open Plan		177	1223.8	13173
Total Ancillary			588.6	6336
Total Support			882.4	9498
Total Vacant			68.0	732
TOTAL NET USABLE AREA			3153	33942

NUA/Staff   14.98
(excl. vacant space)
(excl. messenger, catering & maintenance)
Productive Space/Staff   10.69
(excl. support space)
(excl. vacant space)
(excl. messenger, catering & maintenance)

FIGURE 13-10. Summary Space Budget of Group with Proposed Space Standards

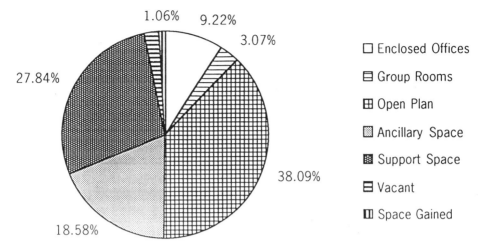

FIGURE 13-11.   Breakdown of NVA Based on Proposed Space Budget

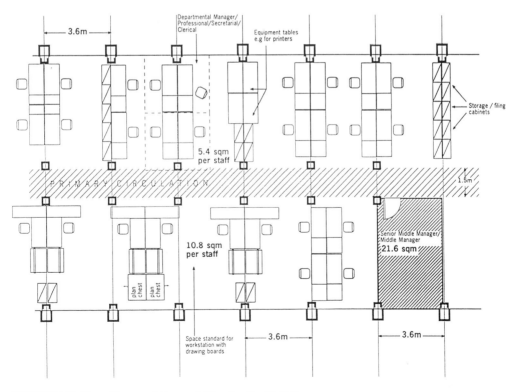

FIGURE 13-12.   Proposed Concept Plan for the Building

Planning for a Captive Audience: Approaches and Problems in Programming Correctional Facilities

Mark Goldman and Frieda D. Peatross

INTRODUCTION

Can a good facility programmer who knows almost nothing about prisons, jails, or juvenile halls develop a competent program for a correctional facility? How does programming these facilities differ from programming other building types? What are the approaches and methods used? What challenges does the correctional facility programmer face?

These questions and others are addressed in this chapter. Many of the answers are based, in part, on the firsthand experience of practicing correctional programmers who responded to a national survey. Rather than a presentation of a single case study, the intent of this chapter is to provide an overview of the programming process for a specific building type.

Correctional facility programming is a fairly recent phenomenon. Beginning in the 1960s, as correctional administrators became more educated and professional, they began to understand the need for specialists in correctional facility planning and the interrelationships between correctional philosophy and design. At about the same time, architects began to realize the magnitude of operational and technical information needed to make good design decisions. Planners thus became facilitators between correctional clients and the designers, as well as sources of state-of-the-art information and design innovations. It became their task to draw on available research and work closely with building operators to understand specific needs. The active involvement of clients and users in the planning process, along with the success of radically different plans, gave new direction to the design of correctional facilities. Programming—the clarification, exploration, and detailing of facility requirements for the client, the user, and the architect—is now an essential ingredient of correctional facility design.

WHAT IS A CORRECTIONAL FACILITY?

Correctional facilities are categorized into a number of types operated by federal, state, county, or city governments:

- prisons
- jails
- camps/farms/stockades
- juvenile detention centers
- juvenile training schools

Correctional facilities also vary by types of populations incarcerated. Some hold only misdemeanants or felons, sentenced or pre-sentenced adults or juveniles, males or females, or a combination of any of these (although males and females and adults and juveniles must be kept separate from each other). Facilities also differ in security levels, in programs and services they offer, and in inmates' length of confinement.

Correctional facilities consist of much more than cells. In reality, a correctional facility is a small, self-contained community. While the components vary somewhat depending on facility category and mission, virtually all contemporary facilities contain distinct areas for the following:

inmate processing	food preparation
medical services	commissary
library	recreation
education	religion
visiting	counseling
administration	staff support and training
warehousing	laundry
maintenance	sleeping, grooming, etc.

Housing accounts for about half the total space in most correctional facilities. Cells take up about half the space in housing units. Often special housing units serve specific populations, such as those requiring segregation, or the mentally ill. Sometimes facilities include factories, a central plant, and a firehouse. Prisons and training schools house longer-term inmates and usually devote more space to inmate programs and services as well as vocational education and industries. Some facilities are part of justice complexes or contain arraignment courts or sheriffs' departments.

Programming a prison is like programming a small city (Figure 14-1). The variety of correctional facility types and their services require that correctional programmers understand the various components and the range of their respective activities.

IS CORRECTIONAL FACILITY PROGRAMMING DIFFERENT FROM OTHER PROGRAMMING?

Programming a correctional facility often requires more intense, longer-term attention than programming a less complex building type. The facility development process is somewhat unique relative to other building types (Figure 14-2).

Programming a correctional facility usually involves hiring specialists who may be either part of or separate from the architecture firm that will design the project. A separate programming firm may subcontract to the architect or contract directly with the client. In some cases, the architect is not hired until after the program is completed. Very often, part of the selection process may be an evaluation of the architects' conceptual responses to a previously written program.

Before the 1960s, "programmer" was just one of many hats worn by the architect or decision maker. Today, intricate bureaucratic structures and large, complex construction programs justify bringing programming specialists on the team. Rather than relying on accepted practices and traditional solutions, architects now realize that a crucial ingredient to a successful correctional facility is effective communication between those who design it and those who must live with it. The programmers' specific task is to understand, analyze, recommend, and document the particular needs of the correctional facility client and users. As a result, correctional facilities may require more "players" and more contracts during programming than do other building types.

SPECIAL PERFORMANCE CRITERIA FOR CORRECTIONAL FACILITIES

Specific to correctional facility programming are issues of security and safety as well as staff and inmate control. These issues intertwine with activities and physical requirements during all programming meetings and must be the foremost concern of programmers of this building type.

Security and Safety

All correctional administrators and elected officials want to ensure that "their" correctional facilities are safe and secure. Escapes produce fear in adjoining communities, embarrass public officials and administrators, and indicate failure. Therefore, security issues permeate programming meetings and documents.

Security, however, can mean many different things, depending on inmate category and clients. Some facilities house minimum-security inmates; others are designed for maximum security, while most facilities include a range of security levels. Further confounding this issue is the fact that one jurisdiction's "medium" security may be equivalent to another jurisdiction's "maximum." The correctional facility programmer must understand each client's definitions of such labels.

Often the correctional programmer develops population projections, inmate profiles, and classification requirements to help determine viable security levels. Whether security levels are determined in advance or developed by the planning team, the programmer must work with clients in developing appropriate operational and architectural responses.

Safety goes hand in hand with security. Inmates, staff, and visitors should be safe from physical or sexual attacks from (other) inmates. Inmates should be deterred from harming themselves, and design of the physical environment should minimize the risk of accidental injuries (such as falling down stairs or slipping in showers). All these issues must be discussed and resolved.

Rehabilitation, Privacy, and Safety and Security

One of the major dilemmas facing correctional programmers is providing an environment that is conducive to rehabilitation, privacy, and safety and security. Maximizing one of these major objectives can compromise another. For instance, complete visibility of inmates' cells and showers limits inmates' privacy. It projects the idea that inmates are untrustworthy and thus interferes with efforts to improve their self-esteem and abilities to lead positive, normal lives.

Hence, a major challenge for correctional programmers is to find the right balance of facility characteristics that encourage rehabilitation, safety, and security. Correctional objectives and inmate programs have little chance of success unless they are supported by the physical plant. These features must be appropriate for each inmate category and consistent with the client's philosophies and objectives (Figure 14-3).

Normalization and Aesthetics

Although any place that locks up people is certainly not "normal," a term often connected to rehabilitation is "normalization." Behind this concept lies the question, "How can anyone who has been detained for a long period of time readjust to society and 'make it' once released?" Normalization advocates believe that readjustment is facilitated if the correctional environment includes "normal" features such as movable furniture, "dry" cells (ones without toilets), and inmates having keys to their rooms. A "normal" environment, together with well-trained, positive staff, can help inmates develop self-trust, pride, and responsibility. A normalized environment is often considered "soft." Its opposite—a "hard" environment at its extreme—implies concrete and steel, fixed furniture, stainless steel toilets, and unbreakable light fixtures and windows (Figure 14-4).

While many long-term correctional staff feel more comfortable with a hard environment, knowledgeable correctional programmers can detail the benefits of softer environments for some populations, with varying degrees of soft or hard. More normalized correctional environments have gained popularity in recent years in juvenile facilities and in lower-security prison and jail units. Research has also provided insight into some of the specific benefits of more normalized environments (Wener and Olsen, 1980; Zimring, 1981; Zimring, Munyon, and Ard, 1991; Zupan, Menke, and Lovrich, 1986).

More so than with most other building types, aesthetics often become a controversial programming issue in correctional facilities. Many clients, fearing budgetary problems and bad press, demand that their correctional facilities "do not look like the Taj Mahal." They fear public complaints about excessive spending, especially in an era when governments are decreasing budgets for schools, libraries, and other politically popular and socially responsible services. Although "attractive" does not have to be expensive, too many constituents associate the two (Figure 14-5).

A factor that often arises in connection with this issue is the morale of staff and inmates. Numerous studies associate attractive environments with more positive attitudes, dispositions, and morale. Most correctional facility clients are concerned about staff and realize the need to create an attractive (although not expensive) workplace with natural light, pleasant colors, sound-absorbing materials, and comfortable and functional furniture.

However, correctional facility clients often debate the merits of attractive environments for inmates. Their opinions are influenced by costs, their attitudes and personal experiences, and how the programmer presents this issue. The programmer's attitude and approach has a major impact on the client's decisions regarding aesthetics as well as other characteristics of the correctional facility.

Long-Term Decisions

Decisions made during the programming of correctional facilities are more permanent than decisions for most other building types. To meet security requirements, walls and ceilings usually consist of reinforced concrete. Reconfiguring the space within existing facilities can be very expensive and is rarely done. Similarly, it is difficult and costly once a jail is built to add wiring for an intercom system, enlarge windows, or change a housing unit from forty to fifty cells.

For these reasons, the client and programmer must take every issue very seriously and objectively explore alternatives. The operators' children and grandchildren and several generations of inmates and taxpayers will live with decisions made during programming, whether they like it or not.

PROGRAMMING MODELS: "DIFFERENT STROKES FOR DIFFERENT FOLKS"

No single model exists for programming and designing correctional facilities. Multiple processes can work, but depend on time lines, sophistication of the client, size of the facility, available budget, and other contextual issues.

Little information is available on current practices in programming correctional facilities. The remainder of this chapter will describe the programming process as currently practiced by many nationally recognized correctional planners. National firms noted for their expertise in the area of correctional facility planning were recently surveyed with a questionnaire that included both closed and open-ended questions. Sixteen (73 percent) of the twenty-two firms contacted responded. The responding firms range in size from seven to 1,275 employees. On average, 17 percent of the firms' individuals devote over 60 percent of their time to programming and planning, although this percentage is higher in smaller firms and lower in larger firms. Similarly, the percentage of the firms' practice devoted to correctional facility planning varies along the same lines. Smaller firms devote more of their practice to correctional facility planning than do larger firms. Three of the sixteen firms responding specialize in planning and programming and are not associated with an architectural or engineering firm.

The goal of the survey was to identify the various methods and approaches that planning, architectural, and engineering firms use to solicit information, and the special challenges faced in correctional facility programming. Because of possible bias in the selection of firms and the open nature of the questionnaire, the results are discussed qualitatively in the following sections.

PREPARING FOR PROGRAMMING

Identifying the Client

Before the programming process can begin, it is critical to identify the decision makers and define the decision-making process. Because many bureaucratic layers and agencies are often involved, it is frequently difficult to identify the main decision makers and players. Almost always, the correctional client is "multiheaded." The client roster may include the following (Figure 14-6):

- elected officials, such as county commissioners and sheriffs
- appointed officials, such as chief probation officers
- correctional facility operators, such as wardens and their staffs
- funding managers and analysts, such as county administrative officers and their staffs
- public works and building maintenance officials and staff
- citizen groups representing taxpayers

In addition, there are often several tiers of clients. Top decision makers give the go or no-go on big-ticket items such as costs and design concepts, but infrequently interact with programmers. Facility administrators and mid-level managers make many decisions involving daily operations and generally work closely with programmers. Finally, facility operators, including correctional officers, cooks, teachers, secretaries, and chaplains, provide a great deal of input about what they do, how they currently do it, and how they would like to do it in an ideal future facility.

Establishing the Programming Team

The success of the planning process hinges in large part on the makeup of the groups involved in programming meetings. Correctional administrators, supervisors, and program/service staff are almost always the main components of the planning team, with correctional officers, maintenance staff, and outside consultants also often participating. Generally, representatives from various levels in the institution and from the local governing bodies are also team members. Interestingly, the primary users of correctional facilities are seldom represented in programming meetings; only 27 percent of the surveyed firms ever involve inmate representatives. Inmates are more likely to be interviewed once or observed in activities; rarely are they a continuous part of the process. Reasons for this stem more from administrators' concerns than programmers' methods.

The ideal programming team is balanced. If top-level decision makers are not involved during programming, they may reject the result, even though the program may be the same as it would have been with their involvement. If only top-level decision makers are involved, the future operators of the facility may feel resentful, sabotage the program, and keep the building from working as intended. There is also danger in relying exclusively on current operators, especially in communities with aging facilities and "We've always done it like this, so why change now" mentalities. As one respondent stated, the greatest challenge to programmers is "educating sheriffs, jail administrators, and state prison directors and wardens of the benefits of changing traditional practices to facilitate improved and more cost-effective inmate management methods."

A frequently heard complaint is "No one asked me." It is important, therefore, to plan the team as broadly as possible and to gain a wide consensus. Participants generally buy into a system they help plan. Those who are involved are more likely to help make the building work once it is built (Figure 14-7).

Committees

To facilitate the programming process, some firms suggest establishing two committees—a policy committee composed of upper-level administrators and officials and a working committee composed of managers and operators. This recently proved both beneficial and expeditious in the programming of the San Bernardino County Juvenile Detention Center. The working committee worked closely with the programmers in providing input, discussing and reviewing operational and design needs, and formulating recommendations. The policy committee was guided by the working committee's recommendations, but made the major, strategic decisions. These two bodies were supplemented by representatives from areas such as health care and education on an as-needed basis. Scheduled meetings, complete with goals and agendas, also facilitated the process.

The Professional Team

Ideally, programming consultants are knowledgeable in many areas—corrections operations, architecture, engineering, interior design, and security. Other needed skills include project management, personnel, scheduling, and verbal and written communications.

The programming team should consist of two to eight people with experience and training in the areas listed above. Two are necessary to lead meetings and record information. As many as eight over the life of the project can provide special skills, such as cost estimating and providing information on mechanical systems. The primary programmers include the project manager and experienced programmers. At least one programmer should have a background in corrections operations.

Team Group Sizes and Meeting Structure

Most planning firms surveyed prefer smaller groups (ranging from two to eight persons) and shorter meetings over an extended period of time rather than intense, marathon meetings. The type of meeting, however, is highly dependent on the client, the size of the project, and proximity and schedule demands. As one respondent noted, marathon meetings may work for smaller or more remote clients, but more frequent, shorter meetings allow for more user feedback and more needs clarification, and result in better relations with the clients. Furthermore, most clients cannot forsake their other responsibilities during programming—they need time to attend to usual tasks.

Changing Decision Makers: Potential Problems

One of the difficulties in correctional programming is the changing status of team members. Very often, initial members transfer, drop out, or are voted out of office, thereby necessitating the reintroduction and education of new members. This can be a frustrating, time-consuming, and costly process. A common scenario shows the difficulties involved:

Sheriff Smith dominated the programming committee, insisting on an indirect-supervision jail with staff in control rooms and little staff-inmate communication.

The design, based on this method of operations, is very far along. Joe Jones, however, opposes Smith in the current sheriff election and wins. He advocates shelving the plans and restarting the design process for high staff-inmate contact in a direct supervision setting. The county commissioners oppose this, since it will cost $1 million more in fees and another year in construction time.

The above scenario is not an uncommon dilemma in the correctional arena. Elected officials come and go, power shifts, and some players simply change their minds as planning progresses. How can the programmer minimize the likelihood of major changes?

The programmer can encourage wider involvement in the decision-making process and can expose recalcitrant clients to more options through the use of comparison tables, slides, and tours of other facilities. Encouraging conversations with other operators may also prove effective weapons in combating such problems.

THE PROGRAMMING PROCESS

Project Initiation

Almost all correctional projects have fixed budgets and prescribed scopes before programming begins. Ideally, the programmer or another firm conducts a needs assessment study to determine the number of beds for each population and to estimate square footage and costs. The scope and budget thus become the foundation on which the subsequent program is built.

Figure 14-8 briefly outlines the various steps in the correctional programming process. As the flow chart illustrates, some functions occur simultaneously. For example, it is beneficial to tour the existing facility while developing the mission and objectives for the facility being planned. It is helpful to tour other facilities when considering solutions to existing problems. Likewise, value engineering should be an ongoing activity. Each of these steps is explained more fully in the following paragraphs.

Development of Mission and Objectives

Most correctional facility clients are individuals with their own goals and agendas. The "multiheaded" client has multiple viewpoints. Survey respondents frequently cited difficulties in dealing with correctional clients whose team members held widely divergent views. Because jurisdictions and decision makers within the same jurisdictions often have a wide range of philosophies, missions, and objectives for their corrections facilities, the programming process starts with the identification or clarification of mission and objectives. These goals provide a valuable guide to subsequent programming activities and are used as a tool to resolve issues. Correctional programmers work with client representatives in clarifying, confirming, or developing these brief expressions, which direct operations and programs that must be spatially accommodated and for which design criteria are formulated (Figure 14-9).

Mission statements often include a reference to treatment or rehabilitation. While it is debatable whether facilities can "correct" behavior, it is generally agreed that if any buildings affect behavior, correctional facilities do—because people are held in them for concentrated and often lengthy periods of time. Generally, attitudes are more liberal and rehabilitation-oriented for juvenile than for adult facilities and for minimum-security than for maximum-security facilities. While with some clients the word "rehabilitation" is taboo, almost all correctional facilities provide at least some minimal programs that could be considered "rehabilitative," including religious services, recreation, visiting, and high school equivalency preparation classes.

Other common missions and objectives concern the following:

safety and security	staffing effectiveness
cost-efficiency	manageability and control
flexibility and expandability	meeting codes and standards

Meetings to Determine Operational and Physical Requirements

After outlining the mission and objectives, programmers concentrate on the activities, programs, and services that must be accommodated. Generally, programming team meetings focus on specific components such as intake and release, housing, and education. The working committees are often supplemented by personnel working in each component. For example, in programming the educational component for the Mt. Olive Correctional Complex in West Virginia, meeting participants included the warden, the prison educational coordinator, the vocational education coordinator, and instructors from both the prison and the local community college.

Operations meetings cover the purpose and objectives of each component, specific activities within them, numbers and types of users, hours of operation, and communication and security provisions.

After establishing operational requirements, programming meetings focus on the physical response, concentrating on spaces and adjacencies, engineering requirements, and desired ambiance, finishes, and materials. Often, operators working in the components under discussion present the positive and negative attributes of the operational issues under review. Staffing and operational costs are also estimated and discussed before knowledge-based decisions are made.

While "rules of thumb" for programming are constantly being challenged and are changing, some benchmarks should be followed:

- About half of gross square footage in prisons is for housing; jails have a slightly higher percentage.
- Generally, about 400 to 600 square feet must be planned per inmate; a somewhat higher square footage is appropriate for very small facilities

(because of economies of scale) and for facilities with a heavy emphasis on industries or other programs. Post-adjudicated juvenile facilities also require more space per person.

- Staff/inmate ratios are critical (since staffing accounts for the largest percentage of all costs). Counting all shifts and positions, programmers should aim for a ratio of 1:2.5 to 1:4.5 staff per inmates housed. A greater number of staff per inmate is needed for reception and diagnostic centers, juvenile facilities, maximum-security prisons, and small facilities. A careful assessment of the client's goals and budgets uncovers additional guidelines that affect operational and design outcomes.

Programmers' Approach During Meetings

Correctional planners agree that their role is to recommend proven practices or, at the least, to inform the client of options and then let the client decide. While these are not mutually exclusive activities, 60 percent of the survey respondents regard themselves primarily as advocates of successful practices, while 40 percent regard themselves primarily as informational sources rather than active advocates. The advocate role is often a difficult one, calling for skillful diplomacy. Indeed, as one planner noted: "We take a strong professional stand for direct supervision, unit management, and use of the least restrictive environment appropriate for each custody or classification level. Doing so requires the staff expertise and will to debate and convince a client to change."

Other firms denounce this approach, arguing that clients who are pushed in directions in which they are uncomfortable may have more trouble operating their facilities and may never feel at ease in the buildings. On the other hand, some "learn to love" what was previously unacceptable.

Value Engineering During Programming

Value engineering—the science of reducing space or changing furniture, finishes, equipment, or building systems to bring a project within budget—is often necessary during programming.

Many clients have longer "wish lists" than their budgets allow. While many architects value-engineer after design is underway, the earlier in a project that changes are made, the smaller the impact these changes will have on project schedule and redesign efforts. Hence, responsible correctional programmers keep a running tab on square footage and estimated construction costs, starting with the first space. If over budget at any point, ensuing discussions will focus on the following:

- reducing the number of spaces and resulting operational implications (e.g., can two adjoining housing units share one visiting area?),
- reducing the sizes of spaces and resulting operational consequences (e.g., is there furniture that will allow the staff training room to be reduced by 5 square feet per person, and will this adversely affect learning?),

- reducing security requirements (e.g., using vitreous china toilets rather than stainless steel toilets in medium-security units, or using "dry cells"),
- changing furniture (also reflected in security requirements), and
- changing finishes in some components (e.g., concrete versus vinyl versus carpeted floors).

Since value engineering can result in increased staffing or maintenance costs, part of the evaluation of value engineering options is a life-cycle cost analysis. For example, value engineering during the planning of Palm Beach County Pretrial Detention Facility in Palm Beach, Florida, resulted in matching existing spaces with some of the expanded functions and reducing the magnitude of added space (Figure 14-10).

Documentation and Presentation to Client

Based on compilation of the data collected and analyzed and the programming team's recommendations, a draft operational and architectural program is produced. The final product for the client is almost always a lengthy textual document consisting of a mission statement, goals and objectives, descriptions of operational and design requirements, and desired adjacency diagrams. While most firms (80 percent of the respondents) consistently provide written architectural guidelines and security requirements, only 33 percent "always" include written operational guidelines. Lists and descriptions of spaces are common. Sometimes, firms provide adjacency matrices in addition to, or as substitution for, adjacency diagrams of spatial relationships, along with sketches, photographs, and conceptual plans. Sixty percent of the questionnaire respondents generally provide cost estimates and project schedules.

Once the draft program is distributed, the client reviews it and comments on it. The programmer reviews all comments, meets with reviewers to resolve any conflicts, then revises and finalizes the document. The final program acts as a project sourcebook during the design phase.

Sometimes, jurisdictions want a formal presentation of the correctional facility program. Audiences may include the programming committees, elected officials, correctional staff, and the public. Such a presentation can be part of a public relations campaign, help sell a bond referendum, or promote a particular site.

The Correctional Program and Programmer During Design

Many programmers have a raft of stories about how the program they sweated over for months was partially or totally ignored, with the resultant building falling short of client needs. Experienced correctional programmers follow several avenues to avoid such disappointments.

First, the programmer ideally is involved at least through schematic design and design development. All project architects and engineers should develop good working relationships with both the program document and the programmers. The programmers should conduct informal "over the shoulder" reviews and should participate in structured review meetings to ensure that the program is followed. An example of where this worked well is the Forsyth County Detention Center (Figure 14-11). Following completion of the program, the lead programmers actively participated in design review, noting discrepancies and consistencies between the program and the designs. One programmer developed a space-by-space comparison of the program and the design to confirm that spaces were not left out, or made too small or excessive for their function.

Second, when design compromises are necessary, the programmer ensures that the operational and design intent are not altered. Finally, if cost reductions are needed, programmers can help identify and evaluate ways to reduce space, materials, or furnishings.

Correctional Programming and Post-Occupancy Evaluation (POE)

Evaluations of an existing facility and its operations are a common means of collecting data on which to base future programs. Post-occupancy evaluations (POEs) inform programmers where the client is coming from, clarify the clients' perspective of reality, and provide a wealth of information on how the client currently does everything, from scrubbing floors to screening incoming inmates infected with AIDS.

For clients with recently completed or older buildings who want a closer fit between design and operations, a POE can be used to fine-tune the facility. Because of the time and money associated with new construction, the idea of a refined building often has appeal. For clients with multiple building projects, there is much merit to developing prototype facilities, evaluating them, and, based on the analyses, modifying the prototype designs. For instance, for the California Department of Corrections' multibillion-dollar construction program, housing units, kitchens, warehouses, and other buildings were programmed, designed, built, and evaluated, and then reprogrammed (and so forth) numerous times.

Pre-programming POEs are a critical part of the planning process, whether they are formal, highly structured evaluations or more casual assessments of what to repeat and what to change.

METHODS OF DATA COLLECTION AND THE EXPLORATION OF ALTERNATIVES

Most firms use hands-on data collection methods. In addition to specific focus meetings centered on component activities, 73 percent of the respondents gather information through individual interviews, surveys, walk-throughs, report and study reviews, and site visits to other facilities. Respondents regard touring other facilities as an effective way to expand the clients' field of possibilities, open recalcitrant minds to new options, and generate solutions to existing problems. Such visits allow the programming committee to understand the numerous operational and design possibilities and to explore, firsthand, which great-sounding ideas work well and which ones to rule out. Programming consultants help identify the facilities that are worth seeing and then join the client or user on these visits.

One planning firm uses videotaped field trips to other facilities as a substitute for actual site visits. While this greatly expands the range of facilities that might be seen and saves the client money, it limits direct feedback from facility staff as to what works and what doesn't.

Approximately 70 percent of the responding planners feel it is important to conduct an observational audit of all existing spaces and activities by taking walks through the facility or conducting structured observations with data forms. These are simple ways to determine how existing spaces meet programmatic needs and their potential for continued use, if the task is one of retrofitting.

In addition, while only 20 percent of the respondents "mostly" depend on literature review, 73 percent generally review other studies and reports for background information. Only one firm (7 percent) stated it uses behavioral mapping or subcontracted consultants for collecting data (Figure 14-12).

While many of the so-called "new techniques" for data collection often catch on and may save time, there is no substitute for good, old-fashioned client/user/planner interaction. An unsophisticated client, for example, may be uncomfortable with computerized space program-based cost modeling and prefer face-to-face reports. It often takes time and a few initial forays into various data collection formats before being able to gauge the client's responsiveness. The programmer needs to be astute enough to know when and how to involve others or to change the meeting approach if the dynamics of the client/consultant relationship is unresponsive. As one planner put it, "There is no substitute for hard and efficient work and the commitment to spend substantial time with a client until the necessary information is obtained and consensus is achieved." This commitment to clients and how they prefer to gather information is more successful than any particular single technique.

THE TOOLS OF THE TRADE

For as many data collection methods as there are, an equal number of "tools" aid the information gathering process. Correctional facility programmers usually convey ideas of movement, access to areas, and desired proximities by sketching or diagramming ideas. "Wallpaper" or flip charts commonly are used to capture key thoughts expressed during programming meetings. Several firms use three-dimensional modeling or full-size mock-ups of facility components to explore alternatives and facilitate client understanding. These methods help clients assess options and save money.

Gaming, "fantasizing," brainstorming, and options ranking also are used effectively by correctional planners. Gaming and brainstorming encourage concentration on specific needs. Ranking available options forces the client to prioritize. One firm relies on papers written by those in custody for information from the often under-represented or unrepresented inmate users. Slides or photographs are also sometimes used to stimulate ideas and to compare options. Rarely used are videotaping and vendor or subconsultant presentations. Again, the use of these tools is in part client-dependent and thus varies from situation to situation.

COSTS

Project Costs

Correctional facilities are among the most expensive building types, largely because of the high costs of security features. These costs are a major reason for programming facilities appropriately for security levels. A minimum-security facility (or portion of a facility) can be considerably less expensive than one where everything is designed for the worse-case inmate. Using dormitories instead of cells, "dry" cells instead of "wet," solid-core wood doors and other more standard building materials also can help reduce costs.

Other major determinants of construction costs are site, capacity, configuration, facility type, and the amount of space. Because of economies of scale, small facilities (under 100 beds) provide more space and cost more per inmate. At design capacity (without double-celling or overcrowding), current construction costs per inmate range from about $20,000 to $200,000, with most facilities costing between $40,000 and $80,000 per inmate to be housed.

Clients often want a Cadillac for the price of a small Ford. Too often, in an effort to get the job, design teams promise more space, higher security, and lower staffing for fewer construction dollars than competitors. Clients and consultants both need to be realistic about costs—another justification for a programming team with extensive correctional experience and knowledge.

Operational Costs

In the long run, the total cost of construction is very small compared with the operational costs of a correctional facility. By far, the biggest operational cost is staff; other major costs are food, clothing, supplies, maintenance, and utilities. Controlling both construction costs and operational objectives can be challenging. Sometimes a slight increase in the construction budget can result in greater staffing efficiencies, thereby reducing overall operating costs.

Recent studies indicate that over a thirty-year period, operational costs in correctional facilities account for as much as 94 percent of life-cycle costs, with cumulative operating costs surpassing initial design and construction costs in *less than three years* (California Board of Corrections, 1990). A $10 million jail, therefore, is likely to cost more than $156 million to operate over thirty years; a $200 million prison may cost over $3 billion to operate in its first thirty years!

The high costs associated with this building type underline the importance of understanding correctional operations—ranging from food service delivery systems to management of inmate sick call, central versus decentralized laundry, housing supervision and case management ratios, methods of greeting and processing inmate visitors, and countless other operational issues. The typical client (except for populous states and counties) has never built a correctional facility and may never have an opportunity to build another. Hence, the client may be totally unaware of recent options and trends in operations, such as cook/chill food preparation and delivery systems, that have a huge impact on future costs. For these reasons, the programming firm must have expertise in correctional facility operations as well as design.

Programming Costs

While talking with as many potential users as possible is advisable, time and budget restrictions often constrain this process. The traditional fee structure for programming facilities is approximately .075 percent of total construction costs (Preiser, 1985). Correctional facility programmers generally charge a flat hourly rate, a flat consultation fee, or part of the design fee; each of these is "sometimes" used by over 80 percent of the survey respondents. Programming costs are a mere fraction (approximately .04 percent) of lifetime operational costs, based on the fact that all initial costs total only about 6 percent of total life-cycle costs (California Board of Corrections, 1990) (Figure 14-13).

Correctional programmers underscore the difficulty of providing quality service within the often meager fee budget generally allocated to programming. Understanding the clients' complex operations and confirming client understanding is a time-consuming process. However, repeat correctional clients are becoming increasingly aware that programming has long-term benefits. Because of the high costs of correctional facility construction and the lasting human ramifications of errors in judgment, many correctional facility policymakers and administrators are taking an increasingly proactive stance on programming services.

THE BENEFITS OF CORRECTIONAL PROGRAMMING

Programming correctional facilities pays off in more ways than in just eventual construction and operational savings. Clients generally benefit greatly from improved facility management after they go through the often agonizing process of defining, analyzing, and refining functional activities and needs. Space planning is generally enhanced for the same reasons. Staff relations and morale often improve because those in charge of operations have undergone an iterative process of defining options and weighing the trade-offs that often result in operational refinements.

The public can benefit from cost reductions, particularly in staffing. Inmates also benefit—with environments that are safe and secure, and that, ideally, help them change their behaviors and learn to become responsible members of society.

CONCLUDING RECOMMENDATIONS

Survey respondents and the authors offer these recommendations to those who will plan correctional facilities:

- Initially, develop a detailed schedule and work plan, indicating all programming activities, committee meetings, and review periods—then follow the schedule.
- Before programming begins, clarify all players, including those who provide input and those who make decisions.
- Even if the team has programmed hundreds of other correctional facilities, do not make assumptions about subsequent clients' wants and needs.
- Understand how the client operates everything now—before proposals are made about repeating or changing procedures.
- With the client, tour "state-of-the-art" facilities that are similar in mission and scope.
- Understand alternative means of providing inmate programs and services, and security and supervision. Where knowledge is weak, hire subconsultants.
- Listen to and empathize with each of the client's many "hats."
- Advocate, but never be pushy.
- Meet their objectives and requirements—do not let "yours" interfere with "theirs."
- Encourage objectivity on everyone's part.
- Be cost-conscious from day one.

For a programmer, it is helpful to remember that the human beings who live and work in correctional facilities twenty-four hours a day, seven days a week will be affected by their environment. It is also wise to recall that almost all inmates eventually return to society. The operational framework under which the programmer operates can thus be guided by this question: How *should* inmates and staff be affected?

ACKNOWLEDGMENTS

Most of the projects described and shown in this chapter were planned by Rosser Fabrap/Justice Systems.

We would like to thank the following leaders in the field of correctional facility planning for their input into this chapter: Carter Goble Associates, Inc.; The Design Partnership; Jay Farbstein and Associates, Inc.; Grad Associates, P.A.; Hansen Lind Meyer; Hennings, Durham and Richardson,

Inc.; Patrick and Associates; Phillips Swager Associates; Rosser Fabrap/Justice Systems; Scarlett Carp and Associates, Inc.; Silver and Ziskind; Steinmann, Grayson and Smylie, Inc.; and the Vitetta Group. We also gratefully acknowledge the other planning firms who responded to our informal survey but who wish to remain anonymous.

We also thank all of our previous clients for what they have taught us over the years. When we speak of problems with clients, we are, of course, not speaking of our own!

Final thanks to Barbara Emmons and Greg Priest for illustrations and Marlene Goldman for editing.

References

California Board of Corrections. 1990. *The state of the jails in California—report no. 5: Jail operating costs.* Sacramento, Calif.: Board of Corrections.

Moos, R. 1975. *Evaluating community and correctional settings.* Palo Alto, Calif.: Consulting Psychologists Press.

Preiser, Wolfgang F.E. (ed.) 1985. *Programming the built environment.* New York: Van Nostrand Reinhold Company.

Wener, R., and R. Olsen. 1980. Innovative correctional information: A user assessment. *Environment and behavior,* 478-94: Vol. 12, No. 4.

Zimring, C.M. 1981. Stress and the designed environment. *Journal of social issues* 37:1, 145-71.

Zimring, C.M., W.H. Munyon, and L. Ard. 1991. *Reducing stress in a third generation jail.* (unpublished manuscript).

Zupan, L., B.A. Menke, and N.P. Lovrich. 1986. Podular/direct supervision detention facilities. Proceedings of the First Annual Symposium of New Generation Jail, National Institute of Corrections.

FIGURE 14-1.   The Correctional Facility as a Small City

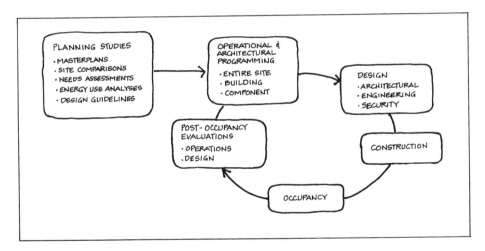

FIGURE 14-2.   The Correctional Facility Development Process

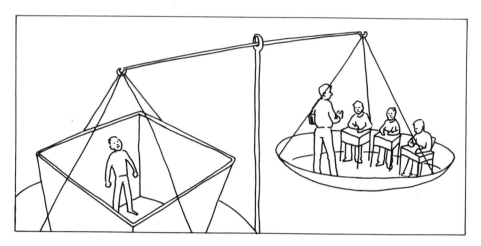

FIGURE 14-3.   Safety and Security versus Rehabilitation

FIGURE 14-4.   "Hard" and "Soft" Correctional Environments

FIGURE 14-5.   "We Don't Want the Taj Mahal!"

FIGURE 14-6.   The Multiheaded Client

FIGURE 14-7. A Rigid Client and an Open-Minded Client

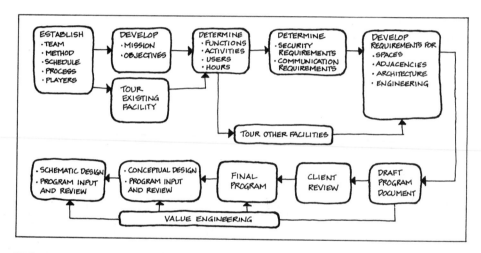

FIGURE 14-8. The Correctional Facility Planning Process

FIGURE 14-9. The Road to Consensus

FIGURE 14-10. The Palm Beach County Pretrial Detention Facility

379

FIGURE 14-11.   Elevation of Forsyth County Detention Center

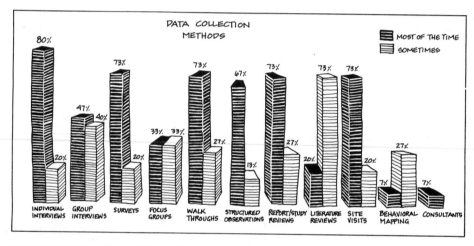

FIGURE 14-12.   Uses of Data Collection Methods

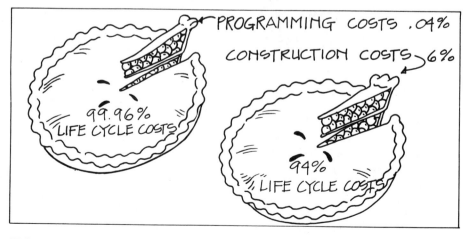

FIGURE 14-13.   Relative Costs

PART III

Issues in Facility Programming

CHAPTER 15

The Impact of the Client Organization on the Programming Process

Jay Farbstein

INTRODUCTION

Facility programming, as a formally recognized process, is perhaps twenty-five to thirty years old. The relatively limited literature on programming consists mostly, on the one hand, of case studies and, on the other hand, of methodological treatises that present arguments in favor of programming and describe how it is or should be done (Palmer, 1981; Peña, 1977; Preiser, 1978 and 1985; Sanoff, 1977). There is an implication that the programmer can choose among the methods as from a toolbox, selecting those that are appropriate to a given project. Various approaches to programming—such as the CRS method of "problem seeking" (Peña, 1977) or more behaviorally based approaches, such as Sanoff's (1977)—seem to imply that the approaches or methods are equally applicable to all projects and for all clients. Little research has been done concerning the effectiveness or appropriateness of programming methods or techniques, and little if any guidance is given as to how one would choose among programming methods for a project, as compared to the selection of research methods, about which much guidance is offered (Michelson, 1975).

Among the primary purposes of programming is to develop information about needed qualities or features of a facility so that design (and, of course, the finished facility) can be responsive to these needs. Almost always implicit—and very often explicit—is the assumption or assertion that the needs to be taken into account are those of the facility's users and/or owners (which are sometimes recognized as being in potential or actual conflict; see Farbstein, 1978; and Silverstein and Jacobson, 1978). It is generally made clear that the owners, in their role as the client for services, have the last word about design decisions, and therefore about the programming process, as well.

Organizational aspects of the client entity—such as the structure of operating divisions, the status relationships among staff, and so on—are not infrequently addressed during programming in terms of their impact on facility needs and performance requirements (Duffy, 1969; Steele, 1986). But rarely are organizational issues discussed or taken into account in looking at how the programming process is or should be structured, even how it proceeds.

Yet, in reviewing my firm's experience in programming dozens of projects, client organizational factors seem to have had a great deal of impact, on both the process and its outcomes—arguably having more to do with the success or failure of the program than did the methods we used, which, while not uniform, varied within our chosen palette. Therefore, I have taken this opportunity to reflect on my experience and to speculate about how and why organizational factors affect programming.

My assessment is based upon—and perhaps limited by—the range of work with our clients, most of whom have been medium-sized to large government agencies. Facility types have ranged from a variety of institutions (jails, prison, homes for abused children) to offices, laboratories, fire stations, courthouses, libraries, post offices, community centers, and border-crossing stations. In almost all cases, the owner (a government entity) has *not* been the occupant or user of the facility. Rather, occupants have been agencies, their staff, their clients or wards, and the general public.

Based upon my limited experience in the private sector, I would assert that facilities owned by corporate bureaucracies (and their attendant planning processes) appear to be subject to organizational structures and forces similar to those at work in governmental organizations. It is possible, however, that facilities owned by other types of entities, such as private individuals or entrepreneurs, might be subject to quite different forces (perhaps with more direct communications). The reader will have to judge the extent to which my experience in programming government facilities is applicable to other settings.

This chapter begins by listing key *organizational factors* that may affect the programming process, goes on to examine the types of *roles and responsibilities* taken by different players in the programming process (and how they may vary in different organizations), and then discusses *situational* or contextual *factors* that may affect the program. The intention is to identify patterns that may emerge in the interplay of these factors. As the chapter proceeds, conclusions are drawn about which programming approaches or methods seem to fit better with a given organizational structure or climate.

ORGANIZATIONAL FACTORS

While this chapter cannot review the literature of organizational analysis (see Pugh, 1971, for such a review), key perspectives on the organization include the following. First, the rather older *structural* approach focuses on the formal patterns of relationships within an organization, such as how delegation of authority and responsibility flow through channels that might be represented on an organization chart (Pugh, 1971). Subsequently, organizational studies shifted focus to examine the *informal* patterns of communications, such as who talks with or works with whom and how things really get done (Etzioni, 1961). More recent models concern themselves with the *"technology"* of the organization; that is, with what the organization makes and how it interacts with its "environment," broadly defined as the complex of forces outside it (Perrow, 1967). Still more recent studies concern themselves with the organization's values, *culture,* and climate, sometimes emphasizing different value systems' relative ability to perform effectively (Ouchi, 1981; Pascale and Athos, 1981).

Looking at organizations from each of these four perspectives can tell us something useful about how they approach and respond to facility planning and programming.

Organizational Structure

Several aspects of the client organization's structure are worth considering in terms of their impact on programming. For example, it is informative to *locate* on the client's organization chart the person or group with responsibility for managing programming. This identifies the organizational "home" of the client's project manager. Then, for comparison, one would locate the facility's users on the organization chart (see Figure 15-1). In a highly differentiated organization, architectural or facility management expertise is very likely to exist within an administrative or support division. But, if the organization is large enough, the user's division may have its own facilities expertise.

One question is whether the two groups can even be found on the same organizational chart. For example, one would have to obtain an organizational chart of the entire U.S. government to find both the General Services Administration (GSA) and the agencies for which it constructs and manages buildings (such as the U.S. Geological Survey or the Immigration and Naturalization Service, each of which would have pages of organizational charts just describing itself). GSA often builds and manages buildings that house unrelated government agencies, acting in effect like a private landlord with tenants (except that the agencies are often a "captive audience").

Another example can be seen in the state of California, where some departments (e.g., Corrections) have gained the power to plan their own projects (circumventing the state's project development agency—at least partially because, historically, that central support agency may not have been responsive to their special needs). For similar reasons, powerful federal agencies, such as the General Accounting Office, gain permission to manage their own buildings and procure their own consultant services.

In principle, to program effectively, one must understand the *relationships* between the parts of the organization that provide programming services and the parts that will use the facilities. More specifically, the analytical questions that need to be addressed are as follows.

How Shallow or Deep Is the Organization?

Organizations differ in terms of the channels they follow and the number of layers of management review they require to make various decisions. The nature of this hierarchy affects programming procedures, such as the number of reviews and who is involved in which review cycle. Shallower organizations are probably able to make decisions faster and, therefore, are easier to work with. For example, the New York State Division for Youth recently reorganized itself so that there are only three steps from the director of facilities planning to the executive director (and the deputy director for administration formally leads the programming process, leaving only two steps to the top (Thyagarajan, 1990). As a result, decisions could be made and ratified rapidly. In fact, with such a short distance to the top, informal knowledge and communications (see the subsequent section on the informal organization) would likely ensure from the start that only acceptable recommendations would be made to the top. This is not to categorize too arbitrarily about the effect of the number of levels: Even in "deep" organizations, decisions may be delegated to lower levels, enabling them to act effectively.

To Whom Does Each Part Report?

Another worthwhile exercise can be performed with the organization chart. One can trace the lines of reporting from the group with responsibility for managing programming to the entity that makes decisions about resource allocations, and then do the same for the future occupants of the building. One can then establish which has the shorter path. It is a good bet that the group with the shorter path to ultimate authority will be able to ensure that its goals are realized through programming. In other words, the group closest to power will effectively control the programming process.

When programming is guided by a service department (such as a public works or facilities management division) rather than by the user agency, such a department may be more likely to function as a coordinator or conduit rather than as an active participant. The facilities group is more likely to be an active participant if it is part of the user agency. For example, the New York State Division for Youth has its own facilities group, which is very familiar with its functions and personnel, and, of course, is directly accountable to the agency's executives. In managing a programming process, the facilities group was able to be an active participant and contribute greatly.

How Is the Group Responsible for Programming
Held Accountable for the Quality of Its Services?

While the previous paragraphs discussed authority and formal channels of communications, here we consider responsibility and accountability. In most formal organizations, performance is measured, at least to some extent, in terms of the degree to which objectives are met. In business and many government organizations, financial measures (such as meeting a budget, getting value for money, or making a profit) are part of the set of objectives.

But other measures, such as customer or client satisfaction, quality of product, and social utility, may also be important. If the group responsible for programming does not share the same objectives as the building occupants—or is not dedicated to helping them achieve these objectives—structural conflicts may arise during the process. To be more specific, if the group responsible for programming is evaluated mainly on its ability to deliver buildings on time and within budget (reporting, for example, to a fiscal manager), it may not be predisposed to take the time needed to reflect the occupant group's needs during the programming phase. I have been involved in a few projects where, unfortunately, schedule deadlines related to saving money severely limited the time allocated to programming of the occupants' requirements, resulting in a less responsive project. (Note that this emphasis on—or clash of—certain values can also be a function of organizational culture, as discussed in a later section.)

In other cases, an operational department (such as production or sales) may have more clout in the organization than does the facility department. (This is not unusual, as the operational departments are more directly involved in carrying out the agency's mission, while the facility department is in a support role.) In this case, the operational department may be better able to ensure that its functional needs are studied, documented, and met.

How Are Resources Allocated to Pay for
Facilities and Programming Services?

In many organizations, the user agency pays from its own budget (even if it is only on an internal accounting system) for buildings (e.g., as rent) or professional services such as programming. If the user agency pays, it may have a greater say in what is done, and may perhaps even hire its own consultants. Even if the user agency only has the *option* of managing its own project, this may be an added incentive for the facilities group to provide responsive service. On the other hand, if the organization allocates space and services through its facilities group, there may be greater central control over resources and less responsiveness to the needs of the parts of the organization. The programmer may be caught on the horns of a dilemma, reporting to a group that is not inclined to allow him or her to respond to user department needs.

These are interesting arenas in which the balance of power between departments can play itself out. For example, the Judicial Council of California (1991) recently recommended that local courts hire independent consultants (including, by implication and practice, programmers) to review the work of courts planners hired by and reporting to county government. This is justified in terms of the separation of powers (since the court is an independent branch of government), but undoubtedly grows out of the perhaps occasional lack of responsiveness of facilities groups and fiscal authorities to the needs of this occupant agency. Interestingly, the federal courts are currently attempting to achieve independence from the General Services Administration's role as their landlord. They do not, however, require independent review of GSA's hired courts planning consultants.

To summarize this section, examination of several structural aspects of the formal organization can shed light on the relationships between the group responsible for programming and the occupants and users of the building.

The Informal Organization

When social scientists started spending time observing organizations at work, they learned that there was much more going on than appeared on an organization chart. They discovered the informal organization; that is, the informal networks of relationships and patterns of communications that overlap and cross formal organizational boundaries. These informal patterns often dictate how things happen in the organization — the way things really work in order to get something done. Here the programmer turns his or her attention to discovering answers to such questions as these:

- Where does decision authority lie?
- Who makes which decisions?
- How are decisions made?
- Whose recommendations get listened to and whose are ignored? (This can be important in determining to whom to talk or whom one would want to carry the torch for a project.) and
- How are conflicting interests balanced?

Where Does Decision Authority Lie?

While one might start by consulting the organization chart, one would also want to observe (or ask about) who really makes which types of decisions; in common parlance, "where is the 'juice'?" For example, in more than one of our projects, consensus decision making by a committee broadly representative of the organization has been encouraged. However, at the same time, tough and powerful decision makers lurked in the background (to make it sound a bit more sinister than it really was), ready to step in if they sensed that things were going in a direction they might not sanction. The programmer must know where the real influence lies, if only to keep informal communications channels open so that weeks or months of work are not suddenly overthrown.

How Are Decisions Made?

Organizations have widely varying patterns of decision making. Some organizations follow strict hierarchical reporting and decision structures, where findings and decisions must be reviewed and ratified at each level before being passed up to the next one. In others, individuals at apparently relatively low positions may in fact control much of what goes on. This may be achieved through networking, through being persuasive, or through knowing to whom to talk or how to get directly to higher-ups, circumventing the standard decision structure. To the extent that the programmer can discover how decisions are made, the process for making programming decisions can be tailored to the organization and effective review and reporting procedures can be set up.

How Are Competing Interests Balanced?

In organizations, various parts (and people) compete for resources. In programming (and design), priorities are established and resources are allocated among various uses and users who are in competition for these resources. The programmer must learn about the relative power of the parts and people in the organization, and consider how these interests are involved in and balanced through the programming process.

The Organization's Technology and Its Environment

An organization's "technology" refers to what it does and how it does it. Viewing the organization from the perspective of its technology can be fruitful for the programmer—and may be a familiar approach, since it deals with the rather concrete issues of activities, processes, and movement. One starts by looking at the organization's *mandate;* for example, does it perform functions related to social services, public services, production, information processing, or social control? Then one considers *how* the organization goes about fulfilling its mandate and how that "technology" may be changing. Are the organization and its environment stable or subject to rapid changes because of shifting markets, social mandates, or available resources?

The answers to these questions can tell the programmer a great deal about the types of issues that need to be addressed in programming and the kinds of methods to use. For example, consider the contrasts among a public service organization (such as a library), an industrial production company, and an institution of social control (such as a jail). The topics discussed (or at least their relative emphasis), the parts of the organization that need to or will be allowed to be involved in programming, and the techniques that are appropriate for programming will differ greatly among these hypothetical organizations (though I would not assert a complete correspondence between an organization's technology or mission and the programming environment it creates).

For example, in the *library,* the mandate is making information accessible to the public. It would be common for staff and the public to be involved in programming in an open, cooperative process. In an *industrial* organization, technical issues such as the processes, flows of materials, and requirements of machines would occupy the foreground during programming. Senior managers and industrial engineers would be primary participants. In planning a *jail,* issues of security, rehabilitation, and prisoner flow would predominate. Participants would include jail management and staff, perhaps supplemented by representatives of related agencies. It would be unusual, but not unprecedented, for inmates to be involved (see the discussion about jail programs in Chapter 14 and in the next section).

Organizational Values, Culture, and Climate

There has been great interest in recent years in organizational effectiveness and, as one strategy, in maximizing the contribution of individuals within the organization. This interest results, in part, from the success of Japanese competitors to North American businesses. One can observe private corporations and government agencies (such as the U.S. Postal Service) adopting Japanese-inspired techniques, such as quality circles, to improve productivity. Some of the precepts of this movement revolve around reorienting the organization's culture and climate, perhaps even calling into question its basic values.

Authoritarian or Participatory Style?

Different organizations, of course, have very different styles of operation and decision making. Authoritarian and participatory styles represent a classic dichotomy. Where an organization falls on this spectrum will greatly affect its willingness to consider gaining input from, and/or delegating programming and design decisions to, its various levels. This basic orientation can affect the programmer's access to user agencies, work groups, their clients, the public, and informal users. A programmer who is committed to broad input may mesh well with an organization whose values are consistent with participation, or poorly with one whose values are hierarchical and authoritarian. Since they depend on the breadth and quality of available information, the nature and quality of the program itself will be affected by the organization's orientation. While it is the programmer's responsibility to attempt to obtain the best possible information, it may not be possible to overcome an organization's orientation if it is opposed to participation. To work effectively, the programmer must adapt to the organization's style, even though his or her personal philosophy may be at odds with it. Accepting certain limits may allow the programmer to do the best achievable job for that client. If the programmer cannot accept these limits, he or she would have to withdraw from the project.

By way of comparison, we recently programmed two jails: one for a coastal county whose culture is permeated by participation, and another for a rural, conservative county. In each case, cultural proclivities penetrated government in general, and the sheriff's department in particular. In the first county, a programming committee was assembled by the client (the programmer did not have to ask for one, and the programmer's willingness to work with such a committee was a selection criterion in being hired). The committee included—in addition to jail administrators—representatives of five other county departments, line supervisors and staff, the jail nurse, a community volunteer coordinator, and the head of a community-based organization that provides services to inmates. At various times, program workshops were also attended by inmates and a member of an inmate's family (to discuss the experience of visiting). Options were widely debated and divergent opinions were expressed, but consensus was reached in the end. The sheriff delegated programming to the committee (and his senior managers), but reviewed decisions and draft reports.

In the other county, programming workshops were attended by the sheriff, undersheriff, jail administrator, a line supervisor, and representatives of two other county departments. There was little interest expressed in hearing from other potential participants. While divergent opinions were expressed, decisions tended to be made by the highest-ranking member of the group who was present, generally the sheriff.

Trend Setter or Trend Follower?

Other aspects of the organization's values and culture may also affect the programming process. An example of this would be the question of whether the organization sees itself as a trend setter or, more conservatively, as a follower of tried and true directions. If the organization is a trend setter, there may be much more attention paid to articulating first principles (e.g., mission, goals, and objectives) as the basis for new departures, many more options generated, and extensive modeling and analysis of their implications. Performance-based programming may be preferred, to allow greater exploration and creativity during design. More conservative client organizations may be content to identify and follow well-established precedents. They may also prefer a more prescriptive program document to ensure that the selected precedents are executed as expected.

Rapid or Slow Decisions?

Another aspect of organization style concerns how quickly decisions are made. Some clients are prepared to expedite decisions, others mull or even agonize over them. Governmental clients tend to have to justify decisions very thoroughly, owing perhaps to their degree of public or interagency scrutiny. An entrepreneurial style is foreign to them. On the other hand, time pressures can overcome this "natural" resistance to speed. Sometimes a project is very badly needed or external pressures are strong (for example, a jail is under court order not to overcrowd its cells). At other times, funding sources carry time limits (for example, money for the program may be available from the current budget but must be expended before fiscal year end, or the facility will be paid for from a grant or bond that has a time deadline). When time deadlines are pressing programming, it is essential to institute especially effective and efficient review and design decision-making processes. Often this is done by including the key decision makers on the programming team, so that they are directly involved rather than basing their decisions on after-the-fact review of reports. While it is always desirable that decision makers be on the programming team, it may only be under situations of some duress that they are willing to serve. An alternative to direct involvement might include frequent special briefings.

ROLES AND RESPONSIBILITIES

The aspects of the organization discussed previously are manifested in the way it decides to do programming. In assessing an organization's programming process, it is worth considering how essential roles are filled and how responsibilities are allocated. The following sections review these key assignments and discuss how organizational factors affect the way they are handled. They begin with a list enumerating the potential roles to be played in the programming process and go on to discuss which player will take each role and how this may depend on organizational factors. Roles are summarized in Figure 15-2.

Roles

Client/Owner Roles
The client or owner is typically responsible for the following tasks:

- Define the *need* for the project (before the decision is made to prepare a program) and then for the program.
- Establish the *terms of reference* for the programmer and the scope of programming work.
- *Select* the programmer (perhaps based on the programmer's proposed approach and specialized expertise in programming or with the subject building type).
- Define the *approach* to programming and scope of work (or the programmer may propose the scope for the client's approval).
- Negotiate the *fee* and contract with the programmer.
- Enter into (sign) a *contract* for programming services.
- *Pay* for the programming work.
- *Manage* the programming project:
  set and maintain the schedule,
  determine the composition of the project team (e.g., steering committee and/or task forces),
  determine the level of participation by user groups, and
  secure and coordinate participation by user representatives.
- *Approve* draft and final reports.
- *Adopt* the final report and its recommendations.
- *Act on* recommendations (e.g., procure financing, acquire a site, hire an architect, proceed with design, etc.).

Client/User Roles
The client or user agency is typically responsible for the following tasks:

- *Give input* to the program (e.g., be interviewed by the programmer or serve on a task force).
- *Participate in decision making* (e.g., serve on a steering committee).
- *Review* and comment on drafts.
- Make *recommendations* (which may be advisory or definitive).

Programmer Roles
The programmer is typically responsible for the following tasks:

- Propose the *approach* to programming and the scope of work (or the owner may do this).
- Assemble the programming *team,* including consultants as needed.

- *Guide* the programming process.
- Conduct or *facilitate* programming team meetings.
- *Conduct* participatory programming sessions (may be the same as above).
- Carry out *information-gathering* activities (archival searches, observations, and user contact methods, such as interviews, surveys, and so forth).
- *Analyze* and present information.
- Identify *issues* and options.
- Conduct *technical analysis* of options.
- Make *recommendations* (if called for).
- Assist with group *decision making.*
- *Record* the programming process, including preparing meeting notes and other documentation.
- Prepare working papers, draft and final *reports.*
- Make *presentations* to the owner or other interested parties.
- *Work* with the architect.
- *Review the design* as part of the client's (or the architect's) team, *or* (if the programmer is also the architect),
- Be part of the design team (i.e., *design the project*).

Players in the Process

The following paragraphs review key players in the programming process and discuss the ways their roles may vary among organizations (see Figures 15-3 and 15-4).

Client/Building Owner

The owner is the entity with authority over—and responsibility for—the project, usually including holding title to the property where the project will be built. The owner has the ultimate authority to approve programming work and results. There are many organizational and legal forms the owner may take, from a corporate or governmental body to a partnership or an individual person.

The owner may also delegate authority to his or her appointed executive or agent (a person or an entity; e.g., the county executive officer), who may have effective decision-making authority for some or all aspects of the project, with or without having to go back to the owner to ratify certain decisions.

The nature of the entity that controls the project should be carefully considered by the programmer, since its form, responsibilities, and charter can strongly influence the process. For example, there is a great difference in the public exposure (and scrutiny) of a project owned by a publicly elected governmental body compared with a corporate board of directors or a private individual, either of which may be able to keep many more decisions to itself.

Owner's Representative

On most projects, the owner designates a representative who has direct, day-to-day responsibility for doing or administering programming work. This entity could be a facilities management, design, or construction group; a public works agency; the county architect; or a private program management consultant. Generally, though not necessarily, it will have some degree of technical expertise. This entity will function as or appoint an individual as *project manager.* The project manager can also be an agent hired to act on the owner's behalf, such as a program manager or construction manager. The programmer needs to consider the position, interests, strength, and experience of the client's project manager, since he or she will greatly influence the daily flow, and perhaps the outcome, of the work.

"Official" Users

I use the term "official" users to designate those groups or individuals who will occupy the building and are formally part of the owner's organization. Typically, these would be paid employees. Official users may be single or multiple agencies, departments, or functional groups. In many cases, they are like tenants, who have the *use* of the building, but do not *own* it. As stated above in the discussion of organization structure, it is very important for the programmer to understand the relationships among the owner, the owner's representative, and the user group or agency. Will the programmer have access to these official users, and at what level within their own internal organization? Does the owner want them to be involved? Should the programmer suggest or insist that they be?

Nonoffical Users

Most buildings we may program have many users who are not official members of the owner's organization. These include visitors, clients, patients, inmates, customers, the public at large, and staff unions, among many others. What is the organization's concern about these types of users, and how will their needs be reflected in the program? Do they have any power (or representation) in the programming process, or is it up to the owner (or perhaps the programmer) either to attempt to anticipate their needs (perhaps paternalistically, if they are not directly involved) or to suggest that they be involved and contacted directly? To be sure, most prisons have been built without input from the inmates and, perhaps more surprisingly, many hospitals have been built without input from patients (though the work of Carpman, et al., 1986, attempts to counter this trend). Some organizations have official recognition and representation of nonofficial users. For example, inmates, patients, and social service clients may be represented by an ombudsman.

Interested Parties

Interested parties may not necessarily be users, but may still have legitimate concerns about the project. Such parties could include the public, neighbors, watchdog groups, environmental groups, other levels of government, financial backers or lending institutions, and so forth. The programmer should take care to uncover their existence and to understand their concerns and their relationship to the client organization.

Regulatory Agencies

Regulatory agencies have statutory power to review and approve certain aspects of a project. At the least, a building official will review plans for conformance with building codes and issue a permit for construction. Other agencies may also be involved, reviewing concerns such as environmental impact, compliance with funding requirements, and so forth. It is critical that the programmer ascertain which agencies have jurisdiction, as well as their substantive and procedural requirements, so that the program can conform to their requirements.

Planning Committees and Task Forces

An advisory committee or task force, representing the owner and any or all of the groups listed above, may be a primary source of input to the program. Generally, such a group is ad hoc—that is, assembled specifically for the project—though some organizations may have standing facilities or capital program committees. The task (and authority) of such a group depends on what is delegated to it. It may be given the power to make decisions itself or may be limited to making recommendations to the decision makers. The programmer should ascertain the degree of responsibility and authority attached to such a group. If the group does not contain representatives that the programmer feels should be there, he or she should discuss this with the project manager (or higher authority, if necessary).

The Programmer

The programmer is, of course, the entity responsible for developing the program. Three main issues are discussed here about the role of the programmer: first, options for the programmer to be drawn from the owner's in-house staff or contracted from outside; second, whether programming is done by a specialist or by the design architect; and, third, whose programming process is followed— the client's or the programmer's.

Programming may be done *in-house* by the organization itself or, alternatively, by a programming *consultant* hired from outside the organization. The in-house option may be preferred in larger organizations that have specialized facility management sections with experience in programming. An advantage of doing programming in-house is that such groups already know the organization and its needs quite well. A disadvantage may be that they have little distance from the organization to gain perspective in how they view it, and may have limited knowledge of what other, similar organizations are doing or of the state of the art of their building type. In-house programmers may also have limited credibility, perhaps being perceived as less than objective, or not allocating resources fairly. A consultant programmer may be able to bring these desired qualities, or overcome the deficits, sometimes simply by being an outsider. Some organizations may prefer to have an outsider come in to take responsibility for making recommendations with which insiders may not wish (or have the courage) to be identified.

A second issue is whether the programmer is a *specialist* or an *architect* who offers programming services. It is not my intention to take sides on this issue (though I am an architect whose practice is limited to programming and related services), but rather to point out that the options suggest different roles and relationships within the project and may imply a different process. For example, if programming is done as an identified phase with a separate contract, a specialist is more likely to be hired, and the transition to design becomes an issue that must be addressed. More attention and effort may need to be directed toward documentation and communication of program requirements. On the other hand, if programming is done as part of the design contract, it may imply less differentiation in the team and a more seamless transition to design. However, there are risks that the programming process may not get as full attention from the client or the consultant team, and that the architect may not be fully objective with regard to the program, either in establishing a scope that could increase his or her fee, or in allowing design preconceptions to creep into the program. In addition, the architect may not have the level of skill of a specialist programmer, though the specialist could be a consultant to the architect. Along these lines, it is interesting to compare the difference between the programmer working directly for the client organization and the programmer working through the architect. When the programmer works for the owner, communication to the owner is direct and complete. When the programmer works through the architect, the architect can filter and control the communications, sometimes leading to a diminution of the programmer's effectiveness (see the discussion in the following paragraphs). Yet, if the architect is involved during programming, he or she will be more fully cognizant of the issues and alternatives considered, as well as the nuances of and reasons behind many decisions. Further, the architect can raise legitimate issues to be considered during programming and contribute a valuable perspective to the team.

The third issue is whether programming follows a *process set by the programmer or the client*. A relatively few large, experienced clients may have an established programming process (e.g., the U.S. General Services Administration; see reference). More commonly, clients may have identified certain features or types of information that they want to have covered by the program. Still others will look to the programmer to propose or provide the methods and to structure the process. Clients with established programming processes may not wish to hire programmers who use a different process, while programmers may or may not be flexible enough to adapt. For each organization, it is worth considering which aspects of the process are generated by the programmer and which come from the client.

The Architect and Other Design Professionals
Once design begins, the team will include the architect as well as a host of other potential consultants (engineers, planners, environmental specialists, etc.). In terms of roles in the process, the key issue is whether the design architect has

been present and/or involved in the programming work. If not, how is the transition handled from programming to design? Methods vary, from simply giving the program report to the architect, to holding a transition meeting with the programmer, to keeping the programmer involved to review the design. In terms of the organization, the key issues are to ensure effective communication and coordination so that the knowledge gained during programming is not lost or ignored. Again, each arrangement of roles has its advantages and disadvantages.

It is also important for the programmer to understand that the architect has certain important responsibilities and liabilities, which may cause him or her to deviate from the program (if, or where, the program is perceived as being inconsistent with meeting these obligations). For example, the architect is generally responsible by contract for delivering the project within the budget. If the architect has this obligation, he or she is generally given the right to reduce the scope of the project to make it affordable. If the program calls for more space or a higher-quality building than can be afforded, the architect may have to cut it down (in consultation with the client, and perhaps the programmer). Here, the setting of priorities in the program can be of great value.

SITUATIONAL FACTORS

In addition to the structural role, and functional issues discussed previously, there are many situational or contextual factors that surround the program. These factors concern the nature of the project as well as the meaning and importance it has to the client organization.

The first issue is how *important* the project is perceived as being. Does it have a high—or a low—profile to the organization, its controllers (e.g., an executive or legislative body), or the public? The more important the project, the more likely the organization may be to make a serious commitment to its programming. For an important project, the organization can be expected to devote to it adequate resources of money, personnel, and time. For a less important project, it may be difficult for the programmer to have an adequate budget or access to needed participants. Sometimes, programming may be done in a perfunctory way, as when it is a required hurdle that must be surmounted (e.g., in order to obtain funding).

The amount of *time available* for programming may also depend on the project's time line. If the organization is in a hurry to get the building on-line, there may be less time for programming. Paradoxically, in situations where programming may be most important, there may be less time available to do it. These situations may include an organization that is growing rapidly and needs space for new personnel or an institution that is stressed from crowding and may be under court order to remedy conditions.

One indicator of time pressure may be measured by examining the project's funding. Is the money for design and construction already budgeted, or is the program a necessary step to help establish the commitment to fund it (and to determine the need for the facility, its scope, and cost)? While organizations that already have funding on hand or authorized may be in a hurry to use it, those who must define the project in order to get funding allocated may also be in a hurry (e.g., to gain consideration during the next budget cycle or to meet a deadline for getting a bond issue on a ballot). Looking at the project schedule will show whether programming is on the "critical path"; usually it is, since programming must be done before design can proceed.

Organizational *culture and style* may influence the way programming is perceived. Contemplative and analytical organizations that expect to have decisions carefully considered and fully documented will be very comfortable with programming and may see it as a way to control the more irrational and creative forces unleashed with design. Organizations that are more action-oriented, and those in which documentation is less valued, may feel more comfortable exploring issues and ideas during design rather than programming.

The *stage of planning* during which programming is done can also affect the nature of the program. Programming may be initiated during strategic planning, project definition, feasibility analysis, master planning, or design. Obviously, the level of detail that is needed increases as one gets closer to design. At an early strategic planning level, it may be adequate to determine the total size and general quality of the project. For a master plan, only the most general design objectives and relationships may be added. Even for design, some projects may phase (or fast-track) programming to first develop and report key requirements for schematic design, then elaborate on detailed requirements (e.g., for room finishes or furnishings) while schematic design proceeds.

DIMENSIONS AND OUTCOMES OF THE PROGRAM

Each of the factors discussed previously has an impact on the programming process and product. Some of these outcomes include the following:

- The amount of *information* and objective *analysis* that is appropriate or required.
- The amount and type of *documentation* that is appropriate.
- The level of *detail* that is needed in the program and the report.
- Whether *performance*-based or *prescriptive* programming is preferred by the client.
- What happens with the *report* (who acts on it and how; what happens during design).
- How the *transition* from program to design is accomplished: whether it is seamless (with the same team or overlapping involvement) or there is a structured hand-off.

Finally, organizational factors affect how *satisfying* it is to work with the client. In my experience, several factors have contributed to making a programming experience satisfying and successful. More satisfying programming experiences generally include several of the following features:

- The project is *important* to the organization.
- Programming is recognized as being of *value* in the process of developing the project.
- The organization is *committed* to the process.
- Adequate *time* and resources are allocated for programming.
- *Involved* individuals from the organization take part in programming.
- Programming is *participatory* and involves many levels of users.
- *Issues* crucial to the success of the organization are explored and found to be affected by design.
- Telling *debate* and *analysis* lead to program recommendations.
- There is a smooth or even *seamless hand-off* to design.
- The design team takes the program *seriously* (though perhaps challenging it).
- The design *reflects* the program.
- The building is a *success* and the organization is happy with it.

IMPACT ON PRACTICE

This chapter has suggested many issues that programmers may find valuable to consider when assessing the appropriate methods and techniques to use for a given client organization. Conducting an initial reconnaissance and analysis of the organization can help the programmer respond more appropriately and effectively to its needs. The programmer can ask questions that help to ensure appropriate representation in the process as well as communication of issues, findings, and recommendations. Being smart about the organization can also help avoid problems that occur when programming methods and client needs or priorities are out of synchronization.

In our programming practice, we look for clients and situations that have the potential to be satisfying. When we face more challenging situations, we do our best to turn them into satisfying ones by setting up a process that responds as well as possible to organizational needs and contextual requirements.

ACKNOWLEDGMENTS

I thank Professor Donna Duerk for her comments on an early version of this chapter and S. Thyagarajan for his comments on a later version.

References

Building Research Board, National Research Council. 1986. *Programming practices in the building process: Opportunities for improvement.* W.F.E. Preiser, Committee Chair. Washington, D.C.: National Academy Press.

Carpman, Jan, M. Grant, and D. Simmons. 1986. *Design that cares: Planning health facilities for patients and visitors.* Chicago: American Hospital Publishing.

Duffy, Francis. 1969. Role and status in the office. *Architectural association quarterly* 1, pp. 4-13.

Etzioni, Amitai. 1961. *A sociological reader in complex organizations,* 2d ed. New York: Holt, Rinehart and Winston.

Farbstein, Jay. 1978. A juvenile services center program. In *Facility programming,* ed. Wolfgang F.E. Preiser, 67-84. Stroudsburg, Pa.: Dowden, Hutchinson & Ross.

Farbstein, Jay. 1985. Using the program: Applications for design, occupancy, and evaluation. In *Programming the built environment,* ed. Wolfgang F.E. Preiser. New York: Van Nostrand Reinhold Company.

Farbstein, Jay, M. Kantrowitz, B. Schermer, and J. Hughes-Caley. 1989. Post-occupancy evaluation and organizational development: The experience of the United States Postal Service. In *Building evaluation: Advances in methods and applications,* ed. Wolfgang F.E. Preiser. New York: Plenum.

Judicial Council of California, Administrative Office of the Courts. 1991. *Proposed California trial court facilities standards.* San Francisco, Calif.

Michelson, William. 1975. *Behavioral research methods in environmental design.* Stroudsburg, Pa.: Dowden, Hutchinson & Ross.

Ouchi, William G. 1981. *Theory Z.* New York: Avon.

Pascale, Richard T., and Anthony G. Athos. 1981. *The art of Japanese management.* New York: Warner Books.

Palmer, Mickey. 1981. *The architect's guide to facility programming.* Washington, D.C.: American Institute of Architects/New York: McGraw-Hill.

Peña, William. 1977. *Problem seeking: An architectural programming primer.* Boston: Cahners.

Perrow, Charles. 1967. A framework for the comparative analysis of organizations. *American sociological review* 32, pp. 194-208.

Preiser, Wolfgang F.E. 1978. *Facility programming.* Stroudsburg, Pa.: Dowden, Hutchinson & Ross.

Preiser, Wolfgang F.E. 1985. *Programming the built environment.* New York: Van Nostrand Reinhold Company.

Pugh, D.S., ed. 1971. *Organization theory.* Harmondsworth (England): Penguin.

Sanoff, Henry. 1977. *Methods of architectural programming.* Stroudsburg, Pa.: Dowden, Hutchinson & Ross.

Silverstein, Murray, and Max Jacobson. 1978. Restructuring the hidden program. In *Facility programming,* ed. Wolfgang F.E. Preiser, 7-26. Stroudsburg, Pa.: Dowden, Hutchinson & Ross.

Steele, Fritz. 1986. *Making and managing high quality workplaces: An organizational ecology.* New York: Teachers College Press.

Thyagarajan, S. 1990. A case study of the evolution of a planning process in an agency setting: Implications for planning and organizational change. Unpublished course paper, University of Albany, New York.

U.S. General Services Administration. No date. *Design programming.* Document PBS 3430.2. Washington, D.C.: draft.

Wener, Richard, and F. Schneiger. July 1990. The role of POE within the organization: Toward an integrated assessment. In *Proceedings of the seminar on critical approaches of environmental design evaluation,* ed. Michel Conan and Craig Zimring. Volume 2. Paris: Centre Scientifique et Technique du Batiment.

Zimring, Craig. July 1990. Normative rationality and evaluation by large building delivery organizations. In *Proceedings of the seminar on critical approaches of environmental design evaluation,* ed. Michel Conan and Craig Zimring. Volume 2. Paris: Centre Scientifique et Technique du Batiment.

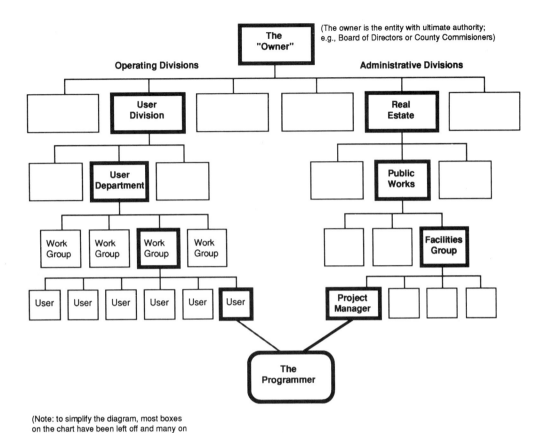

FIGURE 15-1.   Using an Organization Chart to Assess Relationships in the Programming Process (The chart can be used to identify relationships among the owner, project representative, user agency, users, and the programmer.)

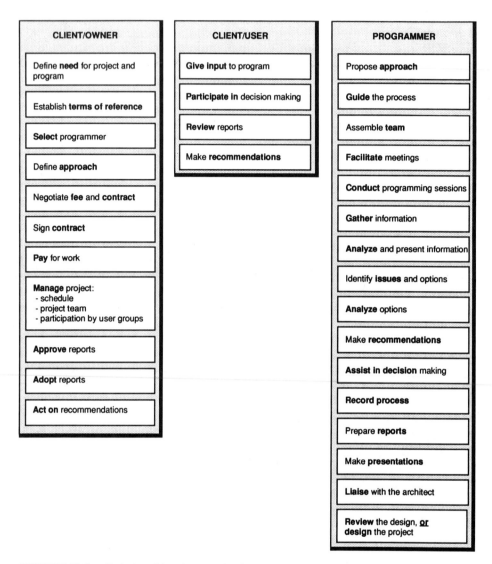

CLIENT/OWNER

Define **need** for project and program

Establish **terms of reference**

Select programmer

Define **approach**

Negotiate **fee** and **contract**

Sign **contract**

Pay for work

Manage project:
- schedule
- project team
- participation by user groups

Approve reports

Adopt reports

Act on recommendations

CLIENT/USER

Give input to program

Participate in decision making

Review reports

Make **recommendations**

PROGRAMMER

Propose **approach**

Guide the process

Assemble **team**

Facilitate meetings

Conduct programming sessions

Gather information

Analyze and present information

Identify **issues** and options

Analyze options

Make **recommendations**

Assist in decision making

Record process

Prepare **reports**

Make **presentations**

Liaise with the architect

Review the design, **or** **design** the project

FIGURE 15-2.   Relationships Among the Owner, Users, and Programmer

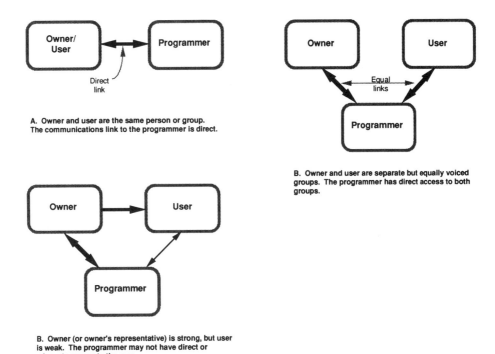

A. Owner and user are the same person or group. The communications link to the programmer is direct.

B. Owner and user are separate but equally voiced groups. The programmer has direct access to both groups.

B. Owner (or owner's representative) is strong, but user is weak. The programmer may not have direct or adequate access to the user.

FIGURE 15-3.   Roles in the Programming Process

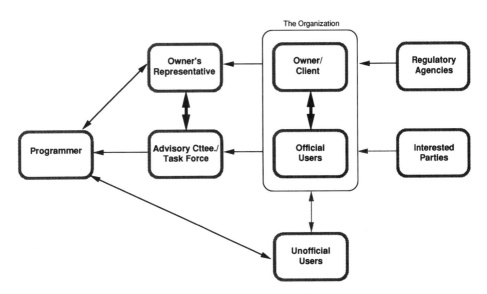

FIGURE 15-4.   Relationships Among Entities

CHAPTER 16

The Role of the Programmer as Interpreter and Translator

Raymond Bertrand

INTRODUCTION

Facility programming, as a field of practice, has been discussed for many years from the methodological point of view, mostly in the United States. Various *know-how* approaches were developed and several presentations—at EDRA conferences, for example—were made on the results of such applications. One question that arises, however, is the role of the person who does the actual programming and the key issues that are part of that process.

This chapter discusses the activities involved in the role of the programmer and how the programmer fits into the programming process, which is seen here as a system of inquiry. Some questions to ask are these: Which philosophy, or paradigm, should the programmer adopt? How can we define the programming process? Can we adequately describe a facility in order to ensure its understanding by the designer? What are the major factors influencing the role of the programmer? And finally, should the programmer be seen as a specialist or a generalist in the field of environmental design?

TOWARD A PARADIGM SHIFT

Trends in research and professional practice are situated within philosophies. A quick overview of the practice of facility programming would reveal a philosophy strongly characterized by empiricism (Palmer, 1981; Preiser, 1985; Building Research Board, 1986). Levy (1987) argues that subjective factors are rarely used, and indeed often ignored, in practice to the benefit of quantitative, generalizable data. Nevertheless, these data are critical if we want a system that assigns importance to the design stage. In effect, qualitative factors are crucial in the definition of a site-specific program exactly because of the specificity of the institution it describes. Notably, Schneekloth (1987) discusses the features and strengths of critical theory: "The purpose of engaging in critical theory is to reveal socially constructed worldviews by asking questions about the history and societal purpose of any institution . . . and how the environment is used to support and maintain the agreed-upon purposes of the social form."

Critical theory may provide us with a paradigm for research seen as an inquiry into social and physical form. Lecomte (1980) submits that a paradigm is a fundamental scheme that serves to set out and limit the phenomena that we observe and to help us perceive reality as well as understand the role of values in determining research methodology.

One question that arises from the foregoing is as follows: How may we arrive at a more comprehensive understanding of what elements constitute a program? A program should not be seen as a mere "shopping list" of elements, but as a set of information, human and physical, that is interdependent and that is often mutually supportive.

A SYSTEMS APPROACH

A systemic view of programming would focus on information transformation, on an epistemological approach based on the principles of complexity, uncertainty, and chaos. This approach takes human and spatial culture into account, in addition to the functions themselves. These are, in turn, largely situated within the realm of positivist science (that is, the instrumentality of space through experience).

In order to set forth a systems approach, we may think of building an integrated, nonreductive, and interrelated triad comprising the programmer, the informant, and the organization (see Figure 16-1). Positivist science has spawned a methodology within which subjectivity and reflection are excluded, resulting in supposedly value-free investigation. In reality, the question we must ask is to what degree the culture of the researcher, as well as the culture of the users, influences the arrangement of programming data. Within this anthropological and social relationship three questions arise:

1. What is the role of self-criticism within this system?
2. What is the organization?
3. What is meant by complexity?

In this respect, Morin (1977) seeks a cyclical methodology aimed at reconstructing knowledge (i.e., the environment). The systems paradigm does not obey the principles of order, neutrality, and objectivity, but rather those of complexity, participation, and communication. We often call large facilities "complex" because of the multiple uses, organizations, and settings that they involve. Complexity does not mean "complicated," but comes from the Latin word *complecti*, meaning "to contain" many elements. Participation and communication, on the other hand, are essential to the understanding of what is really meant behind what is said or observed.

PROGRAMMING AS AN OPERATIONAL DEFINITION

The term *operational definition* denotes the meaning acquired by a space, including the steps and processes needed in order to conceive an architectural milieu. The interpretation designers give to a defined space is its meaning. Steel used in buildings, for example, often connotes technology for people. In summary, an operational definition delineates the terms and boundaries of a given program. Such a definition may be arrived at in three ways:

- Causality, which allows us to consider the elements that contribute to a particular phenomenon. The size and location of tables in a cafeteria, for example, affect the nature and pattern of social interactions in the room.
- Function, which defines the dynamic properties of a space and the way in which it performs. We may think of "appropriation," for example, as a kind of behavior that seeks to maintain control over a specific space. In this case, it is sufficient to observe how the behavior functions.
- Resemblance, which focuses on the structure of a setting and what it resembles when compared to other settings. The "laboratory" has, for example, served as the model for the modern kitchen in most Western cultures. A kitchen may thus be defined by its ease of maintenance, its flexibility, or its furniture arrangement.

Accordingly, the operational definition is based on the observable characteristics of what is defined. Observation, therefore, is of central importance in determining the operational definition of an environment. This type of definition is fundamental to programming, since the information in question is mainly gathered through observable events and features. Among the various methods used to collect data in research, two sources are most useful for an operational definition:

1. *Observations:* Observations are a prime source of data for the programming of similar settings. The programmer can move around and get an overall "feel" for the place, including his or her own responses to it. Also very helpful are patterns of use that can be observed:
   - where people go freely and where they do not
   - the physical and behavioral cues that are received while looking around
   - the extent to which flexibility in a setting is being used or not
   - where people choose to be when they have real choice
   - who can get together and who cannot

2. *Interviews:* Interviews with occupants and users are essential, since the programmer's reaction to a place may differ from those of the people who have to use it all the time or whose experiences differ from his or hers. The users can also direct the programmer to symbolic messages that he or she would not pick up, not knowing the spatial language of a particular organization or group.   .

A time-saver, the *touring interview* is really a combination of observation and interviews. The programmer walks around with users and asks them to talk about what they see and feel. The aim of this method is to get inside the world of the user. The touring interview can be used with a very different environmental scale. The tour process can be used for a neighborhood, a building, a floor, or even an office.

When a space is to be defined operationally, the programmer must select events identifiable by (1) the designer and (2) the client as conceptual indicators, because only those attributes that refer specifically to action are relevant to the exercise of conceptualization. If the facility or environment being programmed is improperly defined, the designer may end up with a wrong image or idea of what is needed (Figure 16-2).

DEFINING THE FACILITY

All definitions, in order to be useful, must have three dimensions: ontological, functional, and historical. The trilogy of *being, doing,* and *becoming* is at the base of programmatic representation and knowledge of the environment. Defining a facility through a program may thus be done by triangulation:

- an ontological definition (what space is)
- a functional definition (what space does)
- a historical definition (what space becomes)

The three orientations of the programmer who attempts to describe what he or she *perceives* (the ontological definition), what he or she *understands* (what space does), and what he or she *conceives* (the genetic definition) suggest the framework within which the facility will be built. The three visions—ontological, functional, and historical—become joined and intertwined (Figure 16-3).

This combination of the three orientations is therefore important to the programmer. The programmer should be able to express the model using basic environmental dimensions:

- the organizational/cultural dimension
- the human/social dimension
- the behavioral dimension
- the spatial/physical dimension
- the judicial/legal dimension

One arduous task for the programmer is to learn about the facility, and to understand it in conceptual terms (and therefore represent it) as a distinct place and a functioning organism. Instead of analyzing facts and reality, defining a facility is conceiving a model. The meaning of the program thus derives directly from the manner in which concepts are defined and represented. For example, providing visual privacy for an office means nothing to a designer unless the concept of privacy is defined and patterns represented. This shift from analysis to conceptualization implies subtle changes in the program's applications and in the role of the programmer. Before, it seemed we had to explain the setting in order to understand it; now, we must interpret it in order to sense its nature.

PROGRAMMING AND DESIGN: THE TRANSLATION PROCESS

For many, the transfer from the written statements of programs to graphics, or design, has caused various dilemmas. This view is also supported by the traditional concept of program as analysis and design as synthesis (Peña, et al., 1977). The so-called "gap" between programming and design lies in the fact that lists of needs or criteria do not readily translate into an architectural form or an environment that properly reflects the programmatic statements. As in the systems approach, the elements of a program have to be explicitly interdependent.

One working assumption is that an architectural program is already a crude social-physical form (Silverstein and Jacobson, 1985). A program is, after all, the definition of a setting or facility in social and physical terms. The program lays out the relationships (or patterns) that, by themselves, are related to the meaning people give to that setting, and are the key to whether or not the form makes human sense.

Robinson and Weeks (1983), for instance, have proposed an innovative approach that they called *Programming as Design*. In their vision, there is intentionally no separation between analysis and synthesis. This model combines the *verbal* (written) and *graphic* media, which tends to allow the programmer to explore physical forms and their implications. To quote: "The verbal ideas inherent in the images married to the words can work together analytically, synthetically, rationally, and intuitively." Verbal concepts are used along with formal concepts, and provide the programmer with tools for analysis by aspect. Each aspect of a facility consists of facts and fact patterns that are again represented verbally and graphically. Finally, an analysis of the whole is conducted using patterns and design alternatives (Figure 16-4).

Within the programming process, one central issue is how the designer will ultimately *interpret* the program content. For this purpose, the author had set forth the importance of meaning in programming. *Meaning* was defined as "a process of interpretation which provides a person with a repertoire that enables him or her to deal with the environment" (Bertrand, 1991). When programmers interpret the needs for a particular environment, they use their repertoires to translate these needs into statements and patterns. Designers ultimately interpret, from their own repertoires, the statements and patterns that enable them to design. However, the final environment may or may not reflect the anticipated one because of the mediation process that occurs (1) when the programmer interprets meaning A, and (2) when the design produces meaning B (see Figure 16-5).

One approach to the inquiry into meaning has been the application of ethnographic research to programming. By far the greatest barrier to a productive program is the use of methods that confuse the intimate relationship between programmer and client/user, as in using traditional social science roles. The act of investigation during programming necessarily means that the researcher and the people studied assume roles. Ethnographic research is a useful approach for programming because it helps the programmer understand organizational and personal cultures. Ethnography, as the "descriptive study of groups," also facilitates the translation process by using observation and interviews, intensively enabling the programmer to situate patterns of use more easily. We have used such an approach for the programming of a new police and fire station. Observation and interviews helped in developing patterns of use that were translated into the program's physical and behavioral requirements (see Figures 16-6 and 16-7). Learning about the firefighters' and police officers' difference in organizational culture, we then proposed to divide the facility in two different buildings, joined by the administration group (see Figure 16-8). A site analysis was then conducted in order to implement the facility (see Figure 16-9). Spradley (1979) has shown the importance of the role of both informants (the people studied) and the researcher in the ethnographic approach. Ethnography adopts a particular stance toward people with whom it works. The ethnographer says: "I want to understand the world from your point of view, I want to understand the meaning of your experience, to feel things as you feel them, to explain things as you explain them. Will you become my teacher and help me understand?"

This frame of reference shows the importance of the role of translation in programming. If we accept the idea that objectivity cannot be promulgated, we can concentrate on the issues that the programmer faces while writing a program.

ISSUES CONCERNING THE ROLE OF THE PROGRAMMER

Several issues will influence the role of the programmer. Some are internal, part of his or her own culture and personal background. Others are external, part of the methods and techniques he or she uses.

INTERPRETATION

As argued previously, architectural programming may be thought of as a process of interpretation. Interpretative thinking—thinking that proceeds from needs and requirements toward design—may be composed of four complementary methods: *hypothesis, analysis, synthesis,* and *globalization.* Together these methods relate interactively. Moreover, they should be understood as cyclical and nonlinear (see Figure 16-10).

Hypothesis

Hypothesis is a way of thinking that results from creative imagination. It takes into account project objectives, needs, and anticipated events. Likewise, a hypothesis explores those alternatives most in line with given goals and objectives. Zeisel (1981) has presented hypotheses as sophisticated possible solutions to a problem that can be thought of as conceptual models, analogous to the physical models designers use. Programmatic hypotheses, for instance, will try to develop tentative answers to questions like these: "What is the nature of the organization? What physical alternatives have been explored?"

Analysis and Synthesis

Analysis and synthesis are two interdependent parts of programming. Without analysis, synthesis constitutes a strategy divorced from a sense of the parts, while analysis without synthesis is a strategy lacking global vision of the human and architectural experience. It is important that the programmer thinks in analytical and synthetical manners simultaneously. In effect, each aspect of a facility being analyzed has to be understood in relationship with others: illumination, for example, has a direct influence on mood, thermal comfort, and eyestrain.

Linking analysis and synthesis interdependently thus moves a program toward concreteness—the design—without relinquishing the abstract qualities of programmatic analysis. To divide the two ways of thinking is to strip programming of its primary role—that of transforming human and physical needs into an architectural system.

Globalization

Globalization is similar to hypothesis in the sense that it too explores solutions to anticipated problems. A global approach allows us to think integratively and construct a vision composed of mutually supportive parameters. This step is crucial for the program, since it explicitly combines the various elements that composed the planned space or facility. Globalization is tested against initial hypotheses to ensure responsiveness of programmatic solutions to hypothesis questions.

Programmatic solutions based on global thinking offer the possibility of joining creative intuition with the programmer's sense of logic. They also bring program concepts a little further toward design to facilitate the designer's interpretation of the anticipated environment.

LEVELS OF PROGRAM INTERPRETATION

Like the approach proposed by Robinson and Weeks (1983), the operational definition leading to a program can be articulated on two principal levels: the *theoretical* level, expressed mainly in graphic form, and the *empirical* level, expressed in written form.

The Theoretical Level of a Program

The program relates the facility's needs to concepts and constructs. A concept is an abstraction, a model, conceived through the organization of thoughts. It is a representation of the specific aspect of a place or an event that characterizes that aspect. A kitchen, for example, is a concept that may contain different meanings, depending upon whether we are American, European, Asian, or from some other culture. A concept's primary value is the simplification of an otherwise complicated task: grouping a number of tasks together.

A construct is another dimension, built from and underpinned by concepts. Accordingly, expressions such as "privacy," "crowding," and "instrumentality" cannot be decoded as easily as "kitchen." In the former case, there is a higher level of abstraction. Therefore, we fabricate a construct from relationships organized within a functional framework. Abstraction is a characteristic of the program, since in information ordering and gathering, the programmer must reduce and conserve the critical aspects of the planned facility.

A construct is built in order to analyze and synthesize events and provide functional explanations of phenomena that we observe. Steele (1973) proposed a system for categorizing functions that communicate the role physical settings play for people. The system is constituted of six functions: shelter and security, social contact, symbolic identification, task instrumentality, pleasure, and growth. Functions of physical settings provide, in this regard, good examples of constructs that serve to represent environmental realities.

The Empirical Level of Programming

The significance of words, in programming vocabulary, must be established in terms of actions that show how a system becomes the operational definition described earlier in this chapter. In an empirical sense, the characteristics of a facility are generally expressed by means of norms or performance criteria. An environment may thus be defined in two complementary ways.

Abstract terms give the environment its general sense—the significance borne out at the semantic level. Metaphors and analogies are rarely used in programming, although they are very useful in describing an image of a building, for example. One can say: "Offices should be designed around individuals' work style and preference. The design should project the industrial image of the firm."

Concrete terms allow us to gauge performance in the context of particular activities. Performance criteria and space functions are the main attributes. For instance, "The maximum interpersonal space should not exceed 12 feet for normal, unamplified voice conversation in a meeting room" is a concept that can be measured.

In the case of analysis and synthesis, therefore, concepts and constructs support the elements of space, but they do not tell us how to measure them or conceive them, since that is the role of the empirical level. Figure 16-11 illustrates the cyclical relationship between theoretical and empirical levels of program interpretation.

PARTICIPATION

A comprehensive approach assigns importance to participation in programming. The notion of participation and participatory observation is derived in particular from anthropology. In architectural programming, real knowledge of needs and values cannot be obtained totally through observation alone. Obtaining such knowledge requires the participation of interested parties. Studies such as those of Hester (1975) and Sanoff (1977) have demonstrated the advantages of user participation in enhancing programmers' understanding of people's basic requirements and specifications.

It follows that in programming as well as in evaluation, a simple, objective description of a facility is no longer valid. We can no longer speak of building performance without discussing subjective perceptions. Participation of the programmer, the users, and the client is therefore of prime importance in order to engage all perceptual capabilities.

INTUITION

For the programmer, the most important role of intuition is in clarifying the issues. A solution then follows logically. The clarification of an issue and its definition is a function of intuition, often confirmed by the experience of users and revealed through interviews. It is here that the importance of the ethnographic approach is confirmed, i.e., knowing the real meaning of a need behind a problem anticipated by the informant. The true role of the programmer is to uncover contrasts and contradictions flowing from differences raised and sensed by users. The programmer should not hesitate to ask questions that bring out the contrasts inherent in an issue.

The important role of creative intuition in architectural programming is stressed here. According to the classical scientific methodology, two types of logic are used: inductive and deductive (which departs from a hypothesis). This paradigm, applied to programming, permits only a limited vision of reality. According to this vision, the program consists of inductive logic (analysis), while design supposedly employs deductive logic (synthesis). The divide between the two phases, as we have seen, is at the origin of problems of interpreting the program. Intuition should serve to construct hypotheses and link analysis and synthesis together so that solutions reflect a global vision of reality.

VALUE DILEMMAS

Contradictory positions often end up in unresolved value conflicts. Rather than attempt to proceed directly to a resolution, we should accept and explore the differences between elements. We should place ourselves in the middle of the debate by adapting our way of thinking. Critical thinking allows the programmer to make decisions based on the problem itself, rather than on personal bias.

Issues raised by the social, political, and cultural position of the programmer may actually help resolve value dilemmas. The programmers' paradigmatic choices with respect to normative measures, data collection methods, and available techniques cannot be made without a clarification of values at the theoretical level. These issues require, moreover, that the programmer understand the true sense of the notion of participation.

Value dilemmas often arise in the programming of facilities where controls over individual liberties are contemplated or the institution has questionable values. This is the case with correctional institutions, hospitals, and the military. It is thus essential that the programmer question the cultural values of the organization in order to properly represent the dignity and rights of the users. Certain questions—"How does the facility promote individual growth? What are the values of the correctional system?"—must be addressed by the programmer.

QUALITY

The qualitative dimension of a program is at the midst of the relationship between the programmer and the project. Quality is the consideration through which programmers become aware of the project and themselves. We know that the principle of duality (so dear to classical scientists) divides the world into parts—into observation and participation, objectivity and subjectivity. This is a fundamental mistake to be avoided. Polarity, rather than duality, integrates differences and does not divide them. Programming research may be seen at once as (1) a system, within which the programmer is situated outside of a planned facility, and as (2) a process within a context of interaction between the programmer and the facility in question.

The programmer may thus proceed in a dichotomous fashion by thinking about one interpretation or the other separately. The programmer thinks in a polarized way, globally—that is to say, by intuition—if he or she realizes the symbiotic relationship between the process and the system envisaged by the project itself. The key is that the approach be a global one. Conversely, the classical programming approach dictates that the programmer's task is to resolve a problem and find a practical solution (Peña, et al., 1977). Such an approach may be useful, as long as we don't devise a solution for a problem that doesn't exist, and we don't leave unresolved issues hanging. This brings us to the notion of reliability in programming.

In qualitative research, for instance, the main objective is to collect data on the behavioral and physical characteristics of an interactional organization and individual perceptions of a particular setting. The nonaxiomatic nature of the programmer, for that matter, makes the program a qualitative product. This non-neutrality of the programmer is of crucial importance and places the notion of traditional research reliability in question.

In programming, the traditional concept of reliability—the similarity of findings in similar settings by independent researchers—is ignored. Since no two programs can, or should, be replicated, and users and clients have different intentions, reliability in this realm is concerned with the manner in which the program is designed and with the systematic character of the protocol. According-ing to Levy (1987), "clear, concise, detailed formulation of the research proce-dure is advanced as the measure of reliability of the research." Validity, on the other hand, is seen as the greatest strength of qualitative research. Levy also declares: "The fundamental criterion in the research is to find the most articulate way of representing the life-world."

In finding the most appropriate way of representing the planned facility, techniques such as extensive informant interviewing, participant observation, and questionnaires help establish comprehensive descriptions of the environ-ment under study. The phenomenological-hermeneutic model, for example, takes a descriptive-interpretative approach, which is distinct from the formal-analytic methods of determining user and building needs. Marton (1981) reminds us that central to the scientific empirical approach is the notion of facts, where facts refer to the directly observable, objectively measured infor-mation about a certain object or environment. Central to phenomenology is the notion of essence, where essence refers to an intersubjective-qualitative meaning of a certain aspect of the world.

CONSCIOUSNESS

Recently, a growing number of scientists have become interested in questions of consciousness; that is, the need to include states of consciousness in research steps. The famous Cartesian proverb, *cogito ergo sum* (I think, therefore I am), led humans to consider only the intellect rather than the global. Today, more than ever, we have to adopt a psychosomatic view of human beings, and an environmental perception of the world in order to represent it adequately. This trend may encourage a more enlightened vision of the rela-tionship between programmer, users, and the environment by producing new approaches.

In programming, as in design, even if we employ various tools and techniques, a constant fact remains: Every search for knowledge is mediated by consciousness.

THE PROGRAMMER: GENERALIST OR SPECIALIST?

Programming, in practice, tends to assign great importance to the setting, to every facet of the physical and human environment, and to the various systems that support the use of a facility. Programming's multidimensional approach helps to resolve antagonisms such as the realization of quality architecture within a limited budget. The multidimensional (or multidisciplinary) approach allows for different visions of the same phenomena. This approach helps to make the programmer a facilitator or an advocate for users' needs and requirements. The programmer may also be called a "specialized generalist" as a result of environmental design. In fact, generalists refer to practice, while specialists require the mastering of state-of-the-art approaches and methods.

Practice, whether as researcher or professional, often figures prominently in debates over programming. Schon (1983) proposed the term "reflective practitioner," meaning a researcher involved in practice. The theory/practice interface is at the heart of this discussion. If too much attention is devoted to theory, we run the risk of dwelling on abstractions that have no application to the real world. Nevertheless, if too much importance is assigned to practice, we risk ignoring innovations and adaptations that then become difficult to interpret from the standpoint of knowledge and values.

A program without a theoretical model underpinning it—without a framework—may be merely a series of amorphous actions, a random collection of elements, a shopping list that precludes valid interpretation.

Ihde (1979) made an interesting interpretation of this duality by referring to the Cartesian mind/body distinction. Theory is perceived as the product of mind, while practice is related to the product of body. It is time to set aside this nomological view of actions and to promote a monistic system without distinctions.

Besides developing programming methods (the know-how), it is equally important to understand how we use the program. This entails, in particular, an interpretation of the meaning of design. To reach for the meaning of design is to begin to understand how and why design is part of the realm of human activities. To understand the use of design is to be able to identify the ideas (political, cultural, economical, psychological, etc.) that are embodied in environmental design. Knowing the values of programming will allow the process of decision making to be more clearly defined. In this manner, the interpretation and judgment of the particular problem will move far beyond the traditional approach based on the practical notions of precision, objectivity, standardization, efficiency, and economy.

Programming must involve not only knowing *what* and knowing *how*, but also knowing *why*, and knowing its ultimate *purpose*.

ACKNOWLEDGMENTS

The fire and police station project program approach was developed in conjunction with Maurice S. Amiel, M. Arch., Professor of Environmental Design, University of Quebec at Montreal.

Many thanks are owed to partners Gaetan Bois, SDEQ, and André Brodeur, CPUQ, for their support. The author also wishes to thank Peter R. Mulvihill for translation of original text and Peter R. Hecht, Ph.D., for comments.

References

Bertrand, R. 1991. Meaning and the built environment: An ethnographic approach to architectural programming. Master's thesis, School of Architecture, McGill University.

Building Research Board, National Research Council. 1986. *Programming practices in the building process: Opportunities for improvement.* Washington, D.C.: National Academy Press.

Hester, R.T. 1975. *Neighborhood space.* Stroudsburg, Pa.: Dowden, Hutchinson & Ross Inc.

Ihde, D. 1979. *Technics and praxis.* Dordrecht: D. Reidel Publishing Company.

Lecomte, R., and L. Rutman. 1980. *Introduction aux méthodes de recherche évaluatives.* Quebec: P.U.L.

Levy, R. 1987. Evaluation of technology: Some arguments for a qualitative approach. *Design studies* 8:4, pp. 224-30.

Marton, F. 1985. Phenomenography—Describing conceptions of the world around us. *Instructional science* 10, pp. 177-200.

Morin, E. 1977. *La méthode—La nature de la nature.* Paris: Editions du Seuil.

Morin, E. 1982. *Science avec conscience.* Paris: Fayard.

Palmer, M.A. 1981. *The architects guide to facility programming.* Washington, D.C.: The American Institute of Architects.

Peña, W., W. Caudill, and J. Focke. 1977. *Problem seeking: An architectural programming primer.* Boston: Cahners.

Preiser, W.F.E. (ed). 1985. *Programming the built environment.* New York: Van Nostrand Reinhold Company.

Robinson, J.W., and J.S. Weeks. 1983. Programming as design. *JAE* 37:2, pp. 5-11.

Sanoff, H. 1977. *Methods of architectural programming.* Stroudsburg, Pa.: Dowden, Hutchinson & Ross Inc.

Schneekloth, L.H. 1987. Advances in practice in environment, behavior, and design. In *Advances in environment, behavior, and design,* ed. Ervin H. Zube and Gary T. Moore, 307-34. New York: Plenum Press.

Schon, D. 1983. *The reflective practitioner: How professionals think in action.* New York: Basic Brooks.

Silverstein, M., and M. Jacobson. 1985. Restructuring the hidden program: Toward an architecture of social change. In *Programming the built environment,* ed. W.F.E. Preiser, 149-64. New York: Van Nostrand Reinhold Company.

Spradley, J.P. 1979. *The ethnographic interview.* New York: Rinehart and Winston.

Steele, F.I. 1973. *Physical settings and organization development.* Reading, Mass.: Addison-Wesley Publishing Company.

Zeisel, J. 1981. *Inquiry by design: Tools for environment-behavior research.* Monterey, Calif.: Brooks/Cole Publishing Company.

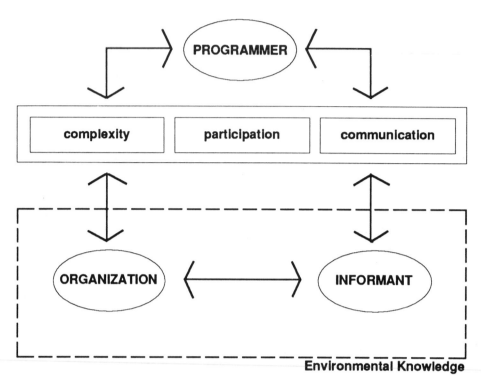

FIGURE 16-1.   The Systems Approach Triad

FIGURE 16-2.   Negotiating a Shared Image

(From Zeisel, 1981)

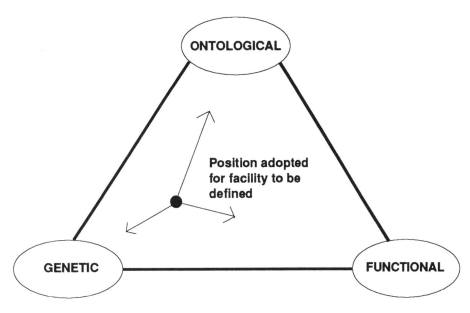

FIGURE 16-3.   Defining the Facility: The Three Dimensions

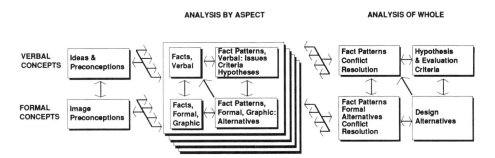

FIGURE 16-4.   Programming as Design

(From Robinson, 1983)

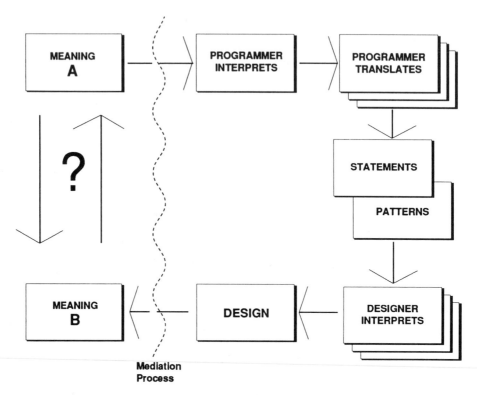

FIGURE 16-5.   The Translation Process

SPACE INVENTORY SHEET

Space: PATROL UNIT COMMANDER

Space no:	17
Amount:	1
Occupants:	1
Floor:	Ground floor
Area:	approx. 170 sq. ft.

Comments:

- •Well located; near Roll Call Room
- •Good visibility to Lobby/Reception Area
- •Good visibility to Communications Center
- •Dimension too small
- •Disorganizéd space
- •Office occupiéd 24 hours/day with shifts from 5 Patrol Unit Commanders

Nature of activities:

- •Supervision of patrol
- •Team briefing (up to 10 people)
- •Writing information for public meetings

Pattern:

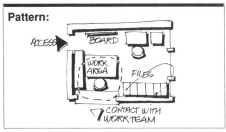

Picture:

FIGURE 16-6.   Example of Space Inventory Sheet

PUBLIC SAFETY DEPARTMENT
FUNCTIONAL   PROGRAM

Patrol Unit Commander

OCCUPANTS

Lieutenant   1

ACTIVITIES

1.This office is used by the Patrol Unit Commander. The activities consist in management of operations and duty team, verifying reports and planning some interventions.

2.This office is occupied 24 hours per day. Three shifts roll each day. During the roll, the Patrol Unit Commander conducts a "debriefing" to the next team in the Patrol Work Room.

3.The Patrol Unit Commander occasionally meets with 1 or 2 persons in his office.

FUNCTIONAL REQUIREMENTS

1.The office includes 1 desk, 1 chair, 6 files, 1 cumputer and 1 speaker in order to hear operational conversations, and 1 CRPQ terminal.

2.The Patrol Unit Commander controls various equipements (flash lights, Walky-Talkies, etc.) and the weapons. The weapons storage room should be adjacent to the office.

3.The location of the office shouls provide visual link with Reception Area while providing privacy needed for conducting operations. For this matter, the office could have large windows.

4.A window should also provide visual link with the Roll Call Room.

5.The design of this office should be sober and the floor materials easy to clean.

6.Access to office should be controlled with keys.

7.Provide visual identification of office beside the door.

ADUM INC

FIGURE 16-7.   Example of Program Requirements Form

PUBLIC SAFETY DEPARTMENT
FUNCTIONAL   PROGRAM

PROXIMITY

- The Roll Call Room   essential
- The Record Storage   essential
- The Weapons Storage   essential
- The Reception Area   essential

- The Detectives' Offices   desirable

SPATIAL REQUIREMENTS

19.5 sq. meters   Type S space

Weapons Storage
7.5 sq. meters   Type S space

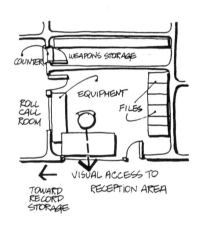

ADUM INC

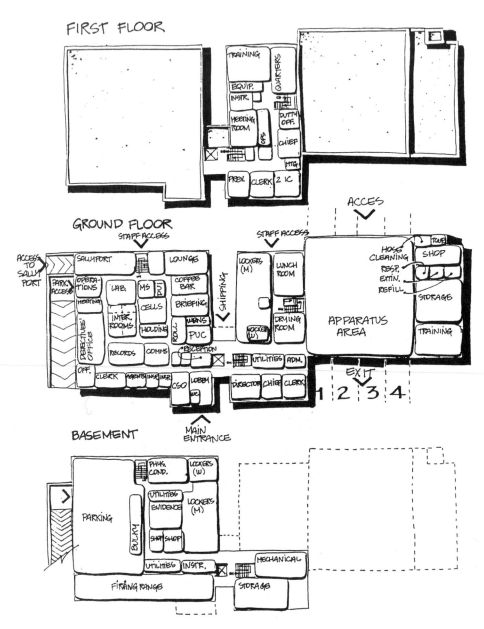

FIGURE 16-8.   Space Arrangement

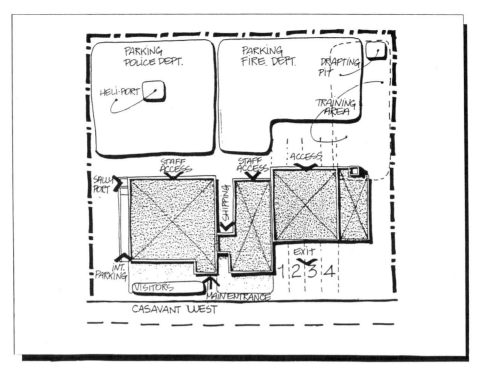

FIGURE 16-9.   Site Plan

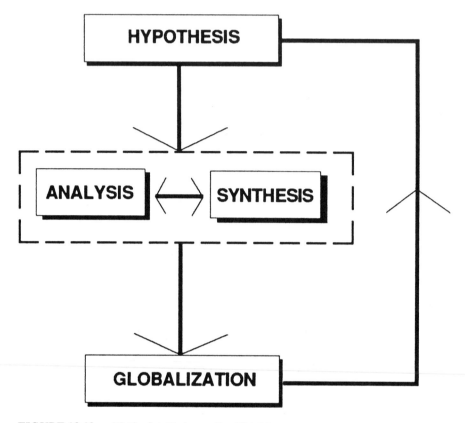

FIGURE 16-10.   Methods of Interpretive Thinking

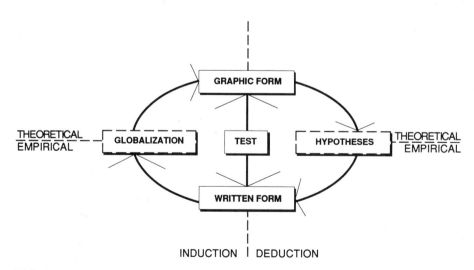

FIGURE 16-11.   Theoretical and Empirical Levels of Program Interpretation

CHAPTER 17

Creating Decision-Support Systems

James Paterson Murray
Roderick M. Gameson
John Hudson

It has been asserted that much of the dissatisfaction displayed by clients with their completed buildings results not only from inadequate strategic planning, but also from an apparent general failure by all involved to acknowledge the significance of the programming process (or briefing process, as it is called in the United Kingdom). The development of a client's facility program is arguably one of the most critical processes to be undertaken on any construction project. If the program does not comprehensively and sensitively reflect the client's needs and aspirations, then the end result—the facility—is likely to be highly unsatisfactory. The limited amount of research that has been carried out, from the British experience, suggests that many of the problems encountered during the programming process stem from defective communications between the client and the construction professionals commissioned to develop the project. These problems are exacerbated and compounded when the client has little or no experience with the construction industry.

The development of a program is a complex, interactive process that requires a client to state and communicate his or her needs explicitly in an unambiguous, logically consistent, and complete form. Evidence tends to suggest, however, that many clients often lack the expertise to formulate and communicate their requirements effectively, with the result that their ideas, objectives, and expectations are frequently misunderstood and misinterpreted by the construction team. The programming process usually involves the client making numerous complex, interrelated decisions, frequently involving the evaluation of both quantitative and qualitative factors. The need for logical inference using a network of decisions suggests that the programming process might benefit from the application of artificial intelligence techniques.

INTRODUCTION

This chapter explores the development of a computer program, the outcome of continuing programming research at the University of Reading in England. The ultimate goal of this research is the promotion of more effective client involvement in, and enhancement of, his or her contribution to the facility programming process. Studies undertaken at Reading in the early 1980s indicated that a major part of client dissatisfaction with the built facility appeared to emanate from the programming process. More specifically, dissatisfaction seemed to be closely related to the level and quality of guidance provided to clients during the initial stages of a project. The university was sufficiently concerned by that degree of client unhappiness that it initiated more detailed research into the programming process in conjunction with the Science and Engineering Research Council (SERC); where possible, its widespread international contacts would be visited to ascertain the response of other interested participants involved in programming. It was considered important then—and still is—to obtain and assess the international perspective on programming. These contacts and many others were later interviewed by Murray during a series of visits; a summary of the major observations from the interviews is contained in Appendix A.

The overall aim of this most recent study, however, was to investigate communication between clients and the construction team during the programming phase. It was considered that the subject of communications was of particular significance in the construction industry, where many different professions have to collaborate in order to fulfill the client's requirements. It was postulated that such a study would provide information to help create a more effective communications model from which a computer-based client-guidance system could be developed. This would constitute an appropriate response to clients who had indicated that they would welcome some form of impartial guidance; such a system could help to improve their understanding of the many issues involved and assist them in establishing their requirements and priorities *before* committing themselves to commissioning a project.

The research identified a core of key issues common to all of the case studies investigated; this core is incorporated in the structure of the computer program. The system developed is intended to be used by inexperienced clients during the earliest stages of a project and certainly before they have committed themselves to a definite and irreversible course of action. The diagnostic program allows clients and their advisers to study the various issues at their own pace; this should enable them to devise a facility program with which all are in agreement and which responds effectively to client needs, expectations, and circumstances.

For most clients, the construction of a new building—or the repair, refurbishment, or extension of an existing one—represents a major investment of resources, not only of money, but also of time and personnel.

For those clients who commission buildings regularly, the prospect of a prolonged encounter with the construction industry and its professionals presents comparatively few problems; for those building infrequently or indeed for the first time, however, the programming, design, and construction processes can appear complex and extremely bewildering.

Each project tends to be a specific solution to a unique combination of a client's diverse requirements and personal aspirations, influenced by prevailing statutory, environmental, and social factors. Many clients, especially the inexperienced, fail to appreciate fully the significance of many of the issues involved; by their inexperience, they unwittingly compound the design team's difficulties from the very inception of the project, especially during the programming stage.

Despite its apparent importance, programming in the United Kingdom seems to have remained a much-neglected part of the development of a project; the provision of guidance for inexperienced clients during that stage also has failed to attract sustained and detailed attention. The reasons for such neglect may be obscure, but they could have their roots in the complexity of the programming process itself, which seeks to address and resolve virtually all the issues fundamental to the successful development of a project from inception through completion to the operation of the facility. It is, by any standards, a formidable challenge.

Nevertheless, if the significance of the programming process, and of the client's role within it, is not acknowledged by all concerned, it is highly unlikely that the completed facility will fulfill all the client's requirements and expectations.

CLIENT ROLE IN THE PROGRAMMING PROCESS

Before a clearer understanding of the client's role in the programming process can be developed, it is essential to remember that no two clients will adopt the same approach to formulating their requirements. There are two key factors, however, common to all types of clients. One is experience; the level of clients' experience in developing a project will largely direct their course of action and control their degree of involvement in preparing the program. The second is client willingness to be involved conscientiously and effectively in programming.

Many participants in the project development process, especially clients themselves, seriously underestimate the crucial role that the committed client can play in assuming responsibility for initiating, directing, and maintaining the momentum of a building project through all the stages from inception to completion. Clients, especially the less experienced, are often reluctant to assume that responsibility, preferring to delegate it to the other participants. Such transference of control, however, can diminish the client's authority and may be interpreted by some as evidence of client weakness and vacillation, which can then be exploited. Failure by clients fully to acknowledge their role and responsibilities as initiators, information providers, communicators, and organizers—in terms of, among other aspects, allocating adequate resources for programming—can have serious repercussions for the successful outcome of the project.

The difficulties involved in formulating and communicating client requirements will vary considerably from project to project. There is no one single type of client; the archetypal client simply does not exist. Indeed he, she, or it may not even be the end user of the facility. If the client is an organization, then it is possible that various sections or departments within that organization may have conflicting objectives; vested interests also could aggravate relations between the client body and the construction team, compounding communication difficulties.

There is some evidence to suggest that failure to communicate effectively in the early stages of programming could lead to significant problems in the design and construction stages and, ultimately, with operating the built facility. Litigation could be the unfortunate end result of ineffective communication.

The client's requirements, therefore, must not only be formulated realistically and efficiently, but they must also be communicated effectively to the construction team during the programming process. Yet these actions presuppose a degree of client experience that simply may not exist. The relatively inexperienced client may be quite unaware—in a construction context—of the significant issues involved and of the strategic and tactical decisions expected of them by the other participants. They may not fully appreciate the extent to which they must be organized to participate successfully in the programming process.

Knowledge and understanding of that process, therefore, is an essential prerequisite of success. Nevertheless, without assistance, inexperienced clients will be unable to participate effectively in the development of their projects. In order for the client role to be enhanced and conscientious involvement to be encouraged, therefore, some measure of guidance must be provided.

Although individual client circumstances will tend to shape and influence programming strategies and procedures, certain issues, factors, and operations during the process seem amenable to systematic techniques. Many of the issues confronting the participants comprise a core common to the majority of clients and projects—the choice of the most appropriate contract form. The resolution of these, it was considered, could be achieved effectively by providing some form of decision-support system to clients during the early stages of project initiation.

While we acknowledge the diversity of approaches to programming adopted by both clients and construction teams, it does appear that, within the programming process, opportunities exist for formalizing many of the procedures. These could be encapsulated within the framework of a computer-based system that could provide a measure of fundamental, impartial, and essentially interactive guidance for the less experienced client during the vital pre-programming and programming stages. In order to develop such a system to benefit clients, however, it was considered that a more comprehensive understanding of the programming process, and especially of communications, was required.

RESEARCH BACKGROUND/ OBJECTIVES

The research project, sponsored by the Science and Engineering Research Council, began with the overall aim of investigating the communication process between clients and construction professionals during the programming phase of construction projects. The two main objectives for the research were these:

1. To develop a formal model of communications in the programming process based on an empirical study of programming in the construction industry.
2. To use the communications model to develop an intelligent knowledge-based system (IKBS) to assist both clients and the design team in the preparation of the facility program.

The project built on previous SERC-sponsored work conducted in the University of Reading's Department of Construction Management in 1982, which partly involved the creation of an embryonic computer-based client guidance system (Goodacre, et al., 1982)

The term *programming*—or briefing, as it is known in the United Kingdom—can cover a wide variety of processes. For the purposes of this project, programming was defined as follows:

> A communication process between a client organization and construction professionals to produce a statement from which a facility which satisfies the client's requirements can be produced.

It was also necessary to define what was encompassed within the programming process; i.e., what were the start and finish points of the process under investigation? The research team was conscious that, because of the diversity of client types and strategies when considering procuring a new facility, the investigation should be limited to covering a process from which valid results could be achieved within the two-year project time frame.

Therefore, the research focused on the process beginning with the client considering that a building in one form or another might be a solution to his or her problem, and ending with the production of a facility program.

RESEARCH METHOD

The initial phase of the project involved a literature search for material relating to programming, communication, and computer systems. Past research into programming is somewhat limited, with only a few major works identified in the United Kingdom (Newman, et al., 1981; O'Reilly, 1987), Europe (Cronberg, 1983; Kuchenmüller, 1983), and the United States (Peña, 1977; Sanoff, 1977; Preiser, 1977, 1978, 1985). Communication is a very wide-ranging term, and therefore it was necessary to focus the accumulation of relevant literature to specific themes, such as interpersonal skills, communication media, language, and professional practice.

For example, the method by which information is communicated to clients by professionals during the programming process can vary considerably. Some professionals use written checklists (of varying detail) to structure their requests for information, while others take a less structured approach. Research studies have confirmed the use of different techniques, such as the use of checklists, photographs, questionnaires, and models (Higgin and Jessop, 1965; Mackinder and Marvin, 1982). One particular research project (Mackinder and Marvin, 1982), which looked at architectural design decision making, discovered that in the few cases in which programming guides developed by the designer or client were used, the guides were found to provide a valuable basis for the development of the design. They also prevented the communication problems that tended to arise in other projects. In 1987 the Building Research Establishment (BRE) published a report that included a suggested checklist to follow during the programming process (O'Reilly, 1987). Currently the British Standards Institutions (BSI) is involved in the development of an international standard checklist for programming (BSI, 1990).

Related work in the information technology field comes primarily from the Royal Institution of Chartered Surveyors (RICS)/Alvey project, from which the expert system "ELSIE" was produced (Brandon, et al., 1988). However, one of the starting assumptions of "ELSIE" is that a project program has already been produced.

The first stage of the development of the research method was to identify key concepts from the information collected during the literature search relating to programming practice and communication. An "ideal" method was developed, which involved researchers observing and recording programming meetings between clients and professionals, supplemented by interviews with individual participants after meetings. The major benefit of this method was that it would enable information to be collected from real-life situations; it also would allow observation of actual programming procedures and communication methods. Although a number of clients and professionals expressed an interest in assisting the research team by providing access to projects, it was not possible to conduct data collection by this "ideal" method. The major reason for this was logistical difficulties of time-tabling and synchronizing meetings within the time frame of the research. An alternative method was devised, therefore, and involved the conducting of retrospective case studies. The objective here was to interview the individual parties involved in recently completed projects.

PILOT STUDY

To test this method, a pilot study was conducted on two recently completed projects. The first was an industrial process facility for a client building for the first time; the second, a new corporate head office facility for a major United Kingdom manufacturing company with previous construction experience. Parties who were interviewed included client representatives, project managers, architects, quantity surveyors, structural engineers, services engineers, and contractors. A full list of projects investigated, and parties interviewed, is shown in Appendix B.

Questionnaires were developed in light of the findings of the literature review of programming and communication-related material, with the main objective being to collect information to be incorporated into the computer system. The following key areas were identified and formed five section headings in the questionnaire:

1. Project Background
2. Programming Process—General Details
3. Interviewee Impressions of Programming Process
4. Post-Programming Facility Development
5. Post-Facility Completion

To enhance the communication aspect of the project, the questionnaires were designed so that opinions could be collected on subject areas from both clients and professionals. This enabled commonalities and discrepancies between parties to be identified, thus highlighting potential problem areas. In addition, the pilot study allowed the team to test questions for clarity and the relevance of responses to them.

Interviews were audio-recorded and transcribed manually, and a qualitative analysis was conducted to extract key points. The main points strongly emphasized as being of importance to the success of the programming process by a majority of interviewees were these:

1. estimates of project cost
2. critical deadlines
3. key building requirements
4. project relationship to its environment
5. organization of the project team

MAIN STUDY

Following the successful completion of the pilot study, an additional five projects were investigated using the same case study approach (see Appendix B). Questionnaires were revised in light of the pilot study's findings and adopted for the main study. Although no observation of participants communicating in real programming meetings was possible using this method, its major advantage was that the responses to semistructured questionnaires allowed for valid comparisons to be made between different projects and participant groups. This led to the identification of specific factors and knowledge for incorporation into the computer system.

During the pilot study, recorded interview data were transcribed and analyzed manually, which proved to be a very labor-intensive and time-consuming process. Therefore, it was clear that with a larger amount of data to be collected for the main study more efficient techniques to assist in data analysis were necessary. The researchers used a qualitative analysis software program called "The Ethnograph" (Seidel, Kjolseth, and Seymour, 1988), which allowed selective retrieval of coded sections of text from word-processed transcripts of interviews. A coding system was developed that related to specific questions asked during the interviews, which allowed for rapid comparisons to be drawn between different project types, clients, and professional groups. This method established a general consensus of key issues that strongly supported the findings of the pilot study. An example of the use of the coding system is presented below. Each question asked during interviews with project participants was allocated a specific code. A question concerning the reasons behind the client's initial decision to build was assigned the code C3. When the interview was coded using The Ethnograph, the printout of the answer given (in this instance from the client's representative in one interview) appeared as follows:

CODED VERSION OF FLOWCL2   7/9/1990   09:11   Page 2

+FLOWCL2

+−C3

CL2:	Looked at a 5 year sales plan, all	35	− +
	very basic stuff. Worked out what	36	:
	machinery capacity we thought we'd	37	:
	need for a 5 year plan. Then we	38	:
	built the factory with that 5 year	39	:
	plan very much in mind, even to	40	:
	the extent of strengthening the	41	:
	end of the existing factory so	42	:
	that we can build a lean-to on for	43	:
	expansion in raw materials stores	44	:
	at a later date.	45	− +

Once all of the interviews had been coded, it was possible to search—using the coding system—to determine if there was a consensus of opinion between projects, clients, and professionals. This analysis method strongly supported the findings of the pilot study.

RESEARCH OUTCOMES

The research confirmed that difficulties were encountered by clients with limited previous experience of building, in that they required a substantial amount of advice and guidance during the early stages of their project's development.

A number of key areas emerged from the overall analysis, which can be broadly divided into two main parts. The first is a common core of key project-related issues; the second, issues relating to the management of the programming process.

The common core of project-related issues concentrated on the following four areas of fundamental importance to all construction projects:

1. Early indications of cost, particularly relating to the client's budget.
2. Early indications of schedule, taking into account client deadlines.
3. Functional constraints, including space and services requirements.
4. Environmental issues, such as planning requirements and site investigation.

There were four areas that emerged as being crucial to the success of the management of the briefing process:

1. Establishing clear points of contact between clients and professionals.
2. Ensuring that client representatives have sufficient authority to participate effectively in decision making.
3. Creating an effective client/professional organization for programming.
4. The necessity of using communication media that can be clearly understood by all of the parties involved in programming.

The issues identified were then used in the computer system as a general framework within which more specific factors were dealt with in more detail.

COMPUTER SYSTEM

Aims and Objectives

The first task involved in the development of the computer system was to define for whom the system was most appropriate and what facilities it should provide.

The research had indicated that the clients most in need of support during the early stages of project definition were those who had little or no previous experience of the construction industry. Those with greater experience might find themselves in need of help from time to time, but their problems were usually specific and more readily addressed by means of conventional professional consultation rather than by use of computers. A decision was therefore made to concentrate on providing advice to inexperienced clients.

The scope for the development of computer-based decision-support systems in this area is immense. The range of issues that might be discussed during the early stages of programming (briefing) is determined by the range of activities that the proposed facility is to accommodate. No computer system could encompass this encyclopedic knowledge. Instead, a more limited aim was adopted: to identify a core of common issues likely to be raised on most projects and to deal with these.

The system was to have a twofold purpose: first, to educate the client in the process of programming; and second, to advise the client on potential problems with the project. The basis of the system would be the case study material compiled during the communications research.

It was considered important that the system be as easy to use as possible. No matter how good the technical content of a computer system, it is of little value if only a few people are prepared to use it. For this reason a great deal of attention was paid to the user interface. It requires only a minimum of keyboard skills and contains built-in explanatory features.

A computer-based system is not suitable for all clients. Those with no computer experience can be intimidated by the thought of the technology. No matter how simple the system is to use, they may be uncomfortable or unhappy using it. Others may see the computer as a dehumanizing threat to the programming process and therefore be unwilling to use it. In cases such as these, it is likely to be more satisfactory to adopt conventional programming methods. However, for clients who feel prepared to try it out, the system can be rewarding.

The emphasis is placed on providing an enjoyable learning experience. In doing so, the objective is to raise client awareness and thereby improve communications between and among all participants in the design process.

The system was developed for IBM-PC-compatible microcomputers. These computers are not ideal for the development of knowledge-based systems, since they are limited in processing speed and memory. However, they are the most common type of machine used by the construction industry in the United Kingdom and it was hoped that the system would be more readily used in practice if it ran on easily available hardware.

Several issues had to be considered when choosing the software with which to develop the system. The most fundamental choice was whether to build from scratch, using a programming language such as Prolog or LISP, or to use a ready-made expert system shell. The advantage of the first option was the flexibility to tailor the system precisely to the project requirements. The disadvantage was the time and resources required for development. As the schedule of the project was relatively short, the researchers decided to adopt the second approach and use a shell. They hoped that any loss in flexibility would be more than compensated for by the rapid development time.

A variety of shells was available on the market at the beginning of the project and a choice had to be made between them. It was anticipated that the knowledge to be represented by the system would be both extensive and complex. For this reason shells based purely on rules of the IF...THEN type were rejected. A more structured method of knowledge representation was required. Several possible systems were investigated. Some required large amounts of computer memory and therefore would not be able to function on the kind of microcomputer used in the offices of most construction professionals and clients. Eventually the Leonardo 3 system was chosen. It provided several forms of knowledge representation and a clear user interface, and it could be run on a basic microcomputer with 640k of memory and a hard disk.

Automating Client Guidance

In addition to using the findings of the research, the system also draws on existing client guidance. A limited number of written guides to programming for the inexperienced client have been produced in the United Kingdom by, for example, the Construction Industry Research and Information Association (CIRIA) (1987), the Building Research Establishment (BRE) (1987), and the National Economic Development Office (NEDO) (1985); some of this material has been incorporated into a draft standard for the International Organization for Standardization (ISO) (1990). Such guidance generally takes the form of checklists that cover the important aspects of a project to be considered by both clients and professionals during the development of a program. Some professional practices have also developed their own checklists, often for use when designing standard facilities for large bureaucratic clients or when dealing with specific technical issues such as air-conditioning.

There are advantages and disadvantages to using such checklists. On the positive side, checklists help to do the following:

1. They prevent oversights in developing a program.
2. They encourage clients to provide information in a form that can be easily used by designers.
3. They can focus the client's attention on the need to define requirements clearly.

But they have a negative side:

1. They may inhibit effective client/professional relationships by constraining communication in too rigid a framework.
2. They may obscure the more subtle aspects of client requirements.
3. They may contain preconceptions about facility types that may channel the client toward a particular kind of design.
4. They may require much information that is not strictly necessary to the design.
5. They may make it difficult to cross-check for consistency of client requirements when the checklist is large.

The computer system can be seen as an extension of the checklist approach to programming that retains its advantages—notably the ability to detect oversights—while overcoming some, but not all, of the disadvantages. It has three particular advantages over written guidance:

1. It can tailor advice to a given project so that only relevant information is given.
2. It can provide automatic cross-checks of project requirements to ensure that consistency is maintained.
3. It can automatically detect and highlight areas that may cause problems later in the construction process.

Such a system may improve client/professional relationships by priming the client with the kinds of issues that are likely to occur during programming. However, it deals in generalities and is unlikely to be able to bring out the intricacies of some client requirements. It should therefore be seen only as an aid to enhance communication in programming and not as a replacement for it.

System Outline

The system operates as a question-and-answer session punctuated with the provision of information and advice by the computer. The length of a session is determined by the type of building and client organization and also by the number of topics on which the user wishes advice. An outline diagram of the system is given in Figure 17-1.

The introduction section gives the user basic instructions on how to use the program. Initially the user is taken through a series of questions designed to establish a project profile; this comprises a basic set of information on the client's requirements as far as they can be known. It includes matters such as project size, budget, availability of site, and so on. After completing the project profile, the user is given a summary of the information given. An example of the project profile, as presented to the system user, is shown in Figure 17-2. The second part of the session then commences.

This second part enables the client to investigate particular aspects of the project in greater depth. A choice of five topic areas or modules is presented, which correspond to the five key areas of concern identified in the research analysis. The topic areas are shown in Figure 17-3.

The sixth option, called "sensitivity," is also available. This allows the user to alter individual variables established in the project profile. Using this facility, "what-if" questions can be asked; for instance, the consequences of shortening the project schedule could be examined.

Each module involves asking the user a series of further questions tailored to the project profile. As the dialogue develops, the system may detect potential problems in the project and will comment on them to the user. At the end of the module, the computer displays a report that gives more details on the identified problems and provides advice on how they may be overcome. An example of such advice is shown in Figure 17-4. Once the advice has been given, the user has the option of beginning another module or ending the session.

System Development

When developing a computer system it is easy to concentrate on its internal logic and to neglect its relationship to the real world. The result can be a product that looks impressive but is of little practical use. To ensure that this did not occur, clients and professionals were consulted at every stage in the system's development process. The original framework and organization of the system came from an analysis of real case studies augmented by other client guidance. Development then took place through the design and testing of prototypes. Rough versions were presented to users for their comments. Their remarks and suggestions were then used to produce a slightly more polished version, and the process was then repeated. In this way it is hoped that the relevance of the system to practice has been maintained throughout the development process.

Reactions of users to the system have been varied but can be said to have fallen into two groups. The first, and largest, group was enthusiastic and saw considerable potential for the system, particularly if it was tailored to suit their own individual requirements. The second group, which was in a minority, expressed the general doubts about the applicability of computers to programming. This criticism seemed to stem from a suspicion that computer systems might erode the architect/client relationship; it did not seem to be directed at the structure or content of the system itself.

Future Possibilities

A number of further developments of the system have been suggested and are under active consideration. In its present form, the system is of necessity a rather general tool dealing with a common core of issues likely to be encountered on most projects regardless of building type. However, many clients and some professionals tend to deal with specific building types. Such clients and professionals have suggested that a system that deals with problems specific to their building type, in addition to the common core issues, would be useful.

Other suggested developments have included a version designed for educating user groups involved in facility programming for large organizations and a version for training young construction professionals about to become involved with clients for the first time.

CONCLUSIONS

Communication is of vital importance in any field of human endeavor. The smooth running of any project from inception to completion depends on a number of factors, but one of the most significant is effective communication.

Failure of client and professional groups to communicate satisfactorily in the early stages of a construction project can lead to considerable problems—not only during the later stages of the project, but also in operating the facility. It must be acknowledged by all the participants, however, that programming is very much a two-way procedure and that the client has a significant role to play. The standard of service that clients receive is very much a function of the effort expended by them in contributing to the programming process.

The primary objective of the computer system, therefore, is to facilitate communications by encouraging more conscientious client participation, thereby enhancing their role. It can be seen, essentially, as a priming tool, enabling clients to understand the processes involved and then to communicate their perceived requirements more clearly and succinctly to their advisers. The system identifies aspects that might not have been adequately considered by the participants; it can also detect contradictions in the programming information and in client responses. Above all, it is designed to ensure that the client and others are aware of the major issues on which decisions have to be made before they commit themselves irrevocably to action.

The interactive processes by which clients' aspirations are transformed into a medium—the program—through which their advisers can act are extremely complex. It is the successful comprehension, manipulation, and communication of clients' requirements, however, in order that the final design accurately reflects their stated objectives, that continues to present such a formidable challenge.

References

Brandon, P.S., A. Basden, I.W. Hamilton, and J. Stockley. 1988. *Expert systems: The strategic planning of construction projects.* University of Salford: Royal Institution of Chartered Surveyors.

BSI. 1990. *Draft international standard ISO/DIS 9699: Performance standards in building—checklist for briefing.* London: British Standards Institution (BSI).

CIRIA. 1987. *Practical advice for the client intending to build.* London: Construction Industry Research and Information Association (CIRIA).

Cronberg, T. 1983. *Design briefing: The brief, the process.* Copenhagen: Danish Building Research Institute (SBI).

Goodacre, P.E., J. Pain, B.M. Noble, and J.P. Murray. 1982. *Client aid program.* Occasional paper no. 5, University of Reading: Department of Construction Management.

Higgin, G., and N. Jessop. 1965. *Communications in the building industry.* London: Tavistock Publications.

Kuchenmüller, R. 1983. *Checklist for the content of a brief.* Copenhagen: Danish Building Research Institute (SBI).

Mackinder, M., and H. Marvin. 1982. *Design decision making in architectural practice.* Research paper no. 19. University of York: Institute of Advanced Architectural Studies.

National Economic Development Office (NEDO). 1985. *Thinking about building.* London: Her Majesty's Stationery Office (HMSO).

Newman, R., M. Jenks, S. Bacon, and S. Dawson. 1981. *Brief formulation and the design of buildings.* Oxford: Oxford Polytechnic.

O'Reilly, J.J.N. 1987. *Better briefing means better building.* Watford: Building Research Establishment.

Palmer, Mickey A. 1981. *The architects' guide to facility programming.* New York: Architectural Record Books.

Paterson, John. 1977. *Information methods for design and construction.* London: John Wiley & Sons.

Peña, William Merriweather, William Caudill, and John Focke. 1977. *Problem seeking: An architectural programming primer.* Boston: Cahners.

Preiser, Wolfgang F.E., ed. 1978. *Facility programming: methods and applications.* Stroudsburg, Pa.: Dowden, Hutchinson & Ross.

Preiser, Wolfgang F.E., ed. 1985. *Programming the built environment.* New York: Van Nostrand Reinhold Company.

Salisbury, Frank. 1990. *Architect's handbook for client briefing.* Cambridge: Butterworth Architecture.

Sanoff, Henry. 1977. *Methods of architectural programming.* Stroudsburg, Pa.: Dowden, Hutchinson & Ross.

Seidel, J., R. Kjolseth, and E. Seymour. 1988. *The Ethnograph—A users guide.* Denver, Colo. Qualis Research Associates.

White, Edward T. 1972. *Introduction to architectural programming.* Tucson, Ariz. Architectural Media Ltd.

White, Edward T. 1982. *Interviews with architects about facility programming.* Tucson, Ariz. Architectural Media Ltd.

APPENDIX A

Observations on Programming Issues Derived from Series of International Visits

ACKNOWLEDGMENT

The authors are extremely grateful to the organizations, institutions, and individuals they visited. Their addresses can be obtained from J. P. Murray at the Department of Construction Management & Engineering, University of Reading, Whiteknights, Reading, England.

The following observations represent a *synoptic view* of only *some* of the significant aspects and issues generated and debated during the programming process. In no way can it be considered, or is it intended to be, comprehensive. The observations, largely commonsense, reflect a *general international concern* that programming is not conducted as *efficiently* as it should be and that relationships with clients could be improved significantly.

Two *key conclusions* can be drawn, nevertheless:

1. There appears to be no consensus on the most appropriate and effective approach to programming strategies and tactics.
2. Active, conscientious client participation in the programming process is the prerequisite for ultimate success in any project.

PROGRAMMING AND THE PROGRAM

- Effective programming is about *identifying the problem, reducing it to key statements, and communicating its essentials* to all concerned. Unless the problem is *clearly stated,* no satisfactory solution can be provided.
- The *broad scale* of the problems must be clearly understood *at the beginning;* however, avoid *too close* a focus *too early.* Concentrate on *concepts.*
- Distinguish between client *needs* and *wants.* Beware of the *"hidden agenda";* what the client really needs may not be immediately obvious. Be *patient,* especially with inexperienced clients! Also be aware of the differences between *real goals* and *"lip-service" goals* (Peña)—*avoid* "impossible" goals.
- Clients *must provide adequate resources* for programming in terms of people, time, and money.
- The program must be concerned more about analyzing the *relationships* between client activities and less about simply compiling a list of

accommodation. Clients appreciate graphic representations of these relationships.

- Programming is *not* a finite process; the program can be a *dynamic document* reflecting *potential changes* in the function of the facility and in the needs of clients. All the participants, however, must be aware of the *implications.*
- *Developing a program jointly* with clients seems widely favored, since during this interactive process significant issues can be raised *that may not always be evident* in a formal, client-generated program.
- Try to discover *why* clients want something; it could provide *clues* to their motives and expectations.

PROJECT ORGANIZATION, ADMINISTRATION, AND DEVELOPMENT

- A competent person *from the client organization* should be appointed to *maintain an overview* of the project from start to finish. That person can then *monitor all activities,* especially programming, so that no one aspect is developed at the expense of others; there must be a *degree of synchronization* at all times — *audit* regularly.
- Encourage clients to *provide a preliminary or outline statement* about themselves, their ambitions, and their projects and to present this at an informal session *before* the formal programming process commences; i.e., at the "big picture" meeting. This encounter helps to "break the ice" and could be *invaluable* in promoting a *rapport* between clients and their consultants. Such a session can reveal, among other aspects, such matters as extent of client experience and expertise, organizational problems, deeply rooted prejudices, and, on occasions, the "hidden agenda."
- *Timing is crucial.* Decide *what* to worry about and *when;* i.e., a *desirable time* versus the *critical point* of *no return* (Zilm).
- Differentiate between *decision-making* sessions and *presentation sessions;* but *record* all program agreements.
- *"Brainstorming"* sessions with clients should be followed by a *"breathing space"* affording adequate *time for reflection.*
- *Define clearly* all questions to which answers are required.

CRITERIA FOR ESTABLISHING SUCCESS OR SATISFACTION

- Early on, establish and agree on *criteria* against which success or client satisfaction can be measured. Such criteria could include, among other items, high comfort levels for users, low energy costs, and maximum flexibility in facility with low costs involved.

- *Problems* can arise if those involved in evaluating the success of the completed facility were not participants in the original programming process: A *degree of reconciliation* may be necessary!

FINANCE

- The importance of a *realistic budget* cannot be overemphasized; budget *constraints* must be identified *as early as possible.*
- Try to avoid *danger* of preliminary budget, however, becoming the final project budget; *very early costings* in the absence of hard project information can be *quite unrealistic.*
- Keep clients *aware* at all times of *cost and other related implications,* especially when *derived from client-induced variations.*
- Prepare an *estimate* of what the initial program *is likely to cost. Compare* with client budget, and *do not proceed* until all anomalies are investigated and reconciled.

PROBLEMS WITH CLIENTS

- Clients are unable *to define the project clearly* and frequently are uncertain about their requirements; they are often unwilling *to produce a realistic budget* to match their needs and expectations. For some, the *total process* of project development is a *complete mystery.*
- Try to *record* clients' *original goals:* Frequently, by the end of the project, they have *forgotten* what they were.
- Client organizations are often reluctant *to appoint senior people* to assist in programming; there should be top-level executive support. *Access* to these key decision makers is often denied to programmers, thereby generating difficulties. Client representatives are often *appointed by default.*
- Clients should *resist* the impulse to start projects *as quickly as possible:* Patience is *not* always a virtue, *but it can help.*
- It is important to determine whether or not *the client* and *the end user* of the facility are *one and the same person: Consultations* with end users are *crucial.*
- Clients frequently *fail to ask the appropriate questions* until the program is *completed* and the preliminary sketches *prepared;* they may often be *very concerned* about *exposing* their lack of knowledge.
- The link between *visualization* and *quantitative information* is difficult for most clients to grasp—abstract design concepts, in particular, can create problems.
- Client insistence on *particular space formulas* is not always helpful to design teams.
- Inexperienced clients may have *problems* forming a "judgment base" when they are building *infrequently.*
- Clients often *unaware* of their responsibilities and the resources required to fulfil them.

GUIDANCE FOR CLIENTS

- Clients, *especially the inexperienced*, would welcome *more informed guidance* from their consultants, on a varied range of aspects:

  evaluation of need to build,
  contract options and characteristics,
  construction industry terminology,
  roles and responsibilities of each of the consultants,
  project development, project stages, and related time frame, especially for
      key decisions,
  spatial considerations: appreciation of 3D,
  criteria for selection of sites,
  relationship between cost and quality in design and construction terms,
  implications of changes,
  environmental issues, including planning implications,
  monitoring building performance—post-occupancy evaluation,
  workplace diagnosis in terms of health, safety, comfort, and productivity,
  quantitative tools for programming, and
  maintenance of facilities.

- It is essential for all consultants *to explore more effective ways* of *communicating* with clients, especially where *qualitative issues* are being debated. All media should be considered:

  Gantt charts,
  photographs/slides,
  models and mock-ups,
  CAD techniques, including walk-through simulations, videotapes, and
      spreadsheets
  material samples, and
  gaming models.

APPENDIX B

Case Study Projects and Interviewees (United Kingdom)

1. *New Sealant Production Facility, Hampshire*
   Client Representative, Architectural Consultant, Project Architect, Quantity Surveyor, Structural Engineer, Mechanical and Electrical Services Engineer.
2. *New Corporate Head Office, Berkshire*
   Client Representative, Architectural Consultant, Quantity Surveyor, Design and Build Contractor.
3. *New Storage Warehouse, Hertfordshire*
   Client Representative, Project Manager, Design and Build Contractor.
4. *New Storage Warehouse, Yorkshire*
   Client Project Manager, Architect, Quantity Surveyor.
5. *Speculative Office Development, Hampshire*
   Client Project Manager, Design and Build Contractor.
6. *New Educational Facility, London*
   Architect, Quantity Surveyor.
7. *New Laboratory Facility, Warwickshire*
   Client Representative, Project Manager, Architect, Quantity Surveyor.

APPENDIX C

Organizations, Institutions, and Individuals Visited to Discuss Programming Issues, Listed in Itinerary Order

1985   Fritz Sigrist
Danish Building Research Institute (SBI)
Copenhagen, Denmark

1988   Ms. Cynthia Milota
Skidmore, Owings and Merrill
Chicago, Ill., USA

Michael Lane/Jerry Reich
Schal Associates
Chicago, Ill., USA

Richard Krauss
Arrowstreet Inc.
Cambridge, Mass., USA

Claude Bernier
General Services Agency
Washington, D.C., USA

James Franklin
American Institute of Architects
Washington, D.C., USA

Gary Silver
Whidden/Silver Inc.
New York, N.Y., USA

Ms. Cindy Froggatt
Haines, Lundberg, Waehler
New York, N.Y., USA

Dr. Robert Gutman
Princeton University
Princeton, N.J., USA

Mrs. B Hillier
Hillier Group
Princeton, N.J., USA

Walter Moleski
Environmental Research Group
Philadelphia, Pa., USA

Ms. Wendy Peck
PHH Interspace
Philadelphia, Pa., USA

1990 Prof. Tom Heath/Dr. David Scott
Faculty of the Built Environment
Queensland University of Technology
Brisbane, Australia

Prof. Peter Johnson/John Wyndham
McConnell, Smith & Johnson Pty. Ltd.
Sydney, Australia

Richard Golombek
c/o Leo Daly
Los Angeles, Calif., USA

Mr. Yerou
c/o The Luckman Partnership Inc.
Los Angeles, Calif., USA

Dr. Wolfgang Preiser
School of Architecture
University of New Mexico
Albuquerque, N.M., USA

John Petronis
Architectural Research
  Consultants Inc.
Albuquerque, N.M., USA

Dan Haas/Lindrea Bernard
3D/International
Houston, Texas, USA

Willie Peña/Steve Parshall
CRS Sirrine Inc.
Houston, Texas, USA

Richard Maxwell/David Wyckoff
Gensler and Associates
Houston, Texas, USA

Don Young/Dr. Lou Guthrie
IFMA
Houston, Texas, USA

Kevin Williams
CPC Space Consultants
Houston, Texas, USA

Dr. Frank Zilm
Frank Zilm & Associates Inc.
Kansas City, Mo., USA

Kent Spreckelmeyer
School of Architecture and
  Urban Design
University of Kansas
Lawrence, Kan., USA

John Hoffman/James Steele
Burns & McDonnell
Kansas City, Mo., USA

Kent Turner/John Van Landingham
Pearce Corporation
Saint Louis, Mo., USA

David Chassin, Bob Osgood,
Janet Brown, Martha Whittaker
HOK
Saint Louis, Mo., USA

Paul Luther Thomas Gyllstrom
Flad & Associates
Gainesville, Fla., USA

Prof. Edward T. White
School of Architecture
Florida A & M University
Tallahassee, Fla., USA

Mike Hearn
MBT Associates
San Francisco, Calif., USA

Tib Tussler
SMP
San Francisco, Calif., USA

Dr. Jay Farbstein
Jay Farbstein & Associates Inc.
San Luis Obispo, Calif., USA

1991   Luke Pollard/ Trent Alston/
            Geoff Brew
        Lend Lease Interiors
        Sydney, Australia

        Prof. Jerry Finrow
        Dept. of Architecture
        School of Architecture &
            Applied Arts
        University of Oregon
        Eugene, Ore., USA

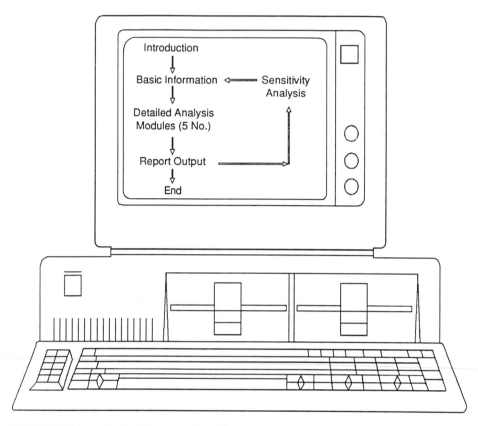

FIGURE 17-1.   Outline Diagram of the System

```
                                          Knowledge Base: CLIENTll
        PRELIMINARY REPORT

        Type of project     industrial

        Location            town          Timescale      12 months

        Budget Limit        £ 500,000     Budget per m2  £ 1000

        Appearance          medium
        Importance                        ┌──────────────────────────┐
                                          │ If any of the entries are │
        Site                none          │ wrong they may be altered │
                                          │ using the sensitivity     │
        Building Area       500m2         │ option on the detailed    │
                                          │ topic menu                │
        Servicing           medium        └──────────────────────────┘

        No of people        50

        m2 per person       10


                          Hit any key to continue
```

FIGURE 17-2.   Basic Project Profile Screen

Knowledge Base: CLIENT11

DETAILED ANALYSIS

A number of topics can be examined in more detail

Please select a topic for further analysis

<u>**cost**</u> time function environment organisation sensitivity	examines the financial details of the project

FIGURE 17-3. System Topic Areas

Knowledge Base: CLIENT11

FLEXIBILITY ADVICE

You are not certain how long you will retain ownership of the new building. It is generally sound practice to build a reasonable level of flexibility into a new building to ensure that it can be adapted to changing user requirements. Even if you do not retain ownership for long a building which can be readily adapted is likely to be more marketable than one which is not.

As you are uncertain whether the building will be extended it may be a good idea to allow for the possibility of expansion. You should ensure that there is sufficient room on the site for this. You should also make clear the possible need for expansion to the design team who can then site the building appropriately and ensure that the structure can easily incorporate the necessary modifications.

Hit any key to continue

FIGURE 17-4. Examples of Advice Screen

CHAPTER 18

Research-Based Programming and Design

Uriel Cohen

INTRODUCTION

The domain of programming for design has matured considerably during the last few decades. Architectural programming is now a formally recognized subfield in architectural education, research, and practice.

Despite its progress and growth, several aspects of programming remain relatively underdeveloped. Some of these aspects are the management of research information regarding human behavior and experience in the environment, the synthesis and communication of this information, and the process of its eventual use in design by architects.

This chapter reviews some of the issues concerning research-based information; describes an approach for informed, user-based programming; and illustrates the application of this approach in a programming and design case study: the planning of special care environments for persons with dementia.

TYPICAL PROBLEMS IN PROGRAMMING FOR SPECIAL USER GROUPS

The state of the art in environment-behavior research has changed considerably since its beginning in the early 1960s. The quality and quantity of knowledge has grown by leaps and bounds. The past two decades also have witnessed the emergence of environmental programming as a subdiscipline focusing on the application of behavioral research in planning and design (Seidel, 1982; Weisman, 1983; Schneekloth, 1987).

Yet some of the old obstacles in applying research information to the design of the environment still persist. More than a decade ago it was noted (Cohen and Moore, 1977) that with the growing recognition of relations between environment and behavior, it was logical to assume that empirical information about how people behave in, or are affected by, various environments would be used as important input in programming for design. Designers expected that the factual foundation for responsive design, coming from the behavioral and social sciences, would be tailored to their needs as decision makers. However, they often found research literature difficult to use because design implications were "buried" in jargon-filled text, were obscured by a cautious, scientific reporting style, or seemed to be totally missing (Francescato, Weideman, Anderson, and Chenoweth, 1976; Reizenstein, 1980; Churchman and Ginsberg, 1984). The result was the perceived "applicability gap." These problems were compounded by the economic constraints typically imposed on architectural programming. The limitations on time and energy devoted to research or information gathering by practitioners rules out from the outset any lengthy programming activity. The common outcome of these problems was a design decision-making process based on inadequate programs, and overreliance on personal experience and guesswork. Recent reviews indicate that these issues are still with us (Seidel, 1985; Schneekloth, 1987).

A CONCEPTUAL APPROACH FOR PROGRAMMING

In an article that examines both problems in architectural programming and possible solutions, Seidel (1982) identifies several strategies to facilitate better use of research information:

1. Improved "translation," "packaging formats," and communication (e.g., Korobkin, 1976; Reizenstein, 1981; Windley and Weisman, 1977).
2. Linkage strategies focusing on information transfer mechanisms (Merrill, 1976).
3. Participatory programming and collaboration between users, researchers, and designers (e.g., Sanoff, 1977).

The work described in this chapter focuses primarily on development of the first strategy. In recent years the author and his colleagues have addressed the issues of extraction, translation, and communication of user-based research information. Different communication methods and formats were put into programming applications in various context areas (Moore, Cohen, Oertel, and Van Ryzin, 1979; Cohen, Moore, and McGinty, 1978; Cohen, Beer, Kidera, and Golden, 1979; Cohen, Hill, Lane, McGinty, and Moore, 1980; Cohen and McMurtry, 1985; Cohen and Weisman, 1991).

The basic programming process that emerged from this cumulative experience over the last two decades is described schematically in Figure 18-1. Its four main phases are these:

1. *Defining goals:* This includes the goals of users, owners, and other parties involved in the environment under consideration.
2. *Identifying, describing, and analyzing problems, issues, and needs:* Critical topics that require informed decision making.
3. *Developing design guidance:* Translating the information gathered in (2) into an integrative, usable communication to be used by designers and others.

    The generic design guide is a typical product of this phase. It supplements specific building programs and other design-guidance products such as case studies. The communication device of design principles is a key feature of our design guides, as described shortly.
4. *Generating solutions:* This is the ultimate goal of the programming process; but since the process is not entirely linear, some good ideas, questions, and information are fed back into the previous phases; this cyclical process is also called "inquiry by design" (Zeisel, 1984).

DESIGN PRINCIPLES: A BASIC TOOL IN PROGRAMMING AND DESIGN

As outlined above, an important part of any program for a building design is the articulation of the basic goals or issues to which the designed environment should respond. For example, in the context of the museum environment, typical and critical issues are "museum fatigue" and "way finding," to name a couple.

Goals and issues form a strong basis for design principles. For example, given the issue of way finding, it is clear from the research literature that a number of design features and environmental qualities such as a coherent path can facilitate easier visitor's way finding. Two design principles that respond to this issue are "understandable structure" and "circulation that overlooks." Both principles are grounded in user-based research information: The former is based on the premise of increased cognitive clarity and predictability; the latter is based on research information about perceptual and physical accessibility.

Design principles suggest critical environmental factors, qualities, and characteristics of those settings that will facilitate the goals or resolve the issues. For example, the main quality of "circulation that overlooks" is expressed in its title: the visitor's commanding view on all or most paths and destinations from the initial point of entry, or from a central location.

Design principles are intended to be abstract, general, evocative, and suggestive of a range of design options. A good design principle should evoke a number of equally good design alternatives, not just one solution.

Although architects use design concepts such as "symmetry" or "central spine" as organizing tools, usually they are form-based, not issue- or user-relevant. Seldom have they been evaluated or questioned seriously. The design principles advanced in our design guides are based on issues that are derived from research of problems in the built environment. Some of these principles come from research literature on basic behavioral issues, others are from disciplinary literature on particular environments, and others yet are organizational issues. The principles are several in number and testable. The intention is to communicate information that may provide a direction and a range of design options. The goal is to inform the reader, to stimulate the designer's imagination and intuition, while avoiding doctrinaire solutions that might inhibit design innovation.

While some design principles are truly universal, a few principles might conflict with other, equally sensible principles. Most principles are useful in any given situation, but—like helpful tools in a toolbox—not all are necessary or appropriate in each problem situation.

Design principles are indeed tools to aid in the design process, and guide the formation of the design environment. Therefore, they should be used selectively, with care and flexibility.

A recent format for organizing and communicating design principles and their constituent parts is described in Figures 18-2a and 18-2b.

A CASE STUDY IN PROGRAMMING: ENVIRONMENTS FOR PEOPLE WITH DEMENTIA[1]

The following discussion describes the key aspects of the generic programming for environments responsive to the needs of people with dementia. A specific design application—a group home for eight persons—illustrates the use of this programming information.

People with Dementia and the Physical Environment

Alzheimer's disease, a special classification of dementia, affects as many as 2.5 million people in the United States. The disease is marked by forgetfulness, trouble with personal care, difficulty with everyday tasks, and mental agitation and confusion. While the disease as yet has no cure, much can be done to improve the quality of life of people with dementia. Sensitive and responsive

---

[1]The discussion of this case study is based on material developed in a series of projects and publications concerning environments for people with dementia. For a comprehensive discussion of the subject, see Cohen, U., and G. Weisman. 1991. *Holding on to home: Designing environments for people with dementia.* Baltimore: The Johns Hopkins University Press.

environmental design can maximize functional independence, efficacy, control, and dignity.

Therapeutic Goals

Review of the literature on dementia and design (Rand, Steiner, Toyne, Cohen, and Weisman, 1987) reveals a variety of therapeutic goals intended to provide direction in the creation of appropriate and supportive environments. While one clearly cannot make specific planning or design decisions on the basis of these global statements, such goals serve to highlight desired relationships between people with dementia and the environments they occupy, and to provide direction for policy, programming, and design decisions. The set of goals in Figure 18-3 has been distilled from the authors' review of the literature, and has proved useful in both the analysis and the design of environments for people with dementia.

These goals are, of course, an abstraction. In some instances, goals may overlap or even conflict with one another. Nevertheless, an understanding of such goals can sensitize the reader to some of the higher-level imperatives to which all environments for people with dementia should respond. Furthermore, it is often through efforts to accommodate therapeutic goals that are inherently and necessarily in conflict that the richest and most creative strategies for problem solving emerge (Alexander, 1969).

Principles for Planning and Design

The design of environments for people with dementia must take into account their special and specific needs, the goals of their care givers (family members and staff care providers), and the organizational needs. However, given the potential impact that the environment may have as a therapeutic tool for this population, designers should view this mandate as an opportunity, rather than as a restriction. Following is an open-ended set of principles for the planning and design of environments for people with dementia, based on the therapeutic goals introduced earlier and upon the nature of the disease and its effect on physical, psychological, emotional, and social functioning.

An extensive literature review, survey of numerous case studies, and exhaustive consultation with both family care givers and experts (in gerontology and Alzheimer's disease, health care provision, and design for the aged) led to the development of the principles for design. However, because of the frequent absence of substantial and conclusive research findings in this area, many design principles should be viewed as working hypotheses, rather than as indisputable directives; designers are encouraged to engage in "inquiry by design," testing the validity of these recommendations and building on them with creative solutions and complementary principles. These design principles are intended to be suggestive, rather than prescriptive, as appropriate solutions will vary with the nature of the users to be served and the characteristics of the specific environment under consideration.

General Planning Principles

This first set of principles addresses broad, initial decisions that must be made when developing environments for people with dementia. Such decisions include the type of services to be provided, the population that will be served by this environment, the location of the facility, and the physical and social organization of the setting. Because of the nature of these decisions, these principles may be most relevant for policymakers, health care planners and administrators, and facility managers, although designers and health care providers can and should question these basic decisions and suggest alternatives where they seem appropriate.

The following are examples for general planning principles:

- tapping local resources
- smaller groups of residents

General Attributes of the Environment

One's experience of and behavior in a particular environment are often more strongly influenced by general qualities or attributes of the setting than by specific architectural features. In the planning and design of various environments for people with dementia, four such attributes appear to be particularly salient: image, negotiability, familiarity, and stimulation. These attributes are a function not only of the physical environment, but also of the interactions of physical, organizational, and social subsystems. Thus, creation of a "home-like" environment requires appropriate furnishings and finishes, patterns of ongoing behavior typical of those found in residential settings, and policies and programs supportive of such residential activities.

Design principles addressing general attributes of the environment include the following (Figure 18-4):

- noninstitutional character
- eliminating environmental barriers
- things from the past
- sensory stimulation without stress

Building Organization

In contrast with preceding guidelines, this group of recommendations and strategies is essentially "physical" in character, focusing on architectural variables rather than characteristics of the policy and program. Specifically, the common theme of these guidelines is the arrangement of spaces relative to one another to support the wandering behavior of people with dementia, define appropriate and varied levels of privacy, and ensure visual and physical access to the exterior.

Design principles in this category include the following:

- opportunities for meaningful wandering
- public to private realms
- positive outdoor spaces
- other living things

Activity Area Guidelines

This final set of guidelines focuses on several distinct types of spaces within the environment, including entrances, public spaces, kitchens, dining rooms, activity alcoves, residents' rooms, bathing and toileting areas, places for visiting, and spaces for staff retreat.

The titles for design principles in this category include the following:

- entry and transition
- common areas for each family
- domestic kitchens
- intimate dining areas
- activity alcoves
- residents' rooms
- dignified bathing and toileting
- places for visiting
- staff retreat

Integration: Illustrative Designs

The illustrative design of a group home for eight persons (Figure 18-5) demonstrates the integration and potential application of the programming information. The annotations identify selected design features that are driven by design principles responsive to issues of persons with dementia.

The group home for eight persons is one of seven illustrative designs for a variety of environments, from adult day-care and respite centers to long-term-care facilities, developed to demonstrate the application of the two dozen design principles presented in this chapter.

CONCLUSIONS: FROM PROGRAMMING TO DESIGN APPLICATIONS

The ultimate goal of a productive programming process is to have a tangible, and hopefully positive, impact on the designed environment.

Our advocacy of structured, clearly communicated, and highly illustrated design guidance extends into the area of design applications.

The use of annotations that relate programming information to design decisions (Figure 18-6) makes for a more compelling and effective presentation of design solutions. This technique is also the designer's "pre-occupancy evaluation" of his or her own work—demonstrating the accountability of the designed environment to important design principles.

References

Alexander, C. 1977. *The pattern language.* New York: Oxford University Press.

Churchman, A., and Y. Ginsberg. 1984. The use of behavioral science research in physical planning: Some inherent limitations. *Journal of architectural and planning research* 1, pp. 57-66.

Cohen, U., J. Beer, L. Kidera, and W. Golden. 1979. *Mainstreaming the handicapped: A design guide*. Milwaukee: University of Wisconsin-Milwaukee, Center for Architecture and Urban Planning Research.

Cohen, U., A.B. Hill, C.G. Lane, T. McGinty, and G.T. Moore. 1979. *Recommendations for child play areas*. Milwaukee: University of Wisconsin-Milwaukee, Center for Architecture and Urban Planning Research with Community Design Center.

Cohen, U., and J. Hunter. 1980. *Teaching design for mainstreaming the handicapped*. Milwaukee: University of Wisconsin-Milwaukee, Center for Architecture and Urban Planning Research.

Cohen, U., and R.M. McMurtry. 1985. *Museums and children: A design guide*. Milwaukee: University of Wisconsin-Milwaukee, Center for Architecture and Urban Planning Research.

Cohen, U., and G.T. Moore. 1977. The organization and communication of behaviorally-based research information. In *Behavior-environment research methods: Proceedings of the Wisconsin conference on research methods in behavior-environment studies*, ed. L. Van Ryzin, 77-93. Madison: University of Wisconsin-Madison, Institute for Environmental Studies.

Cohen, U., G.T. Moore, and T. McGinty. 1978. *Case studies of child play areas and child support facilities*. Milwaukee: Community Design Center Inc. with University of Wisconsin-Milwaukee, Center for Architecture and Urban Planning Research.

Cohen, U., and G. Weisman. 1991. *Holding on to home: Designing environments for people with dementia*. Baltimore: The Johns Hopkins University Press.

Cooper, M.C. 1985. Design guidelines: A bridge between research and decision making. Paper presented at the U.S.-Japan Seminar on Environmental-Behavior Research, October 1985, at Department of Psychology, University of Arizona, Tucson.

Francescato, G., S. Weideman, J. Anderson, and R. Chenoweth. 1976. Impossible dreams, unrealizable hopes? In *The behavioral basis of design*, ed. P. Suedfeld and J.A. Russell, Book 1. Stroudsburg, Pa.: Dowden, Hutchinson & Ross.

Korobkin, B. 1976. *Images for design: Communicating social research to architects*. Cambridge, Mass.: Harvard University, Architecture Research Office.

Merrill, J. 1976. Factors influencing the use of behavioral research in design. Ph.D. dissertation, University of Michigan.

Moore, G.T., U. Cohen, J. Oertel, and L. Van Ryzin. 1979. *Designing environments for handicapped children*. New York: Educational Facilities Laboratories.

Rand, J., R. Toyne, V. Steiner, U. Cohen, and G. Weisman. 1987. *Environments for people with dementia: Annotated bibliography*. Washington, D.C.: Association of Collegiate Schools of Architecture.

Reizenstein, J. 1980. The importance of presentation format. *Environment and behavior* 4:12, pp. 551-58.

Reizenstein, J., and C. Zimring. 1980. Evaluating occupied environments. *Environment and behavior* 12. (A Special Issue.)

Sanoff, H. 1977. *Methods of architectural programming*. Stroudsburg, Pa.: Dowden, Hutchinson & Ross.

Schneekloth, L.H. 1987. Advances in practice in environment, behavior, and design. In *Advances in environment, behavior and design, vol. 1*, ed. E.H. Zube and G.T. Moore, 307-34. New York: Plenum.

Seidel, A. 1982. Usable E.B.R.: What can we learn from other fields? In *Knowledge for design*, ed. P. Bart. Washington, D.C.: Environmental Design Research Association.

Shibley, R.G., L.H. Schneekloth, L. Poltroneri, and E.M. Bruce. 1986. What is a design guide? Unpublished monograph. Buffalo: The State University of New York and the Caucus Partnership.

Weisman, G. 1983. Environmental programming and action research. *Environment and behavior* 15:3, pp. 381-408.

Windley, P., and G. Weisman, 1977. Social science and environmental design: the translation process. *Journal of architectural education* 31:1, pp. 16-19.

Zeisel, J. 1981. *Inquiry by design: Tools for environment-behavior research.* Monterey, CA: Brooks/Cole Publishing Co.

Informed Programming and Design
A Schematic Diagram of the Development Process

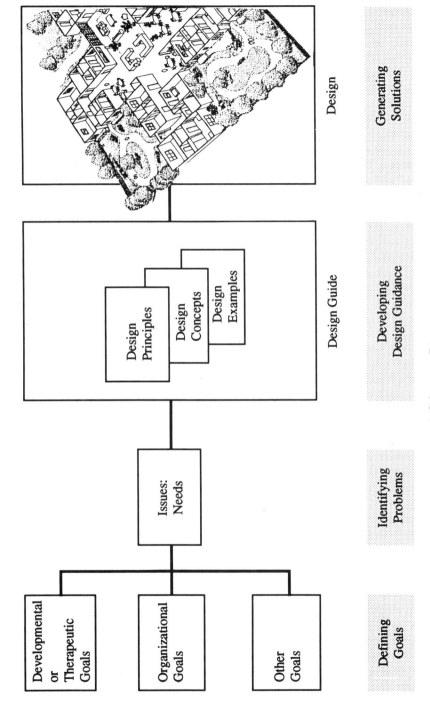

FIGURE 18-1.   Informed Programming Process—A Schematic Diagram

TITLE:
An evocative name that is memorable. It is stated in general terms, usually specifying some quality the environment should have.

DEFINITION:
An expanded description of the title.

ISSUES:
A statement of the problem(s) to be solved and the context for the principle.

QUALITIES & CHARACTERISTICS:
A succinct statement of the the basic qualities and chacteristics the environment should have in order to solve the identified problem(s). The terms used are evocative and open-ended, but directional.

APPROACHES FOR DESIGN:
Basic approaches and design strategies to solve the identified problem. The approaches are generic and several in number.

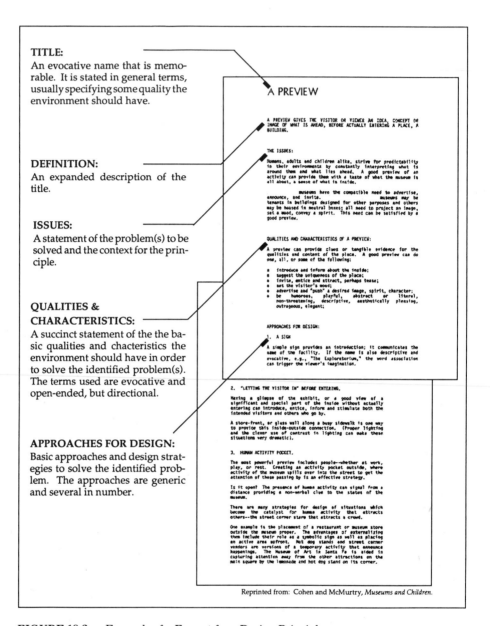

A PREVIEW

A PREVIEW GIVES THE VISITOR OR VIEWER AN IDEA, CONCEPT OR IMAGE OF WHAT IS AHEAD, BEFORE ACTUALLY ENTERING A PLACE, A BUILDING.

THE ISSUES:

Humans, adults and children alike, strive for predictability in their environments by constantly interpreting what is around them and what lies ahead. A good preview of an activity can provide them with a taste of what the museum is all about, a sense of what is inside.

museums have the compatible need to advertise, announce, and invite. museums may be tenants in buildings designed for other purposes and others may be housed in neutral boxes; all need to project an image, set a mood, convey a spirit. This need can be satisfied by a good preview.

QUALITIES AND CHARACTERISTICS OF A PREVIEW:

A preview can provide clues or tangible evidence for the qualities and content of the place. A good preview can do one, all, or some of the following:

● introduce and inform about the inside;
● suggest the uniqueness of the place;
● invite, entice and attract, perhaps tease;
● set the visitor's mood;
● advertise and "push" a desired image, spirit, character;
● be humorous, playful, abstract or literal, non-threatening, descriptive, aesthetically pleasing, outrageous, elegant;

APPROACHES FOR DESIGN:

1. A SIGN

A simple sign provides an introduction; it communicates the name of the facility. If the name is also descriptive and evocative, e.g., "The Exploratorium," the word association can trigger the viewer's imagination.

2. "LETTING THE VISITOR IN" BEFORE ENTERING.

Having a glimpse of the exhibit, or a good view of a significant and special part of the inside without actually entering can introduce, entice, inform and stimulate both the intended visitors and others who go by.

A store-front, or glass wall along a busy sidewalk is one way to provide this inside-outside connection. (Proper lighting and the clever use of contrast in lighting can make these situations very dramatic).

3. HUMAN ACTIVITY POCKET.

The most powerful preview includes people--whether at work, play, or rest. Creating an activity pocket outside, where activity of the museum spills over into the street to get the attention of those passing by is an effective strategy.

Is it open? The presence of human activity can signal from a distance providing a non-verbal clue to the states of the museum.

There are many strategies for design of situations which become the catalyst for human activity that attracts others--the street corner store that attracts a crowd.

One example is the placement of a restaurant or museum store outside the museum proper. The advantages of externalizing them include their role as a symbolic sign as well as placing an active area upfront. Hot dog stands and street corner vendors are versions of a temporary activity that announce happenings. The Museum of Art in Santa Fe is aided in capturing attention away from the other attractions on the main square by the lemonade and hot dog stand on its corner.

Reprinted from: Cohen and McMurtry, *Museums and Children.*

FIGURE 18-2.   Example of a Format for a Design Principle

(adopted from Cohen and McMurtry, 1985)

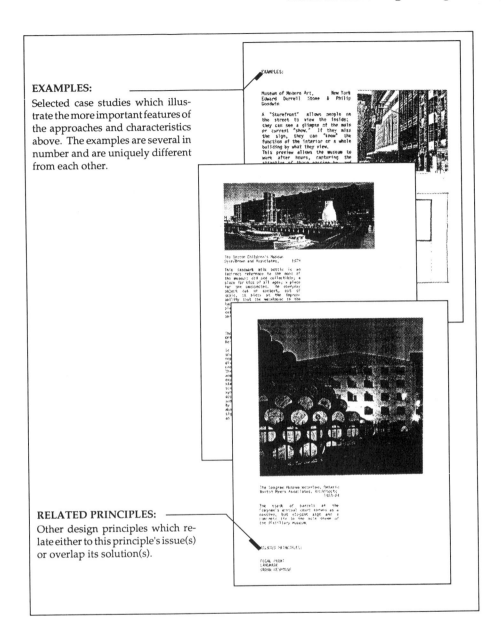

EXAMPLES:

Selected case studies which illustrate the more important features of the approaches and characteristics above. The examples are several in number and are uniquely different from each other.

RELATED PRINCIPLES:

Other design principles which relate either to this principle's issue(s) or overlap its solution(s).

- Ensure safety and security
- Support functional ability through meaningful activity
- Heighten awareness and orientation
- Provide appropriate environmental stimulation and challenge
- Develop a postitive social milieu
- Maximize autonomy and control
- Adapt to changing needs
- Establish links to the health and familar
- Protect the need for privacy

FIGURE 18-3.   Therapeutic Goals to Guide the Development of Environments Responsive to People with Dementia

(from Cohen and Weisman, 1991)

Eliminating environmental barriers.

Physical and cognitive impairments associated with dementia often make movement through and use of the environment difficult. It is critically important to eliminate these barriers to negotiability in environments for people with dementia. In addition to traditional solutions such as ramps or handrails, environmental interventions may include clear and consistent information and easy-to-operate handles and controls.

Things from the past.

Familiar artifacts, activities, and environments can provide valuable associations with the past for people with dementia, and can stimulate opportunities for social interaction and meaningful activity. The total environment may potentially be used to trigger reminiscence.

Opportunities for meaningful wandering.

Wandering is a relatively common behavior among people with dementia. Too often in the past it has been viewed as a problem and has resulted in the use of chemical or physical restraints. A far more positive approach is to view wandering as an opportunity for meaningful activity. Both physical and organizational environments should be supportive of such activity, providing appropriate settings with secure and well-defined paths.

Sensory stimulation without stress.

Levels of sensory and social stimulation in environment for people with dementia should not differ dramatically from those encountered in domestic environments. Both sensory deprivation and over-stimulation are conditions to be avoided. The physical and the organizational environment can both be designed to regulate stimulation, providing interest and challenge without becoming overwhelming. Opportunities should be provided for increasing or reducing levels of stimulation to respond to changing needs and tolerance over the course of a day.

FIGURE 18-4.   A Brief Overview of Selected Design Principles Concerning Environments for People with Dementia

(after Cohen and Weisman, 1991)

Group Home for Eight Residents

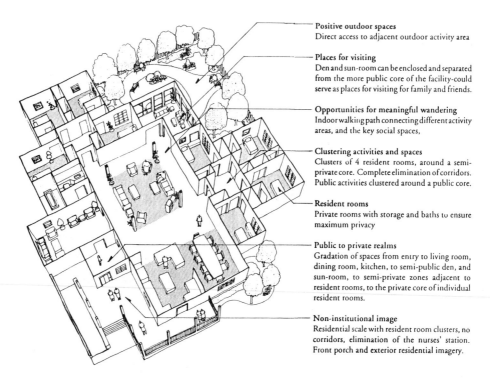

Positive outdoor spaces
Direct access to adjacent outdoor activity area

Places for visiting
Den and sun-room can be enclosed and separated from the more public core of the facility-could serve as places for visiting for family and friends.

Opportunities for meaningful wandering
Indoor walking path connecting different activity areas, and the key social spaces,

Clustering activities and spaces
Clusters of 4 resident rooms, around a semi-private core. Complete elimination of corridors. Public activities clustered around a public core.

Resident rooms
Private rooms with storage and baths to ensure maximum privacy

Public to private realms
Gradation of spaces from entry to living room, dining room, kitchen, to semi-public den, and sun-room, to semi-private zones adjacent to resident rooms, to the private core of individual resident rooms.

Non-institutional image
Residential scale with resident room clusters, no corridors, elimination of the nurses' station. Front porch and exterior residential imagery.

FIGURE 18-5.   Illustrative Design of a Group Home for Eight Residents

(adopted from Cohen and Weisman, 1991)

Plan

Key
1   *Main entry*
2   *Education center*
3   *Entry foyer/lounge*
4   *Activity area*
5   *Religious corner*
6   *Great room*
7   *Sheltered balcony*
8   *Wandering paths*
9   *Living areas*
10 *Dining rooms*
11 *Serving kitchens*

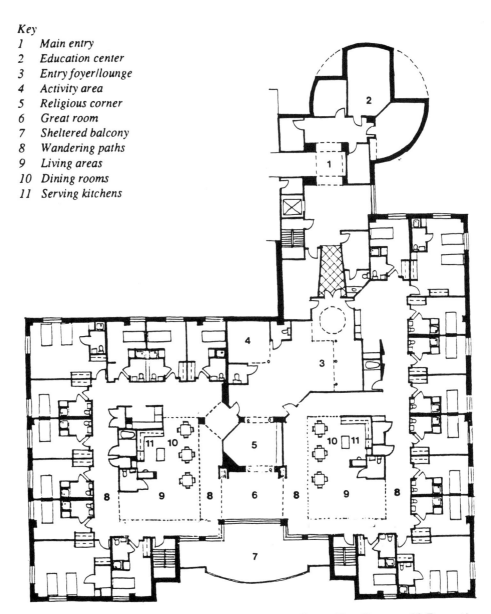

FIGURE 18-6.   A Community-Based Group Home for Twenty-Four Persons with Dementia: Selected Design Principles Are Shown as Influencing Key Design Decisions

(a proposed plan for the Helen Bader Center at the Jewish Home for the Aged, Milwaukee; Miller Meier Kenyon, architects; Cohen and Weisman, programming and design consultants)

See page 470 for explanation of Figure 18-6.

Design for changing needs

+ The great room (6) has sliding walls that allow a variety of space uses: the two households can be joined or separated, or one of them can be enlarged to accommodate different activities and needs at different times.

Things from the past

+ A special activity space (5) has a religious corner with objects and decor with long-time meaning to most current residents. This space can serve as a catalyst for reminiscence as well as a functional space for small group religious practice.

Variety of activity spaces

+ In addition to activity spaces in the residential cluster, simultaneous activities can take place in other shared spaces: (3) the entry foyer; (4) activity—e.g. arts—space; (6) great room; (7) and the sheltered balcony.

Smaller groups of residents

+ The units is divided into two small clusters of 12 residents, each with their own living, dining, and activity spaces.

Tapping local resources

+ The decision to locate this group home on a crowded urban campus was largely influenced by the desire to relate to local resources, places, and people. The adjacent buildings offer a variety of activity spaces and events, for example, a synagogue and a kosher delicatessen restaurant.

Noninstitutional image

The unit is attached to a complex of large mid-rise buildings.

+ A major effort was made to keep the scale of the unit small, to give it a clear and separate identity when viewed from the street, and to decrease the institutional image of the unit.

Entry and transition

− Because of its location on the second floor, and the connection of the entry to an existing building with its own underground parking, the whole entry and transition experience is indirect, lengthy, and potentially disorienting to visitors and residents alike.

FIGURE 18-6.   Continued

CHAPTER 19

Programming for Safety

Roger L. Brauer

INTRODUCTION

Programming

There are several definitions for an architectural program. Peña[1] called a program "a statement of an architectural problem." Sanoff[2] calls a program "a communicable statement of intent," and "a prescription for a desired set of events influenced by local constraints, stating a set of desired conditions and the methods for achieving those conditions." A program may vary in detail, but the basic function is to define what is needed in a facility project. A comprehensive program will lead to a good facility solution.

Programming is the family of procedures and methods for gathering, analyzing, and recording information that forms a program. Designers combine these data, together with a variety of standards, codes, formalized criteria, and principles of design practice, into a facility solution.

A program typically contains both functional and technical requirements. Functional requirements describe building or facility characteristics that will allow occupants or users to perform their activities efficiently and safely. Technical requirements define attributes of a building or facility and its

---

[1]William M. Peña. 1969. *Problem seeking*. Houston: Caudill Rowlett Scott.

[2]Sanoff, Henry. 1977. *Methods of architectural programming*. Stroudsburg, Pa.: Dowden, Hutchinson & Ross.

systems that are essential for meeting a variety of constraints. Examples of such constraints are energy conservation; structural integrity; meeting the demands of weather, earthquakes, and other environmental conditions; aesthetics; maintainability; and economy. To derive the functional and technical requirements, leaders of the programming process formulate requirements data that provide the background or justification for the requirements.

Typical contents of a program are the types and amounts of space, attributes of individual spaces or types of space, attributes of the facility or building, characteristics of the site, types and capacities of building systems, and supporting utilities. An essential part in each element of a program is safety data and safety requirements for various aspects of a project.

Programming for Safety

The purpose of this chapter is to discuss where safety fits into programming. This chapter will give only a brief overview of many safety topics that could be discussed in much greater detail. The discussion here will focus on some basic safety concepts, some approaches for applying safety in programming procedures, and a few examples of safety problems in facilities.

Safety is an essential part of the design process. In fact, the public depends on designers to provide reasonable protection from hazards. There is only one reason why states license designers: "to protect the safety, health, and welfare of the public." In the course of history, designers have failed the public too often, pushing the demand for safety even higher.

In facility projects, programming plays an important role in achieving safety. Safety cannot be left to design; it must begin in project planning. Some aspects of safety may require specialists, but safety must be integrated into the total programming effort. From a safety point of view, programmers are the representatives of the people who will occupy and use a facility. From a liability point of view, programmers represent facility owners and can help minimize potential claims or losses.

Why Safety Is Important

Safety makes good professional sense. Beside the general duty designers have to protect the public, facilities must comply with a wide variety of laws, regulations, standards, and codes promulgated to achieve safety. The programming process should help identify the local, state, and national criteria that apply. Programming should also uncover the professional standards of practice from within the architectural profession and from other disciplines that apply to a facility project.

Safety also makes economic sense. The cost of anticipating, identifying, and ultimately controlling hazards in a project can be recovered through reduced insurance premiums for owners and occupying organizations and fewer opportunities for litigation. In addition, safety is an essential element of productivity for users and occupants. The programming process may have to perform analysis to identify the costs of including certain safety features and the benefits from reduced insurance or legal claims, reduced insurance premiums, and enhanced productivity, quality, and profitability of future occupants. Insurance related to a facility can involve general or special liability, fire, casualty, and workers' compensation insurance. Reduced risk and claims can lead to reduced premiums for owners and occupants. Safety features of a facility or building can enhance productivity and improve quality of products and services, which, in turn, increases profitability of organizations. Analysis during programming may be necessary to demonstrate the return on investment of particular features.

SAFETY CONCEPTS FOR FACILITIES

Many designers have little training in facility safety. Some have gained experience with safety or have worked with safety professionals and the methods they use to identify, evaluate, and control hazards. For those without the training or experience, some general comments on safety are in order. There are many other important considerations for safety in a facility project beside the few reviewed here.

Safety Professions

One can seek help on safety matters from people trained as safety professionals. Often safety professionals are part of facility planning and design teams. Besides safety professionals (who are generalists in safety), there are related specialists, such as industrial hygienists, health physicists, fire protection engineers, sanitation specialists, system safety specialists, and others. Because states have not licensed safety professionals, national peer certification is used commonly to establish competency. Primary certifications include Certified Safety Professional (CSP),[3] Certified Industrial Hygienist (CIH),[4] or Certified Health Physicist (CHP).[5] Many states have a fire protection engineering specialty within engineer registration programs. Two states (Massachusetts and California) have safety engineering specialties. Programmers may look to safety professionals and related specialists for help with safety during facility programming. Major employers will have safety professionals on their staff and may offer their assistance during facility programming activities.

---

[3]Board of Certified Safety Professionals, 208 Burwash Avenue, Savoy, IL 61880 (217) 359-9263

[4]American Board of Industrial Hygiene, Suite 101, 4600 West Saginaw, Lansing, MI 48917 (517) 321-2638

[5]American Board of Health Physics, Suite 400, 8000 Westpark Drive, McLean, VA 22102-3101 (703) 790-1745

Prevention

The primary safety role for design professions is prevention of accidents, injuries, illnesses, and other losses through design. Organizations that use facilities also apply administrative and management techniques to their operations to be sure that workers, guests, or customers are safe.

The main goal is *removal* of hazards. If there are no hazards, it makes little difference what occupants do—the potential for harm has been removed. However, not all hazards can be removed or eliminated. When that is the case, planners and designers should look for ways to *reduce* hazards. This can be accomplished by reducing the potential for an accident event or by reducing the severity if such events occur. The type of hazard dictates what control options are available. When hazards remain, additional approaches include providing warnings and instructions and deferring control to users and their operating procedures. The most effective approaches are correcting hazards through design.

During programming, the primary task is to recognize and even anticipate hazards related to a facility. Additionally, the programming process may include evaluating hazards and recommending appropriate controls. During design, the key goal is eliminating hazards through design or reducing them to acceptable levels through appropriate controls.

Complexity and Cost

The more complex a facility or building and the activities or operations that it houses, the more users depend on analysis by professionals to identify hazards and apply appropriate protection. Users may not have the knowledge, skill, or capability to perform analyses and uncover the interrelationships among various facility elements and systems and the user activities and materials in a facility. Deferring correction of hazards until occupancy is usually much more expensive than controlling hazards early in the facility planning and design process.

Risk

Risk is an important concept in hazard recognition and control. Risk has various meanings. When dealing with hazards and trying to achieve safety, risk infers two parts. The first is the likelihood or frequency of an accident or incident occurring; the second, the severity of consequences if an undesired incident occurs. A subsequent part of risk analysis is evaluating control options for effectiveness and cost. Qualitative and quantitative risk analysis can be valuable tools in making decisions about control for hazards.

High frequency may be defined as having an incident every day, week, or month; after a certain number of hours of operation; or for some number of guests or customers. High severity is having a major loss to a facility, shutting down operations that a facility houses, the loss of one or more lives, or incurring permanent disability.

Haddon's Theory

In the safety field there are several theories about accident causation and control. A brief discussion of one theory will provide some additional ideas for hazard recognition and control.

Haddon[6] focused on the marshaling and release of energy. One must first consider the form of energy. There is potential energy (such as people or objects being at an elevated height). There is also stored energy (such as in springs or steam lines), mechanical energy (such as equipment in motion), internal energy (such as the energy of various fuels and combustible materials), and other forms of energy. The goal for achieving safety is recognizing the energy in situations and applying appropriate protective controls. These are some controls Haddon recommended:

1. Prevent marshaling of energy.
2. Reduce the amount of energy marshaled.
3. Prevent the release of energy.
4. Control the rate of energy release.
5. Separate energy from people and structures through distance, time, or intervening barriers.
6. Distribute forces and energy to reduce the potential damage.
7. Strengthen structures to reduce the effect of energy marshaled or released.

Haddon's concepts are useful during facility programming and design to recognize certain hazards and identify suitable controls.

Defects

Programmers need to understand the theories of liability and their legal implications for design. A brief review of one part of products liability law — kinds of defects — will help illustrate this concept. The type of defect becomes important when a defect is a proximal cause of injury and the case goes to litigation. A building may incorporate several products that fall under these concepts. In an injury lawsuit a design may be tested under similar legal theories.

In dealing with products, there are three kinds of defects: design defects, manufacturing defects, and failure to warn. A design defect is one that results from failure to specify something in a design or from an incorrect specification. All products produced from the design thus have the same deficiency. A manufacturing defect is one that is introduced during assembly; an example is

[6]Haddon, Jr., W. May 1970. On the escape of tigers: An ecological note. *Technology review:* Vol. 73, No. 3.

a faulty bolt or part of a machine or structure. A failure-to-warn exists when a hazard remains in a product and the manufacturer fails to identify the hazard for a user and fails to instruct the user in proper protection from the hazard.

SAFETY IN FACILITIES

Role of Programming

Safety in programming involves at least three functions. The first is anticipating and recognizing hazards. The second is uncovering the standard of protection that is needed. The third is performing preliminary analysis to determine risk and possibly the cost and effectiveness of corrections.

While compiling data on the activities and operations that a facility will support or house, programmers should investigate what safety requirements exist for them. Most important are identifying hazards that the facility design should eliminate or control. Some requirements can be incorporated in general requirements for the facility as a whole. Other safety requirements are related to particular interior or exterior spaces, building systems, or utilities. Programmers need to think in terms of hazards and the degree or type of protection that is necessary to eliminate or minimize the hazards.

The standard of protection may be based on laws, regulations, consensus standards, or codes. An important safety role for programming is identifying what safety rules apply to a facility project. A company may have an internal safety manual that has rules more stringent than prevailing laws, regulations, and codes. Programmers may have to understand the hazards in detail and identify levels of protection that are expected from legal cases or changing public expectations that have not yet found their way into formalized rules. A program may include information about warnings that should be incorporated in a design and their contents, placement, and style. Often warning sign requirements are specified in published standards. A program may include what tests will be used to determine effectiveness and acceptance of safety in systems or a design.

In large, complex facilities, there may be a need to perform detailed analyses that will allow hazards to be quantified or ranked. Risk analysis, fault tree analysis, failure mode and effects analysis, software analysis, energy analysis, and other methods may be needed to determine the frequency and severity of incidents. Cost analysis may be needed to determine cost of controls and benefits of their implementation.

Communicating safety requirements for a facility is a key role for a program. Safety requirements require the same detail that other functional and technical requirements do: Just stating that ventilation or radiation shielding is needed may not be adequate. Providing detailed information about the hazard and the controls required for protecting occupants or the facility will help designers achieve an effective safety solution.

Role of Design

Designers are responsible for final selection of controls for hazards and incorporation of protection in design. They often depend on the safety information in a program to know what hazards must be controlled and what standards of protection the owner or occupants expect. Designers will also have a role in the quality of assembly and correctly implementing safety features.

Well-developed safety requirements can be a valuable tool in design review. Designers become more accountable for their solutions when safety requirements are precise. Owners are confident that proper protection is incorporated in a design if their safety requirements are detailed and used to evaluate design alternatives.

Carry-Over to Occupancy and Use

Designers may not eliminate all hazards in a design or reduce hazards to acceptable levels of safety. As noted earlier, when this occurs, occupants may have to incorporate protective measures in equipment brought into a facility or in operating procedures. Well-developed safety requirements in a facility program provide information about hazards. When a design cannot meet a desired level of safety, designers may need to communicate to owners and occupants what protection is left for them to manage and implement.

A possible extension of safety requirements in a program is a user manual for a facility. The user manual can incorporate information about the hazards, what protection is built into the facility, limitations of the protective features or systems, and what responsibility the owners and occupant organizations have to ensure safety during use. Users need to maintain design features and systems so that protection continues beyond initial occupancy.

APPROACHES

There are several approaches that can help programmers identify hazards and define needed controls. Some methods and procedures are tools of safety professionals; others are derived from architectural principles and other sources. A few approaches are summarized in Table 19-1.

Scale

One good approach for identifying hazards during a programming process is to analyze hazards according to scale in a facility: site, building(s), space types, rooms, work stations. For example, at the site level it is important to look for conflicts in pedestrian and vehicular traffic. Vehicular traffic may be divided into general traffic, delivery traffic, and emergency traffic. At the site level one

TABLE 19-1   Incomplete List of Safety Considerations in Facility Planning.

SITE

DRAINAGE
Prevention of spills, leaks, or activities that may contaminate storm water or to control runoff.
Flood control and protection.

UTILITIES
Prevention of damage to utilities (power lines, pipelines).
Remote shutoff of utilities.
Barricades to protect people from utilities.
Water supply for operations, for fire protection.
Storage of fuels on site.

TRAFFIC
Traffic load on or adjacent to site (pedestrian, vehicular, railroad, public, employees, delivery, etc.).
Need to separate kinds of traffic.
Types and quantities of materials entering or stored on site.
Access for emergency vehicles and equipment.

HOSTILE CONDITIONS
Wind loads and conditions.
Snow loads.
Earthquake zones.
Lightning protection.
Protection from sun, water, weather, or other hazards.

SITE STORAGE
Storage of fuels, water, hazardous materials on site (type and quantity).
Separation requirements.

ADJACENT PROPERTIES AND COMMUNITY
Barricades and fences to keep unauthorized people from dangerous areas or materials.
Protection from hazards of adjacent or nearby properties or transportation routes.
Dangers to adjacent properties from site or operations.
Emergency response plan.
Community right-to-know requirements.
Emissions and controls.

FIRE AND EMERGENCY
Access for emergency vehicles and equipment.
Fire load.
Fire response management.
Fire suppression and extinguishment.

BUILDING

WALKWAYS, STAIRS, AND ACCESS

Adequate lighting at entries, transition points, stairs, landings, etc.

Guard rails for elevated surfaces.

Hand rails for stairs and certain types of pedestrians.

Hand rail dimensions for firm grip.

Floor finishes to minimize slipperiness, prevent corrosion, etc.

Drainage or raised flooring for wet or oily areas or where foreign material is slippery.

Spill isolation to prevent distribution of contaminants.

Minimize changes in surfaces (elevations, irregularities, slipperiness).

Aisle and area markings for pedestrian areas, vehicles, materials handling, or hazardous operations.

Door sizes for vehicles and materials.

HAZARD ZONES

Enclosure, isolation, separation, or other controls for hazardous sources (noise, gaseous or particulate contaminants, etc.).

Exhaust ventilation, hoods, or cabinets for hazardous contaminants.

Barricades for hazardous operations.

Sensors and monitoring equipment for hazardous materials.

Warning signs that meet various standards and markings to identify hazardous areas.

FIRE PROTECTION

Fire loads.

Smoke and heat detectors.

Alarm systems and evacuation management systems.

Sprinklers and other fire suppression equipment.

Fire ratings for materials, finishes, and partitions (walls, ceilings, floors, doors).

Exit signage.

Roof vents and curtain boards.

Explosion venting.

Fire control equipment and systems for flammable operations.

SANITATION AND FIRST AID

Sufficient washrooms.

Clean areas for food and eating, including isolation from contaminated sources.

Lockers, change rooms, and showers for control of contaminants.

Emergency showers.

Emergency eye wash fountains.

GENERAL

Enclosure of dangerous equipment and building systems.

Maintainability to minimize repair, cleaning, and servicing hazards.

Storage areas for hazardous materials.

Proper separation of noncompatible materials.

System, equipment, and operations shutoffs in nonhazardous areas.

may have to define distances between buildings to separate hazardous materials from general occupancy or to separate hazardous materials from public facilities, adjacent properties, or transportation routes. Safety requirements for fuel storage and remote utility shut-offs may be critical.

Today there is a great deal of concern for hazards a facility may bring to adjacent properties and communities. A program may identify requirements based on community right-to-know, fire protection, security, and transportation regulations.

Within a building one may want to separate hazards of one area from others. For example, one may want to isolate certain activities and operations that produce noise, potentially release hazardous materials, or create other environmental or fire dangers. A safety principle is controlling environmental (indoor or outdoor) hazards at their source and minimizing potential distribution of hazardous conditions or materials.

Certain operations or work stations may require special ventilation systems, uninterrupted power supply, or backup systems in the case of failure. Mechanical rooms, rooms or areas with dangerous equipment, and some operating areas may require special locks and access control to keep unauthorized or unqualified people from getting into dangerous situations. Storage areas may require special barriers to separate fuels from oxidizers.

Occupancy and Occupants

Another approach for identifying hazards is to consider the kinds and numbers of occupants present or the kind of occupancy of a facility. Fire protection standards and many building codes use type of occupancy as a classification scheme for particular requirements. A building or facility may have several kinds of occupancy, and a program may identify requirements for different occupancies. Closely associated is type of occupant. Occupants may be young, old, able-bodied, disabled, trained employees, untrained employees, or the public. There may be different safety requirements for particular areas of a facility accessible to different kinds of occupants. A program should discuss the kinds of occupants expected. A program should also define safety requirements associated with each occupancy type.

Facility Type

As with type of occupancy, a programmer may need to analyze the hazards and safety requirements identified for each facility in a project. This approach is most important when there are several types of facilities involved. The safety requirements for an office building, storage building, parking area, manufacturing facility, sales area for the public, or other facility type may be quite different.

Activity

Another approach involves analysis of user activities. In analyzing activities that can occur in a facility, programmers need to identify what hazards exist in these activities and record safety requirements for each. One method found in safety literature is called job safety analysis (JSA). The procedure involves breaking down activities into steps or tasks, identifying hazards for each step, and defining what is needed to eliminate or reduce the hazards. A number of the corrections may be facility requirements that need to be listed in a program or incorporated in a facility user manual.

Analysis Methods

Closely related to analysis of activities are methods for analyzing processes, operations, and systems. These methods help identify what hazards exist at or in a facility or building. Safety specialists have developed a number of rigorous methods to identify and evaluate hazards. Some are relatively simple, while others are quite complex; some are qualitative, others quantitative. The methods are most successful when the analysts work together with those who know processes, equipment, or facilities as well as those who know associated hazards and their controls. Some of these methods are used regularly to evaluate hazards in the design of complex equipment and systems.

A number of these methods were developed in a safety specialty called system safety. A couple of the more commonly known methods are fault tree analysis (used in a famous study of nuclear power plant designs) and failure mode and effects analysis (FMEA). Two more recent requirements for applying such techniques to buildings and facilities are briefly discussed in the following paragraphs. Additionally, a facility or building project may have to meet drainage, emission, or other standards set by the Environmental Protection Agency or other government agencies at the federal, state, or local level. A program should identify whether the project has potential hazards or conditions that need to be analyzed further and resolved during design. (References for this chapter contain details about these methods.)

Department of Defense Facility System Safety

For several years the Department of Defense (DOD) has had a requirement that all DOD facility projects must apply system safety techniques during the design.[7] At a minimum, early design must include a preliminary hazard analysis (PHA). Preliminary hazard analysis is used to identify hazards that may exist in a completed facility. The design must adequately address each of

---

[7]U.S. Army Corps of Engineers, Huntsville Division. 1985. *Facility system safety program manual*, HNDP 385-3-1. Huntsville, Ala.

the hazards and ensure that proper controls are incorporated. If there are significant hazards in a facility, additional analysis is required during later stages of a project. The additional analysis may evaluate the hazards further and evaluate the effectiveness of alternate designs.

During programming of a project, it may be appropriate to complete a preliminary hazard analysis and establish the standards and codes that must be met in controlling each hazard identified.

OSHA Process Safety

In the 1990 Clean Air Act, Congress mandated that OSHA develop a process safety standard. The idea for the standard stems from the disaster in Bhopal, India, and other disasters in which releases of hazardous materials from process plants and other facilities injured and killed people when the materials moved outside the boundaries of the plant. OSHA has proposed such a standard.[8] Any facility that contains a process involving highly hazardous materials must apply at least one of several analyses to the process. A highly hazardous material is one that possesses toxic, flammable, reactive, or explosive properties specified by the OSHA standard. The methods identified in the standard include what-if, checklist, what-if/checklist, hazard and operability study (HAZOP), failure mode and effects analysis (FEMA), or fault tree analysis. For any hazard identified by an analysis procedure, there are a number of requirements to meet, including engineering or administrative controls, training, pre-startup safety reviews, mechanical integrity requirements, emergency planning and response, and other requirements.

If process safety analysis is performed during programming or feasibility studies, the results should identify known or potential hazards, corrective actions or facility design requirements, and methods and standards by which a solution will be evaluated for effectiveness.

Building Systems and Components

A program may need to analyze the safety requirements for each supporting utility system and building subsystem. For example, there may be a need to analyze a water supply for fire protection, or waste handling systems for type and quantity of effluent. There may be requirements for solid waste handling and management. There may be requirements at delivery points to prevent any spills from entering storm water drainage lines. There may be analysis for uninterrupted power supply, backup power, emergency power or generators, lightning protection, special grounding systems, or other electrical capabilities for safety and emergency situations. There may be a need for analysis of exhaust ventilation systems, independence between systems, and prevention of reentry of exhausted contaminants. There may be analysis to determine if exhausted materials exceed allowable standards for public exposure and pro-

---

[8]29 CFR 1910.119, *OSHA process safety management of highly hazardous chemicals.*

tection of the environment. There may be a need to conduct fire propagation and exit simulations to determine effective solutions. There may be a need to simulate potential toxic releases and plume movement and dispersion in surrounding communities. There may be a need to analyze processes involving a variety of systems, identify hazards, conduct risk assessments, and specify the type and degree of control for potential failures of the process. There may be a need to evaluate noise sources and specify the degree of isolation, absorption, or enclosure for certain user equipment or building equipment. There may be a need to analyze seismic risk and specify the kind and level of protection needed.

When there are safety requirements for particular building systems and components, it may be important in a program to identify the evaluation or testing procedures that will be used to determine acceptance or compliance with the requirements. Errors in selection or assembly may render emergency systems ineffective. Testing and evaluation are essential to ensure that the systems at least work properly or meet requirements prior to occupancy or use.

Standards and Codes

In some cases a programming exercise will identify the standards, laws, and codes that apply to a project or portions of it. Designers must remember that codes and published standards are *minimums*. Design solutions can often provide a greater degree of protection than is called for in codes and published standards.

Standards of practice and state-of-the-art methods may not be included in published standards and codes. Unless precise requirements are defined, it is not clear what is expected. Published standards are slow to keep up with changing technology and public expectations. Further, published standards and codes do not always explain what hazard they are trying to control. Completing hazard analyses will help identify what dangers need controls and whether standards and codes adequately control the hazards and protect the future users of the building or facility.

Following are some of the standards to consider:

- *Zoning ordinances:* Often contain site density limits and similar safety requirements.
- *Subdivision ordinances:* Contain traffic visibility and site accessibility requirements.
- *Building codes:* Contain fire, electrical, wind and snow load, exiting, and other safety requirements.
- *Plumbing codes:* Contain sanitation and biological safety requirements.
- *Electrical codes:* Contain fire, power surge, lightning, and related requirements; often part of fire codes.
- *Seismic design codes:* Contain standards for earthquake protection.
- *Fire codes:* Contain standards for fire safety and hazardous materials safety in various buildings, facilities, spaces, and operations. The major

source is the National Fire Protection Association and its *National Fire Code.*

- *Work safety standards:* OSHA regulations (29 CFR 1910) and some state and local work regulations for specific activities and operations.
- *Standards for building systems, components, and equipment:* Consensus/voluntary standards organizations—such as the American National Standards Institute, American Society for Testing and Materials, Underwriter's Laboratory, and Factory Mutual—publish numerous standards for components, assemblies, products, and equipment that may be built into or become part of buildings or facilities. In addition, EPA regulations, found in 40 CFR, contain many requirements for facilities, buildings, and sites that must be met.
- *Community right-to-know or community emergency response laws:* Federal and state laws have established rules on transportation and storage of hazardous materials and the need to develop plans to evacuate or otherwise protect the public if there is a release or spill.

EXAMPLES

One can gain insights into safety matters for facilities from looking at a number of historical events. A few examples will be reviewed next: Each helps increase sensitivity for the importance of safety in programming. Whether one is dealing with noise sources, air quality and airborne contaminants, lighting, signage, exiting, walking surfaces, storage areas, or other elements of buildings, each has a safety component for which rules and standards probably exist. The rules and standards are based on experience from accidents, injuries, and even litigation.

Fires

The Great Chicago Fire

When Mrs. O'Leary's cow kicked over the lantern and set off the Great Chicago Fire of 1871, little did Mrs. O'Leary realize that over 13,000 homes and three-and-a-half square miles of property would be destroyed in a fire that lasted three days, leaving 100,000 people homeless. Neither did Mrs. O'Leary realize that, as a result, ordinances would be adopted that set standards for construction of buildings, limit the amount of land that can be occupied by buildings on lots, and establish strict street layouts to provide emergency access to property.

One factor that contributed to the scale of the disaster was poorly laid out streets and limited access to properties. The fire brigades had difficulty getting through streets and gaining access to properties. Another factor was that a large portion of most lots was covered by houses and outbuildings, and fire easily jumped from one to the next through radiant and convective heat transfer. Nearly all structures in the city were of wood frame construction, and neighborhoods were congested.

When one reviews provisions of zoning and subdivision ordinances today, there is little or no information about the reasons for many of the rules. Many rules for sites, streets, and construction stem from the near elimination of Chicago as a growing industrial and transportation center.

MGM Grand

On November 20, 1980, fire and smoke in the spectacular MGM Grand Hotel in Las Vegas, with its 2,100 guest rooms and lavish casino and restaurants, led to the death of eighty-four people. If only sprinklers had been incorporated throughout the $106 million dollar structure, the small electrical fire in the kitchen area would have not led to such loss of life and millions of dollars in losses and litigation. Post-fire investigations also identified the importance of not having holes in fire stops, having fire walls, and having a fire control and management system built into such a complex facility.

Other Famous Building Fires

There are lessons to be learned from many fires. The Triangle Shirtwaist Factory fire occurred on the eighth, ninth, and tenth floors of a building in New York City in 1911. When fire erupted at quitting time, the paths of garment workers were blocked by inadequate exits. One hundred forty-six workers, mainly young women, died in the fire or fell to their death as they leaped from the upper floors. This and other famous fires—such as the 1903 Iroquois Theater fire in Chicago that killed 602 people and the Beverly Hills Supper Club fire in Southgate, Kentucky, that snuffed out 165 lives—contributed to stricter standards for safe exiting, requirements for smoke and fire detectors, better alarms, and other protection.

Slips, Trips, and Falls

Much architectural literature is nearly silent on flooring selection from a safety point of view. Litigation over flooring materials and conditions have led to standards for assessing slipperiness and recommendation in some codes for minimum level of slip resistance. Studies of stairs and observations of people falling on stairs have led to recommendations such as avoiding textures and patterns on stairs materials and avoiding stairs design that provides people with attention-getting views that distract them from the dangerous task of descending stairs.

One role for facility programs is to establish what standards apply to walkways, stairs, and working surfaces. The requirements may be different for various building types or when young, old, public, or other user populations are expected.

Dark Adaptation

It is not uncommon for people to walk from the bright outdoors into a dark restaurant at midday only to stumble down a step or two. Behavioral and ergonomics literature discusses the time lag in the adjustment of eyes to changes in light level. However, entries and similar transition points for buildings often introduce points where people can trip and fall because the spaces have strange dimensions, sudden changes in light levels to which eyes cannot adjust quickly, backlighting and glare, obscure steps, or small changes in elevation. Minimum light levels in some standards do not account for the physiological limits of light-to-dark or dark-to-light accommodation or images hidden by glare.

Small Elevation Changes

One-step elevation changes are dangerous when one realizes that most people do not look at their feet when walking. The normal position for eyes is about 15 to 20 degrees below horizontal. Irregular surfaces and obscure changes in surfaces go undetected rather easily. Where changes in elevations exist, guardrails, barriers, and visual cues are important. Ramps are preferred when there are one- or two-step changes in elevation. The safest walking surface is one that has no abrupt changes in elevation.

Guard Rail Height

OSHA and other standards call for 42-inch-high guard rails. The standard is based on the mechanics of someone leaning or falling against the rail. First, the guard rail must withstand the forces acting against it. Second, the height must prevent someone from falling over it. The height is based on where the center of gravity acts when someone leans or falls against a guard rail. If the center of gravity is below the rail, the rotation will be under the rail. In this case, infill under the rail can prevent a fall. If the center of gravity is above the rail at impact, the body will tend to rotate over the top of the rail and a person has a good chance of falling.

The center of gravity of a person is about 3 inches above the midpoint of their height. A 42-inch-high guard rail will keep the center of gravity of people who are six-and-a-half feet tall or less below the top of the rail.

The theoretical basis for the rail is violated when people stand on something near the rail or raise a child up to see. To minimize the danger of a fall over the rail, there may be a need to provide visibility through the infill or extend the railing inward to keep people from hanging over the rail. Infill often takes the form of balusters or spindles, which can create hazards if spaced too far apart. Children may fall through them or get their heads caught. One may turn to standards for rails in baby cribs[9] to determine what spacing is safe. In some cases there may be a requirement for a catch platform or net as an extra protection should someone fall over the rail. Figure 19-2 shows a guard rail that meets standards.

Sites

It is not uncommon for a facility to affect the area around it. Chemical releases at facilities in Bhopal, India; Mexico City; and Wheeling, West Virginia, made

---

[9]16 CFR 1508: requirements for full-sized baby cribs.

headlines for days. Chemical releases have caused thousands in communities to evacuate, injured many, and, in the case of Bhopal, killed over 2,500. Disasters like these led to the requirement that facilities that create hazards for those around a site establish emergency response plans and communication of such hazards to community or area emergency planning organizations.

Many facilities create traffic problems, both on and off the site. Large facilities may need turn lanes from arterial streets. Traffic patterns for employee, delivery, emergency, and pedestrian traffic need careful analysis. Figure 19-3 provides an example of a well-developed site plan for all of these.

SUMMARY

Safety is an important part of any facility program. The range of safety topics is very broad and often complex for a particular project. During programming, the important tasks are identifying hazards and setting standards for their control. For some hazards it may be necessary to complete detailed analysis, using safety specialists. It may also be important to define what controls are appropriate. Hazards may be associated with the site and its use, the structures placed on it, the organization and layout of spaces to isolate hazards, and meeting the thousands of standards and regulations that apply.

References

American Institute of Chemical Engineers, 1987. *Guidelines for hazard evaluation procedures.* New York: Center for Chemical Safety.

American Institute of Chemical Engineers, 1989. *Guidelines for chemical process quantitative risk analysis.* New York: Center for Chemical Safety.

American Institute of Chemical Engineers, 1989. *Guidelines for process equipment reliability data with data tables.* New York: Center for Chemical Safety.

Brauer, Roger L. 1986. *Facilities planning: The user requirements method.* New York: AMACOM, American Management Association.

Brauer, Roger L. 1990. *Health and safety for engineers.* New York: Van Nostrand Reinhold Company.

Kohr, Robert L. 1991. *Accident prevention for hotels, motels, and restaurants.* New York: Van Nostrand Reinhold Company.

Loss prevention data books for architects and engineers (2 volumes). Factory Mutual Engineering Corporation, 1151 Boston-Providence Turnpike, P.O. Box 9102, Norwood, MA 02062.

1991. *Fire protection handbook.* 17th ed. Quincy, Mass.: National Fire Protection Association.

Rosen, Stephen I. 1983. *The slip and fall handbook.* Del Mar, Calif.: Hanrow Press.

Roland, H.E., and B. Moriarity. 1990. *System safety engineering and management.* 2d ed. New York: John Wiley & Sons.

Hammer, W. 1991. *Handbook of system and product safety.* 2d ed. Des Plaines, Ill.: American Society of Safety Engineers.

Woodson, E. 1981. *Human factors design handbook.* New York: McGraw-Hill.

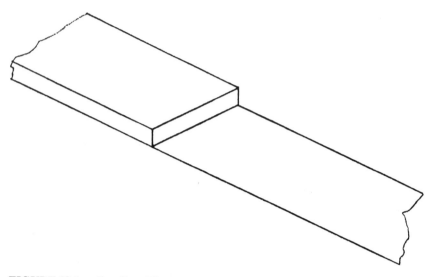

FIGURE 19-1.   One-Step Elevation Changes Are Hazardous

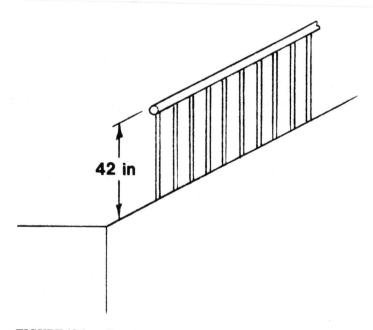

FIGURE 19-2.   Guard Rails Should Be at Least 42 Inches High

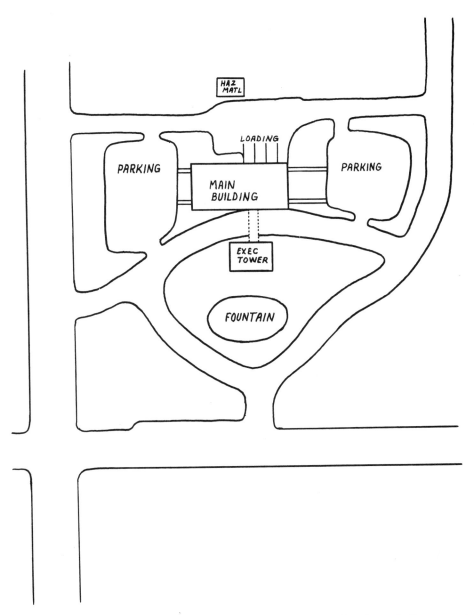

FIGURE 19-3.   A Site Plan That Has a Good Arrangement for Employee, Delivery, Emergency, and Pedestrian Traffic

CHAPTER 20

Programming Architectural Security in Facilities

Randall Atlas

INTRODUCTION

Security is a topic on the minds and budgets of a growing number of clients, as is evidenced by the rapidly expanding supply of security technology products. The demand for more secure facilities, coupled with computerized technology, is making access control and intrusion detection into a science of its own.

Vandalism, terrorism, burglary, shoplifting, employee theft, assault, and espionage are just some of the crimes that endanger lives and threaten our built environment. As crime increases, architects are being called on to address security and crime concerns through the programming and building design process.

Architects and designers can make some of the greatest contributions to meeting a facility's security objectives. Architects generally make the basic design decisions about circulation, access, building materials, fenestration, and many other features that can support or thwart overall security aims. Designing without security in mind can lead to lawsuits, injuries, expensive retrofitting with protection equipment, and the need for additional security personnel. If not properly planned for and installed, the equipment can distort important building design functions, add to security personnel costs, and result in exposed, unsightly alarm systems or blocked doors and windows.

While "form follows function" is a familiar tenet of twentieth-century architecture—originally expressed by the Bauhaus school of design and popularized in America by Frank Lloyd Wright—most of the architecture has focused on form rather than function. It is as if the structure itself, harmony with the site, and integrity of the materials have become the function. Less emphasis has been placed on the activities taking place inside and immediately around the building. Effective security design can integrate form and function into the standard design approaches or highly complex architectural solutions. Design elements that are closely coordinated with security personnel and security technology can form a foundation of a strong and cost-effective security master plan.

The keys to achieving that foundation are for the client and the security specialist to clearly outline the security and protection requirements with the architect's continual input. Once the architect and the client can agree on the overall functional requirements and building image, the security elements can be treated specifically.

To be able to integrate security into a building, the architect and the designer will need to know the basics of security management, the fundamental concepts of crime prevention through environmental design, and the architectural programming and design process.

THE SYSTEMATIC PROCESS OF SECURITY DESIGN

Security design is the systematic process that allows proper design and the effective use of the built environment to reduce the opportunity, incidence, and perception of crime. The security design process can be used on all building types, from the smallest restaurant to a planned urban development. Effective security design need not be complicated or compromise architectural solutions.

All buildings must meet specific functional criteria from which the design will evolve. A building should permit efficient job performance, meet the needs of its occupants, and protect its occupants from the safety hazards and criminal acts that will affect production and service. Architects worry about the "fortress" mentality of security professionals, and security professionals are concerned about architects' failure to include security equipment in their building design. The conflict is not over whether to include security equipment in the building, but between a building's openness versus control of access.

Securing a building that was not originally designed for security is expensive, and architects have to sacrifice much more openness in retrofitting during post-security stages. Protection personnel needs and operating expenses are greater than they need to be because of a lack of foresight during the programming and design of the facility. This condition is particularly evident in many of today's buildings, where modern design and materials result in facilities that are especially vulnerable to criminal activity.

The Architectural Process

To understand the architectural process, it is helpful to recall the sequence of steps that occur before a building can begin undergoing construction.

Phase 1: Programming

Information about the building is provided to the architect by the client. The role of the client is to define precisely the vulnerabilities and threats to people, information, and property. The client also assesses the level and cost of protection and the coverage that will be needed. The client and security director develop the definition of security needs, define who and what needs protection, and define the assets and the importance of each asset worth protecting.

Programming is the problem-seeking process that leads to problem solving in design. The programming should proceed in an objective manner to do the following:

> establish goals and objectives in order to clarify the owner's requirements;
> determine project constraints that include governmental codes, zoning ordinances and regulations, project budget, site conditions, pedestrian and vehicular access, and time limitations;
>   gather information that considers such factors as departmental functions, systems and procedures, movement of materials, personnel and the public, and desired adjacencies;
>   organize and analyze facts which include tabulations of existing square footage and populations, future expansion, special equipment requirements and in general determine the needs of the owner and the people for whom the facility is designed. (Murvin, 1982:B2-2)

The architect verifies that the space requirement program is in balance with the budget. The architect incorporates all of the information of the program to state the design problem that is to be solved with the design process.

The security specialist's role is to help the client describe and elaborate the protection requirements and the level of protection required in each area. The security specialist helps the client assess the threats, security needs, and vulnerabilities. He or she also will help in the planning of access control, security zoning, target hardening, surveillance systems, security manpower allocation, and security operational procedures and policy.

The architect must then incorporate the security program information into effective space and circulation planning.

Phase 2: Schematic Design

The architect processes the programming information and develops diagrams that reflect circulation patterns and proximity relationships. The diagrams evolve into single-line drawings of the floor plan, site plan, and elevations.

The architect can design to provide for clear sightlines for surveillance and access controls for entrances and exits. The architect also can design for the appropriate location of sensitive or restricted areas and design for the planned placement of security personnel. The architect will provide an architectural solution that uses design elements to closely coordinate security technology and personnel considerations.

Phase 3: Design Development

The architect has presented preliminary design ideas to the client and now undertakes drawings that are more sophisticated and include engineering considerations such as structural, mechanical, electric, ventilation, and site planning issues. The architectural drawings are illustrated with double-line drawings to reflect the thickness of walls, door swings, lighting fixtures, reflected ceilings, etc.

The design development drawings are the last real opportunity for any design changes. The design development drawings consist of detailed site plans, floor plans, sections, elevations, schedules, outline specifications, and other documents to establish in greater detail the extent and character of the entire project.

The security consultant makes important contributions to the design development stage by assisting the architect in the development of security equipment schedules. These schedules may include security doors, security glazing, door monitoring, door closers, types of locks, etc. The security electronic consultant may submit conduit riser diagrams and security devices layouts on the floor plans.

Phase 4: Construction Documents

These are the final drawings prepared for construction purposes. The purpose of construction documents or working drawings is to provide detailed graphic representations of the characteristics and scope of the project for the bidding and construction process. The architect produces scaled drawings, which include site plan, floor plans, sections, elevations, details, notes, and schedules. These drawings depict graphically all work to be done with respect to dimensions; arrangement; location of materials and equipment; structural, mechanical, and electrical systems; and all other relevant systems involved in the project.

All technical data are presented in the drawings and are accompanied by technical and written specifications. The final specifications set forth the technical detail requirements for the architectural portion of the work, such as materials, equipment, workmanship, and finishes; related site work; and special equipment. All work is coordinated with structural, mechanical, and electrical layouts. Materials and color schedules are finalized with the owner.

Upon completion of the final plans and specifications by both the architect and the consultants for the complete set of working drawings required for bidding and construction, the architect checks all completed documents for coordination, compliance with program and codes, and accuracy. In addition, the architect advises the owner of any adjustments to construction costs and refinements of scheduling decisions. Upon final client approval, the architect places the necessary architect's seals and signatures on the documents (required by reviewing authorities) and obtains the same from the engineering consultants.

Phase 5: Bids for Construction

The architectural drawings and specifications are publicized for bids by qualified contractors who will provide the service at the lowest price. The bidding documents provide a description of the project to prospective bidders. These documents are prepared, assembled, and distributed to bidders so that they may prepare proposals for the construction of the project.

The architect's professional responsibilities regarding bidding documents include assisting the owner and the owner's attorney in the preparation of the construction contract for the project and awarding of the contract for performing the work to the successful bidder. This assistance involves administration of the bidding process, review of the contractor's qualifications, the analysis of bids or negotiated proposals, and providing guidance on the selection of contractors.

Phase 6: Construction

All phases of the job come together with the implementation of the project. The construction of the project can be guided or directed by a general contractor, a construction management company, or a team of construction professionals.

The architect provides administration of the construction contract, which includes the architect visiting the site at intervals appropriate to the stage of construction to make field observations and evaluations. The architect reviews all construction for conformance with the working drawings and determines the dates of substantial completion and final completion.

The security contractor will be subject to periodical inspections of the security work by building inspectors and the architect's field representative. All of the security systems installation will have to be coordinated with the electrical contractor's work and allow for coordination of the different construction trades.

Phase 7: Operation

The product of the whole process is the moving in and opening of the facility. The realizations of the architect, client, construction team, and security specialist are actualized. If the building users are satisfied, the mission has been accomplished.

The security consultant and security systems contractor conduct a series of tests for the operation of all of the systems: intercoms, alarms, keying systems, card access systems, fence monitoring systems, intrusion detection systems, etc. The security contractor will usually offer the maintenance staff of the new project an intensive training course on how to use all of the security systems technology. Preventive maintenance is discussed, and the building is turned over to the client.

Where Does Security Fit?

The programming phase of design is the most efficient stage in which to consider a building's security requirements or countermeasure development process. This assessment should be conducted by the security specialist and the client. Together they should provide the following:

1. *Asset definition:* which assets are vital, important, or secondary for people, information, and property.
2. *Threat definition:* which threats are highly probable, probable, or unlikely.
3. *Vulnerability analysis:* what is the penetration delay, what are the detection capabilities, access controls, and security force capabilities.
4. *Security measures and strategies:* what are the policies and procedures, what physical barriers are proposed, what mechanical and electronic security devices are proposed, what type of security personnel is available.

Figure 20-1 illustrates the countermeasures' development process. When these six steps have been conducted they provide the basis for the security master plan and the basis of the security program. The information that is developed may include the types and numbers of users in the building, the security procedures for access, what items are of high intrinsic value, which critical property is to be protected, where is sensitive or valuable information stored, what types of threats are posed and how would they be carried out. After all the security needs are identified, the client and security specialist must decide what is the needed level of protection in each area. The architect can suggest design considerations to the client early and continuously during the programming phase as the security plan is being developed.

Once the security plan has identified the vulnerabilities, the architectural program can establish the design goals and criteria. The architect and client may develop fiscal constraints. The architect then proceeds to incorporate the security program features into the schematic design, design development, and construction documents.

The architect and security specialist may develop the preliminary security system design as part of the design process. The security system design is a natural outgrowth of this design process. The system design should be part of the design process, with drawings and specifications; it should *not* be part of the programming phase, which seeks problem definition, not solutions.

ARCHITECTURAL SECURITY PROGRAMMING

Architectural security programming begins with the security professional. It is his or her job to determine the total security needs of the building users. This includes an analysis of the following:

- *What* are the crime problems in the neighborhood surrounding the facility?
- *What* kind of protection is needed?
- *Who* is in need of protection?

- *How* could potential threats be actualized?
- *What* will be the cost, in terms of staff and equipment, of implementing a total protection plan?

At this point, the security professional and the client determine the specific security needs for each level of staff and operation; i.e., administrative staff, corporate executives, loading dock area, employee parking, etc. The program should research who the employees are (their role in the organization), where they work, what work products are involved, and what equipment or technology the employees will use. The security program should also identify all other users of the building, such as public, customers, consultants, sales representatives, delivery people, cleaning crews, etc. While such planning may not prevent all potential security threats, it will certainly make criminal activity more difficult.

The security professional should identify specific threat scenarios and define ways in which the security of the building could be jeopardized. Are the threats external or internal? Does the programming address such threats as sabotage, eavesdropping, natural disasters, and bomb threats?

After the establishment of possible significant threats, the next step is to determine how these threats could occur, how often, and what approaches can be taken to counter them. The architect will use the recommendations of the security professional to develop structural responses for the level of protection needed. An industrial plant might be designed to resist unauthorized entry, or an embassy may be designed to withstand internal or external explosions.

After the security needs have been identified and analyzed, the client and security specialist will decide the level of protection to be designed for. These decisions should be made in consultation with the architect so that they are designed into the building during the schematic design drawing phase. Initial cost estimates of security features should consider and compare the type of security and the cost of potential losses.

The work product of the programming phase is a report and circulation diagrams, along with scenario developments that are integrated into the architectural process. The architect should be active and informed during the security analysis and planning process, and have a clear line of documentation. Once the security program is complete, the architect is ready to respond to the program with security design.

THE SECURITY PROFESSIONAL AND THE ARCHITECT

The security professional is often faced with the challenging task of cooperating with and assisting the architect or design professional on an addition, renovation, or new construction.

The architect will need information from the owner-client to program and design an efficient building. The person who can best provide critical information on security needs is the security director or security consultant. To provide the information in a format that the architect can work with, the security professional must identify which corporate assets are vital. In most applications, it will be a mix of *people, information,* and *property.*

Human resources are the first and most valuable asset to protect. To develop security criteria for the architect, the critical questions are these:

- *Who* are the users? (employees, service crew, visitors, sales)
- *Where* can users go to in the building? (horizontal, vertical)
- *What* do the users do in the building? (task, recreation, work)
- *How* can the users get there? (access methods, circulation)
- *When* do the users get there and leave? (time, shift patterns)
- *Why* are the particular users there? (official business, guests)

When the security professional is clear on the answers, a task summary can be prepared for the architect. Whether the user is the president of the company or a member of the cleaning crew, the same scenario development of asking the six key questions applies. The security professional will then determine the security implications and design implications.

For example, a cleaning crew might have the following security implications: (1) control of after-hour access, (2) verification of cleaning employee status, (3) security personnel to sign in and supervise entry and exit, and (4) key control.

These security concerns could then translate into design implications, such as (1) a sign-in desk for the service trades, (2) design of access control systems to allow staff to control entry and log-in movement, (3) placement of dumpsters, and (4) location systems of offices with control room tie-in. These are just a few aspects that need to be addressed by the architect based on information that the security professional develops.

The second asset for protection is *information.* Critical questions for information protection include the following:

- Who has access to it?
- What information is being protected?
- Why is it worth protecting?
- When is it accessible or vulnerable?
- Where is it available or vulnerable?
- How can the information be acquired or compromised?

A security professional who is clear on the answers to these questions can describe the threats and name proposed solutions to the architect.

The following example will illustrate the protection of information:

1. *Who:* The company president and top management have unrestricted access to all records in a central location. Clerks mainly screen mail and

make copies of memos. Department managers generate and file local personnel data on assigned personnel. They also have access to payroll information for their people. The computer center has personnel files and payroll data on disks and tapes and runs the payroll weekly.

2. *What:* Information includes central personnel files, sensitive department memos, and computer disks and tapes.

3. *Why:* The protection of personnel records preserves individual privacy and minimizes civil legal liability. Reasons can be examined for practicality and cost.

4. *When:* Personnel department records are available for review Monday through Friday, 8:00 a.m. to 5:00 p.m. Operating departments are open from 7:00 a.m. to 5:00 p.m., Monday through Friday. Mail delivery and document copying occur during normal working hours. The computer center operates twenty-four hours a day. The most vulnerable times are during mail breaks and shift changes. Burglary and unauthorized access and cleaning crews at night are after-hour exposures.

5. *Where:* Information is stored in central and departmental files, in managers' desks, and on computer pages and disks located in the computer center.

6. *How:* Department information is most vulnerable to internal compromise through unobserved access owing to the lack of systematic access control. Control personnel files do not generally leave this area. The computer center does not enforce control in admittance of nonassigned personnel and has no "need-to-know" rule for its own people.

Once the security professional has identified the threats and vulnerabilities, counterstrategies can be developed with the architect. Architectural design features that could improve the protection of personnel information include the following:

- Provide clear demarcation of executive areas with layering of access to these zones.
- Limit the number of building entrances and make those established easily observable. Define the entrances for visitors and staff. Design a service entrance that is able to be supervised and secure.
- Control access to central personnel files, and document file access.
- Design a reception desk or counter to screen visitors, vendors, and outsiders. The reception desk should be designed to view all entry doors and elevators.
- Elevators should open in the supervised building core area. Special floors or offices may require special elevator access control programming or dedicated elevators.
- Locate the mail room with a clear, unobstructed line of travel from loading and delivery areas. The mail room should be a secure room and admittance should be monitored. Critical mail could be delivered by way of a closed

automated system to minimize human intervention. Similar systems could be made for other types of sensitive information, such as trade secrets and financial data.

The same processes illustrated above for protecting people and information assets would be applied for protecting *property* resources. Property protection completes the triad of asset and threat analysis. The number of architectural, technological, and operational innovations to security design are almost limitless. The most important thing to remember is to go through the problem-defining process and get the results to the architect in the earliest design stages.

There is a temptation to present a standard list of design solutions for security protection. However, each building has a unique function, operation, and combination of materials. If the security professional uses asset vulnerability analysis to develop criteria for the architect, the correct solutions will emerge.

THE ARCHITECTURAL RESPONSE

Architects and designers can contribute a great deal to a project's security objective: They generally make the basic design decisions about circulation, access, building materials, fenestration, and many other features that can support the overall security aims.

Building clients and design professionals are not the only ones concerned about security during the design process. In addition to safety inspection requirements, many jurisdictions now require security review by the police as part of the building-permit approval process. Inspectors evaluate the plans for obvious spots where assaults, muggings, break-ins, and other crimes of opportunity may exist. Some jurisdictions have security ordinances that require certain lighting levels and secure door and window designs.

The emphasis in security design falls on the design and use of the space, a practice that deviates from the traditional target-hardening approach to crime prevention. Traditional target-hardening focused predominantly on denying access to a crime target through physical or artificial barrier techniques such as locks, alarms, and gates. The traditional approach tends to overlook opportunities for natural access control and surveillance. Sometimes, the natural and normal uses of the environment can accomplish the same effects as mechanical hardening and surveillance.

Security design involves integrating the efforts of community citizens and law enforcement officers to prevent crime through the design and use of the built environment. Design professionals can use three basic strategies for crime prevention through environmental design (also known as CPTED): natural access control, natural surveillance, and territorial reinforcement. The implementation of each of these strategies is carried out through organized methods, mechanical methods, and natural methods (see Figure 20-2).

ACCESS CONTROL

Access control is a design concept directed at reducing the opportunity for crime. Organized methods of access control include security guard forces. Mechanical strategies include target-hardening, locks, and electronic and mechanical key systems. Windows may have protective glazing that withstands blows without breaking. Door and window hardware may have special materials and mounting that make them hard to remove. Walls, floors, or doors may be specially reinforced in high-security areas with materials that are difficult to penetrate (see Figure 20-3).

Natural methods of access control make use of spatial definition and circulation patterns. An example of natural design is the use of security zoning or layering. By dividing space into zones of differing security levels, such as unrestricted, controlled, and restricted, sensitive areas can be more effectively protected. The focus of access control strategies is to deny access to a crime target and create a perception of risk and detection.

SURVEILLANCE

Surveillance strategies keep intruders under observation. Organized surveillance strategies include police and guard patrol. Lighting and closed-circuit television cameras are mechanical strategies for surveillance (see Figure 20-4). Natural strategies include windows, low landscaping, and raised entrances.

TERRITORIAL REINFORCEMENT

Territorial strategies suggest that physical design can create or extend the sphere of territorial influence. Natural access control and surveillance contribute to a sense of territoriality, boosting security by encouraging users to protect their turf. Organized strategies typically include neighborhood crime watches, informed receptionists, and guard stations. Mechanical strategies can be perimeter-sensing systems. Natural territorial strategies include fences, walls, and landscaping (see Figure 20-5).

Security needs must be determined early in the project's programming stage. The design team should analyze how the space or building will be used. Architects should have a basic understanding of security principles and must be able to evaluate and implement security recommendations. Space, function, and occupants must be a part of the plan to support the security objective of detection and delay unwanted or criminal situations.

SITE DEVELOPMENT AND SECURITY ZONING

Security analysis in site planning should begin with an assessment of conditions on-site and off-site. This analysis should take into account topography, vegetation, adjacent land uses, circulation patterns, neighborhood crime patterns, police patrol patterns, sight lines, areas for concealment, and lighting. Other key factors for site security planning are off-site pedestrian circulation, vehicular circulation, access points for service vehicles, employee access and circulation, and visitor access and circulation. Site analysis represents the first of three levels of security defense planning and considers the site perimeter and grounds of the facility.

First Level of Security Design: Site Characteristics

Site design measures are the *first level,* which can include walls, fences, ditches, lighting, natural topographic separations, or a combination of such elements (see Figures 20-6 and 20-7). Here are several factors to consider at this stage:

- What is the physical makeup of the site and how does it influence security?
- What is the land surrounding the site used for?
- What is the type and frequency of criminal activity in the area?

Second Level of Security Design: Building Perimeter

The *second level* of security is the perimeter or exterior of the building. The building shell and its openings represent the crucial second line of defense against intrusion and forced entry. The principal points of entry to be considered are the windows, doors, skylights, storm sewers, roofs, floors, and fire escapes.

Doors are among the weakest links of a building and provide poor resistance to penetration. Attention must be paid to the door frame, latches, locks, hinges, panic hardware, the surrounding wall, and the door leaf. Window considerations for security design include the type of glazing material, window frame, window hardware, and size of the opening.

The building shell is an important security consideration because the type of construction will affect the level of security. Most stud walls and metal deck roof assemblies can be compromised with hand tools in less than two minutes, and unreinforced concrete block walls can be broken quickly with a sledge hammer.

Third Level of Security Design: Internal Space or Point Protection

The *third level* of security that the architect should design for is internal space protection. Sensitive areas within a facility may warrant special protection with security technology and restricted design circulation. The level of protection may be based on zones, with access limited to authorized persons (see Figure 20-8).

Application of the zoning concept determines the control of employees, visitors, vendors, and others. The idea is to allow people to reach their destination, but prevent them from entering certain areas. The controlled access to each department of a building screens out undesirable visitors, reduces congestion, and helps employees identify unauthorized persons.

The zoning design goals are accomplished with unrestricted zones, controlled zones, and restricted zones. Some areas of a facility should be completely unrestricted to persons entering the areas during the hours of designated use. The design of unrestricted zones should encourage persons to conduct their business and leave the facility without entering controlled or restricted zones. Unrestricted zones might include lobbies, reception areas, snack bars, certain personnel and administrative offices, and public meeting rooms.

Controlled zone movement requires a person to have a valid purpose for entry (see Figure 20-9). Once admitted to a controlled area, persons may travel from one department to another without severe restrictions. Controlled zones might include administrative offices, staff dining rooms, security offices, working areas, and loading docks.

Restricted zones are sensitive areas that are limited to certain staff members. Sections within restricted zones frequently require additional access control. Restricted areas might include rooms with vaults, sensitive records, chemicals and drugs, supplies, etc.

The security zoning concept is being used effectively in the design of hospitals, jails, courthouses, laboratories, and industrial plants. Once circulation patterns are successfully resolved through security zoning, physical security systems can be considered. After security needs are identified and outlined, it is up to the client and security specialist to decide the level of protection needed in each area. The architect should be consulted about design considerations early and continuously during the programming phase. He or she should also be consulted as a security master plan is being developed to provide the most cost-effective and operational systems design.

CONCLUSION

If security is treated as one of many design requirements, security measures are not onerous or difficult to implement. A growing number of architects, aided by knowledgeable equipment manufacturers and security specialists, find that society is increasingly concerned with protecting its people and property against the acts of criminals, opportunists, violent political radicals, deranged persons, and saboteurs.

For the architect to be effective in integrating security in the building design, he or she should seek an experienced, independent, nonvested security consultant who will work closely with architects and is knowledgeable about the client's business. Such a consultant can help the architect achieve a fine building design while maintaining good security. The high costs of security renovation and litigation are also good incentives to have a security professional work with the architect.

The architect and security consultant can integrate security needs through the five stages of design. All the security planning features mentioned are geared toward preventing crime in the built environment. The architect plays a key role in the shaping of the environment and the cues and signals that the building sends to users and visitors. How the building turns out in terms of safety, security, and comfort is a good indication of how well the architect understands the intended use of the building. However, good architecture can't prevent all misdeeds. The crimes that a building environment can deter by natural, mechanical, and organized means are overwhelmingly external—that is, crimes from outsiders breaking in, robbery, or assault. These stranger-to-stranger crimes produce the greatest fear, but not the greatest economic losses.

Internal crime is where the real money is lost. The terrorism of the future may not be bomb attacks on a building but rather theft of company secrets, pilferage, and destruction of computer records. Can architecture make a difference in preventing internal crime? It can possibly make a difference. If a living or working environment is perceived by its users as safe, the employees or residents likely will be more responsible and accountable for undesignated and undesired activity.

Environmental design can never eliminate all crime, because it does not attack the root causes. Architectural security design may only move crime to other, more vulnerable areas. It remains easier to remodel a building than to create jobs for teenagers. Design can provide a conducive environment for personnel control, but it cannot create such control if the social control of the community is fragmented. On a small scale, the inclusion of security and life safety functions add greatly to the potential for a safer and more cost-effective work and living environment. A security professional should be made a member of the owner's design team as early as the site selection phase. The security consultant should continue to assist the team right through design, construction, and occupancy. If security is designed into the building from the very beginning, it may again be safe to go back into the building.

References

American Institute of Architects. 1989. Security Design. *AIA memo,* November 5.

Anderson, D., and M.T. McGowan. 1987. Design in security. *Progressive architecture,* March, p. 144.

Atlas, R. 1988. Just when you thought it was safe. . . . *Security management* 32:8.

Atlas, R. 1991. Security design. *Protection of assets bulletin.* Merritt Company.

Atlas, R. 1991. The other side of CPTED. *Security management,* March, p. 135.

Crowe, T. 1991. *Crime prevention through environmental design: Basic training manual.* Louisville, Ky.: National Crime Prevention Institute.

Keller, Steven. 1987. Designing for security. *Building design and construction,* March, p. 127.

Krupat, E., and P. Kubzansky. 1987. Designing to deter crime. *Psychology today,* October, p. 61.

Murvin, H.L. 1982. *The architect's responsibilities in the project delivery process.* Oakland, Calif.: Publisher: American Institute of Architects, Washington, D.C.

Newman, Oscar. 1973. *Defensible space: Crime prevention through urban design.* New York: Macmillan.

Vonier, Thomas. 1987. General building design guidelines for security. *Progressive architecture,* March, p. 143.

COUNTERMEASURES DEVELOPMENT PROCESS

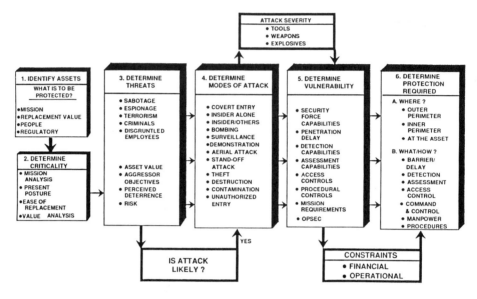

Source : R. Grassie, ASIS Facility Security Design Workshop, 1992.

FIGURE 20-1.   Countermeasures Development Process

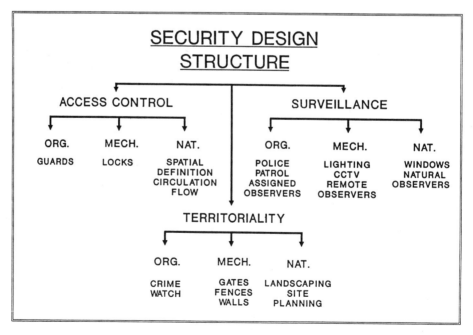

FIGURE 20-2.   Security Design Structure

FIGURE 20-3.   A Control Center at Prince George County Detention Center Illustrates Breakproof Security Glazing and Reinforced Wall Construction, Yet Permits Surveillance and Access to Adjacent Spaces

FIGURE 20-4.   New Computer Chip Video Cameras Provide Excellent Color Imaging of Critical Areas Under Observation

FIGURE 20-5.   The Use of Gates and Fencing Permits Surveillance Through the Material Yet Allows for Distancing from Outsiders and Defining Boundaries

FIGURE 20-6.   The Use of Manpower by a Gate Entry Allows for Screening of Outsiders and Reduces Opportunity for Illegitimate Users of the Space

FIGURE 20-7.   The Use of Fencing Provides the Physical Barrier for Separation of Public Spaces from Semiprivate Property

FIGURE 20-8.   A Control Monitoring Station Permits the Access of Visitors and Staff and Keeps Record of Entry of Persons into Unauthorized Areas

FIGURE 20-9.   Often an Information Booth Will Provide Visible Control of an Area to Deter Criminal Activity; Information and Reception Booths Can Serve a Dual Role of Public Relations and Security Screening

CHAPTER 21

Programming Considerations for Energy Conservation[1]

Fuller Moore

INTRODUCTION

Energy-efficient facilities programming involves making a trade-off between construction costs and operating costs. In general, energy-efficient construction costs more to build but less to operate for heating, cooling, and lighting. While this life-cycle trade-off is relatively simple to evaluate for residential structures, which are occupied continuously with envelope-dominant thermal loads, it is much more complex for commercial and institutional facilities, which are occupied intermittently with internal-dominant thermal loads.

In addition to having lower energy costs, energy-efficient structures are typically more comfortable and preferred by occupants. For example, daylighted facilities reduce lighting, heating, and cooling energy costs if properly designed. In addition, they are preferred by occupants not only for illumination quality but for view and contact with daily and seasonal weather cycles. If this preference reduces absenteeism by even less than 1 percent, it is possible to realize greater economic savings than all of the energy savings combined.

PROGRAMMING ENERGY-EFFICIENT COMMERCIAL BUILDINGS

Facilities, especially continuously occupied residential structures, with thermal loads primarily dominated by the envelope are comparatively simple and

---

[1]Excerpted by permission from Moore, Fuller. 1993. *The Responsive Envelope*. New York: McGraw-Hill.

straightforward to analyze and to adapt to climate. "Commercial"—or non-residential—facilities are much more complex to analyze and to design with a high degree of energy efficiency. The reasons for this complexity are numerous.

Commercial facilities typically have large internal loads owing to equipment, lighting, and people. Even in northern climates, for example, cooling is the dominant thermal load in large office buildings. Cooling systems often are not operated continuously, but on schedules that vary throughout the day and week. Because occupants may be restricted to certain locations, thermal and visual comfort requirements for commercial facilities are typically more stringent than for residences. Because occupants and operational staff are often not financially responsible for energy costs, energy-efficient operation may be neglected. In the case of facilities built for lease where the tenant will pay for energy costs, the owner's objective of minimizing construction cost discourages investing in any energy-efficient improvements.

In the case of companies building for their own occupancy, the capital costs of upgrading construction quality for the purpose of energy efficiency offer less tax benefit than the alternative of higher energy costs, which may be deducted directly as a cost of business operation. When a commercial corporation considers investing in energy-efficient facility features, the rate of return on this investment is compared with other investment alternatives, such as improvements in manufacturing operations. Typically, only energy-efficient strategies with a simple payback period of less than two years will compare favorably with competing investment alternatives.

Effect of Utility Rate Structure

One of the greatest differences between residential and commercial facilities is the difference in the electric utility rate structure that applies to each. In residential buildings, the demand for electric energy is comparatively continuous throughout the day and, depending on climate, throughout the year. Thus, a simple billing rate is used for residential customers based solely on the total quantity of electrical energy consumed throughout the billing period. Because the rate of consumption is fairly constant, this consumption charge fairly compensates the utility both for the cost of generating the consumed energy but also for the long-term cost of building the generating capacity.

In commercial buildings, occupancy is not continuous, and typical daily operation causes a sharp peak in power consumption. This occurs typically during mid-afternoon, when the maximum lighting, cooling, and equipment loads coincide. Thus, in addition to a "consumption" charge based on actual energy consumed, commercial customers are charged an additional "demand" charge based on the peak *rate* of energy use or power demand. This is, in effect, a penalty charge designed to compensate the utility for the costs of building the additional generating capacity necessary to meet infrequent but high power demands. These charges can be quite substantial and typically represent the largest part of commercial facility energy costs. Typically, the monthly demand charge is based on the peak power demand occurring at any time throughout the billing period—even if that period was brief and much higher than the next highest demand during the billing period. In some cases, the demand charge is based on the peak demand during the last several billing periods. In other words, a single brief, heavy consumption period can determine the demand charge for several months (up to a year for some utilities).

Because of the way that demand charges heavily penalize power consumption peaks, there is a great incentive to spread the various loads out so that they do not occur simultaneously. In fact, in commercial buildings, reducing *peak demand*, rather than reducing *consumption*, becomes the predominant strategy for reducing energy costs. *Load shifting* becomes economically more important than *load reduction*.

Occupancy schedule, internal and ventilation loads, heavy lighting requirements, utility rate schedules, cost/benefit economic considerations, occupant behavior, sophisticated control strategies, maintenance, and security are typical of the greater number and complexity of the factors that affect commercial facilities. Because of this, it is important to realize that the relatively simple design strategies and analysis techniques that apply to residences are inadequate or inappropriate for commercial buildings. Today, this complexity necessitates the use of a computer to aid in the design of even comparatively simple commercial buildings, and it is difficult to generalize about their design. However, the emphasis on passive solar heating that applies to residential design in most regions of the United States is replaced by concern for lighting and cooling in commercial buildings.

PASSIVE SOLAR HEATING

A *passive solar heating system* is one in which the thermal energy flow is by radiation, conduction, or natural convection. This is distinguished from an active solar heating system, which uses fans or pumps for forced distribution of heat (Balcomb, et al., 1984).

Key Design Elements

The four most important elements affecting the thermal performance of a passive solar-heated facility are these (Balcomb, et al., 1984): (1) the size of the solar aperture (window, skylight, greenhouse, etc.), (2) the amount of energy conservation achieved, particularly as a result of envelope insulation and infiltration control, (3) the amount and placement of the thermal storage mass (to reduce excessive temperature swings and reduce overheating), and (4) the weather (principally, insulation and air temperature).

Types of Passive Solar Heating Systems

Passive solar heating systems are most commonly classified according to their physical configuration: direct gain, thermal storage wall, sunspace (greenhouse), and convective air loop. Only direct gain and thermal storage wall, which have the greatest application for commercial facilities, will be considered here.

Direct gain is a passive solar heating system type consisting of a facility with south-facing windows that admit the slanting rays of the winter sun. Thermal mass, usually in the form of masonry walls or a masonry floor, stores heat during the day and releases this heat during the night. Most direct gain systems include an overhang above the glazing for summer shading and a means of reducing excessive night heat loss — by using night insulation, for example.

Thermal storage wall is a passive solar heating system type consisting of a south-facing wall constructed of heavy masonry (Trombe wall) or water-filled containers (water wall). The outside, south-facing surface is glazed to admit sunlight and reduce night heat losses. A *Trombe* wall consists of a dark, south-facing masonry wall covered with vertical glazing. Solar heat is absorbed by the dark surface and conducted slowly through the wall to be released to the interior by convection and radiation. Vents can be cut through the top and bottom of the masonry wall to allow prompt transfer of heat to the living space by convection. A *water wall* system consists of water-filled containers located behind a south-facing glazing. Solar heat is absorbed by the water container, and convection currents in the water transfer heat promptly across the wall where it is transferred to the living area by convection and radiation.

Night Insulation

Operable thermal shades or shutters may be positioned to cover solar glazing at night to reduce heat loss, and removed during the day to admit solar radiation. Night insulation improves the heating performance of most passive solar heating systems; however, it is an expensive enhancement that requires operation and maintenance. Its cost-effectiveness should be carefully considered.

For commercial facilities, high-performance, "low-E" (low-emissivity) glazing is an effective alternative to night insulation; however, this type of glazing must be selected on the basis of several factors, including *solar transmittance* where solar heating is desirable, *visible transmittance* where daylight illumination is desirable, and *effective R-value* where reducing heat loss is important.

PASSIVE COOLING

Passive cooling is the counterpart of passive space heating. While passive solar heating is driven only by the sun, passive cooling can utilize several heat sinks and a variety of climatic influences to create thermal comfort in warm regions. While passive heating has been widely adopted only recently, passive cooling has a much longer history of theory and application in indigenous buildings. However, few of these principles are widely found in contemporary facility design. Because a general goal of passive cooling is to avoid overheating, which is primarily generated by the sun, passive cooling is not "solar" at all but is, instead, "non-solar . . . even anti-solar" (Cook, 1984). However, because passive heating and cooling both depend heavily on heat flow by natural means, they share many similar principles.

The primary comfort strategies in overheated climates are defensive: avoiding gains because of solar radiation by shading and reflective barriers, and avoiding heat transfer through the envelope by insulation and infiltration sealing.

"Offensive" Cooling Strategies

Beyond these defensive strategies, passive cooling requires the evacuation of heat from the building to those natural heat sinks of the planet that normally offset the heat gained from the sun: the atmosphere, the sky, and the earth.

Passive Cooling Categories

Passive solar heating is divided into categories according to application configuration. On the other hand, passive cooling is better understood as a series of research fields that focus on the basic heat sinks. While this organization is helpful to scientists and inventors, it is a source of frustration for designers and policymakers because so many workable systems involve multiple heat sinks. Nonetheless, this characterization of passive cooling will be used here (Cook, 1990):

- *Ventilative cooling:* (1) exhausting warm building air and replacing it with cooler outside air; (2) directing moving air across occupants' skin to cool by a combination of convection and evaporation. In passive applications, the required air movement is provided either by the wind or by the "stack effect." In hybrid applications, movement may be assisted by fans.
- *Radiative cooling:* the transfer of heat from a warmer surface to a cooler surrounding surface (or outer space). It may be used to cool the *facility* (where warm building surfaces radiate heat to the sky) or to cool *people* (where warm skin radiates heat to cooler surrounding room surfaces—to the cool walls of an underground facility, for example).
- *Evaporative cooling:* the exchange of sensible heat in air for the latent heat of water droplets of wetted surfaces. It may be used to cool the *facility* (where wetted surfaces are cooled by evaporation), the *building air* (cooled either directly by evaporation, or indirectly by contact with a surface previously cooled by evaporation), or the *occupants* (where evaporation of perspiration cools the skin surface).
- *Dehumidification:* the removal of water vapor from room air by dilution with drier air, condensation, or desiccation. In the case of condensation and desiccation, dehumidification is the exchange of latent heat in air for the sensible heat of water droplets on surfaces; both are the reverse of evaporative cooling and, as such, are adiabatic heating processes.
- *Mass-effect cooling:* the use of thermal storage to absorb heat during the warmest part of a periodic temperature cycle and release it later during a cooler part. "Night flushing" (where cool night air is drawn through a facility to exhaust heat stored during the day in massive floors and walls) is an example of daily-cycle mass-effect cooling and is especially suited to commercial buildings in dry climates.

ENERGY-EFFICIENT LIGHTING

Richard Peters, a noted lighting designer and professor of architecture at Berkeley, has often expressed his disdain for the distinction made between daylighting and electric lighting: "Daylight . . . electric light . . . it's all light!" His point is that the eye perceives both, that the same approach to distribution and control may be used regardless of the original source, and that both can and should be consciously manipulated in order to achieve design goals.

Thus, while the following two design approaches were originally proposed by the Illuminating Engineering Society for electric lighting, they apply equally well to daylighting and have been so adapted here. They are the *luminous environment* design approach and the *visual task* design approach (Kaufman, 1987).

"Luminous Environment" Design Approach
This approach is based on the concept of considering all of the visual surfaces in a room as potential reflectors whose importance is consciously emphasized by their respective brightness. Brightness is controlled by a combination of illumination of these surfaces and their respective reflectances or colors. As such, this method is best suited for general lighting design: for occupant orientation, for organizing the visual priorities within the space, and for revelation of the architecture itself. The method may be considered as the following steps: (1) the determination of the desired visual composition in the space, (2) the determination of the desired appearance of visual tasks and objects in the space, and (3) the selection of luminaires that fit the concept of visual composition and implement the desired appearance of objects.

"Visual Task" Design Approach
In areas where the primary function of the lighting system is to provide illumination for the quick, accurate performance of visual tasks, the task itself is the starting point in the lighting design. The method may be considered as the following steps: (1) identifying the visual task, (2) defining the task environment, (3) luminaire selection, and (4) calculation, layout, and evaluation.

Selecting Illuminance Levels

Lighting guidelines for the illuminance needed to perform a visual task have changed considerably since they were first recommended in 1899. The Illuminating Engineering Society has recommended the following illuminance categories for various activities. The recommended illuminance is for typical adults with normal visual acuity; this can be varied ±33 percent for special conditions (see IES, 1984, for more specific recommendations):

- Public spaces with dark surroundings—3 fc.
- Simple orientation for short, temporary visits—7.5 fc.
- Working spaces where visual tasks are only occasionally performed—15 fc.

- Performance of visual tasks of high contrast or large size — 30 fc.
- Performance of visual tasks of medium contrast or small size — 75 fc.
- Performance of visual tasks of low contrast or very small size — 150 fc.
- Performance of visual tasks of low contrast or very small size over a long period — 300 fc.
- Performance of very prolonged and exacting visual tasks — 750 fc.
- Performance of very special visual tasks or tasks of extremely low contrast and small size — 1,500 fc.

UTILIZING DAYLIGHTING FOR ENERGY EFFICIENCY

Programming for Daylighting

If daylighting is to be used in a proposed facility, it is necessary to determine its availability on the site. Surrounding objects, such as other buildings, trees and land forms, all act as daylight obstructions by blocking either direct sunlight or portions of the sky dome as visible from the facility location. Because of its potentially large contribution to illumination, and because of its directionality, the position of the sun is of particular interest to the designer. In addition to its effect on illumination, solar position is important because of its effect on winter sun penetration for passive heating, and on the design of summer shading devices (Robbins, 1986).

In the early site programming stage, goals should be established to ensure access to daylight. These goals fall into two categories: daylight planning goals, which ensure that daylight is available around and within facilities as needed, and daylight safeguard goals, which protect the site for future development or protect surrounding sites (Robbins, 1986).

Daylight Planning Goals (With Applications)
1. Ensure that daylight is present on and between the facades of buildings in order to provide good interior and exterior illumination (new facilities and land development or zoning).
2. Ensure that daylight is available where it is wanted, either in particular rooms or at particular exterior locations (new buildings, land development or zoning, facility renovation, and site rehabilitation).

Daylight Safeguard Goals (With Applications)
1. Ensure that daylight is safeguarded within all new projects (new facilities and site rehabilitation).
2. Ensure that daylight is safeguarded on all land likely to be developed (land development or zoning).
3. Ensure that daylight is as fully safeguarded in rehabilitated or renovated facilities as possible, given the existing conditions (land development or zoning and facility renovation).

4. Ensure that daylight is safeguarded in facilities and land developments adjacent to the proposed project (new buildings, land development or zoning, facility renovation, and site rehabilitation).

Daylighting Strategies in Buildings

Form

In early design stages, facility shape has a primary effect on daylighting performance. As a general rule, daylighting is a function of the exposure of interior spaces to the sky vault (Moore, 1985).

Single-story structures—and the top story of multistory buildings—are particularly suited for daylighting because of the accessibility of virtually all interior areas to the sky dome. Furthermore, overhead light sources are more efficient for illuminating horizontal task surfaces—such as tables and desks—than are side sources, because the cosine reduction is less. Because overhead sources tend to occur above the normal field of view of the occupants, the potential for direct glare is reduced.

If, as a result of nondaylight considerations, multiple stories are to be used, exposure to the sky dome becomes a function of the narrowness of the plan. The "15/30" rule of thumb is a useful guide in the schematic design phase. With careful fenestration design, a 15-foot perimeter zone can be task-lighted primarily by daylight; the next 15 feet, partially daylighted with supplemental electric lighting; and the remainder requiring entirely electric illumination; this guide is based on high windows and a 10-foot floor-ceiling height.

Prior to the widespread use of air conditioning, office facility plans tended to be narrow (about 65 to 70 feet wide) to provide adequate ventilation. With a center circulation zone, all of the work areas were within about 30 feet of the exterior. With the increased availability of air conditioning, plans became deeper, leading to the present dependence on fluorescent lighting owing to the average increased distances to the exterior wall.

To effectively use daylighting in multistory buildings, use narrow plans to keep work areas within 30 feet of the exterior. "Finger" plans can be used where other conditions make a straight plan undesirable. However, if the structure is tall and the space between wings is narrow, each wing becomes a sky dome obstruction to those adjacent. This effect can be minimized by the use of light-colored exterior surfaces.

Orientation

Small facilities, where daylighting is less of a design priority and where energy performance is dominated by the envelope, must balance the desirability of southern exposure for passive solar heat gain against minimizing perimeter area to reduce heat loss. In larger, daylit buildings, heat loss is less of a concern because of greater internal loads, and the need for exposure to relatively uniform lighting levels predominates. In general, southern and northern exposures are the most desirable, while eastern and western exposures are to be minimized (Moore, 1985).

Because light (and sun) on the south facade is abundant and relatively uniform, and because excess solar gain in the summer can be effectively controlled with overhangs, this is the most desirable facade for daylighting access, and its dimension should be maximized.

Daylight exposure is less abundant on the north facade, but the near-constant availability of diffuse sky light and the absence of summer sunlight make it the second most desirable orientation. The large net heat loss through north glazing is still a disadvantage, but not to the degree associated with smaller facilities with minimum internal gains and large envelope losses.

Both east and west orientations afford only half-day exposure to sunlight, making optimum fenestration design more difficult. Both—especially the west orientation—experience large summer heat gain at unwanted times, while providing little winter passive solar contribution. For these reasons the east and west facade dimensions should be minimized.

Therefore, to the extent permitted by siting and other constraints, the multistory facility plan should be elongated, with the maximum length facades on the north and south. In addition to proportioning facade exposures properly, this results in a narrow building, allowing maximum interior exposure to daylight. In single-story and low-rise buildings, the availability of the roof for admitting daylight makes this plan elongation less important.

Sidelighting

Sidelighting systems are so named because light sweeps across tasks from either side. The oblique incidence angle on the work plane causes a significant reduction of illuminance owing to the cosine effect, but it also results in virtually no veiling reflections and as a result is a valuable source of illumination. Sidelighting apertures also can provide view glazing to maintain a visual connection with the surrounding environment (Robbins, 1986).

Daylight *penetration* is defined as the distance into the room that daylight reaches along the task plane at a predetermined illuminance level. In general, for a given window area, higher windows provide better penetration and more uniform distribution. This desirable height is often in conflict with view requirements. Consider separating the two functions: a high strip of windows for daylighting and relatively narrow vertical slits to frame selected views. In order to reduce the brightness contrast around the windows, locate them adjacent to perpendicular partition walls to utilize the reflectance of the wall to bounce light back on the wall surrounding the window.

Sidelighting, because of its inherently low angle of direction, is particularly subject to interior obstructions. These include furnishings—such as filing cabinets, etc.—as well as interior partitions. As a general rule, work surfaces that cannot "see" the window directly will receive reduced illuminance. This poses a particular problem for the designer because of his or her lack of control over the placement of movable obstructions during the life of the building. When the architect does not control the interior design directly, considerable collaboration with interior designers and occupants is required to avoid decisions that reduce daylight penetration.

Toplighting

In addition to the sidelighting strategies described previously, single-story buildings and the top story of multistory structures can employ skylights (horizontal and shallow-sloped glazing) and monitors (vertical and steeply sloped glazing) to introduce daylight. This is particularly advantageous for large-area floor plans with interior areas remote from perimeter windows.

Because of the large amount of sunlight hitting horizontal surfaces during the summer, *skylights* introduce considerable heat gain and are often avoided in order to reduce cooling loads. However, if the aperture area is carefully controlled so that all admitted sunlight can be effectively used for lighting, the increase in cooling load will actually be less than would result from comparable electric lighting. This is because of the high efficacy of the sunlight (about 95 lumens per watt) compared with the supplemental fluorescent lighting (about 60 lumens per watt), together with the modest aperture areas that prevent "overlighting." In other words, even though daylighting results in heat gain, it introduces less heat than a comparable amount of electric lighting. The key to preventing unnecessary cooling loads is the use of moderate aperture areas to ensure that all admitted daylight can be necessary to achieve the design lighting level.

Roof monitors are structures that use vertical or steeply sloped glazing. This allows contribution of roof-reflected light, and, in the case of south-oriented glazing, more direct exposure to winter sunlight. Typically, north-facing monitors employ clear glazing for maximum transmission since diffusion is inherent in the skylight and roof-reflected sunlight. South-facing monitors must employ translucent glass or white baffles to diffuse direct sunlight.

The combination of direct north skylight and twice-reflected sunlight (roof plus monitor interior) provides about half the illumination with similar distribution as does a horizontal translucent skylight. A comparable south-facing monitor with translucent glazing transmits illuminance comparable to the flat skylight, but the greatest illuminance occurs slightly north of the opening.

Courtyards and Atria

Courtyards and atria (covered courtyards) are a traditional response to climate. The courtyard plan is the most compact variation of the "finger" plan, and thus creates the most "self-obstruction" of the sky dome. It does, however, provide some daylight access to the center of an otherwise deep plan. Because interior locations typically are unable to "see" the sky in a courtyard configuration, illuminance is particularly sensitive to exterior wall illuminance. A horizontal light shelf or scoop is particularly effective. There is one advantage inherent in the geometry of courtyards. While the opposite wall obstructs the sky dome, it also obstructs low-angle direct sunlight, reducing glare problems and the need for wide overhangs.

The enclosed atrium is a buffer space providing a transition zone between inside and out. In the process, this central buffer space has assumed such large proportion as to become the focal space in the building. The lighting performance of an atrium is very similar to that of a courtyard of similar dimensions because the sky dome obstructions are present. A clear atrium roof glazing simply replaces courtyard window glazing. There are, however, major thermal differences. In cold climates, the atrium remains habitable in the winter, at the expense of considerable summer heat gain. If an opaque roof, with clerestories, is used to cover the atrium, sky dome obstruction is increased, and illuminance is reduced accordingly. Based on the monitored performance of a small number of atrium office facilities, it is not clear that life-cycle costs are lower for facilities with an atrium than for comparable courtyard buildings.

THE DOE COMMERCIAL BUILDINGS PROGRAM

In order to examine the potential of energy-efficient nonresidential facilities through a process of careful design, construction, and field testing, in 1979 the U.S. Department of Energy (DOE) instituted a large design development and field test program in response to these questions. The program, the Nonresidential Experimental Buildings Program, built a body of practical information on the design, construction, and performance of nonresidential energy-efficient facilities and investigated the potential of passive solar technologies to meet commercial facility energy requirements. The program is the largest known attempt to guide design and simultaneously evaluate construction and operational costs, actual energy use, occupancy effects, and reactions in climate-responsive, nonresidential buildings.

The DOE Program Conclusions

- Vertical glazing was found generally superior to sloped glazing and definitely superior to horizontal skylights in internal-load-dominated buildings.
- Glazing sloped toward the sun admitted too much direct-beam sunlight and was difficult to shade with overhangs.
- Core daylighting was best achieved using roof monitors.
- Roof monitors should face south whenever there was even a modest heating load and they work best as small, distributed apertures instead of a single large opening.
- Daylight distribution to core areas was necessary for good perimeter lighting because light distributed evenly across the room reduces bothersome brightness contrast caused by unilateral exposure.
- The best cooling strategies are defensive: shading and insulation.
- The next best cooling strategy is natural ventilation and night flushing in massive construction.
- Ventilation air flow must be direct; convoluted paths that wind through a building are a designer's fantasy.

- Venetian blinds effectively obstruct natural ventilation when in the closed position.
- Well-controlled daylighting will reduce cooling since, lumen for lumen, daylight generates less heat than does artificial light. The design's objective is to admit modest amounts of light distributed over large areas. Excessive light will generate excessive heat gains, and poor distribution will require more electric light use in interior areas than is otherwise necessary.
- Nonresidential-quality movable insulation is not generally available; consider low-E glazing or selective surface alternatives. While project designers worked hard to develop custom movable insulation systems, the end results were mixed. In five cases, there were either delays in the original installation, problems with operation once installed, or such poor performance that the original system had to be replaced.
- Occupants enjoy and appreciate climate-responsive buildings. In several of the projects, there was a significant increase over anticipated facility use. Owners claim that employee productivity is up because employees like the spaces in which they work. Occupant surveys leave no doubt that most occupants enjoy these facilities more than comparable conventional alternatives.
- Operable windows should not be used for night-flushing ventilation in facilities that are not occupied at night. For reasons of security and precipitation, facility staff will not leave windows open when the facility is not occupied. Instead, use screened, louvered openings with weather-stripped interior shutters.
- Passive devices must be simple to install, and both function and operation must be intuitively obvious. In the project buildings, devices that were difficult to install or seemed counterintuitive to construction personnel were usually built incorrectly, and (in some cases) were sabotaged by construction personnel. In one case, the auxiliary electric resistance space heaters were wired to operate continually because the electrical contractor did not believe that the passive techniques would provide sufficient heating; the problem was discovered during the performance monitoring phase and easily corrected.
- Manual light control can be more energy conserving than automated dimming or switching controls. This was particularly true in facilities where users perceived that they had a greater level of control over the interior environment. Occupants were found to be often willing to work at lower lighting levels than those recommended by industry standards. This voluntary action is apparently connected to the high degree of personal control that users perceived in those buildings.
- The bottom line is that climate-responsive facilities can reduce energy consumption and costs; those participating in the DOE program used 47 percent less energy than their conventional "base care" counterparts.

High-Mass vs. Low-Mass Buildings

Both high-mass and low-mass facilities work well, but each must be carefully examined with respect to climate, facility use, and occupancy schedules.

High-mass buildings work well under the following conditions:

1. Where there is extended evening and weekend use; such schedules can take advantage of stored heat.
2. In sunny climates; solar energy can charge the mass.
3. With high-cooling-load buildings; high mass absorbs gains during the day and allows discharge at night by night-flushing ventilation.
4. In climates with large diurnal temperature swings; mass allows for storing up heat during the day for release at night. In the heating season, this release is to the interior; in the cooling season, it is to the outside.

Low-mass buildings work well under the following conditions:

1. Where facility hours follow typical forty-hour-per-week schedules. For more continuous operating schedules, night and weekend setback may contribute higher savings than will thermal mass, which dampens temperature setback savings. In general, setback is difficult in high-mass buildings because heating systems must recharge the mass before the facility opens; occupants feel cold with cool walls and floors, even though the air temperature is sufficiently high.
2. In cloudy climates; solar energy should meet the immediate—or instantaneous—heating load before being stored in thermal mass. This makes storage less important with limited solar energy.
3. In facilities with large internal volume; high ceilings can be used to collect heat for redistribution to areas needing heat.
4. In facilities with relatively small solar collection apertures (compared with the heat loss); all of the available solar energy goes to meeting the immediate heating load, and little is left over for storage.

The Importance of Daylighting Distribution

Daylighting resulted in significant cost and energy savings while contributing to user comfort; approximately 55 percent of the savings over the base case lighting energy was achieved through these daylighting strategies. Successful daylight design shared a number of characteristics; the most important of these was distribution. If daylight was well distributed, a visually comfortable and largely glare-free environment was attained. The most successful design solutions had the following characteristics:

- Glare and contrast were controlled.
- Direct sunlight was not allowed to enter an occupied space; instead, baffles, diffusing reflecting surfaces, and/or diffusing glazing were used to break up beam lighting.

- Occupants were not able to see the light source directly from the spaces they usually occupied.
- Light was admitted high on the wall plane or at the ceiling plane.
- The view was retained.
- A number of smaller roof apertures (clerestories and monitors) were used rather than fewer larger openings.
- Roof monitors and clerestories were oriented south with vertical glazing.

References

American Institute of Architects. 1981. *Energy in architecture: Level 3a applications.* Washington, D.C.: American Institute of Architects, as cited by Franta, Gregory. 1990. Thermal energy distribution in building interiors. In *Solar facilities architecture,* ed. Jeffery Cook. Cambridge, Mass.: MIT Press.

Balcomb, Douglas, Robert Jones, Robert McFarland, and William Wray. 1984. *Passive solar heating analysis: A design manual.* Atlanta: American Society of Heating, Refrigerating and Air-Conditioning Engineers.

Burt Hill Kosar Rittelman Associates and Min Kantrowitz Associates. 1987. *Commercial building design: Integrating climate, comfort, and cost.* New York: Van Nostrand Reinhold Company.

Cook, Jeffery. 1990. Introduction. In *Passive cooling,* ed. Jeffery Cook, 1-42. Cambridge, Mass.: MIT Press.

Kaufman, John. 1984. *IES lighting handbook 1984 reference volume.* New York: Illuminating Engineering Society.

Kaufman, John. 1987. *IES lighting handbook 1987 application volume.* New York: Illuminating Engineering Society.

Moore, Fuller. 1985. *Concepts and practice of architectural daylighting.* New York: McGraw-Hill.

Robbins, Claude. 1986. *Daylighting: Design and analysis.* New York: Van Nostrand Reinhold Company.

Ternoey, Steve, Larry Bickle, Claude Robbins, Richard Rusch, and Kenneth McCord. 1983. *The design of energy-responsive commercial buildings.* New York: John Wiley & Sons.

EPILOGUE

Robert G. Hershberger

Since architectural programming was recognized in the early to mid-1960s as an activity having the potential for profound personal, social, and cultural impact through design, it has developed as an area of importance and undergone a number of changes, to the point where its current practice, as evidenced by the chapters in this book, has become very sophisticated in both its theories and its methods. The idea of the architect going to a client to obtain a list of the required spaces, equipment, and budget, or even to spend a few hours with the client to develop this information, is not even discussed by the authors as something to be avoided. It is simply as if programming no longer is done this way.

The authors in this book discuss developing new knowledge about the interactions of built form and social organizations; how special needs of the elderly, prisoners, and other populations can best be accommodated; how safety and security issues can be addressed; and even how built form can affect energy savings and resource conservation. They write about the development of sophisticated computer databases available to programmers and designers that contain knowledge about the interface of built form with human institutions of every kind.

John Eberhard's prediction in *Facility Programming*—that computerized databases were developed from post-occupancy evaluations and linked to programming and design in a comprehensive system—seems on the verge of becoming a reality.[1] Indeed, it *is* a reality within some of the organizations represented by authors. Ched Reeder's chapter on "Computer Usage in Facility Programming" focuses on this area. Murray, Gameson, and Hudson's chapter on "Creating Decision-Support Systems" also explores the use of computers to set up a framework for the interaction of clients and construction professionals. Database access would, of course, be a natural outgrowth of such computer-aided systems. However, the ability to link various databases in a national or international network is still in the future, because of both the limited capabilities of most potential users and reluctance by some design firms to share knowledge (because of perceived marketing advantages). It seems inevitable, however, that such linkage will occur as leading design and programming firms realize the advantages of sharing information and university research groups generate databases from their research studies.

There are some other themes running through the chapters of the book that portend interesting developments in programming. Several of the authors—Henry Sanoff and Francis Duffy in particular—emphasize the importance of user (nonpaying client) research and participation in the development of programmatic information and design decisions. Duffy stresses the particular importance of facility managers as knowledgeable users in office facility programming. Sanoff advocates that users be active participants throughout the programming and design process. Uriel Cohen emphasizes the importance of research-based programming to generate "design principles" from which the designer can develop appropriate design concepts. Cohen's work with dementia, Roger Brauer's on safety, Randy Atlas's on security, and Fuller Moore's on energy conservation all demonstrate how research can be used to identify issues and generate useful information to be used in the design of various facilities. Similarly, Janet Mackey Brown's chapter on the NCR Corporation sets forth a particularly systematic and effective research methodology for programming for a particular client—including literature search, photo record review, walk-through observation, executive interviews, and data analysis—to get at the important issues to be addressed in the design of corporate facilities through company-wide design guidance. Gary Miciunas, in the chapter about the renovation of the World Headquarters of the British Petroleum Company, discusses how extensive user interviews can be helpful in developing a program document. Peter McLennan, also with DEGW, Ltd., joins Duffy in encouraging interaction with facility managers in office programming and discusses the advantages of using systematic analysis of existing building stock to establish appropriate programming guidelines.

Another theme that runs through several of the chapters of the book is that programming and design should not be distinct phases of a project, but rather that they should run concurrently, that the programmer should be involved in design, and that the designer should be involved in programming. For example,

---

[1]Eberhard, John. 1978. Prospects for facility programming. In *Facility programming*, ed. Wolfgang F.E. Preiser, 325-29. Stroudsburg, Pa.: Dowden, Hutchinson & Ross Inc.

Zeisel and Maxwell's chapter on relocating the H-E-B Arsenal Headquarters presents an approach that involves programmers, designers, clients, and users working together throughout the design process in a "fast-track" system with programming, master planning, and design starting at the same time and informing the next phase of each. Coleman and Olson's work on the Mattel Toys Worldwide Headquarters included quite active and beneficial involvement of independent programming and design firms throughout the entire programming, design, and building process. Tusler, Zilm, Hannon, and Newman's chapter supports this approach in health care architecture. Maxwell and Wyckoff's chapter on "Stacking and Blocking for Society National Bank" reinforces this notion by showing how the design concept had to precede specific floor-by-floor programming activities.

The chapter by Maxwell and Wyckoff also points out another theme found in several chapters—that "facility programming never fully ends, considering the dynamic nature of most corporations." The chapter by Maxwell and Brown on military health care facilities makes this point very clear in an argument for "in-house programming" in large governmental organizations. They also support the idea that clients and users should be major participants in developing programmatic and design concepts. Goldman and Peatross's chapter, dealing with correctional facility programming, advocates that the programmer be an active participant at least through the schematic design and design development phases of a project.

The themes relating to the importance of user-based research and the active involvement of users, clients, and programmers throughout the design process are important conceptual changes from earlier attitudes about programming and design and, indeed, the architecture profession's position that programming is not even an essential service in the practice of architecture. The themes about the continuing nature and interlocking of programming and design are also important evolutionary steps in the advancement of the design profession. There is a distinct potential for an ever-improving built environment resulting from well-developed theory, knowledge, and methods for discovering particular values, goals, and needs of organizations as outlined in the book. It is clear that this potential is beginning to be realized in some architectural firms. It will become a more pervasive characteristic of the architectural profession as other firms try to emulate their success.

Yet, as an architectural practitioner and educator, I share some of Wolf Preiser's concerns expressed in the introduction as I look around me and realize that the vast majority of practitioners are not involved in such careful and systematic programming activities. Most programs are, in fact, a list of requirements and budget obtained from the owner or similar ones produced by architects after an interview or two with the client. Similarly, the schools of architecture, while required by the National Architectural Accrediting Board (NAAB) to cover architectural programming in their curricula, are very uneven in how this is accomplished. The faculty at my college, for example, have seen fit to require only one two-credit programming course in the professional program. Fortunately, it is taught very well and followed by a six-credit design studio, which emphasizes the development of programmatic information as a basis for design. Other design studios treat programming very unevenly, depending on the specific orientation of the instructor. The students are expected to develop a program for their final project, but have no course work or credit given for this activity, have no required programming product, and, as Preiser has stated, rarely are held to any programmatic standards in final reviews. Our college is by no means alone in this lack of emphasis on programming in the architectural curriculum.

Until the idea becomes widely accepted within the academy that effective architectural programming is an essential part of design practice, it will be difficult to realize its full potential within the profession.

What, primarily, is hindering this acceptance?

1. Faculty who were educated at a time when programming was not even taught, or who have themselves been taught that programming is not an essential part of architectural practice.
2. An architectural profession that still considers programming an "additional service" that may or may not be necessary in designing a facility.
3. Clients who want to pay for the minimum service necessary to receive governmental approvals to proceed with a project.

What can make this change?

1. Architectural firms, such as those represented by the authors in this book, that prove that they do better architecture and get better commissions because they do effective programming.
2. Satisfied clients/users who realize the value of programming and, hence, are willing to pay sufficient fees to allow effective programming to occur.
3. Educators who come out of the few schools and firms that advocate effective programming and convince other faculty and students of the essential nature of this activity in design.

This is beginning to happen, but there is one more theme running through several of the chapters of the book that is an essential ingredient in making the adoption of programming pervasive within the architectural academy and profession:

4. It is essential that the important bottom-line values of design-oriented architects be adopted during programming.

As long as programming is seen as a method only to ensure that better, more user-responsive facilities are designed by architects, it will have little appeal to educators or practitioners. The profession, by tradition and philosophical orientation, is dedicated to the development of not only useful objects, but also aesthetic objects! Aesthetic objects bring much more to the design problem than the solution of user problems. The potential to express the highest aspirations of the client, the essential purposes of the institution, the values held by contemporary society, and the convictions of the architect regarding appropriate form is the "blood running through the veins" of most leading architectural designers. It is what makes architecture, Architecture![2]

As Raymond Bertrand has pointed out in his chapter on "The Role of the Programmer as Interpreter and Translator," a paradigm shift is needed. Programmers must be more concerned with subjective, less empirical data. A methodology is needed that allows programmers to explore the larger issues relating to a project, so that data acquisition can be informed by an understanding of these larger issues. As he points out:

> Rather than outlining a step-by-step analytical approach, then, we should seek to know the place, and to understand it in conceptual terms (and therefore represent it) as a distinct place and a functioning organism. Instead of analyzing facts and reality, we are conceiving a model. The meaning of the program thus derives directly from its conception.
>
> This shift from analysis to conception implies subtle change in the program's applications and in the role of the programmer. Before, we had to explain the setting in order to understand it; now we must interpret it in order to sense its nature.

Adoption of this paradigm shift, not by designers, but by programmers, is mandatory before designers will be completely willing to accept programming as an essential part of architectural services.

My teacher, Louis I. Kahn, railed at the programs he was given by clients because they prescribed objects or activities (design and performance requirements) without ever exploring or understanding the essential institutional purposes or meanings. In consequence, the specifications were almost always wrong! Quoting Kahn (Tyng, 1984):

> If we get a program from a school board which says: Don't forget the nine-foot fence around your school, a lobby so many square feet, corridors nine feet wide, all classrooms alike—you have a red light budget that goes with it. I think nothing can come out of it in the way of what the architect is able to do.
>
> If you were to define architecture in a few words you would say architecture is the thoughtful making of spaces. It is the duty of the architect to find what is this thoughtful realm of space, what is school—and not just take the program of the institution but try to develop something which the institution itself can realize is valid.[3]

---

[2]Hershberger, Robert. 1985. Values: A theoretical foundation for architectural programming. In *Programming the built environment*, ed. Wolfgang F.E. Preiser, 7-12. New York: Van Nostrand Reinhold Company.

[3]Tyng, Alexandra. 1984. *Beginnings: Louis I. Kahn's philosophy of architecture.* New York: John Wiley & Sons.

Traditional programmers characteristically have not looked for the underlying values associated with architectural problems. These values generally remain a kind of "hidden dimension," the programmer accepting the usual way of doing things without really understanding why.[4] But this is not the case with the programmers represented in the book. Jay Farbstein and Murray, Gameson, and Hudson in their chapters analyze the impact of the client organization on the programming process. Farbstein, for example, concludes that the closer the client/user is to the key decision makers in an organization, the more likely that they will be able to realize their goals in programming. Furthermore, if the activities of the programming group are evaluated by a group charged with "bringing in facilities on time and within budget," there is little likelihood that time will be allocated for a thorough assessment of occupant group needs. And, of course, who pays the bills has a profound effect on the kind of a study that can be accomplished. In other words, it is not always the programmer's decision as to how a program will be developed. Programming is not all objective research activity in which good analysis will ensure a good program. Subjective issues, such as those discussed above, will play a role and must be considered.

Goldman and Peatross's chapter dealing with prisons discusses value conflicts that arise in correctional facility programming and design. What are prisons really for? Punishment? Correction? Rehabilitation? Custody? There are apparently very strong and differing views in this regard held by the public, government officials, clients, and programmers. Indeed, the authors indicate that some programmers serve as advocates for one position or another, not as "interpreters and translators," as Bertrand might advocate. The viewpoint finally adopted by client and programmer will, of course, have a profound affect on every aspect of the program and design that follows. For example, Coleman and Olson discovered in the Mattel Toy project that the key values were very different from any of the underlying values related to prison design. They discovered that the aesthetic values were very important and somewhat different for the two facilities on which they were working. The goals developed from these values (playfulness? sophistication?) were to do the following:

1. Develop a "free," "entertaining," and "light" interior environment appropriate for a toy company.
2. Develop a professional interior environment appropriate for a Fortune 500 company.

The design of these facilities certainly would not result in anything like a correctional facility. The important issues are totally different!

Zeisel/Maxwell and Maxwell/Wyckoff also support the need for a paradigm shift in their chapters as they discuss the necessity of involvement of the designer in identifying important issues to be addressed in the program.

---

[4]Hall, Edward T. 1966. *The hidden dimension.* Garden City, N.Y.: Doubleday.

Tusler, Zilm, Hannon, and Newman in "Programming: The Third Dimension" state the need for this paradigm shift directly:

> Great architecture requires interaction between programming and design. That is, a *third dimension* is needed in programming. The program must be derived from the concept and at the same time define the concept. It must speak about the building as a piece of architecture as well as a place to house users. It must define and establish the aesthetic goals for the building. It must also establish in the collective client's mind the possibilities that a well-designed building can reveal. . . . Thus, the programmer and the designer must collaborate and work simultaneously, not sequentially as at present, with the client as an integral part of this collaboration. A shared vision . . . must exist between all three.

Most of the authors also question the traditional idea of a sequential, two-step process in which the program is seen as analysis and design as synthesis. This idea about programming and design is generally attributed to Peña, et al.[5] But please recall that designers at CRSS always participate on the programming team—to ensure that this separation is not complete and that programming and design proceed based on concepts that the client, user, programmer, and designer all understand and accept. CRSS typically follows up this "schematic programming" phase with "development programming," which takes place while schematic design and design development studies are underway. Interestingly, in advocating "The Problem-Seeking Approach to Engineering Programming," Brown and Scarbrough, in their chapter, emphasize the importance of the separation and sequential nature of programming and design. This is interesting because engineering typically defines its whole mission as problem solving—art is not a consideration. The programmer in architecture, however, must be in a position to define the important human, institutional, and cultural values relating to the project so that the designer can explore the formal means to accommodate and express these central issues in a design concept. Then programming can proceed within the adopted conceptual framework to develop secondary levels of information. Design can proceed in an iterative, integrative fashion with programming until the last detail is designed. This is the way to architecture of great meaning and substance, architecture that responds to user requirements in a creative and responsible way while creating aesthetic objects. Programming and design are inextricably linked in this paradigm.

If we accept this proposed paradigm shift, can we continue to accept the idea that complete facility programs can be prepared by a programming team prior to engaging the design architect? Possibly so, if the programming team would limit its activities to value identification, goal setting, facts, and needs development appropriate only for schematic programming so that the design firm would be involved in setting formal concepts and continue to be involved during design development programming. Another alternative would be for

---

[5]Peña, William, and John Focke. 1977. *Problem seeking*. Boston: Cahners.

the programming team or client to have individuals on it capable of determining both the definitional (programmatic) and the formal (design) concepts appropriate for the project. Many architects would be delighted to receive such a well-conceived program, especially if convinced of the appropriateness of the concepts previously adopted by the programming team. On the other hand, some very capable designers would not readily accept such programs, because they would bring with them strongly held views not just about form, but also about society, culture, and even quite possibly about the institution for which the program is being prepared. These ideas of the designer would need to be factored into the initial conceptual definitions of the design problem from which program development would follow. Otherwise, even the most well-developed facility program might be challenged and reformulated from beginning to end, from broadest issue to smallest detail, so that the design problem can be assimilated into the designer's conceptual framework.

In any case, the authors have made an important point. Programmers must accept as one of their primary objectives the development and translation of the reasons for being of any institution and its essential relatedness to place and time before proceeding to more routine activities of identifying specific space requirements. If they do this, it will be possible for most architectural educators and practitioners to embrace programming as an essential activity in the practice of architecture. Programmers will be programming for architecture, not merely for facilities.[6] This is an important distinction currently lost on all too many programmers.

---

[6]Hershberger, Robert. 1992. *Programming for architecture* (to be published by Van Nostrand Reinhold Company).

Index

A

Agron, George, 156
Analysis cards, wall displays of, 51
Architectural security programming,
    491-510
    access control, 501, 507
    construction phases, 495-96
        bids, 495
        documents, 494
    countermeasure development process,
        495, 506
    design development phase, 494
    operation phase, 495
    programming phase, 493
    schematic design phase, 493
    security design structure, 500, 506
    security professionals, 496-97
      and architect, 497-501
    site development/security zoning, 501-3
      building perimeter, 502
      internal space/point protection,
        502-3, 509, 510
      site characteristics, 502, 508, 509
    surveillance, 501, 507
    systematic process of, 492-96
      architectural process, 492-95
      security process, 495-96
    territorial reinforcement, 501, 508
ARRIS F/X (Sigma Design), 114

Asset audit, 28, 40-41
    Asset Audit Evaluation Form, 28, 40-41
    preparation of, 26
Atlas, Randall, 491

B

Bechtel, Robert, 156
Bertrand, Raymond, 405
Blocking, 202
Brauer, Roger L., 471
British Petroleum Company plc, 279-301
    Britannic House, architectural renovation
      of, 280-81, 294
    changing office, 290-92
    corporate reorganization of, 282
    elements/outcomes, 286-89
      boardroom functions, 287
      conference center, 286-87
      directors' suite, 287, 298
      food service, 287, 298
      general office areas, 288, 301
    furniture and space standards, 297
    furniture solution options, 299-300
    organizational design, 295
    process/methods, 282-86
      client's brief to architect, 283-84
      client/user interviews, 284-86
      discussion of, 288-89

British Petroleum Company plc *(cont.)*
    space planning reviews, 286
    project team working relationships, 296
    relocation planning, 281-82
    teamwork, shift to, 290-91
Broadgate project, 85-92, 94
    factors for change, 87-88
    illustration of, 96
    key user research documents, 97
    programming of, 88-89
    typical city office design
      recommendations, 98
Brown, Conny R., 47
Brown, Dale R., 249
Brown, Janet Mackey, 65-84

C

CADG+FM (Ospro/CADG), 113-14
Campus child-care facilities, 131-51
    case study, 136-38
      activity data sheets, 136, 145
      design criteria, 138
      facility design, 138-39, 148-51
      spatial planning, 136-37, 146-47
    client awareness techniques, 135
    design participation, 134-35, 144-45
      effectiveness of, 141-42
    planning for outdoor play, 139-40, 151
    research findings, 133-34
    teachers' response to process, 140
Capital outlay plan, overview of, 30, 45
Capital project coding scheme, 29, 44
Central office, changes in, 291-92
Client organization, 383-403
    dimensions/outcomes of program,
      398-99
    impact on practice, 399
    informal organizations, 388-89
    organization chart, assessing
      programming process relationships
      with, 401
    roles/responsibilities, 391-97, 403
      architect/design professionals, 396-97
      client/building owner, 393
      interested parties, 394
      nonofficial users, 294
      "official" users, 394

owner's representative, 393-94
      planning committees/task forces,
        395
      programmer, 395-96
      regulatory agencies, 395
    situational factors, 397-98
    structure, 385-88
    technology, 389
    values/culture/climate, 390-91
Cohen, Uriel, 453
Coleman, William T., 303
Communication, with clients, 430
Computer usage, 103-29
    adjacency matrix, 111, 126
    aging of information, 108
    architectural program, 107, 124
    benefits of, 109-10
    costs of, 110-11
    data gathering/processing, cost of, 108
    end user problems, 116
    evolution of, 112-13
      database, 112
      files, 112, 127
      spreadsheet, 113, 128
    facility management group
      problems, 116
    future of, 116-17
    general characteristics of programs,
      111-12
    general management problems, 115-16
    integration of facility progamming data,
      114-15, 129
    interior/space planning program, 107-8,
      115, 125
    inventory, 114
    layout, 115
    master planning program, 106-7, 114-15,
      123
    programming techniques, 104-6
      archival record analysis, 105-6, 122
      interviews/focus groups, 105
      simulations, 105, 120, 121
      structured observation, 106
      surveys, 104-5, 118-19
    program overview, 113-14
Correctional facilities programming, 357-81
    benefits of, 373-74
    compared to other programming, 359
    correctional facility, defined, 358-59

costs, 371-72, 380
    operational costs, 371-72
    programming costs, 372
    project costs, 371
data collection methods, 369-70, 380
documentation/presentation to client,
    368
facility development process, 375
mission/objectives, development of,
    365-66
operational/physical requirements,
    meetings to determine, 366-67
post-occupancy evaluations (POEs), 369
preparing for, 362-65
    client identification, 362-63
    committees, 363-64
    potential problems, 364-65
    professional team, 364
    programming team formation, 363
    team group sizes/meeting structure,
        364
programmers:
    approach during meetings, 367
    during design, 368-69
programming models, 362
project initiation, 365
special performance criteria, 359-61
    long-term decisions, 361
    normalization/aesthetics, 360-61
    rehabilitation/privacy/safety/
        security, 360, 367
    security/safety, 359-60, 376
tools, 370-71
value engineering, 367-68
Cox, Warren, 154
CRSS Architects, Inc., 51-56

D

Dark adaptation, 485-86
Data collection, 48
    computer and, 108
    correctional facilities programming and,
        369-70, 380
    pilot survey, 11
Daylighting, 517-21
    courtyards/atria, 520-21
    facility shape/form, 518

orientation, 518-19
    planning goals, 517
    safeguard goals, 517-18
    sidelighting systems, 519
    toplighting, 520
Decentralization, shift toward, 291
Decision-support systems, 427-52
Defects, safety and, 475-76
DEGW Ltd., 337-55
    area measurement graph, 340, 350
    building area data/diagrams, 344, 351-52
    Chatham Place, analysis of, 343-46
    facility management framework, 338-40
    facility planning hierarchy, 339, 350
    net usable area, 347, 355
    organizational demand, 346-48
    planning analysis, 345, 353
    proposed concept plan, 347, 355
    service charter, 346, 354
    space taxonomy and measurement, 340
    space use, 345, 352-53
    strategic facility recommendations,
        342-43
    supply and demand, 341
    user analysis, model of, 341, 351
    user requirements, identifying, 341
    work space standards, 347, 354
Dehumidification, 515
Department of Defense (DOD), facility
    system safety, 481-82
DOE, See U.S. Department of Energy (DOE)
Duffy, Francis, 85-101

E

Eberhard, John, 2
Economic life cycle of a facility, 32
Elevation changes, 486, 488
Empirical level of programming, 412-13
Employee productivity, office design and,
    292-93
Energy conservation, 501-24
    daylighting, 517-21
        courtyards/atria, 520-21
        facility shape/form, 518
        orientation, 518-19
        planning goals, 517
        safeguard goals, 517-18

Energy conservation *(cont.)*
     sidelighting systems, 519
     toplighting, 520
  DOE commercial buildings program,
     521-24
     daylighting distribution, 523-24
     high-mass vs. low-mass buildings, 523
     program conclusions, 521-22
  energy-efficient lighting, 516-17
     luminous environment design
        approach, 516
     selecting illuminance levels, 516-17
     visual task design approach, 516
  passive cooling, 514-15
     categories of, 515
     defined, 514
     "offensive" cooling strategies, 515
  passive solar heating, 513-14
     defined, 513
     key design elements, 513
     night insulation, 514
     system types, 513-14
  utility rate structure, effect of, 512-13
Engineering programming case study, 51-56
  Engineering Information Index, 52, 58
  problem seeking in action, 52-54
  process flow diagram, 55, 62
  programming schedule, 52, 59
  project schedule, 52, 60
  project summary, 51-52
  site selection criteria, 53, 61
  system definition, 54-56
  system operation/maintenance, 56
  work sessions, 52, 61
Evaporative cooling, 515
Exley, Chuck, 66-67

F

Facilities managers:
  developers and, 86
  new developments and, 85-101
Facility delivery cycle, 23, 24, 32
Facility Programming, 2
Facility programming:
  architectural education and, 5-8
  client organization and, 383-403
  computer usage in, 103-29
  current trends in, 8-14

definition of, 23-24
field of, 2-8
focus of, 23-24
problem-seeking approach, 47-63
recent developments in, 1-19
strategic asset management, 23-45
See also Pilot survey; Strategic asset
  management
Farbstein, Jay, 383
Final design program, preparation/
  submission of, 6-7
Fire safety, 484-85
FM:Space-Management (FM:Systems),
  113

G

Gameson, Roderick M., 427
Geographical dispersion/decentralization,
  shift toward, 291
Goal setting, 48, 50
Goldman, Mark, 357
Guard rail height, 486-87, 488

H

Haddon's theory, 475
Haddon, W. May Jr., 475
Hannon, James T., 227
Hartman-Cox Architects, 154
Hartman, George, 156
Health care programming, 227-42
  alternatives, visualizing, 237-38
  amenities, building, 241-42
  budgetary control, 240
  building re-use, 239-40
  building sections, 248
  character, building, 241-42
  circulation and movement systems,
     240-41
  client needs, serving, 230
  data analysis tools, 234-35
  existing site plan, 244
  expansion strategies, 240
  ground floor plan, 245
  integration of architectural design and,
     228-30
  interdepartmental collaboration, 236-37

organizational concept, establishing,
    232-34
planning schedule summary, 247
programming-design interrelationships,
    238-39
simultaneous design and, 230-32
stacking and relationship issues, 239
statistical techniques, 234-35
user group organization, 246
H-E-B arsenal headquarters case study,
153-83
    architect selection, 155
    architect's experience with programming,
        155-56
    briefing report, 161
    client, 156-57
    design team tripod, 178
    diagnostic program staffing report, 162-63
    facilities design program, 163
    final plan, 180-83
    goals and objectives report, 161
    master planning applications, 163-65
    program-design double helix, 179
    programmers, 157-58
        selection of, 156
    programming/design, connecting, 156
    programming methodology, 158-60
        fast-track programming design, 159
        initial independent planning/design
            decisions, 159-60
        program organization/methods, 160
    project definition/scope, 154-55
    reprogramming, 166-68
    research report, revision spiral, 179
    rules of thumb, 168-75
        common amenities, 172
        individual work space planning, 170-71
        In Search of Excellence parallels,
            173-75
        planning principles, 169-70
        work group planning, 171-72
    space planning program applications,
        165-66
    space standards report, 161-62
Hellmuth, Obata & Kassabaum (HOK), 65,
    72, 283-86, 293
Hershberger, Robert G., 525
HFPA, *See* U.S. Army Health Facility
    Planning Agency (HFPA)
Hudson, John, 427

Inquiry by Design (Zeisel), 159, 160
Institutional audit, preparation of, 25-26
Interactive work sessions, 50-51
Intergraph STPL module, 113
Interior programming, *See* Society National
    Bank case study
Interpretation, 410-14
    analysis and synthesis, 411
    empirical level, 412-13
    globalization, 411
    hypothesis, 411
    theoretical level, 412
Interpretive thinking, methods of, 426
Interviews, 105, 196-98, 284-86, 408, 446
Intuition, 413-14

J

Jones, Peter, 92

L

Labor costs, computer usage, 110
Lighting, 516-17
    illuminance levels, selecting, 516-17
    luminous environment design approach,
        516
    visual task design approach, 516
Lipton, Stuart, 92

M

McLennan, Peter, 337
Maintenance, 24-25, 32
Mass-effect cooling, 515
Mattel Toys Worldwide Headquarters,
    303-35
    concept space plan for tower, 332
    corporate functional organization chart,
        329
    database spreadsheet, example of, 330
    design center, 333-35
        staff interaction node, 333
    diverse space types, 304

Mattel Toys Worldwide Headquarters *(cont.)*
    elements/outcomes, 311-16
        occupancy alternatives, 311-12
        planning/design guidelines, 313-15
        space plan review, 315
        space requirements, 311
    existing facility, evaluation of, 305
    implementation, 306
    master planning process, 327
    methodology, 306-11
        evaluation, 308-9
        familiarization, 306-7
        implementation, 310-11
        recommendations, 309-10
    new building/alternative uses, evaluation
        of, 305-6
    open systems work station standards, 328
    pre-design focus, 303-4
    program success, actions contributing
        to, 315-16
    project objectives/elements, 304-5
    questionnaire, 318-26
    stacking diagrams, 310, 331
Maxwell, Clarence E., 249
Maxwell, Marc A., 153, 158
Maxwell, Richard C., 187
M.D. Anderson Cancer Center, 227-48
    See also Health care programming
Miciunas, Gary A., 279
Military health facilities, 249-77
    analysis, 260-65
    changes influencing programming, 263,
        276
    continuous programming, 269
    facility planning continuum, 268
    guide plates, 258, 273-74
    overview, 258-60
    participatory decision preparing, 263-64,
        277
    planning environment, 268
    program for design (PFD), 258, 271
    programming:
        influence on designing, 254-55
        methods/tools, 255-58
        within life-cycle systems planning,
            251-54, 269
    programming and change requirements,
        261, 276
    relationship matrix, 258, 272
    space planning criteria, 258, 270

Moore, Fuller, 511
Mountain Top CAD Information
    Management (Accugraph), 113
Murray, James Paterson, 427, 442

N

NCR Corporation worldwide facilities
    design guidelines, 65-84
    application of, 68
    approach/methodology, 68-72
        data analysis, 70
        design process, 71
        information gathering, 69-70
        manual design/preparation, 71-72
    descriptors, 72, 79
    elements/outcomes, 72-73
    "Guidelines Structure," 68, 77
    guidelines users, 67-68
    manual, 72-73, 79-84
    NCR Look Agenda, 74-76
    process diagram, 69, 78
    scope of, 67
Needs determination, 26, 49
Newman, Mary Ann, 227

O

Observations, 407-8
Office space programming, *See* H-E-B
    arsenal headquarters case study
Olson, Branka V., 303
ORBIT 1/2, 89-91
OSHA, process safety, 482
Ostrander, Edward, 156
O'Toole, James, 73

P

Parsons, Talcot, 164
Participatory decision preparing, 263-64, 277
Passive cooling, 514-15
    categories of, 515
    defined, 514
    "offensive" cooling strategies, 515
Passive solar heating, 513-14
    defined, 513

key design elements, 513
night insulation, 514
system types, 513-14
Peatross, Frieda D., 375
Peed, Shelton, 156
Peña, William, 47, 471
Petronis, John, 23
Pilot survey, 8-20
    billing methods, 12
    data gathering, methods of, 11
    educational level of programmers, 13
    future research, 13-14
    programming clients, 10-11
    programming information, formats for
        communicating, 11-12
    programming specialists, 10
    questionnaire, 15-16
    respondents to, 8-9
    tables, 17-20
Post-occupancy evaluations (POEs), 369
Preiser, Wolfgang F. E., 15-16
Prime FM+ (Prime), 114
"Principle of Idoniety," 263
Problem seeking, 47-63
    analysis cards, wall displays of, 51
    fact collection/organization/analysis, 48
    goal setting, 48, 50
    interactive work sessions, 50-51
    needs determination, 49
    problem statement, 49-50
    specialists, use of, 51
    uncovering/testing concepts, 49
    See also Engineering programming case
        study
Problem Seeking (Peña), 47
Product-line/market-segment team
    organization, 291
Professional Practice in Facility
    Programming (Preiser), 15
Program development, 427-52
    advice screen, example of, 452
    case study projects/interviewees, 446
    clients:
        guidance for, 445
        problems with, 444
        role in development, 429-31
    computer system:
        aims/objectives, 435-37
        client guidance automation, 437-38
        future possibilities, 439

system development, 439
    system outline, 438-39
criteria for establishing success/
    satisfaction, 443-44
finance, 444
organizations/institutions/individuals
    visited, 447-49
outline diagram of system, 450
programming and the program, 442
project organization/administration/
    development, 443
project profile screen, 451
research:
    background/objectives, 431
    main study, 433-34
    method, 431-33
    outcomes, 435
    pilot study, 433
system topic areas, 452
Programmer:
    as generalist vs. specialist, 416
    interpreter/translator role of, 405-26
Programming, 227-48
    client organization and, 383-403
    client role in, 429-31
    conceptual approach to, 454-55
    consciousness, 415
    courses in, 7
    definition of, 260-61, 471-72
    -design interrelationships, 238-39
    educational questions, 7-9
    facility, defining, 408-9, 419
    "good" programs, components of,
        262-65
    and greater design environment, 261-62
    interpretation, 410-14
        analysis and synthesis, 411
        empirical level, 412-13
        globalization, 411
        hypothesis, 411
        theoretical level, 412
    intuition, 413-14
    as operational definition, 407-8
    participation, 413
    as part of final design project, 6-7
    quality, 414-15
    for safety, 471-89
    for special user groups, problems in,
        453-54
    systemic view of, 406-7

Programming *(cont.)*
    translation process, 409-10, 420
    value dilemmas, 414
Programming-intensive projects, 12
Programming the Built Environment, 2
Program requirements form, example of,
    422-23

R

Radiative cooling, 515
Reeder, Chad, 103
Research-based programming/design,
    453-70
    case study, 456-59, 467-70
    conceptual approach for programming,
        454-55
    design principles, 455-56
        format for, 464-65
    informed programming/design,
        schematic diagram, 463
    special user groups, problems in
        programming for, 453-54
Reticular organization, 291
Royal Institution of Chartered Surveyors
    (RICS)/Alvey project, 432

S

Safety, 471-89
    carry-over to occupancy/use, 477
    complexity/cost, 474
    considerations, 478-79
    defects, 475-76
    design's role in, 477
    fires, 484-85
        Great Chicago Fire, 484-85
        Iroquois Club fire, 485
        MGM Grand Hotel, 485
        Triangle Shirtwaist Factory, 485
    Haddon's theory, 475
    importance of, 472-73
    prevention, 474
    professions, 473
    programming approaches, 477-84
        activity, 481
        analysis methods, 481-82

    building systems/components, 482-83
    facility type, 480
    occupancy/occupants, 480
    scale, 477-80
    standards/codes, 483-84
    programming's role in, 476
    risk, 474-75
    slips/trips/falls, 485-87
        dark adaptation, 485-86
        guard rail height, 486-87, 488
        small elevation changes, 486, 488
Sanoff, Henry, 131, 471
Sauer, Louis, 156
Scarbrough, Timothy K., 47
Sidelighting systems, 519
Society National Bank case study,
    187-225
    add-on factor, 199, 207
    bar graph schedule, 191, 204
    blocking, 202
    computer database, 198-99
    CPM schedule, 191, 204
    current layouts/potential locations,
        191-92
    detail report, 200
    forms completion/interview scheduling,
        196-97
    interviews, 197-98
    kick-off presentation, 196
    modifications, 203, 213-14
    organization, 195-96, 205, 206
    program directives, 189-90
    program objectives, confirmation of, 188
    reports, 199-201, 208-10
    schedule, 191
    SF summary (report), 200, 209
    space requirements survey forms, 193-95,
        216-25
    space standards, 192-93, 205
    stacking, 201-2, 210-12
        report, 200, 210
    team, 188-89
Sommer, Robert, 156
Space inventory sheet, example of, 421
Specialists, use of, 51
Stacking, 201-2, 210-12, 239
Stockley Park project, 85-89, 92-93, 94
    factors for change, 87-88
    illustration, 99

key user research documents, 100
    programming of, 88-89
    typical business park design
        recommendations, 101
Strategic asset management, 23-45
    asset audit:
        Asset Audit Evaluation Form, 28,
            40-41
        preparation of, 26
    capital outlay plan overview, 30, 45
    capital project coding scheme, 29, 44
    case study, 28-30
        context, 28
        planning process highlights, 28-30
        purpose, 28
    classroom need projections, 29, 43
    considerations, 25, 34
    enrollment projections, 29, 42
    Facilities Master Plan Flow Chart, 28, 37
    facilities standards, 28, 38-39
    facility delivery cycle, 23, 32
    flow chart, 25, 33
    focus of, 25
    growth/change, assessment of, 26
    institutional audit, preparation of, 25-26
    maintenance, 24, 32
    management (work) plan, 27, 36
    needs determination, 26
    plan formulation, 26
    plan implementation, 26-27
    successful planning, formula for, 27, 35
Systems approach triad, 418

T

Technical Programming Guidebook (Zeisel),
    157

Theoretical level of programming, 412
Time and cost billing, 12
Tool costs, computer usage, 110
Toplighting, 520
Tusler, Wilbur H., 227

U

U.S. Army Health Facility Planning
    Agency (HFPA), 249-50, 257
U.S. Department of Energy (DOE):
    commercial buildings program, 521-24
        daylighting distribution, 523-24
        high-mass vs. low-mass buildings, 523
        program conclusions, 521-22

V

Vanguard Management (O'Toole), 73
Ventilative cooling, 515

W

Walk throughs, 135
Whidden-Silver modules, 114
Woll, Ed, 158
Work-group organization, 290-91
Wright, Frank Lloyd, 491
Wyckoff, David J., 187

Z

Zeisel, John, 153, 156, 157-60
Zilm, Frank, 227